Jesus Christ
in
History and Scripture

A Poetic and Sectarian Perspective

For our grandchildren:

Heather, Forrest, and William.

Jesus Christ
in
History and Scripture

A Poetic and Sectarian Perspective

by
Edgar V. McKnight

MERCER UNIVERSITY PRESS
1979 ■ 1999
TWENTY YEARS OF PUBLISHING EXCELLENCE

ISBN 0-86554-653-3   MUP/H486
ISBN 0-86554-677-0   MUP/P202

BT
303.2
.M33
1999

Jesus Christ in History and Scripture
A Poetic and Sectarian Perspective
Copyright ©1999
Mercer University Press, Macon, Georgia 31210-3960

Library of Congress Cataloging-in-Publication Data

Jesus Christ in history and Scripture :
a poetic and sectarian perspective /
by Edgar V. McKnight.
xiv+332pp. 6x9" (15x23cm.)
Includes bibliographical references and index.
ISBN 0-86554-653-3 (casebound : alk. paper).
ISBN 0-86554-677-0 (alk. paper).
1. Jesus Christ—Historicity.
2. Bible. N.T. Gospels—Criticism, interpretation, etc.
I. Title.
BT303.2.M33   1999
232.9'08—dc21   99-35521
CIP

Contents

Prologue

A Poetic
and Sectarian Perspective

This book began as a series of lectures on the study of Jesus at the First Baptist Church in Greenville, South Carolina. The Christian Education Committee of the congregation wanted me to share with nonspecialists some of the information included in lectures given during my recent sabbatical.[1] The committee had become aware of an intense interest in Jesus among New Testament specialists, students of religion in general, and a multitude of "ordinary" people, and they wanted a scholar within the community of faith to help them make sense of those developments.

Developments in Jesus studies in recent years are astounding. Cherished critical presuppositions that earlier had limited historical reconstruction of the life of Jesus have been overturned. A revolution has taken place! Scholars have always been interested in historical and theological questions about Jesus, and they have carried out discussions in specialized journals and monographs. These discussions have been rather academic and marked by scholarly timidity, and they have been of only passing interest to nonspecialists. In mainline academic circles this timidity was a result of the opinion that sources do not allow reconstruction of the life and personality of Jesus, that such a reconstruction is unnecessary since the Jesus Christ of real concern is the Christ proclaimed by the church,

---

[1]In 1995–1996 I had a Fulbright appointment as Senior Research Professor at the University of Münster. That year I gave lectures at Münster, Dortmund, Bielefeld, Padaborn, and Hamburg in Germany; at Sheffield, Durham, and Newcastle in England; at Lund in Sweden; and at Karoli Gaspar and Pazmany Peter Universities and the Center for Hermeneutical Research in Budapest, Hungary. In the spring of the year, I gave the Bailey Lectures at the American Baptist Seminary of the West in Berkeley, California. I am especially grateful for my hosts for these series of lectures, Detlev Dormeyer in Germany, William R. Telford in England, Birger Olsson in Sweden, Tibor Fabiny in Hungary, and Joel Green in Berkeley.

and that reconstruction of the historical figure of Jesus is an illegitimate crutch for Christian faith.

In recent years scholars have overcome the timidity related to the reconstruction of the life and personality of Jesus. This recovery of nerve is not due to the discovery of radically new sources or methods. It is accompanied, to be sure, by the expansion of critical studies to include sociological and anthropological methods and by the fuller appreciation of literary studies. But the recovery of confidence in Jesus study results essentially from a new perspective. A simple change of opinion as to the possibility, desirability, and legitimacy of genuine historical study of Jesus has created a revolution in "Jesus-talk."

Since perspectives and a change of perspectives are so important in understanding developments in the study of Jesus, in that series at the First Baptist Church I first of all shared my worldview, a critically chastened worldview, and compared it with precritical and severely critical worldviews, knowing that members of my audience embraced a variety of different worldviews that influenced their approaches to the Bible and the study of Jesus. Some held precritical or noncritical attitudes toward the Bible and the study of Jesus. They would make no distinction between the historical figure of Jesus, the Jesus presented in the canonical Gospels, and the Christ defined by the creeds of the Church. Their robust, naïve, and noncritical attitude allowed them to read the New Testament accounts of Jesus and relate these accounts directly to their lives today. The distance between the time of Jesus and the present was dissolved. The gulf separating the human and historical from the sacred was spanned or obviated. Critical questions about authorship and date of the Gospels, the relationship of the Gospels to earlier oral and written sources, and the relationship of these sources to Jesus as a historical individual did not arise for these readers.

Other members of the audience were properly modern and critical. Their attitude toward the Bible and toward Jesus was colored by critical and rational presuppositions. They did not modernize Jesus but saw him as a first-century figure. They made a distinction between the earthly Jesus, the Jesus of the Gospels, and the Christ of the creeds. They distinguished between the contingent historical world and a transcendent world. They distanced the Bible so that the Bible could become an object of critical scrutiny. They questioned how the Gospels are related to earlier oral and written sources and to the earthly Jesus.

These critical members of the audience were not antagonistic toward their noncritical fellow church members. As believers, their agenda in the church was one with that of their fellow church members in that it did not end with critical explanation of the Bible. Some of these judicious members of the congregation were able to use the texts for personal and congregational edification by bracketing the critical questions as they read themselves into the stories of Jesus. Some of the more thoroughly critical members sought to establish their theological and religious response on thoroughly critical foundations. But the desire and ability to find personal, congregational, and churchly meaning and significance in the scriptures remained vital as those members of the audience had moved from pre-critical to thoroughly critical attitudes. They had somewhat intuitively achieved what Paul Ricoeur refers to as a second naïveté—a naïveté that takes full account of critical knowledge and insights.

The identification of members of the congregation with a Radical Reformation whose approach to scripture was churchly and oriented to praxis may help explain the ability of the members to work together with their differing precritical, critical, and postcritical assumptions. The Baptist theologian James Wm. McClendon cites the biblical agenda of the heirs of the Radical Reformation that influence the members of the moderate First Baptist Church. The Bible is read within a local community that sees itself in the framework of both the New Testament church and the church of the end time. The reading of Scripture has to do with faith and practice, and that faith and practice have essentially to do with mission, liberty, discipleship, and community. In the reading of the Bible and the practice of biblical insights within the church, there is a tentativeness, a provisionality. The church is "by nature provisional, subject to correction arising from further Bible reading . . . the church must change, for God is on the move, and the end is not yet."[2] The Baptist[3] or "sectarian" way of doing church and understanding the Scriptures, in my estimation, can be brought to consciousness and made relevant in understanding and in carrying out contemporary studies of Jesus of Nazareth.

---

[2]McClendon, *Doctrine*, vol. 2 of *Systematic Theology* (Nashville: Abingdon Press, 1994) 344.

[3]McClendon uses the term "baptist" to refer to the Christian bodies of the Radical Reformation and their descendants. Others use terms such as "free church" or "believers' church." See McClendon, *Ethics*, vol. 1 of *Systematic Theology* (Nashville: Abingdon Press, 1986) 19.

The distinction between precritical, critical, and postcritical approaches to Scripture and the appreciation of the different sorts of interpretation involved are vital for pursuing honesty and integrity and for fairness in working with fellow Christians who may be at different locations from our own in this pilgrimage. In a precritical epoch, the Bible was accepted as the unquestioned source of premises to be used in theology. In fact, early terms for what became theology were "sacred scriptures," "sacred knowledge," and "divine pages." The Bible and divine revelation were not distinguished. With the Enlightenment, the Bible became data to be subjected to human reason.

Theological use of the Bible continued, of course, with criteria for evaluation and use being theological. But the dominant approach to the critical study of the Bible was historical, beginning with historical questions about the development of a canon of Scripture. Against the background of theological understanding and use of the Bible, historical-critical study was valuable, but eventually the historical-critical approach came to be seen by many biblical scholars as the gatekeeper to biblical truth. The historical meaning was to be determined first of all and then religious and theological significance was to be ascertained. Today, scholars increasingly see that critical and rational approaches to knowledge overreached themselves, that factors other than the rational and empirical cooperate with the rational and empirical in a complete system of knowledge and learning.

The "poetic" perspective assumed in this volume recognizes the creative contribution that readers of the Gospels make in their reconstruction of Jesus. Contemporary readers are recapitulating the creative activities of the early evangelists. In the sessions at the First Baptist Church, I suggested that the precritical, critical, and postcritical epochs and attitudes support different sorts of knowledge concerning Jesus. Different images and constructions of Jesus Christ are combined in the Gospels: historical reconstructions; historic memory and appropriations; imaginative, poetic, and artistic creations; and theological formulations.

Chapter 1 ("Who Is Jesus Christ Today?") treats this theme. Values of contemporary critically oriented readers support a historical Jesus, a Jesus consistent with history in general and with what we know of the historical situation in Palestine in the first century in particular. At times, a severely historical approach is followed with rigorous demands for validation of historical information about Jesus. At other times, (and often integrated with historical information) the historic Jesus is emphasized, stressing that Jesus (just as individuals like Socrates and George Washington) transcends his first-century historical context. With historic appropriation, creative memory is at work. The past and the present coalesce. Historical knowledge and historic knowledge are not distinguished in the Gospels. With our contemporary historical sensibility, it is important to anchor the historic depiction of Jesus in historical reality, but it is not necessary to limit the significance of Jesus to what can be established by severe historical-critical study.

Jesus is also a figure in literature and art. The poetic and metaphorical understanding, depiction, and appreciation of Jesus is not finally limited by historical or historic criteria and appropriation. But the metaphorical and poetic understanding and appreciation of Jesus is able to mediate historical and historic concerns and theological concerns. In the New Testament, the Jesus event is interpreted by means of images and categories provided in large measure by Jewish thought. What had happened was seen as saving act of God. The God of Israel revealed in Jesus was the creator who controlled the course of history and gave meaning to that history, the God who was revealed through the actual happenings of human history.

Chapters 2 and 3 ("The Gospels and Historical Sources" and "The Gospels and Religious Literature") discuss the materials used in the study of the earthly Jesus, emphasizing that the church's basic sources (the canonical Gospels) are "compounds." They were composed at different times and places in the final third of the first century by Christians who combine historical information and historic memory in imaginative ways to present a Jesus who was relevant to their congregations as he was to the earliest disciples and to subsequent followers. The Gospels challenge readers to accept the way of Jesus as a revelation of the nature of the sacred. The affective and volitional are combined with the historical and theological. The Gospels do not exist as a simple mixture with some parts referring to historical events, other parts witnessing to ahistorical existential or theological truths, while yet other parts propose historic models for admiration, emulation, and contemporary guidance, and so on.

Early critical approaches could not appreciate the complexity of the Gospels. These approaches were historical-critical in nature. They sought to recover the earliest written sources with the idea that once those sources were recovered we would be back to the time of Jesus himself. (This study is called *source criticism*.) The documentary sources, however, were seen to be more than simple primary accounts of Jesus'

acts and teachings. Oral sources were obviously utilized by the evangelists (see Luke 1:1-2), and scholars attempted to ascertain what sorts of
oral sources would have been used in the early church before the composition of the Gospels. (This study is called *form criticism*.) Source and
form criticism as practiced by historical-critical scholars treated the
Gospels as mixtures, with the idea that historical data could be separated
from historic, poetic, and theological application and interpretation.

When scholars saw the Gospels as one of the sorts (forms) of literature used by the early church, the Gospels began to be seen as compounds, as literary-theological and historical-historic unities. At first,
older ideas of historical and literary influence were used in what is called
redaction criticism (with the idea that the evangelists were redactors or
editors of previously existing material). Then the evangelists were seen
as actual authors in their own right, utilizing earlier material, to be sure,
but using their own creative talents as evangelists to present compelling
accounts of Jesus. When the Gospels are seen as literary unities, the importance of readers and the reaction of readers must be taken into
account.[4]

The contemporary quest for Jesus is historically oriented, just as
earlier quests, and the nature and character of this historical interest, as
well as the limitations of the historical approach, must be appreciated.
The concern for objective historical data referring to objective historical
individuals and events as over against ideas, values, and a transcendent
realm of reality (the empiricist versus the rational) is a heritage not only
of the Enlightenment but also of the different classical ways of defining
what is real and how that reality is to be discovered (Platonism and
Aristotelianism).

Chapter 4 ("Philosophical Constraints for Jesus Study") discusses
philosophical presuppositions that play a part in the distinction between

---

[4]In lectures, I traced the trajectory of Gospel study from source criticism to literary
criticism, and in this volume I do the same, including revisions of material previously
published. I am grateful for permission from publishers for the use of this material: "Form
and Redaction Criticism," in *The New Testament and Its Modern Interpreters*, ed. Eldon
Jay Epp and George W. MacRae, The Bible and Its Modern Interpreters 3 (Philadelphia:
Fortress Press; Atlanta: Scholars Press, 1989) 149-74; "Literary Criticism," in *Dictionary
of Jesus and the Gospels*, ed. Joel B. Green and Scott McKnight, with I. Howard Marshall
(Downers Grove IL: InterVarsity Press, 1992) 473-81; and "Reader-Response Criticism,"
in *To Each Its Own Meaning: An Introduction to Biblical Criticisms and Their Applica-
tion*, ed. Stephen R. Haynes and Steven L. McKenzie (Louisville: Westminster/John Knox
Press, 1993) 197-219.

the historical-critical methods of biblical scholars and the rationalist methods of theologians.

Chapter 5 ("Hermeneutical Possibilities for Jesus Study") treats the hermeneutical tradition from the days of Schleiermacher, a tradition that attempts to correlate modern Enlightenment modes of knowledge with feeling, lived experience, and praxis.

The history of the attempts to do justice to the historical Jesus is then traced in chapters 6 and 7 ("The Precritical Horizon and the Original Quest" and "From Bultmann to Crossan and Wright") by means of concentration on three "quests" for the historical Jesus. A first critical quest was inaugurated by developments in the Enlightenment, especially in Germany, and came to a climax and conclusion at the beginning of this century with Albert Schweitzer's two volumes[5] sketching the life of Jesus as a failed apocalyptic prophet and tracing the history of the quest of the historical Jesus up to the recovery of this apocalyptic perspective. Schweitzer's alternative to the old liberal quest was so shocking and his demolishing of the old quest so successful that scholars after Schweitzer did not really do serious work on Jesus until a second quest by students of Rudolf Bultmann in the middle of the century. The post-Bultmannian quest for the historical Jesus may be seen from contemporary studies as an aborted attempt, satisfied too quickly with assurance of some sort of relationship between the Jesus of history and the Christ of the church and thwarted by Bultmann's perspective on the impossibility of going beyond this and recovering the personality of Jesus. Now a third set of quests for the historical Jesus is eclipsing the accomplishments of earlier quests, with varying connections to earlier quests and the post-Bultmannian quest.

Chapter 7 ("From Bultmann to Crossan and Wright") includes a discussion of the church's stake in the question of historical research on Jesus. The relationship of the Jesus of history (a figure in history as such) and the Jesus recovered by historical-critical methods (a figure recoverable by historical research as such) to each other and to the Christ proclaimed by the church and presented in the Gospels is discussed. A

---

[5]*The Mystery of the Kingdom of God: The Secret of Jesus' Messiahship and Passion*, trans. Walter Lowrie (London: Adam & Charles Black, 1914; original 1901) and *The Quest of the Historical Jesus: A Critical Study of Its Progress from Reimarus to Wrede*, trans. William Montgomery, with a preface by F. C. Burkitt (London, New York: A. & C. Black; Macmillan, 1910; original 1906).

defense is made for the church's engagement in the critical enterprise and for a *critical* refusal to limit the significance of Jesus to what can be ascertained by historical-critical research.

The final three chapters discuss the relevance of nonfoundationalist hermeneutical approaches for the broader questions of the use and authority of the Bible.

Chapter 8 discusses "The Significance of Literary Criticism for New Testament Hermeneutics: Bultmann Revisited,"[6] showing how the hermeneutical task in the tradition of Schleiermacher and Bultmann may be reconceived and advanced by literary insights.

Chapter 9 ("A Sheep in Wolf's Clothing: Feminist and Sectarian Hermeneutics"[7]) compares contemporary moves in feminist biblical interpretation with approaches of the Radical Reformers.

Chapter 10, "How to Read the Bible and How Not to Read the Bible: Lessons from the Münster Anabaptists,"[8] concludes the study by comparing the approach of the Radical Reformation with Roman Catholic, mainline Reformation, and historical-critical approaches. In the end, an ecumenical rather than a divisive sectarian approach is advocated. Different ways of doing church and different ways of discovering and creating truth demand an ecumenical approach.

I am glad *Jesus Christ in History and Scripture* is among the volumes published by Mercer University Press during its twentieth year. I am especially grateful to the publisher, Cecil P. Staton, Jr., a longtime friend and colleague; the assistant publisher, Marc A. Jolley, who encouraged me to submit the manuscript to the Press; and the senior editor, Edmon L. Rowell, Jr., who saw the book through the press with his usual knowledge and skill. The dedication to "our" grandchildren is a way of acknowledging with gratitude and love the important part that my wife has played not only in our family life but also in our professional activities.

---

[6]This is a translation and revision of my essay in *Biblische Zeitschrift* (1997) "Der hermeneutische Gewinn der neuen literarischen Zugänge in der neutestamentlischen Bibel-interpretation."

[7]The essay was included in *The New Literary Criticism and the New Testament*, ed. Elizabeth Struthers Malbon and Edgar V. McKnight (Valley Forge PA: Trinity Press International; Sheffield UK: Sheffield Academic Press, 1994) 326-47 and is used by permission of the publishers.

[8]The essay was published originally in *Perspectives in Religious Studies* 24/1 (1997): 77-99, and is used by permission.

Chapter 1

Who Is Jesus Christ Today?

Jesus may be understood and spoken about as a historical figure, as a historic figure transcending his historical origins, as the subject of art and literature, and as a model and revelation of the nature of the divine. To be honest to the data that exist about Jesus, all of the ways of understanding Jesus must be acknowledged. But each way of understanding Jesus presents its problems and the coordination of knowledge from these approaches is a staggering task. Paralleling the different sorts of knowledge related to Jesus are the different functions of the Gospels and other sources of information about Jesus—the different functions of language and literature. Language in general and the language of the Gospels in particular may serve to convey information—historical information and theological convictions and truth. But language serves noncognitive affective functions. The two Gospels that indicate their objectives give evidence of these functions.

Luke stresses assurance:

> Since many have undertaken to set down an orderly account of the events that have been fulfilled among us, just as they were handed on to us by those who from the beginning were eyewitnesses and servants of the word, I too decided, after investigating everything carefully from the very first, to write an orderly account for you, most excellent Theophilus, so that you may know the truth concerning the things about which you have been instructed. (Luke 1:1-4)[1]

John emphasizes belief:

> Now Jesus did many other signs in the presence of his disciples, which are not written in this book. But these are written so that you may

---

[1]Unless otherwise noted, biblical quotations are from the New Revised Standard Version (NRSV).

come to believe that Jesus is the Messiah, the Son of God, and that through believing you may have life in his name. (John 20:30-31)

These evangelists along with Matthew and Mark did not distinguish between different uses of language. The affective and the cognitive were combined, making each use more and not less vital. Different perspectives of Jesus utilized in the different uses of language were combined, or better, amalgamated into a unity. The evangelists' presentation of what is (from a contemporary scholarly perspective) clearly historical fact is always stamped theologically or ideologically. But theological statement about Jesus is historically anchored. What we see today as historical or theological is transformed in the Gospels. The earthly Jesus is in continuity with the risen Lord, and the experience of the risen Lord in the church is reflected in the presentation of the story of Jesus. But the represented actions of the earthly Jesus are not simply the expressions of timeless transcendent truths; they are reflections of conscious willful acts of the human Jesus and may be seen not only as a revelation of the nature of the sacred but as heroic activities of the individual Jesus of Nazareth.

The theological assumptions of the evangelists and their churches made the unified poetic-historical-historic-sacred portraits of Jesus a possibility that became problematic in the later church. The difference between mixtures and compounds in chemistry may be used to help us understand the nature of the Gospels and the complexity of separating out one element from the other elements. A mixture would result from different sorts of information and knowledge being combined without the knowledge being transformed in some way. Salt and pepper can be mixed, but with care the salt can be separated from the mixture. When the Gospels are considered as mixtures, the historical information is seen as separable from other sorts of knowledge. A compound is not simply a mixture; it is the result of a chemical reaction between elements such that a new product results. Sodium and chloride enter into chemical combination and produce something new, the salt we use daily. The sodium and the chloride cannot be so easily separated from each other; another chemical process is required. The Gospels are much like compounds. They were composed at different times and places in the final third of the first century by Christians who compounded historical information with historic memory in imaginative ways to present a Jesus who was relevant to their congregations as he was to the earliest disciples and to subsequent followers.

The Gospel text, then, is like a compound. It is to be understood as a unity. The various parts form a nexus; they do not simply exist as a mixture with some parts referring to historical events, other parts witnessing to ahistorical existential or theological truths, while other parts propose historic models for admiration, emulation, and contemporary guidance, and so on. The historic Jesus is a historical figure. But this historical figure is for Christians a revelation of the nature of the sacred. To attempt to separate out one sort of knowledge is to do violence to the unity of the Gospel. Moreover, ideas and literary units in each of the Gospels are to be understood as they are related to other ideas and units in that Gospel and other Gospels. And these ideas and units (and the Gospels as units themselves) are to be understood canonically—in relation to the Scriptures of which they are a part, including the Hebrew Bible.

When the Gospels are studied as literary units, the world revealed in the Gospel becomes primary. Instead of picking and choosing what is acceptable from a contemporary perspective, the story is accepted at face value. The world of the Gospel of Luke, for example, is one in which God intervenes through miraculous conception, angels mediate between heaven and earth, and evil forces are active. The Jesus of Luke is presented within the world of Luke. The world of Luke presupposes the possibility of miraculous healing, and Jesus is, among other things, a healer. This healing activity is interpreted within the broader scriptural (Old Testament) context and used to present the narrative of a Jesus who brings near the blessings of the kingdom of God. The Gospels challenge readers to accept the way of Jesus as a revelation of the nature of the sacred. The affective and volitional are profoundly linked with the historical and theological.

We are unable to read the Gospels in exactly the same way as the earliest readers. We read the Gospels after the development of careful analysis of the uses of language and after the nineteenth- and twentieth-century revolutions in historical study. The remainder of this chapter will delineate the different ways contemporary readers may view Jesus and the Gospels' treatment of Jesus and then ask whether and how contemporary readers may be able to repeat the naïve reading of the earliest readers in our critical or postcritical epochs.

Historical and Historic Knowledge of Jesus

Historical Knowledge about Jesus. The Gospels of Matthew, Mark, Luke, and John constitute the major sources of information about Jesus.

They, along with other information from the New Testament as well as from other Christian sources and from Jewish and Roman sources, present a historical figure. New Testament historians are generally (not necessarily unanimously) agreed about basic historical facts concerning Jesus. Jesus was a Galilean Jew who carried out a ministry to Israel. Jesus appeared on the scene historically when he responded positively to the preaching and baptism of John the Baptist. Jesus himself carried out a ministry involving preaching and healing. His preaching centered on the kingdom of God, the reign of God that signified God's triumph. Jesus called twelve disciples to be associated with him in his role as herald of God's kingdom. The ministry of Jesus involved exorcisms and cures and also involved an initiative toward social outcasts. Jesus undertook a mission to Jerusalem that concluded with his execution outside Jerusalem by Roman authorities.

Historical data must be sorted out, related to each other, and evaluated according to historical criteria; and factual information is always susceptible to different historical evaluations. We must, therefore, distinguish between historical events, that is events that took place at particular times and particular places involving particular individuals, and our reconstruction of those events. We use the term "history" to refer to the events *and* to the reconstructions we make of those events. But there is obviously a gap between the actual events and the historical reconstructions of those events. That Jesus was an actual figure in history is more certain than any reconstruction we can make of the life of Jesus. Reconstructions of the life of Jesus involve determination of basic historical data and the arrangement and interpretation of those data according to some sort of framework that transcends that data. The data itself do not provide the framework, rather the way the data are conceived or even conceivable (the worldview of an epoch) provides constraints upon the framework that is found satisfying. The successful approach to the material world on the basis of reason and scientific principles is responsible for altering the view of the human world in the nineteenth and twentieth centuries. It led to the conclusion that the human sciences were also susceptible to being investigated critically and scientifically. The earlier theological framework for making sense of the human world was replaced by a historical framework emphasizing the historicality of cultural phenomena in general and literary documents in particular. That is, the cultural documents and artifacts are to be understood essentially within the temporally and spatially limited context of their origins.

Accompanying the emphasis on the historicality of the phenomena was the insight into historical process. The scientific principle of evolution and the idea of progress, then, went hand in hand with the development of the historical method in the nineteenth century. A particular event is to be understood in its place in a chain of events proceeding in a cause-and-effect relationship. This principle of *correlation* is one of the three interrelated principles on which historical inquiry rests. The historical cycles of human life influence and intersect one another in such a way that a change at any one point in the historical nexus effects a change in the entire set of relationships. Ernst Troeltsch declared that "the sole task of history in its specifically theoretical aspect is to explain every movement, process, state, and nexus of things by reference to the web of its causal relations." He discerned that the development of the historical-critical explanation of cause presupposed a revolution in the consciousness of the West.

> The causal explanation of all that happens, the setting of the individual life in its true relations, the interpretation of events in their most intricate interaction, the placing of mankind in a rounded system of ceaseless change—these constitute the essential function and result of modern historical reflection. The latter, viewed as a whole, forms a new scientific mode of representing man and his development, and, as such, shows at all points an absolute contrast to the biblical-theological views of late antiquity.[2]

Two additional principles or assumptions are necessary for the scientific historical approach. The principle of *criticism* affirms that judgments about the past are not to be classified simply as true or false but are to be seen as claiming only a greater or lesser degree of probability. Historical judgments are always open to revision. The principle of *analogy* affirms that humans are able to make such judgments of probability only by presupposing that their own present experience is similar to the experience of people of past epochs. By the nineteenth century, the assumptions of the historical method had penetrated so deeply into Western consciousness that it was impossible even to think about the assumptions. These had become "a part of the furniture" of Western mentality.

---

[2]Ernst Troeltsch, "Historiography," in *Encyclopedia of Religion and Ethics*, ed. James Hastings (New York: Charles Scribner's Sons, 1925) 4:718. See also his essay on "Contingency."

Although the Gospels were not composed or read originally by those whose worldview found the historical approach congenial, many scholars influenced by that worldview have attempted to establish the essential historicity of the Gospels by claiming that the evangelists intended to present historical accounts. The fact that the Gospels are narratives of events set in the first century would seem to support the idea, and Luke's statement of purpose seems to support Luke, at any rate, as a historical record. Present-day conservative scholars, such as Joel Green, however, agree with scholars in general that the Gospels, including the Gospel of Luke, is persuasive narrative, not history in the modern sense. Green gives attention to historical and narrative aspects of Luke, indicating that the narrative representation of history is always partial in terms of its selectivity of material and its orientation to a hermeneutical vantage point. "Historiography—in its choice of events to foreground at all, and in its ordering of those events in terms of temporal and causal relations— inevitably provides more, and less, than 'what actually happened.' "[3] One vantage point from which to evaluate the ordering of events in Luke is seen by Green as provided by the fact that it is a cultural product and must be seen as "a representation of the values and contexts within which it was generated." But

> at the same time, Luke's narrative gives expression to a vision of the world that cannot be equated with the first-century context insofar as this can be reconstructed via historical inquiry. . . . Luke has provided . . . an interpretation that must of necessity escape the historian concerned primarily with the scientific verification of particular events. . . . Indeed, it is not too much to say that the Lukan narrative is an invitation to embrace an alternative worldview and to live as if the reign of God had already revolutionized this age.[4]

A full appreciation of the Gospels will result from discovering the theological and religious viewpoint of the Gospels and discerning the creative ways that the Gospel writers have used traditional materials to set forth that viewpoint and to persuade their readers to share that viewpoint. A genuinely historical approach will not attempt to support the theological and religious conviction expressed in the narrative as the historical framework but will attempt to separate out the historical data and place

---

[3]Joel B. Green, *The Gospel of Luke*, New International Commentary on the New Testament (Grand Rapids MI: Eerdmans, 1997) 2.

[4]Ibid., 11.

that data in a framework that is acceptable to historical scholarship. Different frameworks are possible. Some are more conducive to the theological and religious agendas of the evangelists than others.

Jesus as a Historic Figure. Historic individuals are historic because they are seen by later individuals to have put their mark on history and to be significant for later generations. Socrates' acceptance of his death and his drinking of the hemlock as the consequence of his own convictions is historical knowledge that may become historic as it assumes direct significance for a future time. When the historical Jesus and historical knowledge of Jesus assumes a direct significance for the present, we have moved from historical knowledge to historic knowledge. Historic knowledge is related to historical knowledge, but these two types of knowledge are not the same. Historic knowledge is acknowledged to be related to the present. In some way historic figures are exemplary individuals. The significance of these individuals, the way they are exemplary, is not static. That Jesus died on the cross is historical knowledge. Historical knowledge might also include the fact that Jesus accepted his death as the inevitable consequence of his life, his proclamation of the kingdom, and his initiative toward social outcasts. Jesus' acceptance of the cross may become historic knowledge as it influences our time and we find ourselves touched or moved by it in some way.

Just as knowledge of Jesus as a historical individual is related to but not the same as the significance of Jesus for later epochs as a historic figure, historic knowledge and appropriation is related to but not the same as confession of faith in Jesus Christ as one who affects the world as revealer and makes known the nature of the sacred. Acceptance of Jesus Christ as Word of God has to do with faith. This faith knowledge is not necessarily opposed to historic knowledge, but it acknowledges and views the Jesus event as in some way revelatory of God and God's relationship to humankind. It is not knowledge that is verifiable by historical research or established through conceiving of Jesus as a heroic example.

The presentations of Jesus in critical study following the Enlightenment were influenced by the desire to present a Jesus purged of false dogmatic accretions, one consistent with the historical knowledge opened up by humanistic studies. From today's perspective it may be suggested that in much, if not all, of the study of the historical Jesus since the Enlightenment an unstated and perhaps unconscious goal has been to present a purely this-worldly Jesus who is as compelling as the dogmatic Jesus of the pre-Enlightenment period.

Herbert Samuel Reimarus (1694–1768), influenced by the antidog-
matic trends of the early Enlightenment and by deism, saw the Gospels'
story of Jesus and his resurrection as a creation of the disciples of Jesus
after their disappointment over Jesus' crucifixion. The real Jesus was a
political revolutionary who led an aborted revolt against the Romans. A
figure of Jesus who is able to speak to his own and later generations does
exist, however. This is the Jesus who was a moral enlightener and who
attempted to improve humanity inwardly through the cultivation of high
ideals, humility, gentleness, self-denial, and love of God and neighbor.[5]
     In different editions of the *Life of Jesus Critically Examined*, David
Friedrich Strauss (1808–1874) presented different reconstructions. In all
of them, the traditional explanation of Jesus was forsaken. In an initial
portrait, Jesus was presented as a disciple of John the Baptist who
ministered in Galilee, regarded himself a messiah, called disciples,
journeyed to Jerusalem with plans for his kingdom, had premonitions of
his death, predicted his second coming as Son of Man, and was condemned and crucified. Later, under the influence of Hegel's philosophy,
Strauss omitted the apocalyptic aspects of his earlier portrait of Jesus and
presented him as a man with an intense consciousness of the sacred.
"Jesus belongs to the category of highly gifted individuals who . . . are
called to raise the development of spirit in humanity to higher levels." He
claimed that "nothing higher can be imagined than the peculiar excellence
of the religious personality and work of Jesus himself."[6] This understanding of Jesus, as a human transcending (but not transgressing) normal
human sensibilities, had been stated earlier by Schleiermacher who
emphasized the constant potency of Jesus' God consciousness. It has been
stated in later epochs. Bultmann emphasized Jesus' existential relation to
the transcendent. John Macquarrie emphasizes Jesus as the human being
who actualized the possibility of human transcendence in manifesting the
fullness of the image of God (understood not in terms of dominion or
reason, but in terms of spirit that goes out from oneself and forms rela-

---

     [5]Reimarus's conclusions were published only after his death by G. E. Lessing. See
Reimarus: Fragments, ed. Charles H. Talbert, trans. Ralph S. Fraser, Lives of Jesus series
(Philadelphia: Fortress Press, 1970; London: SCM Press, 1971).
     [6]Cited from the third edition of Strauss's *Life of Jesus* by Leander E. Keck in
"Editor's Introduction" to *The Christ of Faith and the Jesus of History: A Critique of
Schleiermacher's "Life of Jesus"* by David Friedrich Strauss, trans. and ed. Leander E.
Keck, Lives of Jesus series (Philadelphia: Fortress Press, 1977) lxiv-lxv.

tionship with the other and that, therefore, opens out toward God and finds its completion in God).

In the liberal lives of Jesus, ethical questions about the ordering of human life in the world were the focus. The Jesus constructed by the liberal scholars was one consistent with an emphasis on moral values. Harnack sought the essence of Christianity in a way of life, and he found the original gospel in the ethical preaching of Jesus. The foundations of Jesus' teachings were the kingdom of God as a universal moral common-wealth, the fatherhood of God, and the infinite value of the human soul. The distinctive Christian element was the higher righteousness and the command of love. The gospel Jesus preached and Jesus' own person and history were closely connected. According to Harnack, Jesus Christ "was what he taught; to steep ourselves in him is still the chief matter."[7]

In America, the liberal Baptist pastor and seminary professor Walter Rauschenbusch propounded a "social gospel" and saw Jesus in relation to that gospel. He reminded the church of the concern of the prophets for justice and the concern of Jesus for the neighbor. He called the churches to become involved in the "social movement." For Rauschenbusch, then, Jesus is primarily the initiator of the kingdom of God. Jesus set in motion the historical forces of redemption that aim at the transformation of human society into the kingdom.[8]

Albert Schweitzer highlighted the apocalyptic aspect of the Gospels' presentation of Jesus (acknowledged by Reimarus and the early Strauss but ignored by the liberals) because he saw the apocalyptic mentality as a key to understanding the historical Jesus. In an ironic fashion, the relevance of the apocalyptic strain in Jesus is the lack of relevance that allows a more ethical view of salvation to be loosed. In Jesus' life this ethical view may be glimpsed, but it is historically subordinated to the apocalyptic view. Theologically and religiously, however, it is the more significant. In his autobiography, Schweitzer explains this relevance:

> The religion of love taught by Jesus has been freed from any dogmatism which clung to it by the disappearance of the late Jewish expectation of the immediate end of the world. The mold in which the casting was made has been broken. We are now at liberty to let the religion of Jesus

---

[7]*What Is Christianity?*, trans. Thomas Bailey Saunders, intro. by Rudolf Bultmann, Harper Torchbooks TB17 (New York: Harper & Row, 1957; orig. 1900) 11.

[8]See Walter Rauschenbusch, *Christianity and the Social Crisis* (New York: Macmillan, 1907).

become a living force in our thought, as its purely spiritual and ethical nature demands."[9]

Although Rudolf Bultmann was not inclined to use the Gospels' proclamation of Jesus as a "source" to reconstruct the "historical Jesus" with his "messianic consciousness," his "inwardness," or his "heroic character," Bultmann ties the historical figure of Jesus to what he sees as the theme of Jesus' teachings.[10] In the teachings of Jesus, an understanding of existence is revealed that challenges us in our understanding of our own existence. Jesus himself may be seen as an example of existential relationship to the transcendent.

The contemporary situation is extremely pluralistic, allowing a variety of portraits of a historic Jesus, an actual historical figure who transcends historical facticity and who is relevant for contemporary life. Some of the factors supporting a variety of positions are: (1) the breakdown of the Bultmannian hegemony in New Testament studies with no replacement for Bultmann (the post-Bultmannian quest may now be seen as maintaining major Bultmannian theological and historical tenets); (2) the different academic and ecclesiastical contexts of scholars involved in the study with different constructions appropriate to the different contexts; (3) the postmodern (or postcritical) challenges to cherished modern (or critical) notions of Enlightenment rationality; (4) the related emphasis upon experience and praxis, the historical nature of human existence, and the historically constrained nature of human knowledge; and (5) appreciation of the literary nature of the Gospels, a return to the emphasis of Strauss upon the creative artistic nature of the Gospel tradition with particular emphasis that the Gospel tradition and the Gospels as wholes are to be viewed in light of linguistic and literary conventions.

The different historic constructions of Jesus by members of the Jesus seminar and by scholars involved in a "third quest" show the influence

---

[9]*Out of My Life and Thought* (New York: Mentor, 1963) 50.

[10]See *Jesus and the Word*, trans. Louise Pettibone Smith and Erminie Huntress Lantero, new ed. (New York: Scribner's, 1958; [1]1934; orig. 1926).

The series of books in which Bultmann's book on Jesus appeared was entitled "The Immortals: The Intellectual Heros of Humankind in Their Life and Accomplishment" ("Die Unsterblichen. Die geistigen Heroen der Menschheit in ihrem Leben und Wirken"). Bultmann, of course, did not present Jesus as a hero in the normal sense of the word. This would have been an objectifying of one to be known in living experience, the transformation of an event that takes place when the word of Christ is heard as word of God into an object to be examined, taken apart, and put together again.

of different presuppositions. In its work on the teachings of Jesus, the Jesus Seminar came to the conclusion that Jesus was a visionary Galilean sage. Robert Funk provides a glimpse of a sage for whom the cross was the symbol of an uncompromising integrity:

> Jesus was originally a disciple of John the Baptist who called on people to repent in the face of the coming wrath of God. Jesus eventually rejected the ascetic life of John, along with his apocalyptic message, and returned to urban Galilee eating and drinking in profane style in celebration of the arrival of God's reign. . . . Jesus attracted dozens of followers. They followed him about as he wandered from village to village telling his stories, coining his epigrams, and living on handouts. . . . Jesus was drawn to Jerusalem to announce God's rule. He instigated an incident in the temple area when thousands of pilgrims were gathered to celebrate Passover and the weeklong festival of Unleavened Bread. The authorities took his invective against those who sold animals for sacrifice and changed currencies for the temple tax as a hostile act. He was arrested and summarily executed. His friends fled in terror. . . . [T]he theme of Jesus public discourse was the kingdom of God or God's domain. God's domain was that region or sphere where God's dominion was immediate and absolute. Jesus believed God's reign to be present but not discernible to ordinary eyes. . . . Jesus always talked about God's reign in everyday, mundane terms—dinner parties, travelers being mugged, truant sons, laborers in a vineyard, the hungry and tearful. . . . Although his language was drawn from the mundane world about him, he did not have ordinary reality in mind when he spoke about God's estate. . . . Jesus was not merely a victim; he was the victim of his own vision. The cross for Jesus and the hemlock for Socrates are symbols of uncompromising integrity.[11]

James M. Robinson constructs a picture of "an undomesticated Jesus, what one might call a real idealistic, a committed radical, in any case a profound person who proposed a solution to the human dilemma."

> What Jesus had to say centered around the ideal of God's rule ("the kingdom of God"), the main theological category Jesus created. Calling the ideal God's rule puts it in an antithetical relation both to other political and social systems, and to individual self interest—"looking out for number one." . . . God will not give a stone when asked for bread, or a snake when asked for fish, but can be counted on to give what one really needs. Indeed, people should trust God to know what they need

---

[11]"Jesus of Nazareth: A Glimpse," *The Fourth R* 9/1-2 (January–April 1996): 17-19.

even before they ask. This utopian vision was the core of what Jesus had to say. It was both good news—reassurance that good would happen to undo one's plight in actual experience—and the call upon people to do that good in actual practice. . . . This radical trust in and responsiveness to God is what makes society function as God's society. This is, for Jesus, what faith and discipleship were all about. Nothing else has a right to claim any functional relationship to him.[12]

Roy W. Hoover presents a profile of Jesus as a "remarkably perceptive and courageous young man who had a new vision of life as it ought to be, life under God's reign."

His gifts of mind and language made him a sage. His vision of God's order or life for his contemporaries made him an iconoclast and a reformer. As a sage with a vision he was provocatively and memorably clear. As a reformer, however, he was rather enigmatic. There is a moral vision expressed in exhortation to give to everyone who asks, for example, but there is no economic plan, no help on how to implement the moral vision. The author of a moral vision may not give much thought to the questions of limited resources and the costs of production, but the authors and managers of an economic plan always have to. God's generosity can be infinite because God's resources are infinite; human generosity can only be finite because human resources are always finite. It seems clear that Jesus thought that there was too little generosity in the life of his time and that in a good society there would be a lot of it. But he had little to say about how his vision of social generosity could be sustained, and he had little time to think about that. So as a reformer, he was enigmatic. . . . The reign of God is an ideal kingdom in Jesus' ordering vision, an ideal goodness that may inform, but ultimately transcends the moral virtual attained or attainable by any society. It was and is a goodness that transcends what is realizable in history even when it offers history a sense of direction. How to respond to an inspiring, ennobling, but impossible ideal is the challenge that all of Jesus' spiritual heirs were and are obliged to deal with. That is the legacy he has left to any who may choose to treasure it.[13]

The three representatives of the Jesus Seminar present a nontraditional Jesus with heroic traits that appeal to contemporary men and women in light of the values of their own world. The most popular and

---

[12]"What Jesus Had to Say," *The Fourth R* 8/5-6 (September–December 1995): 9-11.
[13]"The Jesus of History: A Profile in Courage," *The Fourth R* 9/3-4 (May–August 1996): 25-26.

prolific writer representing a traditional perspective is N. T. Wright. Wright sees the same data as those who portray Jesus as an iconoclastic teacher of wisdom. But he places that data within a more-or-less traditional view of Jesus as "a prophet bearing an urgent eschatological, and indeed apocalyptic, message for Israel." The main arguments for this prophetic portrayal is "the sense it makes in the total context of Judaism in general, of popular movements in particular, and of John the Baptist above all."[14]

As a Jewish prophet, Jesus believed that "Israel was the true people of the one creator God, called to be the light of the world, called to accomplish her vocation through suffering." The Jewish hope for "the coming kingdom of Israel's god, which would bring about the real return from exile, the final defeat of evil, and the return of YHWH to Zion" was thematic for Jesus' own work. Wright's Jesus may be seen as a heroic figure, not as the "supernatural" figure defined by some who are concerned to maintain a high Christology. Jesus' awareness of his vocation, for example, was of "a more risky" type than the "supernatural" knowledge often supposed in traditional approaches. Jesus' knowledge of his vocation was like knowing that one is loved. "One cannot 'prove' it except by living by it. Jesus' prophetic vocation thus included within it the vocation to enact, symbolically, the return of YHWH to Zion."[15]

Wright encourages his readers to focus on "a young Jewish prophet telling a story about YHWH returning to Zion as judge and redeemer, and then embodying it by riding into the city in tears, symbolizing the Temple's destruction in celebrating the final exodus." Wright proposes that "Jesus of Nazareth was conscious of a vocation, a vocation given him by the one he knew as "father,' to enact in himself what, in Israel's scriptures, God had promised to accomplish all by himself. He would be the pillar of cloud and fire for the people of the new exodus. He would embody in himself the returning and redeeming action of the covenant God."[16]

---

[14]*Jesus and the Victory of God*, vol. 2 of *Christian Origins and the Question of God* (Minneapolis: Fortress Press, 1996) 150.

[15]Ibid., 652-53.

[16]Ibid., 653.

The Jesus of History and the Christ of Faith

The most challenging task today is not the attack upon or defense of the Gospels as factually accurate presentations of the life of Jesus. As suggested earlier, the evangelists are not historians in the sense that they intended to present an account of the life of Jesus in terms of cause and effect on the human historical level. Of course, a continuing task for the church as well as the academy is the examination of the Gospels as sources for the study of the life of Jesus as a historical figure of the first century. The critical examination of these sources cannot move methodologically to the level of the sacred when the sacred is philosophically, theologically, and practically separated from the human and historical. The critical task, then, is to reconceptualize the relationship between the human and the divine, between the historical Jesus (however he may be portrayed by historians) and the sacred.

Accidental Truths of History and Necessary Truths of Reason. What is the relationship between the Jesus who is susceptible to historical investigation and the Christ who is the object of Christian faith? Can the transcendence of God over creation be reconceptualized so as to make a relationship between the human and divine conceivable? The study of Jesus has proceeded along two different paths, one path following philosophical and theological presuppositions and methods and the other following historical-critical presuppositions and methods. The very fact that this is the case may lead to the assumption that this bifurcation is inevitable.[17]

Appreciation for the different paths and the possibilities of reconvergence must begin with recognizing that the division goes back to the classical arguments over what is really real and how the really real is known. The idealist/realist dichotomy of the classical period was translated into the different theological approaches of Augustine and Aquinas and into the rationalist/empiricist dichotomy of the Enlightenment. The presuppositions behind Lessing's dictum that "accidental truths of history can never become the proof of necessary truths of reason"[18] forms the basis for the philosophical and theological dichotomies and the different

---

[17]Robert Morgan has traced the history of this division of tasks and pointed out earlier moments when the theological and historical-critical tasks coincided. See Robert Morgan with John Barton, *Biblical Interpretation* (London: Oxford University Press, 1988).

[18]*On the Proof of the Spirit and the Power* (1777).

paths in the study of Jesus. It is interesting and perhaps instructive that Lessing sometimes viewed reason as a destructive force removing humankind from a primitive innocence. A precritical return to this "primitive innocence" requires a reexamination and revision of the presuppositions behind Lessing's dictum. Against the background of a classical Christology from above, this section will trace attempts to develop a Christology from below and to revisit the question of the transcendence of God over God's creation in general and humankind in particular.

It will be noted that the current attempts to relate the eternal and the finite, the sacred and the historical, are imaginative and creative. They recognize that in a postcritical epoch our rational and empirical tools and methods have their limits. The models that guide these attempts are not foundations. They posit relationships between theory and praxis, between the rational and the empirical. In some measure, the conclusions reached mirror the models used, emphasizing the truth that is reached in terms of a nexus of relationships.

Human Transcendance. In his masterful treatment of Christology, John Macquarrie describes the development of classical Christology as an attempt to "assimilate Jesus Christ more and more to the being of God, and to obscure his humanity."[19] The Chalcedonian fathers came down on the side of divinity in their attempt to do justice to opposing sides in the controversy that had gone on since New Testament times. They declared:

> Therefore, following the holy Fathers, we all with one accord teach men to acknowledge one and the same Son, our Lord Jesus Christ, at once complete in Godhead and complete in manhood, truly God and truly man, consisting also of a reasonable soul and body; of one substance [ὁμοούσιος (*homoousios*)] with the Father as regards his Godhead, and at the same time of one substance with us as regards his manhood; like us in all respects, apart from sin; as regards his Godhead, begotten of the Father before the ages, but yet as regards his manhood begotten, for us men and for our salvation, of Mary the Virgin, the God-bearer [Θεοτόκος (*Theotokos*)]; one and the same Christ, Son, Lord, Only-begotten, recognized IN TWO NATURES, WITHOUT CONFUSION, WITHOUT CHANGE, WITHOUT DIVISION, WITHOUT SEPARATION; the distinction of natures being in no way annulled by the union, but rather the characteristics of each nature being preserved and coming together to form one person and sub-

---

[19]*Jesus Christ in Modern Thought* (London: SCM Press; Philadelphia: Trinity Press International, 1990) 166.

sistence [ὑπόστασις (*hypostasis*)], not as parted or separated into two persons, but one and the same Son and Only-begotten God the Word, Lord Jesus Christ; even as the prophets from earliest times spoke of him, and our Lord Jesus Christ himself taught us, and the creed of the Fathers has handed down to us.[20]

The Christology of Chalcedon answered the questions, "How does God become man?" or "How does the Word assume humanity?" But another question is implicit in the Chalcedonian statement that Jesus Christ as a human being is "consubstantial" with ourselves. This new question became explicit in developments in Enlightenment and post-Enlightenment philosophical, theological, and biblical studies. This question Macquarrie tries to answer: "How does a man become God?" or "How does a human life embody or manifest the divine life?"[21]

Macquarrie's strategy in answering the question is the strategy followed by philosophical anthropologies that are not satisfied to reduce humanity to a part of nature. It is the strategy of discovering a "transcendence" in humanity. Macquarrie points out that "some of the most profound anthropologies of modern times, both religious and secular, have made the idea of transcendence central to their understanding of the human condition" and that there is, in fact, great difficulty "in saying where the limits of human transcendence lie." (He deals with existentialism, Marxism or neo-Marxism, process philosophy, and transcendental Thomism.) Macquarrie concludes in reference to Jesus Christ:

> To call him the God-man (or whatever the preferred expression may be) is to claim that in him human transcendence has reached that point at which the human life has become so closely united with the divine life that, in the traditional language, it has been "deified." It has not, however, ceased to be human—rather, for the first time, we learn what true humanity is.[22]

In a separate chapter on "The Divinity of Jesus Christ," Macquarrie deals with the thesis that "if there is a capacity for God in human being, that can be the case only because there is already . . . a humanity in God."[23] Macquarrie finds a simple and direct doctrine of divine imma-

---

[20]Henry Bettenson, ed., *Documents of the Christian Church*, The World's Classics series (London and New York: Oxford University Press, 1943) 73.

[21]*Jesus Christ in Modern Thought*, 360.

[22]Ibid., 370.

[23]Ibid., 376.

nence to be problematic in light of features of the Old Testament that conceive of God predominately in transcendent terms and in light of historical association of immanence with paganism and polytheism.[24] Nevertheless, Macquarrie finds features of the Old Testament that qualify the transcendence of God over the creation and he declares that the Bible certainly does not teach the doctrine of a distant God typical of the deists of the Enlightenment.

The Christian statement of the relationship between the sacred and the mundane, however, comes not in the "form of a directly stated doctrine of divine immanence, but in the specifically Christian doctrine of the Trinity or triune God. Through Jesus Christ, the members of the Christian community had had a new experience of God, nothing less than a 'revelation', to use the technical term. Their new experience of God was so closely bound up with Jesus Christ that they could not now think or speak of God apart from Christ, or of Christ apart from God."[25] But Macquarrie argues:

> Only if there is *in all human beings* a possibility for transcendence and a capacity for God, can there be such a possibility and capacity in the man Jesus; and only if God makes himself present and known in and through the creation generally can there be a particular point at which he is present and known in a single way. Jesus Christ would not be a revelation if he was only an anomaly in the creation. He is revelation because he sums up and makes clear a presence that is obscurely communicated throughout the cosmos.[26]

Macquarrie finds the possibility of the divine becoming manifest on the finite human level in the idea of the creation of humankind in the image of God.

> Then God said, "Let us make humankind in our image, according to our likeness; and let them have dominion over the fish of the sea, and over the birds of the air, and over the cattle, and over all the wild animals of the earth, and over every creeping thing that creeps upon the earth."
> So God created humankind in his image,
>   in the image of God he created them;
>   male and female he created them. (Genesis 1:26-27)

---

[24]Ibid., 378.
[25]Ibid., 377-78.
[26]Ibid., 381.

The image in which God created the first human couple, according to Macquarrie, is best understood not as dominion or even reason, but spirit. By spirit, Macquarrie understands "the capacity of the human being to go out from himself or herself to form relations with that which is other." It is that which in the human being "opens out toward God and finds its completion in God."[27]

Personal Presence and Friendship between Humans and God. In *The Distancing of God*, Bernard J. Cooke expresses dissatisfaction with the view that humans participate in the divine in that they are the image of God and with the parallel philosophical reflection on the way in which effects participate in the perfection of a cause. "The ontological participation of some physical effects in its cause" is quite different from truly personal presence as "a reality constituted by a communication of consciousness from one person to another." In personal presence, "it is a question not of sharing some aspect of being with another but of sharing self as such."[28] Cooke is not criticizing Macquarrie's dynamic interpretation of the image of God. Rather he is dissatisfied with the way the understanding of the image of God was used in the Christian tradition to distance God rather than make God closer. Indeed, Cooke's conceptualization emphasizes experience and relationship.

In Jewish and Christian tradition, God was viewed as revealed through the actual events of human history. The God of Jesus Christ is the God of Israel who had been nurturing God's people for past centuries, and God was expressed by Jesus in the ordinariness in life—above all in caring concern for people. The earliest generations of Christians had a sense of God's presence such that the division between the sacred and the ordinary tended to disappear. Cooke declared, "The experience of being Jesus' followers was not of belonging to a new religion; it was the experience of existing humanly in a new world, in a new and final but not yet fully realized period of history."[29]

In both the Jewish world of primitive Christianity and the Hellenistic world of the later church, however, a process took place whereby the sacred was distanced from ordinary happenings in the lives of believers. Cooke points out that in the postexilic period Judaism's contact with

---

[27]Ibid., 370.
[28]Cooke, *The Distancing of God: The Ambiguity of Symbol in History and Theology* (Minneapolis: Fortress Press, 1990) 5.
[29]Ibid., 11.

Yahweh was crystallized in Bible and in Temple liturgy and that early Christianity was influenced by this earlier Jewish distancing of the sacred. But it was in the wedding of Christian tradition and Greek interpretation, particularly the Platonic tradition, that the understanding and practice of Christian faith was excessively spiritualized, leading to a "God thrice-distanced." It is because the victory of the Greek outlook can be traced in the changes and understanding of the "image of God," the idea that humans symbolize the divine, that Cooke finds that idea limiting.

> In its original biblical usage (Genesis 1:26-28), both man and woman are created in the image of God and are so in their total being as bodily persons, imaging the Creator precisely by their sexual creativity. By the third century it is only *man*, because of his rationality who is *imago Dei*; and he becomes more fully "image of God" in proportion as he turns away from involvement with the material world and commits himself to the "things of the spirit."[30]

The distancing of God in the early church affected Christology. The church began with the insight that in a special way God's saving presence is revealed in Jesus' human career, but "within a very short time there began a spiritualizing of the human/divine coincidence in Jesus as the Christ, with increasing emphasis on his identity and function as divine logos/son of God."[31] Instead of beginning the process of understanding Jesus as the Christ by reflection on his human career, the procedure now becomes one of starting with the eternal word in reflecting on how this word of God relates to God the Father and then relates to humans in its "descent" among us.

Cooke, however, is less interested in Christology than in divine contact with humans, with the possibilities of reestablishing a contact made problematic with developments in the church. This may explain his dissatisfaction with humans being the image of God according to their rational nature or imaging God by moral perfection. Nevertheless, Cooke finds that these "come together in something that transcends both." This is *"friendship* between humans and God."[32]

Cooke compares the relationship of friendship between humans and God and the resultant understanding of Jesus Christ with magical and miraculous understanding of God's relationship to humans. Magical and

---

[30]Ibid., 39-40.
[31]Ibid., 39.
[32]Ibid., 6.

miraculous views of providence seemed to salvage a biblical view of providence, but in fact leads to the "death of God." In magical terms, "all reality, including the divine, was considered a closed system that functioned according to a predetermined pattern in which ultimately irresistible forces interacted in fatalistic fashion. In the last analysis, humans had no freedom in determining their destiny; their only hope was to discover the magical formula of ritualized words or rituals and, having discovered it, to control the happenings of their lives. Belief in astrology is today's remnant of this magical view of providence."[33] The miraculous view "sees God as constantly involved in working minor miracles, moving directly, though unseen, the forces of nature and the actions of humans. What this entails is a two-level world: a sensible level in which the physical laws and the free choices of humans seem to be the effective causes of what happens, and a behind-the-scenes level where the real determining action is being carried on by God or by spiritual legates of God such as the angels."[34]

Human experience itself, rather than magic or miracle, may be seen as "the bridging medium of communication between God and humans."[35] This human experience is the basic awareness of self and world existing. "It is each person's experience that is for that individual the fundamental "Word of God." It is one's experience of being blessed or not, of self-esteem or self-depreciation, of being cared for or isolated and abandoned, that speaks concretely about God-for-us."[36] This raw word of daily experience requires interpretation and "for Christians this immediate exposure to divine self-expressing finds a unique fullness in Jesus of Nazareth and his human experience. His experienced life and death and resurrection is, as some contemporary scholars name it, 'God's parable'; it is the story through which the divine reveals what it means for God to be for humans and how humans in response should be for God."[37]

Cooke points out how the career of Jesus has undergone constant interpretation (and he does not suggest that we have a record of Jesus' career apart from interpretation), but he finds that that career itself "embodies the divine self-revelation, the 'Word of God.' " The distinctive

---

[33]Ibid., 361-62.
[34]Ibid., 362.
[35]Ibid., 363.
[36]Ibid.
[37]Ibid., 364.

Word cannot be seen in isolation, the fullness of that communication is achieved in extension of the mystery throughout history, in the relation of that core of meaning to the experienced meanings of other people's lives. According to Cooke,

> A basic reorientation of theological epistemology and methods is occurring; Christian life itself, particularly in its ritual moments, now functions in theological reflection as starting point rather than as "practical application." It is in experience in Christian discipleship—and here theologies of liberation, especially feminist theology, have made a major contribution—and in realizing its sacramental dimension that the presence of the risen Christ is experienced in the sharing of his Spirit.[38]

Cooke's conclusion that "God-for-us can be experienced as loving, caring, nondominating, exercising power as Servant rather than Lord, opposing oppression of the weak, forgiving human frailty"[39] sounds much like Peter C. Hodgson's thesis that

> God is efficaciously present in the world . . . in specific shapes or patterns of praxis that have a configuring, transformative power within historical process, moving the process in a determinate direction, that of the creative unification of multiplicities of elements into new wholes, into creative syntheses that build human solidarity, enhance freedom, break systemic oppression, heal the injured and broken, and care for the natural.[40]

The work of Cooke and Hodgson challenges the presupposition (underlining the dictum of Lessing) that accidental historical experience and truth and the necessary and universal reality of the sacred and truth belong to different conceptual realms. Hodgson (whose work is treated more fully below in chapter 8) may be seen as revising the philosophical tradition that distanced God. This philosophical revision and Cooke's emphasis on "friendship" are not the same, but both the cognitive and affective play their part in a reconceptualization of the sacred and therefore of Christology. Hodgson is primarily concerned with a rereading or revision of Hegel's scheme that seemed to overrate the sacred at the expense of the historical, to deny the essentially accidental and contingent nature of historical experience. When the contingent character of historical

---

[38]Ibid.
[39]Ibid.
[40]*God in History: Shapes of Freedom* (Nashville: Abingdon Press, 1989) 205.

experience is taken seriously, God will be understood as incapable of being God apart from nature and history. "What God 'does' in history is not simply to 'be there' as God, or to 'call us forward,' or to assume a personal 'role,' but to 'shape'—to shape a multifaceted transfigurative praxis. God does this by giving, disclosing, in some sense *being*, the normative shape, the paradigm of such a praxis."[41]

The Imaginative Construal of Jesus

How can a contemporary Christian be "honest to Jesus"[42] in light of the different ways of conceptualizing and imaging Jesus? Simplistic ways would be to select one way of knowing Jesus as foundational or primary and other ways as secondary and/or derivative. More complex ways would see a dialectical relationship between the different sorts of knowledge. In the history of the church's understanding of Jesus, there was movement from a dogmatic Jesus to a historical Jesus, with historical understandings correcting and modifying traditional dogmatic perspectives. This continues to be a helpful procedure for those who recognize the creative constructive nature of dogma and who are open to and aware of the nature and limitations of historical research. When such a procedure becomes the basis for a contemporary model of investigation, other elements become important. The end in mind becomes important. Praxis—in and out of the church—impinges upon the dogmatic/historical dialectic. For those approaching Jesus solely as a historic figure able to serve as a moral exemplar (like Socrates), the reconstructions of the historical personality of Jesus may be the focus—with this reconstruction able to impinge upon contemporary life. For those in the church, the practice of doctrine may be the end in mind, following Jesus as he reveals and actualizes a divine love, justice, and peace. Praxis has the capacity to focus and bring to satisfying completion the incomplete intellectual exercise involved in dogmatic and historical investigation.

The Creative and Poetic Imaging of Jesus. Honesty requires that the creative and poetic imaging of Jesus be recognized. As Robert Funk puts it, the early church's memory of Jesus was influenced by its convictions. Funk speaks of this as cheating, as the primitive Christian community felt

---

[41]Ibid., 205.

[42]This is the title given to his work presenting "Jesus for a new millennium" by Robert W. Funk, the founder of the Jesus Seminar (*Honest to Jesus: Jesus for a New Millennium* (San Francisco: HarperSanFrancisco, 1996).

free "to adapt their memories to their convictions."[43] When genuine literary insights are applied to the work of the evangelists, the charge of "cheating" must not only be modified but contemporary Christians must be freed to follow the very same procedures as the evangelists. To be sure, there is a difference between the first century and the twentieth century. Historical revolutions have occurred, revolutions in terms of historical study. (Even though we are in the age of a "new historicism," this historicism continues to feed upon an older positivistic historicism.)

Honesty in terms of poetic presentations of Jesus allows and demands a distinction between simple historical depictions and poetic heightening of those depictions, between historical occurrences in the life of Jesus and creative adaptation of traditional material (especially the Old Testament) to the life of Jesus. When readers are sensitive to the conventions of language and literature, it will be seen that all that the Gospel material relates (even the depictions of the most certain historical events) is shaped poetically in its structure and content. Readers may search for historical kernels in the life of Jesus lying behind the biblical texts or they may seek the historical experience in the life of the church that is impressed upon the text and expressed by the text. They may seek to recapitulate the experience that is expressed in the text and so to follow Jesus.

Literary capacity is not a static capacity. It involves a capacity to observe different levels of meaning, a narrative or story level whereby elements in the narrative fit together to tell a story, a more-or-less "literal" level whereby the text is referring to events in a real historical world, and levels of significance beyond the story and literal level. Literary capacity involves the capacity to observe conventional poetic meanings involved in simile and metaphor, parable and story—meanings that are clearly intended and discerned by ancient authors and readers. But literary capacity involves moving beyond those conventional meanings to new meanings that are appropriate for contemporary readers.

A literary approach, then, will not be constrained by so-called original "intentions" of ancient authors. These intentions, as they may be discerned, may be seen as involved in the originating circumstances of the text. A literary approach to the life of Jesus may even come to be less concerned with Jesus' understanding of himself and/or our inability to

---

[43]Robert W. Funk, "Letter to Fellows of the Jesus Seminar," 8 February 1996, as included in "Exchange of Letters" in *Jesus Seminar Papers, Santa Rosa, February 1996* (Santa Rosa CA: The Seminar, 1996).

prove scientifically some original self-understanding because Jesus' self-understanding would not be a final limiting constraint upon Jesus' meaning and significance.

Honesty demands that individual readers and readers in community make sense of Jesus and different presentations of Jesus in light of their need and capacity. But honesty demands that readers acknowledge that others have discerned other meanings, that the meanings we presently discern are genuine meanings but that they do not exhaust the meaningfulness of Jesus.

Revelation and Contemporary Readers. When the contemporary reader recognizes the literary and poetic aspect of the evangelists and assumes the same sort of creative approach, the reader is closer to being able to coordinate the different sorts of knowledge involved in the Gospels. The coordination is not the result of reducing other sorts of knowledge to one sort of knowledge—establishing a historical or theological foundation or even a foundation emphasizing praxis (related to the historic knowledge of Jesus). A reader may consider a comprehensive approach to Jesus Christ as a system involving different "worlds," the world of the text, the world of the historical Jesus, the world of the sacred, and the actual world of the reader. Each of these worlds is related to the others and the reader moves back and forth from the reader's own world to these other worlds. The worlds do not exist as independent entities. They are not unreal, but they exist essentially in relationship with each other.

Dan O. Via has dealt with the revelation of God in the New Testament from a perspective that parallels this reader-oriented perspective. Via takes statements of Paul in the first two chapters of 1 Thessalonians as paradigmatic in their emphasis on (1) the word of God or content, (2) the power of the Holy Spirit, (3) the way a particular situation influences the expression of the gospel, and (4) the place of human reception:

> Paul refers to the gospel (1:5; 2:4) or word of God (2:13) as rational content or *logos* (1:5a) and as empowered by the Holy Spirit (1:5b). He also speaks of the way in which the Thessalonians have received the gospel (1:6; 2:13) and of the historical circumstances in which he had worked and they had received the word (1:6; 2:2, 4-7, 14-17). These four factors recur regularly in the New Testament witnesses although not with the same emphasis or degree of explicitness. My argument will be that

for the New Testament, revelation is actual only when all four elements are operative. Only the four together are sufficient.[44]

Via sees his work in relation to that of Peter Hodgson. As observed, Hodgson's concern is the analysis of the interaction between God and humans in history from a contemporary theological standpoint. Via's questions is: "How does the recital of God's acts in the Bible, naïvely portrayed as historical, function in the revelation situation—primarily for the New Testament writers but by implication also for us."[45] Hodgson emphasizes the theological and ethical while Via emphasizes the herme-neutical and the configuration of all four elements, of which history is only one.

In his chapter on "Event and Word: The Historical Jesus," Via deals with the question of the relationship between historical actuality and revelation from the perspective of contemporary attitudes about history as human ways of creating meaning.

> If history is about the creation of meaning, what does it mean to say that God reveals God's self in history? What is the import of revelation in history if we have no unmediated access to the past? The locus of reve-lation becomes the imaginative construction of history writing, the narra-tive, the interpretative word, the kerygmatic proclamation, the literary text. Does that mean that historical event has simply been swallowed up in the word, in the language about the event?[46]

Via's answer is a definite no. He argues that historical actuality (as distinguished from linguistic representation) is in a certain way a neces-sary factor in the revelation situation. In the life process these two ele-ments are dialogically interactive. In light of the fact that revelation in the New Testament "is so materially constructed from theological intentions and imaginative decisions (to which we have access only through our own imaginative, theological, and theoretical decisions)," Via would reverse the normal connection between event and language while main-taining the close relationship between the two: "God reveals God's self in the language, the word, the text—language as the event of revelation—and the historical events narrated are a set of symbols for the event character of the word and for the capacity of a present situation to be a

---

[44]Dan O. Via, *The Revelation of God and/as Human Reception in the New Testament* (Philadelphia: Trinity Press International, 1997) 8-9.

[45]Ibid., 63.

[46]Ibid., 70-71.

new, redemptive event under the impact of the word." In that case, Via argues, "It is not so much that the word interprets the event as that the event narrated interprets the narrative word about the event *as* event."[47]

The claim that God is eschatologically active in the ministry of Jesus "is a *theological* affirmation derived from the *faith* experience or existential experience in which the merging of the Jesus tradition and one's present situation is experienced powerfully."[48] The story of the event and the event that is narrated itself have the same power—the power of revelation to liberate and transform.

There is, then, an ontological connection between the event and the story. The power of the narrative does not rest merely on its literary qualities. The question as to how much factual correspondence there must have been between event and narrative to justify claim of an ontological relationship is absorbed in the systemic approach. Not only is there a dialogue between event and narrative but there is also a dialogue between event/narrative, the imaginative reception and configuration of the word by human beings, and a historical-cultural situation in which the received word is meaningful.

Conclusion

This chapter began with the recognition that in the Gospels contemporary readers can recognize reflections or expressions of different perspectives concerning Jesus: an actual historical figure, a historic individual transcending his first-century constraints, a literary product, and a revelation of the nature of God. The Gospels unite these (and doubtless other) perspectives in a way difficult for contemporary readers to emulate. In the history of the study of Jesus, we have had to isolate these different perspectives and approaches. In the following chapters, these different approaches will be traced in some detail. But from the systemic dialogical reader-oriented approach, these different approaches will be see as playing their part—not in isolation but in conjunction with other approaches.

---

[47]Ibid., 77.
[48]Ibid., 78.

Chapter 2

The Gospels and Historical Sources

Jesus was a first-century Galilean Jew who carried out a ministry of teaching, preaching, and healing in Palestine. His followers continued his ministry, first in Palestine and then in the larger Hellenistic world. Strictly speaking, we do not have primary sources for the study of the historical Jesus. Jesus left no writings. We are dependent upon the writings of his followers in our attempts to discover what can be known about the historical figure of Jesus. In this chapter, I will discuss the Jesus traditions of the Christian community, along with the limited references to Jesus in non-Christian writings, as historical sources. This discussion will be along the lines of the order of study followed by scholars in their attempt to move back to the early first-century Jesus movement from the late first- and early second-century churches of the evangelists in the larger Mediterranean world.

The methods known as *source criticism* and *form criticism* were appropriate in light of the historical assumptions of scholars in the nineteenth and early twentieth centuries. The assumption was basically that scholars would be able to discover sources behind the canonical Gospels that would transport them back to the time of Jesus. When sources of the Gospels were seen not to reflect an "innocent" nonideological period but to share the theological agendas of the Gospels, attempts were made to move behind those sources by means of the study of the "forms" assumed by individual units of the Gospels that would have been transmitted orally and formulated for use in the primitive Christian communities. The major exponent of form criticism, however, was a scholar who was very slow to accept individual units as going back to the historical Jesus. The assumptions and conclusions of source criticism and form criticism are responsible for the "failure of nerve" in attempts to reconstruct the life of Jesus. We are left with fragments that have a tenuous relationship with the life of Jesus and that do not provide a satisfying framework for understanding those fragments judged to be "authentic."

In this chapter, I will first of all catalogue the multiplicity of sources for a study of the historical Jesus and then discuss the results of source and form criticism of the Gospels. The next chapter will then show how the focus changed from concern with the sources and forms of the Gospels to the Gospels themselves, first as reflections of the churches of the evangelists and their historical and theological situations and then as genuine literary productions of real authors.

Sources for a Study of Jesus

Jesus was an actual person who lived in Palestine during the first third of the first century. Facts concerning the historical Jesus, as facts concerning any other person in ancient history, must be gleaned from the ancient sources that deal directly and indirectly with him. The Four Gospels of the New Testament are the most complete sources for a study of Jesus. They are not the only sources, however, and Jesus is so central to the Christian movement that attention must be given to all of the possible sources of information.

Sources apart from the Gospels. The sources other than the Gospels give limited information. Jesus is mentioned merely in passing by some early Jewish and Roman writers. Early Christian writers whose works did not gain a place in the New Testament treat Jesus and his teachings more frequently and directly. Most important, however, among the sources apart from the Gospels are other New Testament writings that give some information about Jesus.

Jewish and Roman Writers. During the early Christian centuries, Jewish and Roman writings were flourishing. Of course, none of these writings deal primarily with Jesus. The writers were interested in interpreting the Jewish traditions, recording Jewish and Roman history, and composing "lives" of leading Roman officials. But Jesus is mentioned in passing by several of these authors.

a. The Talmud. The major part of Jesus' ministry was spent in Galilee, which was not a center of Jewish literary activity, and there is no evidence of Jesus' contact with contemporary Jewish writers, such as Philo, the Jewish writer in Alexandria, Egypt. It is not surprising, therefore, that Jesus is mentioned only infrequently in contemporary Jewish literature. References do occur in the Jewish materials that came into fixed form in the Talmud, the repository of Jewish interpretation of the Law from the time of Ezra to the middle of the sixth century CE. The Talmud contains legal materials, moral reflections, homilies, apologies, maxims of worldly wisdom, metaphysical speculations, traditions of Israel's past, visions of its future, and other materials. Just as Christian literature of this period of conflict between Jews and Christians contains references to the Jews, so the Jewish literature mentions Jesus Christ and his followers. References on both sides are often polemical or defensive, however, and their historical value is questionable. One of the passages that refer to Jesus in the Babylonian Talmud, for example, is declared by the Jewish scholar Joseph Klausner to have "greater historical value" than the others.[1]

> On the eve of the passover Yeshu was hanged. For forty days before the execution took place, a herald went forth and cried, "He is going forth to be stoned because he has practiced sorcery and enticed Israel to apostasy. Anyone who can say anything in his favor, let him come forward and plead on his behalf." But since nothing was brought forward in his favor, he was hanged on the eve of the Passover. (Talmud, *b.Sanhedrin* 43a)

This statement, and the other references in the Talmud, oppose the claims of Christian tradition, and it is difficult to assign independent historical value to the Talmudic traditions. They are probably dependent upon the various Christian traditions that they attempt to discredit. Note, for example, that in the passage quoted above, Jesus is sentenced to be stoned. According to Jewish tradition, this is the correct punishment;[2] but according to the passage quoted, Jesus is hung instead of stoned. It seems that the passage attempts to justify Jesus' condemnation from the Jewish point of view; the tradition that Jesus was crucified was so firmly fixed, however, that the writers could not go so far as to say that the sentence of stoning was carried out.[3]

In spite of its polemical bias the witness of the most ancient rabbis as given in the Talmud has some value. The texts attempt to destroy the validity of Christian truth by altering and interpreting the Christian tradition; they do not deny its basis. The Talmudic evidence is sufficient to make clear that there is no reason at all to doubt the existence of Jesus.

---

[1] Joseph Klausner, *Jesus of Nazareth: His Life, Times, and Teaching* (New York: Macmillan, 1925) 27.

[2] The Mishnah. *m.Sanhedrin* 7.4.

[3] See Maurice Goguel, *The Life of Jesus*, trans. Olive Wyon (New York: Macmillan, 1933) 72.

Moreover Klausner regards the early statements in the Talmud as substantiating some facts about Jesus.

> There are reliable statements to the effect that his name was Yeshu'a (Yeshu) of Nazareth; that he "practiced sorcery" (i.e., performed miracles, as was usual in those days) and beguiled and led Israel astray; that he mocked at the words of the wise; that he expounded Scripture in the same manner as the Pharisees; that he had five disciples; that he said that he had not come to take aught away from the Law or to add to it; that he was hanged (crucified) as a false teacher and beguiler on the eve of the Passover which happened on a Sabbath; and that his disciples healed the sick in his name.[4]

b. Josephus. Additional information about Jesus comes from Flavius Josephus, a Jewish historian born in Jerusalem in the late 30s CE. He was a member of a priestly family, received a good education, and became a member of the party of the Pharisees. During the Jewish war with Rome (66–70 CE), Josephus first fought as an officer with the Jewish forces and later was captured by the Romans. Gaining their favor, however, he was set free and lived thereafter in Rome, devoting himself to historical and literary work. Four works of Josephus have been preserved[5] and, although these works treat the period when early Christianity was active, no allusion to the Christian movement appears in any of them. Josephus' silence on the Christian movement, along with the scarcity of allusion to the general messianism of the first century, is probably due to his overall apologetic purpose. He is writing to present Judaism to his Roman readers in the best possible light, and references to Christianity and other Jewish messianic movements might have detracted from that purpose. In his *Antiquities,* however, two passages do mention Jesus:

> About the same time came Jesus, a wise man, if indeed we should call him a man. For he was a doer of miracles and the master of men who received the truth with joy. And he attracted to himself many of the Jews and many Greeks. He was the Christ, and, when after his denunciation by our leading citizens, Pilate condemned him to be crucified, those who had cared for him previously did not cease to do so, for he appeared three

---

[4]Klausner, *Jesus of Nazareth,* 46.

[5]*The Jewish War,* a history of Jewish nationalism from around 175 BCE to the Jewish War of 66-70 CE; *The Antiquities of the Jews,* a history of the Jews from creation to the revolt of 66 CE; *A Life,* a sequel to the *Antiquities,* defending his career and earlier writings; and *Against Apion,* a reply to criticisms of himself and the Jewish people.

days afterwards, risen from the dead, just as the prophets of the Lord had announced this and many other marvels concerning him. And the group which is called that of the Christians has not yet disappeared. (*Antiquities* 18.3.3.)

Ananus called a Sanhedrin together, brought before it James, the brother of Jesus, who was called the Christ, and certain others . . . and he caused them to be stoned. (*Antiquities* 20.9.1.)

The authenticity of the first passage is open to rather serious question. It does exist in the earliest Greek manuscripts of Josephus' works, but none of the manuscripts goes back earlier than the eleventh century. The real question of origin, however, arises from an internal study of the passage. Could Josephus actually say such things about Jesus? It seems that only a Christian could have made these statements and Josephus was not a Christian. It seems best to conclude that Josephus originally made some passing reference to Jesus that was expanded by later Christian writers to make the passage more of a confessional statement about Jesus. This modification must have taken place fairly early, for Eusebius, a Christian leader of the early fourth century, knew the passage.[6]

The second passage more probably comes directly from Josephus. Early Christian writers attributed the statement to the Jewish historian and no real reason precludes assigning its authorship to him. Both passages together, however, add no essential data to the canonical story of Jesus. But they do affirm that he really lived.

c. Pliny. Information concerning Jesus and the early Christian movement in Roman writers is scanty. That this is so may at first be a surprise because the Roman dominance assumed by Christianity in later centuries leads easily to a belief that it always had this importance. For first-century Roman society, however, Christianity was simply another superstition from the East. It was important only as the cause of political and social disturbances, hence the Roman writers Pliny the Younger, Tacitus, and Suetonius speak of Christ and his disciples in the context of political and social ferment.

One of the more important Roman references to early Christianity occurs in a letter written by Pliny the Younger to the Roman emperor Trajan. At the beginning of the second century Pliny had been sent by

---

[6]See Edgar Hennecke and Wilhelm Schneemelcher, eds., *New Testament Apocrypha*, 2 vols. (Philadelphia: Westminster Press, 1963, 1965) 1:436-37, for a brief treatment of the authenticity of the quotations and for a bibliography.

Trajan to be the governor of Bithynia. The senate usually appointed the provincial governor, but Bithynia had fallen into such a poor state of affairs that the emperor himself sent the "upright and conscientious, but irresolute [and] pedantic"[7] Pliny to reorganize affairs in the province. Among other difficulties, he faced an unusual set of problems with the Christians, and in a letter dated about 110 CE he asked the emperor for instructions. Pliny was convinced that Christianity was merely a "perverse and extravagant superstition." The Christians themselves, he stated in the letter,

> maintained . . . that the amount of their fault or error had been this, that it was their habit on a fixed day to assemble before daylight and recite by turns a form of words to Christ as a God; and that they bound themselves with an oath, not for any crime, but not to commit theft or robbery or adultery nor to break their word, and not to deny a deposit when demanded.[8]

Pliny's letter affirms the presence of Christianity in Bithynia and illustrates the conflict with the authorities that sometimes occurred. The specific descriptions of Christian beliefs and practices, however, arise from an examination of Christians about their faith and cannot be taken to represent an independent non-Christian source for information concerning Jesus.

d. Tacitus. The *Annals* of Tacitus provides another important reference to Christianity. Tacitus was a Roman historian who had earlier held political office, serving as a provincial governor from 112 to 116 CE. He wrote two important historical works: *Histories*, which covers the period of Roman history from 68 to 96 CE, and *Annals*, which covers the period from 14 to 68. Tacitus intended to paint a vivid picture of Roman life under the Caesars of the first century. The bitterness which the historian felt toward the tyrannical rulers of the period is not hidden.

In his *Annals*, Tacitus gives information concerning the great fire of Rome and tells of the people's suspicions that Nero was responsible. In the context of the report he mentions Christians and Christ.

> But all human effort, all the lavish gifts of the emperor, and the propitiations of the gods, did not banish the sinister belief that the

---

[7]James Stevenson, ed., *A New Eusebius: Documents Illustrative of the History of the Church to A.D. 337* (London: S.P.C.K.; New York: Macmillan, 1957) 13.

[8]Ibid., 14.

conflagration was the result of an order. Consequently, to get rid of the report, Nero fastened the guilt and inflicted the most exquisite tortures on a class hated for their abominations, called Christians by the populace. Christus, from whom the name had its origin, suffered the extreme penalty during the reign of Tiberius at the hands of one of our procurators, Pontius Pilate, and a deadly superstition, thus checked for the moment, again broke out not only in Judaea, the first source of the evil, but also in the City, where all things hideous and shameful from every part of the world meet and become popular.[9]

Tacitus is obviously drawing upon information procured from some source. The generally negative attitude toward the "deadly superstition" and the view that the Christian movement did not reawaken until the time of Nero show clearly that Tacitus was not drawing upon a Christian source. A Christian would not have been so derogatory toward the Christian faith. Nor does Tacitus seem to be dependent upon a Jewish source. The statement refers to Jesus as "the Christ" and seemingly suggests that Christianity is tied to the Jewish nationalistic movement, which affirmations a Jew would not make. Apparently Tacitus knew a secular source that connected Christianity with the Christ, who was crucified under Pontius Pilate.

The evidence from Tacitus is important, not because it gives information that the Christian sources do not give, but because it confirms some of the information we have in the Christian sources.

e. Suetonius. Two important references appear in the work of Suetonius, a young friend of Pliny. In about the year 120 CE, while he was secretary to the emperor Hadrian, Suetonius published *The Lives of the Twelve Caesars*. The work is not history in any scientific sense. "It is a mere assemblage of superficial facts, spiced with gossip or even scandal,"[10] but at two places in the work mention is made of Christianity. In his *Life of Nero*, Suetonius mentions the persecution of the Christians, "Punishment was inflicted on the Christians, a class of men given to a new and wicked superstition."[11] Nothing is said, however, about Jesus Christ. In his *Life of Claudius*, he tells of the expulsion of the Jews from Rome. "Since the Jews constantly made disturbances at the instigation of

---

[9]Ibid. 2.
[10]Dean Putnam Lockwood, *A Survey of Classical Roman Literature*, 2 vols. (Chicago: University of Chicago Press, 1962) 2:242.
[11]*A New Eusebius*, 3.

Chrestus, he expelled them from Rome."[12] The interest in this passage centers around the name "Chrestus," whose similarity to "Christus" is obvious. Is he simply an unknown Jewish agitator who stirred up trouble among the Jews at Rome? Or is this a reference to Jesus Christ? Possibly Suetonius, viewing the Christian message as an outsider, was referring to Jesus Christ and thought that this "Chrestus" about whom the people were speaking was actually in Rome at the time.

Obviously the Roman historians do not give us a great deal of information concerning Jesus Christ. The evidence from Tacitus is solid evidence against any theory of the nonhistoricity of Jesus, but neither Tacitus nor the other writers have preserved information to supplement the knowledge of the life of Jesus which we have in the Christian sources.

Early Noncanonical Christian Sources. In addition to the New Testament a great deal of early Christian literature has been transmitted that contains information about Jesus and teachings purported to come from Jesus. Much of this early Christian literature has been collected and published and can be consulted with ease.[13]

a. Agrapha. A variety of documents contain words ascribed to Jesus that are not in the best manuscripts of the four canonical Gospels. These sayings, or "agrapha" (literally, "unwritten things"), were perhaps remembered by his disciples, transmitted in oral form, and eventually written down. Some of these sayings of Jesus are found in New Testament writings outside the Gospels. First Corinthians 11:23-25 and Acts 20:35 contain sayings that are clearly attributed to Jesus:

> For I received from the Lord what I also handed on to you, that the Lord Jesus on the night when he was betrayed took a loaf of bread, and when he had given thanks, he broke it and said, "This is my body that is for you. Do this in remembrance of me." In the same way he took the cup also, after supper, saying, "This cup is the new covenant in my blood. Do this, as often as you drink it, in remembrance of me." (1 Cor. 11:23-25)

> In all this I have given you an example that by such work we must support the weak, remembering the words of the Lord Jesus, for he himself said, "It is more blessed to give than to receive." (Acts 20:35)

---

[12]*A New Eusebius*, 1.

[13]An introductory guide is M. R. James, *The Apocryphal New Testament* (Oxford: Clarendon, 1924). A more recent work is Hennecke and Schneemelcher, eds., *New Testament Apocrypha*, vol. 1.

Some of the inferior manuscripts of the canonical Gospels also contain sayings attributed to Jesus that are not contained in the oldest and best manuscripts. A frequently noted saying is found in Codex Bezae at Luke 6:4, addressed by Jesus to the man found working on the Sabbath: "Man! if you know what you are doing, you are blessed! But if you do not know, you are cursed and a transgressor of the law." The fact that a reading does not belong to the genuine text of the Gospel does not preclude the possibility that it does go back to Jesus himself. Statements like the one just quoted could well be genuine teachings from Jesus that for some reason or another were not incorporated in the Gospels.

Early Christian, and some non-Christian, writings outside the New Testament also contain some quotations attributed to Jesus. Some of these may go back directly or indirectly to the Synoptic tradition, others are from extant apocryphal gospels, but some derive from sources with which we are not familiar. Among papyri discovered at the turn of the twentieth century in Egypt were copies of short sayings ascribed to Jesus. The sayings, copied from apocryphal sources, are contained in fragments of codices, papyrus rolls, and even on the back of a property writ. Following are a few samples of important agrapha from various sources.[14]

"There will be dissensions and squabbles." (Justin Martyr, *Dialogue with Trypho* 25.3)

"No one can attain the kingdom of heaven who has not gone through temptation." (Tertullian, *On Baptism* 20.2)

"Ask for the great things, and God will add to you what is small." (Clement of Alexandria, *Stromaties* 1.24.158)

"He who is near me is near the fire; he who is far from me is far from the kingdom." (Origen, *On Jeremiah*, Homily 20.3; *Gospel of Thomas*, logion 82)

"(He who today) stands far-off will tomorrow be (near) (to you)." (Papyrus Oxyrhynchus, 1224)

---

[14]These and other agrapha are quoted in Henneeke and Schneemelcher, eds., *New Testament Apocrypha* 1:85-116. Some of the most important of the sayings that parallel sayings in the first three Gospels are noted in *Gospel Parallels. A Synopsis of the First Three Gospels / A Comparison of the Synoptic Gospels*, ed. Burton H. Throckmorton, Jr., 3rd rev. ed. (Nashville: Thomas Nelson, RSV 1949–1979; NRSV 1992).

While it is probable that some of the agrapha may represent an authentic tradition that may in some way be traced back to Jesus, they offer no significant supplement for knowledge of the historical Jesus.[15]

  b. Apocryphal Gospels. Still another possible source of information about Jesus is noncanonical or apocryphal "gospels," a number of which are known today.[16] Some are known only through quotations or references in early writers; the names of others are known only through lists of noncanonical books issued by early ecclesiastical groups. But some noncanonical gospels have survived from the date of origin being copied and transmitted through the centuries, and some of these that had been lost for centuries have been rediscovered in modern times. The most valuable discovery of "lost" gospels was made at Nag Hammadi, in upper Egypt, in 1946. Thirteen Coptic codices (manuscripts in book form) with nearly 800 pages were uncovered. They have been dated as early as the third century and are thought to be based upon Greek originals. The codices contain about fifty different works, some previously unknown and some known only by title, quotations in early writers, or translation in other languages. Once work began on the manuscripts, nearly a decade after the discovery, it was learned that the writings once belonged to a church or monastery, the ruins of which were near the site of discovery. It is obvious that the documents were preserved by Gnostics, for some of the writings are plainly Gnostic writings and others show Gnostic tendencies.

  Even a cursory reading of the noncanonical gospels shows that they do not compare with the canonical Gospels. Some of them are similar to

---

[15]Joachim Jeremias judges that the agrapha may be seen as consisting: "(a) Of tendentious coinings of sayings of the Lord; (b) of barefaced legendary inventions or legendary transferences to Jesus . . . ; (c) of biblical and extrabiblical citations which, because of slips of memory, have inadvertently been transferred to Jesus; (d) of sayings of Jesus given in the Gospels, which have been remodelled and worked up; [and] (e) of sayings the attestation of which occasions doubt. . . . There remains: (f) a very small residue of sayings in the case of which content, form, and attestation justify the opinion that they stand on a level with the sayings of our Lord (themselves historically of very differing value) contained in our four Gospels." Jeremias, "Isolated Sayings of the Lord," in Hennecke and Schneemelcher, eds., *New Testament Apocrypha* 1:86-87. Jeremias quotes eleven sayings which may belong in the last category. But he gives some reasons for doubting a few of these, and he also lists five other sayings that may belong in that category.
[16]See Hennecke and Schneemelcher, eds., *New Testament Apocrypha* 1:71-84, 117-531.

modern biblical novels in that they attempt to write fuller lives of Jesus and the disciples than the canonical Gospels do by supplying incidents and information some of which is plausible, some of which is not. Other apocryphal gospels support a particular religious viewpoint or interpret Jesus in the light of a particular heresy. The *Protevangelium of James*, for example, provides an imaginary account of the birth of the Virgin Mary, her upbringing, and the birth of Jesus. The *Infancy Story of Thomas* gives a group of miracles purportedly wrought by Jesus as a small boy. Some of the materials in these apocryphal gospels may come from the early tradition. In them traditions about Jesus and his disciples not recorded in the canonical Gospels may be preserved and forms of the traditions that are also recorded in the Gospels may be earlier than those in the Gospels.

The Coptic *Gospel of Thomas* (to be differentiated from the *Infancy Story of Thomas*), one of the volumes of the Coptic Gnostic library found in Egypt, is a collection of purported sayings of the exalted Lord that are to be considered revelatory discourses and are to mediate "gnosis" (knowledge) and bring "life." No fewer than 68 of the 114 sayings of the *Gospel of Thomas* have parallels in the Synoptic Gospels, and if the *Gospel of Thomas* (in its present form or even in an earlier form) is independent of the Synoptic Gospels, the form of sayings in the *Gospel of Thomas* may be closer to the original than the forms in the Synoptics.[17]

New Testament Writings apart from the Gospels. The earliest data in the New Testament about Jesus come from the Pauline epistles, and there is additional material about Jesus in some of the later writings. Although information about Jesus in nongospel New Testament material is not plentiful, it is valuable, for it confirms the viewpoint of the Gospels that Jesus was an actual historical figure. The way that notices of Jesus are

---

[17]An account of the discovery and contents of the writings from Nag Hammadi is given by Willem C. van Unnik in *Newly Discovered Gnostic Writings: A Preliminary Survey of the Nag-Hammadi Find*, Studies in Biblical Theology 30 (London: SCM Press, 1958; Naperville IL: Allenson, 1960). Another, and fuller, description of the discovery with a translation of the Gospel of Thomas is Jean Doresse et al., *The Secret Books of the Egyptian Gnostics*, trans. Leonard Johnston (New York: Viking Press, 1960). Kendrick Grobel edited and translated *The Gospel of Truth* (New York: Abingdon) in 1960; and *The Gospel of Thomas* with text and translation was published by Harper and Row in 1959. For a concise and authoritative discussion of the question of the relationship of the Gospel of Thomas to the synoptic Gospels, see Ron Cameron, "Gospel of Thomas," *The Anchor Bible Dictionary*, 6 vols., ed. David Noel Freedman et al. (New York: Doubleday, 1992) 6:535-40.

given shows that the early Christians presupposed both the historicity of Jesus and some knowledge of his life and teaching.

a. Letters of Paul. Paul's major letters, the undisputed ones, tell that Jesus was a man born of a woman and subject to the law (Gal. 4:4). He was an Israelite, a descendant of David (Rom. 1:3; 9:5). Jesus' brothers are mentioned (1 Cor. 9:5) and one is named as "James" (Gal. 1:19). Jesus carried on a ministry among Jews (Rom. 15:8) with a circle of disciples known as "the Twelve" (1 Cor. 11:23-26). He was betrayed. He was crucified, buried, and on the third day he was raised from the dead (2 Cor. 13:4; 1 Thess. 2:14-15; 1 Cor. 15:4).

In addition to references to the life of Jesus, Paul refers to teachings of Jesus, some of which are clearly related to the Synoptic tradition. A most important saying of Jesus in Paul has been quoted above (1 Cor. 11:23-25). It tells of the institution of the Lord's Supper, citing Jesus' words as a part of the ritual. In 1 Corinthians 7:10-11 Paul writes, "To the married I give this command—not I but the Lord—that the wife should not separate from her husband (but if she does separate, let her remain unmarried or else be reconciled to her husband), and that the husband should not divorce his wife."[18] That Paul is confident of giving an actual quotation from Jesus is seen as Paul later, in the case of the unmarried, admits that he has "no command of the Lord" (1 Cor. 7:25). And the instruction he gives to Christians married to pagans is clearly his own instruction, "To the rest I say—I and not the Lord— ... " (1 Cor. 7:12). In 1 Corinthians 9:14—"In the same way, the Lord commanded that those who proclaim the gospel should get their living by the gospel"—Paul establishes the right of those who proclaim the gospel to be supported by the churches through an appeal to a command from Jesus. Paul also gives evidence that his readers are aware of other facts from the life of Jesus. These facts are not reported by Paul, but knowledge of them is necessary to make sense of Paul's writings.[19]

b. Later New Testament Writings. The later New Testament writings report some facts from the life of Jesus, and, perhaps more importantly, presuppose the historicity of Jesus and knowledge of his life. The Epistle to the Hebrews not only contains details concerning Jesus, but also rests its teachings upon the foundation of Jesus and his death. It is obvious in Hebrews that the manifestation of Christ had taken place recently (1:2),

---

[18]Compare Mark 10: 11-12 and Matthew 5:32.
[19]See Romans 15:8; 1 Corinthians 13; Galatians 3:1; and Philippians 2:5-11.

and that his message had been passed on by those who had received his teachings (2:3). The sufferings and temptations of Jesus are used to encourage Christians who are enduring persecution (2:18; 4:15; 5:8) and the epistle treats the fate of Jesus as comparable to the fate that every person faces (9:27-28). Beyond Hebrews, the books of 2 Peter and Revelation are helpful. Second Peter alludes to the transfiguration (1:16-18). The Book of Revelation is aware of the Gospel tradition and alludes to some specific facts in the life of Christ. Jesus Christ had a human history (1:5; 5:9; 11:8); he was slain and, because of this, is worthy to open the seals (5:6); he is the one who was dead and is alive again (1:18; 2:8). The Book of Revelation also reflects the belief in Jesus' Davidic descent (5:5; 22:16).

Clearly the materials in the New Testament apart from the Gospels provide no great amount of information that is not contained in the canonical Gospels. Yet the writers of the New Testament presuppose information about the historical Jesus and build their writings upon this knowledge, and what information is contained in their writings confirms the information of the Gospels. One historian of the life of Jesus asserts that in the light of extremely skeptical judgments of the validity of the Gospels' witness to Jesus "it is important for the historian to be able to state that the testimony of Paul confirms that of the Gospels, and confirms its reliability."[20] Thus the nongospel material in the New Testament, like noncanonical references to Jesus, add little to the overall picture of Jesus, but it does confirm the historicity of Jesus and some of the events recorded in the Synoptic Gospels.

The Canonical Gospels. The scanty data available outside the Gospels make it clear that no serious study of Jesus can proceed on the basis of such limited information. A historical figure emerges, but no real story of Jesus can be reconstructed. Any large-scale presentation of the life and teachings of Jesus then depends upon the four canonical Gospels. However, as with sources for any other historical person or event, the nature of the Gospels must be determined and appropriate means devised for their use in a study of Jesus.[21]

---

[20]Goguel, *The Life of Jesus*, 119.
[21]See Stephen C. Neill and N. Thomas Wright, *The Interpretation of the New Testament, 1861-1986*, 2nd ed. (Oxford and New York: Oxford University Press, 1988) for a survey of developments in the study of the life of Jesus by means of the Gospels.

The Nature of the Gospels. a. Religious Literature. The Gospels are plainly not simple and objective presentations of Jesus' life and teachings. The writers were Christians who had accepted Jesus as Christ and Lord and who were writing because of this very fact. The Christians believed that what God had promised in the Hebrew Scriptures had begun to be accomplished in Jesus of Nazareth. The new age had been inaugurated in his coming, a beginning adequately attested by his resurrection. The report in the Book of Acts on Peter's sermon in Jerusalem sounds this note:

> You that are Israelites, listen to what I have to say: Jesus of Nazareth, a man attested to you by God with deeds of power, wonders, and signs that God did through him among you, as you yourselves know—this man, handed over to you according to the definite plan and foreknowledge of God, you crucified and killed by the hands of those outside the law. But God raised him up, having freed him from death, because it was impossible for him to be held in its power. (Acts 2:22-24)

The Gospels are written from this Christian perspective for quite definite religious purposes. The writer of the Gospel of John frankly gives his evangelistic aim in telling about Jesus: "These are written that you may believe that Jesus is the Christ, the Son of God, and that believing you may have life in his name" (John 20:31). He was not primarily interested in discussing the questions about what Jesus did and what Jesus said. Rather, he is concerned with who Jesus was, that is, the meaning of the entire Christ event. In some sense Jesus' words and deeds are presupposed and questions of theological import are asked, "Who was the One who did these things? Who was the man who taught these things?" John's testimony is that he is the "father's only son" (1:14), "the Lamb of God" (1:29), "Rabbi" (1:38), "the Messiah" (1:41), and consequently attention must be given to his deeds and words. Although the Synoptic Gospels do not state their purpose in such a direct way, that they are controlled by a theological purpose is seen from their general content, organization, and specific treatment of Jesus Christ.

b. Written by Later Disciples. As written documents the Gospels date from a period sometime after Jesus' life and ministry. The Synoptic Gospels, acknowledged by scholars to stand closest to traditions going back to Jesus, were written not by original disciples of Jesus but by later Christians. The earliest was written sometime around 65 CE. The names of Mark and Luke are connected with the Second and Third Gospels although these men were not among the earliest disciples. Matthew's name is connected with the First Gospel, but there is good reason to believe that the apostle Matthew did not write the Gospel in its present form. None of the Gospels, therefore, were written by eyewitnesses or companions of Jesus.

c. Dependent Upon Oral Sources. Since the Gospels are not the stenographic reports of those who had seen and heard Jesus, they are necessarily dependent upon earlier sources—originally oral sources. This lack of direct relationship of the Gospels to the historical events in the life of Jesus is both advantageous and disadvantageous. From the perspective of a scientific history, the Gospels suffer severe limitations. The traditions contained in them have been selected and modified by the Christians who were passing them on. The faith of the Christian community could not have failed to affect the selection of the tradition and the formation of each unit of the tradition. When the Gospels are studied, account must be taken not only of the events reported but also of the faith that molded the Gospel tradition.

However, the process of oral transmission did preserve narratives and sayings of Jesus that would otherwise have been lost. Had there been no oral transmission, no information would be available. Further, the process of oral transmission was a relatively dependable method of preservation in the first century. The orally transmitted word was more highly valued among the Jews of the first century than it is today, actually being regarded as important as the written word, perhaps more highly valued by some. One rabbi paid the tribute to a disciple that "he was like a well-plastered cistern that loses not a drop."[22]

Paul gives evidence of the transmission of the Jesus tradition among early Christians. In a letter to the church at Corinth Paul declared that his message was that which he had received from those Christians before him. "For *I handed on to you* as of first importance *what I in turn had received*: that Christ died for our sins in accordance with the scriptures, that he was buried, and that he was raised on the third day in accordance with the scriptures, and that he appeared to Cephas, then to the twelve" (1 Cor. 15:3-5, italics added). The verb Paul uses means "to pass on what

---

[22]Quoted in Francis Wright Beare, *The Earliest Records at Jesus: A Companion to the Synopsis of the First Three Gospels by Albert Huck* (New York and Nashville: Abingdon Press, 1962) 54.

one has received." It is equivalent to the Latin word *traditio* from which derives the English word "tradition."[23]

The process of oral transmission continued even during and after the tradition in the Gospels was written down. The author of the Gospel of Luke acknowledged dependence upon oral tradition:

> Since many have undertaken to set down an orderly account of the things that have been fulfilled among us, just as they were handed on to us by those who from the beginning were eyewitnesses and ministers of the word, I too decided, after investigating everything carefully from the very first, to write an orderly account for you, most excellent Theophilus, so that you may know the truth concerning the things about which you have been instructed. (Luke 1:1-4)

A comparison of different treatments of the same sayings of Jesus suggests that, although these were transmitted in a manner analogous to the transmission of the teachings of other rabbis, the words of Jesus were presented and transmitted with the freedom gained from the awareness that their meaning, not their form, was the important thing. A great English New Testament scholar, Brook Foss Westcott, declared concerning this fact, "Thank God, we are not called to rehearse a stereotyped tradition, but to unfold a growing message."[24]

d. Dependent upon Written Sources. Written materials as well as oral materials are mentioned in Luke's prologue, indicating that the Gospels utilized written sources as well as oral traditions. The Synoptic Gospels' dependence upon written sources is confirmed by a comparison of the Gospels with one another. When the three are studied side by side, it becomes clear that (1) their content and arrangement of materials are closely related; (2) the basic course of Jesus' activities is the same in each; (3) the narratives portraying Jesus' ministry are used in a similar way; and (4) the discourses of Jesus share the same characteristics in the Synoptics. The close relationship extends to matters of style, language, and even specific wording. Such marked similarity in subject matter, arrangement, and external form leads to the inevitable conclusion that the Synoptics are somehow literarily related to one another. But the literary relationship cannot be a simple one, for at places the three Gospels differ significantly from one another in form and content.

---

[23]See also 1 Cor. 11:23ff.
[24]Quoted in Beare, *The Earliest Records of Jesus*, 54n.

The Gospels are certainly far from being carbon copies of each other. For example, each Gospel has its own way of beginning its story. Mark opens with the ministry of John and the baptism of Jesus; Matthew and Luke both have rather extensive birth narratives, but these birth stories differ from one another in essential features. Even such a routine item as Jesus' genealogy is molded differently in terms of each Gospel's purpose. Matthew and Luke have great amounts of discourse material that is missing in Mark, but in turn they vary considerably in their presentation of the discourse material. Matthew presents the material in five long discourses, while Luke collects it along with narrative materials in the sections 6:2–8:3 and 9:51–18:14. Each Gospel also has unique material, Matthew and Luke containing much more than Mark. Clearly, the Synoptics use their sources, both oral and written, to develop distinctive theological interpretation of Jesus, considered by all these to be pivotal to the church's life and faith.

Source Criticism

The scientific study of the literary relationships of the Synoptic Gospels has been carried on since the eighteenth century and some positive results have assisted in a study of the historical Jesus.[25] The solution of the "Synoptic Problem" (that is, the possible literary relationships between Mark, Matthew, and Luke) has led to three basic affirmations: (1) Mark is the earliest written Gospel and was used as a source by both Matthew and Luke; (2) Matthew and Luke share a large body of material not present in Mark, called Q (from the German *Quelle*, "source"); (3) Matthew and Luke each had sources peculiar to themselves. M is used to designate Matthew's peculiar material, L for Luke's.

The Priority of Mark. A number of facts combine to make the priority of Mark a logical conclusion. The material of Mark is almost completely contained in Matthew and Luke--only six short sections of Mark

---

[25]The ancients, of course, noted the similarities and differences between the Synoptic Gospels, but they assumed that these were due to the different eyewitnesses of the same events. The Fathers, especially Augustine, held Matthew as the original Gospel with Mark as a condensed version of Matthew and Luke depending upon both Mark and Matthew. See Burnett H. Streeter, *The Four Gospels: A Study of Origins* (London: Macmillan, 1924) for a full treatment of evidence concerning the relationships of the Gospels. See Paul Feine, Johannes Behm, and Werner G. Kümmel, *Introduction to the New Testament*, 17th rev. ed., trans. Howard Clark Kee (Nashville: Abingdon Press, 1975) 38-80, for a concise treatment of the "Synoptic Problem."

are found in neither Matthew nor Luke. Within the material common to Mark, Matthew, and Luke there is extensive agreement in vocabulary. The most logical explanation seems to be that Mark was written first and later Matthew and Luke used Mark, incorporating large blocks of Mark's material and often utilizing his vocabulary. The following sections from the Synoptic Gospels illustrate the literary relationship between the three. A careful comparison clearly shows that the three accounts are essentially the same with some minor editorial additions by Matthew and Luke.

Matthew 22:15-22	Mark 12:13-17	Luke 20:20-26
Then the Pharisees went and plotted to entrap him in what he said. So they sent their disciples to him, along with the Herodians, saying, "Teacher, we know that you are sincere, and teach the way of God in accordance with truth, and show deference to no one; for you do not regard people with partiality. Tell us, then, what you think. Is it lawful to pay taxes to the emperor, or not?" But Jesus, aware of their malice, said, "Why are you putting me to the test, you hypocrites? Show me the coin used for the tax." And they brought him a denarius. Then he said to them, "Whose head is this, and whose title?" They answered, "The emperor's." Then he said to them, "Give therefore to the emperor the things that are the emperor's, and to God the things that are God's." When they heard this, they were amazed; and they left him and went away.	Then they sent to him some Pharisees and some Herodians to trap him in what he said. And they came and said to him, "Teacher, we know that you are sincere, and show deference to no one; for you do not regard people with partiality, but teach the way of God in accordance with truth. Is it lawful to pay taxes to the emperor, or not? Should we pay them, or should we not?" But knowing their hypocrisy, he said to them, "Why are you putting me to the test? Bring me a denarius and let me see it." And they brought one. Then he said to them, "Whose head is this, and whose title?" They answered, "The emperor's." Jesus said to them, "Give to the emperor the things that are the emperor's, and to God the things that are God's." And they were utterly amazed at him.	So they watched him and sent spies who pretended to be honest, in order to trap him by what he said, so as to hand him over to the jurisdiction and authority of the governor. So they asked him, "Teacher, we know that you are right in what you say and teach, and you show deference to no one, but teach the way of God in accordance with truth. Is it lawful for us to pay taxes to the emperor, or not?" But he perceived their craftiness and said to them, "Show me a denarius. Whose head and whose title does it bear?" They said, "The emperor's." He said to them, "Then give to the emperor the things that are the emperor's, and to God the things that are God's." And they were not able in the presence of the people to trap him by what he said; and being amazed by his answer, they became silent.

The sequence of the narratives in the Gospels also points to the priority of Mark. In the material parallel to Mark, Matthew and Luke generally agree with the Marcan sequence. When the Marcan sequence is not followed, Matthew and Luke rarely agree with each other.

Changes in the language and subject matter in the materials common to Matthew, Mark, and Luke is a third argument for the priority of Mark. Matthew and Luke often modify the Semitic-colored Greek of Mark and other awkward Greek constructions to a better form of Greek. Changes in the subject matter also constitute important evidence. In Matthew 3:16, for example, the word "immediately" is not understandable in the context, but it is easily explained when Mark's use by Matthew is assumed, for Mark 1:10—"And when he came up out of the water, immediately he saw the heavens opened and the Spirit descending upon him like a dove" (RSV)—provides the word. Again, in Matthew 9:2 there is no indication of a cause for Jesus observing the faith of the men who brought the paralytic; but Mark 2:4 tells about the unusual task of bringing the sick through the dug-up roof, which is evidence of their faith. Matthew and Luke clearly seem to be dependent upon Mark.

The Existence of Q. Matthew and Luke have an extensive amount of common material that is not taken from Mark. This body of material is usually referred to as Q and may be illustrated from numerous places in Matthew and Luke. Compare Jesus' saying on the watchful householder in Matthew and Luke.

Matthew 24:43-44	**Luke 12:39-40**
"But understand this: if the owner of the house had known in what part of the night the thief was coming, he would have stayed awake and would not have let his house be broken into. Therefore you also must be ready, for the Son of Man is coming at an unexpected hour."	"But know this: if the owner of the house had known at what hour the thief was coming, he would not have let his house be broken into. You also must be ready, for the Son of Man is coming at an unexpected hour."

These and many other passages in Matthew and Luke are almost identical to each other, but have no parallel in Mark. Obviously these passages bear some literary relationship to each other. The simplest possibilities are (1) that Matthew used Luke, (2) that Luke used Matthew, or (3) that both Matthew and Luke used a common source.

Explanations (1) and (2) are generally rejected for several reasons. The different arrangement of the material in each Gospel points away from this solution. In Luke this common material is mainly in two sections inserted into the Marcan narratives;[26] in Matthew the material is

---

[26]Luke 6:20–8:3 and 9:51–18:14.

contained mainly in five major discourses of Jesus.[27] If Matthew used Luke or Luke used Matthew, it is difficult to explain why either rearranged the material.

Perhaps as important is the internal evidence. At times the material appears in a more original form in Matthew and at times it is more original in Luke. This certainly argues against either one being used by the other.

Hence the most likely resolution of their literary relationship is the third possibility. Matthew and Luke not only used Mark, but also a non-Marcan source (already referred to as Q).

It is, of course, impossible to reconstruct the original source from the materials in Matthew and Luke (just as Mark could not be reproduced precisely from the Marcan content of Matthew and Luke). Yet the basic character of Q is evident. It is mainly a collection of the sayings of Jesus to which are added also some material about John the Baptist, a narrative of the temptations of Jesus, several controversy stories, and miracles.

Why the Q collection was created and whether it was written or oral are matters of continuing speculation and debate. The frequent verbal agreements of Matthew and Luke suggest, but do not prove, that the source was written, and, generally, Q must have come into existence to meet needs of the Christian community. The sayings of Jesus, now the risen Lord, would have given continuing direction to the life of the Christian community. Nonetheless more is unknown than known about this illusive document.

Material Peculiar to Matthew and Luke. Both Matthew and Luke contain material the origin of which is unexplained from this assumption of the sources Mark and Q. That is to say, both Matthew and Luke contain material peculiar to themselves. Some of the material peculiar to either Gospel could have come from Q, and some is perhaps the direct composition of the authors of the Gospels; but all of the material peculiar to Matthew and Luke cannot be explained on these bases. Likely some other sources were used.

A number of years ago the assumption was that there were two written documents roughly equal to the unique material of each Gospel. Matthew's special source was called "M" and Luke's was designated "L." Today there is great hesitation in crediting the special material of Matthew and Luke to written sources. It is still possible that one or both

---

[27]Matthew 5–7; 10; 13; 18; and 23–25.

Gospel writers drew heavily from one important written collection, each selecting materials of special interest to himself, but more probably the symbols M and L should be used to designate simply the special material of Matthew and Luke without pronouncing a judgment about either the existence or the nature of these sources.

This analysis of the sources of the Synoptic Gospels does give some help in a treatment of the life ar.• teachings of Jesus. It shows that the framework of the life as presented by the Synoptics was not independently designed by three writers, but came from Mark. The analysis also demonstrates that the teachings of Jesus were not originally placed in an unalterable chronological or topical order but that Matthew and Luke arranged them freely as best fitted their confessional portrait of Jesus. Source criticism is a valuable tool to study specific sayings and narratives, but even its most scientific use fails to take account of all aspects of the nature of the Gospels.

Form Criticism.

An analysis of the sources of the Synoptic Gospels obviously does not carry us back to Jesus himself. Not only do Matthew and Luke use earlier written and oral traditions produced for religious purposes, but Mark itself developed out of earlier materials. The literary analysis of the Gospels, then, forces us back to the oral period, and this is exactly the history of Gospel criticism. At the beginning of the twentieth century a school of study known as "form criticism" developed as a tool to study the traditions of the Gospel in the oral period.[28]

Origin of Form Criticism. Form criticism of the Gospels developed out of the scholarly concern to get beyond study of the literary relationships of the Gospels to each other. Vincent Taylor characterized it as "the child of disappointment of source criticism."[29] But it was also influenced

---

[28]For an introduction to the discipline of form criticism, see E. Basil Redlich, *Form Criticism: Its Value and Limitations*, Studies in Theology (London: Duckworth, 1939); Rudolf Bultmann and Karl Kundsin, *Form Criticism: Two Essays on New Testament Research*, trans. Frederick C. Grant, Harper Torchbooks TB96 (New York: Harper & Row, 1962); and Edgar V. McKnight, *What Is Form Criticism?* (Philadelphia: Fortress Press, 1969). See also Martin Dibelius, *From Tradition to Gospel*, Scribner Library SL 124 (repr.: New York: Scribner, 1965; 1934); and Rudolf Bultmann, *The History of the Synoptic Tradition*, trans. John Marsh (Oxford: Basil Blackwell; New York: Harper & Row, 1963).

[29]Vincent Taylor, *The Gospels. A Short Introduction* (London: Epworth, 1930) 16; and

by developments of studies in Greek literature and in Old Testament literature that dealt with recurring literary forms that were altered in the process of transmission. By careful study of the forms scholars were able to trace the traditional forms to earlier stages. Hermann Gunkel, an Old Testament scholar, applied the method of form criticism to the narratives of Genesis, and when two of his students applied his principles to the study of the Gospels, New Testament form criticism was born. These men were Martin Dibelius and Rudolf Bultmann.[30]

The term "form" is used because it was held that the traditions in the Gospels could be analyzed in terms of the forms in which they circulated in the oral period. It was also supposed that the process of transmission effected changes and developments in the forms. The challenge was to determine the history of the tradition so that the earliest forms of the narratives and sayings of Jesus could be determined.

Presuppositions of Form Criticism. The method of form criticism becomes logical only when two basic presuppositions are accepted. First, the sayings of Jesus and narratives about Jesus circulated orally as independent units. For numerous reasons it is generally thought that the chronological and topographical framework of Mark does not go back to Jesus himself but is at least partly the creation of the author. Attention is called especially to the vague notices of time and place in the Gospel of Mark. Orally transmitted units lie behind the organization in Mark. Very early, even before the writing of Mark, oral units may have been joined into connected narratives. One of the earliest of these was the passion narrative with the basic scheme of Last Supper, arrest, trial, crucifixion, and resurrection appearances. The second basic presupposition is that the needs of the early Christian community played an important role in the selection, formation, and transmission of the sayings and narratives. Both of these presuppositions are accepted by all who use form criticism.

Within this context of agreement, however, scholarly opinion varies widely about the original form of the sayings and narratives and their history in the life of the early church. Some see the church as the formulator of the tradition with little concern for historical events; others

---

see Taylor, *The Formation of the Gospel Tradition*, 2nd ed. (London: Macmillan; New York: St. Martin's, 1935; [1]1933) 10-11.

[30]See Dibelius, *From Tradition to Gospel*, and Bultmann, *History of the Synoptic Tradition*. The original German editions of both works appeared after World War I (1919 and 1921, respectively). Both works have passed through several editions and have long since been translated into English.

believe that the Christian community only molded historical reality in the form of its own faith, that the tradition is essentially trustworthy historically. Some emphasize preaching as the most important factor in transmitting the material; others stress worship. Other factors would certainly include teaching or instruction, conflict and debate with the Jews, and church administration. There is general agreement about some of the forms that the materials took, but there is also some disagreement, especially about the terms to be used and the specific form to be attributed to certain passages.[31]

Method of Form Criticism. Vincent Taylor provided a useful, although not necessarily unique, vocabulary for the study of form criticism. Taylor is a cautious form critic who evaluated the method in 1933, more than a decade after it was introduced.[32] He classified the forms of the units of tradition as pronouncement stories, sayings, parables, miracle stories, and stories about Jesus.[33]

Pronouncement Stories. Pronouncement stories are brief narratives of an encounter of Jesus with one or more persons that culminate in a statement or pronouncement of Jesus. The stories contain words of Jesus useful in preaching, teaching, and controversy with outside opponents. It is possible that some of the narratives are "typical" scenes created out of the church's memory of Jesus to act as a carrier for the saying. Mark 12:13-17 (cited above with the parallel passages from Matthew and Luke) illustrates the pronouncement story at its best. The pronouncement concludes the narrative: "Render to Caesar the things that are Caesar's, and to God the things that are God's" (Mark 12:17 RSV).

---

[31]The form critics also vary in their estimate of the historical value of the individual sections of the Synoptic tradition. Bultmann in particular is noted for his "skeptical" position regarding the historicity of much of the material of the Synoptic tradition.

[32]Taylor, *The Formation of the Gospel Tradition.*

[33]Bultmann divides the sayings of the Gospel tradition into (1) logia, or wisdom sayings; (2) prophetic and apocalyptic sayings; (3) legal sayings and church rules; (4) I-sayings in which Jesus speaks of himself; (5) parables; and (6) apothegms, a decisive saying or pronouncement as the climax of a brief narrative. He also gives narrative materials as: (1) miracle stories and (2) historical narratives and legends. Martin Dibelius divides the narrative material into five forms: (1) paradigms; (2) novellen or wonder stories; (3) legends, edifying stories of a holy person; (4) the passion story; and (5) myths which tell of the invasion of human life by supernatural power. Sayings are organized by Dibelius into: (1) similitudes; (3) narrative parables; (4) prophetic utterances; (5) concise commands; (6) more elaborate demands; and (7) sayings concerning the nature of the speaker.

Sayings. Many sayings of Jesus circulated independently of the narrative framework of the pronouncement story. The Gospels contain collections of such sayings. Some of these seem to be collections of sayings that were grouped somewhat artificially during the oral period. Mark 4:21-25 is such a collection.

> He said to them, "Is a lamp brought in to be put under the bushel basket, or under the bed, and not on the lampstand? For there is nothing hidden, except to be disclosed; nor is anything secret, except to come to light. Let anyone with ears to hear listen." And he said to them, "Pay attention to what you hear; the measure you give will be the measure you get, and still more will be given you. For to those who have, more will be given; and from those who have nothing, even what they have will be taken away."

But in certain instances the collections in our Gospels may go back to a sequence of sayings given in that form by Jesus and transmitted as a group until they were written down. This form is illustrated by Luke 6:27-38.

> "But I say to you that listen, Love your enemies, do good to those who hate you, bless those who curse you, pray for those who abuse you. If anyone strikes you on the cheek, offer the other also; and from anyone who takes away your coat do not withhold even your shirt. Give to everyone who begs from you; and if anyone takes away your goods, do not ask for them again. Do to others as you would have them do to you.
> "If you love those who love you, what credit is that to you? For even sinners love those who love them. If you do good to those who do good to you, what credit is that to you? For even sinners do the same. If you lend to those from whom you hope to receive, what credit is that to you? Even sinners lend to sinners, to receive as much again. But love your enemies, do good, and lend, expecting nothing in return. Your reward will be great, and you will be children of the Most High; for he is kind to the ungrateful and the wicked. Be merciful, just as your Father is merciful.
> "Do not judge, and you will not be judged; do not condemn, and you will not be condemned. Forgive, and you will be forgiven; give, and it will be given to you. A good measure, pressed down, shaken together, running over, will be put into your lap; for the measure you give will be the measure you get back."

Parables. A rich element in the early Christian tradition is the parables. A parable is a narrative of a commonplace experience that suggests an analogy to a spiritual truth. The Gospels, of course, contain numerous parables. A well-known one appears in Mark 4:3-8.

> "Listen! A sower went out to sow. And as be sowed, some seed fell on the path, and the birds came and ate it up. Other seed fell on rocky ground, where it did not have much soil, and it sprang up quickly, since it had no depth of soil. And when the sun rose, it was scorched; and since it had no root, it withered away. Other seed fell among thorns, and the thorns grew up and choked it, and it yielded no grain. Other seed fell into good soil and brought forth grain, growing up and increasing and yielding thirty and sixty and a hundredfold."

The parable is used to express a single truth independent of the parable itself, but in transmission the parable sometimes tended to be allegorized. Mark 4:13-20 is an allegory based on the parable in Mark 4:3-8.

> And he said to them, "Do you not understand this parable? Then how will you understand all the parables? The sower sows the word. These are the ones on the path where the word is sown: when they hear, Satan immediately comes and takes away the word that is sown in them. And these are the ones sown on rocky ground: when they hear the word, they immediately receive it with joy. But they have no root, and endure only for a while; then, when trouble or persecution arises on account of the word, immediately they fall away. And others are those sown among the thorns: these are the ones who hear the word, but the cares of the world, and the lure of wealth, and the desire for other things come in and choke the word, and it yields nothing. And these are the ones sown on the good soil: they hear the word and accept it and bear fruit, thirty and sixty and a hundredfold."

Miracle Stories. Numerous miracle stories narrate miraculous acts of Jesus. The form of the Synoptic miracle stories is the same as the form of Jewish and Hellenistic miracle stories. The general pattern includes three elements: a description of the circumstances, a statement of the miraculous act, and a description of the consequences. Mark 1:40-45 shows the pattern of the miracle story.

> A leper came to him begging him, and kneeling he said to him, "If you choose, you can make me clean." Moved with pity, Jesus stretched out his hand and touched him, and said to him, "I do choose. Be made clean!" Immediately the leprosy left him, and he was made clean. After sternly warning him he sent him away at once, saying to him, "See that you say nothing to anyone; but go, show yourself to the priest, and offer for your cleansing what Moses commanded, as a testimony to them." But

he went out and began to proclaim it freely, and to spread the word, so that Jesus could no longer go into a town openly, but stayed out in the country; and people came to him from every quarter.

Certain narratives of a miraculous act are included among the pronouncement stories[34] and in at least one instance two miracle stories are combined in the same narrative.[35]

Stories about Jesus. Taylor classifies as "Stories about Jesus" all the narrative material that does not fit into the categories above. He admits that the stories in the category "Stories about Jesus" have no common structural form but almost all of them center upon Jesus.[36] Taylor suggests that practical aims and not narrative interests were responsible for the formation of these stories. As the stories were transmitted, the figure of Jesus came into stronger focus and secondary features faded out.

Form criticism is clearly very subjective and not a method that supersedes all other methods of study. However, it can be used as an important tool for clarifying the early forms of the Gospel tradition and elaborating the meaning of Jesus for early believers. Taylor declared:

> Form-Criticism is not an instrument by which we can solve the problems of Gospel Origins, but it can play its part in that task. It will break in our hands if we use it for ends for which it was never intended; for other purposes it cannot be bettered. It has certainly succeeded in pointing out definite narrative-forms which meet us in popular tradition, and has made important suggestions regarding the life-story of these and the causes which gave them shape. But its most valuable service is that it helps us to penetrate the hinterland of the decades from 30 to 50 A.D. and place ourselves in imagination among the young Palestinian communities, so that we can enter the "twilight-period" and, in the words of A[rnold] Myer, "are permitted still to be earwitnesses, to hear the disciples of Jesus and through them Jesus himself"[37]

Source and Form Criticism and the Study of Jesus

Important lives of Jesus were written during each of the various steps in the study of the Gospels. In the ascendancy of both source and form

---

[34]See Mark 2:3-12.

[35]Mark 5:21-43.

[36]Some of them are about other persons, such as the story of the birth of John the Baptist.

[37]Taylor, *The Formation of the Gospel Tradition*, 20-21.

criticism, scholars were agreed that the canonical Gospels constitute the basic primary sources for the study (this is questioned by some who are involved in the contemporary quest). Even with this assumption, widely different Jesus books were written as Gospel study proceeded.

Prior to the "assured result" of Marcan priority, the framework and content of the Fourth Gospel were used as well as the framework of the Synoptic Gospels (Matthew and Luke following the same narrative outline as Mark). Schleiermacher's life of Jesus, for example, was dependent on the Fourth Gospel. For Schleiermacher, the Fourth Gospel forms an organic whole because it is the narrative of an eyewitness. The Synoptic Gospels, on the other hand, present no clear ordering of events because they are compilations of narratives and sayings that had arisen independently of each other.

With the assumption of the priority of Mark and the existence of a sayings source (Q), two widely different historical sources were highlighted. But different uses were made of these sources based on different assumptions. Mark could be seen as a rather unsophisticated collection of traditions (as with Albert Schweitzer) or as the imposition by an editor of dogmatic elements into the tradition about Jesus (as with Wilhelm Wrede). The framework of Mark could be seen as a relatively reliable outline of Jesus' ministry or as an artificial creation of the evangelist. When the sayings were emphasized, both traditional and nontraditional assumptions and procedures were followed. (Schweitzer concluded that the Sermon on the Mount, for example, was delivered essentially as it exists in the Gospel of Matthew and form critics in general concluded that the sayings were transmitted as independent units.)

In the mid-twentieth century, the results of source and form criticism brought scholars to the conclusion that the Gospel writers were not concerned to present a comprehensive biography of Jesus and that a scientific biography of Jesus could not be written by using their work. The initial result of this insight, perhaps particularly the result of the work of Rudolf Bultmann and his followers, was a profound skepticism concerning any knowledge of the historical Jesus. In a work written in 1926 Bultmann said, "I do indeed think that we can now know almost nothing concerning the life and personality of Jesus, since the early Christian sources show no interest in either, are moreover fragmentary and often legendary; and other sources about Jesus do not exist."[38]

In light of such radical skepticism some scholars refused to take the form critical method seriously. Generally, however, the method was accepted but some initial extreme conclusions of form critics were challenged and modified. Many of these revisions gave more serious consideration to the impact of the activities and sayings of Jesus on followers who formed the core of the early Christian community and to the importance of the presence of eyewitnesses in the early Christian community during the very period when the traditions about Jesus were remembered, interpreted, and transmitted.

In the mid-twentieth century a more-or-less positivistic approach was taken to the Gospels by those who used scholarly methods of study. Differences could be observed between conservative scholars and liberal scholars but the same tools were used. I was convinced of the necessity of the rather positivistic approach in the academy and felt that this approach did not challenge the church's faith in Jesus Christ as Lord. Even then, before I began to emphasize literary approaches to the Bible, I distinguished the relatively meager results of scientific study of the Gospel tradition as source for knowledge of the earthly Jesus from study and experience of the Word that came to light in the Gospels. Later I would relate the two by emphasizing the present-day power of the text to enable the same sort of experience of the Word of God that the original event and succeeding reports of the event engendered. With such a view, the literary and theological questions involved are different from the questions involving the sort of historical proof required by a severe source- and form-critical approach. With confidence that the approach to the Gospels as sources for knowledge of the historical Jesus did not challenge Christian faith, I delineated this critical approach as it had developed to the mid-twentieth century in *What Is Form Criticism?* and in *Introduction to the New Testament* (with Robert W. Crapps and David A. Smith).[39]

---

[38]*Jesus and the Word*, trans. Louise Pettibone Smith and Erminie Huntress Lantero (New York: Scribner's, 1934; new ed. 1958) 8.

[39]Edgar V. McKnight, *What Is Form Criticism?* (Philadelphia: Fortress Press, 1969); Robert W. Crapps, Edgar V. McKnight, and David A. Smith, *Introduction to the New Testament* (New York: Ronald Press; New York: John Wiley & Sons, 1969.

Chapters 6 and 7 of this volume deal with some of the lives of Jesus written on the basis of source and form criticism, but lives of Jesus today (discussed in chapter 7) are being written against the background of more recent approaches to the Gospels. The following chapter will trace developments in redaction criticism and in genuine literary approaches to the Gospels. The current studies of the historical Jesus do not ignore the methods and results of studies developed and refined in the nineteenth and first half of the twentieth centuries. They utilize these tools from a poetic (rather than a positivistic) perspective.

Chapter 3

The Gospels and Religious Literature

Source and Form criticism and the presuppositions and worldview within which these methods made sense fostered the search for an objective photograph-like knowledge of the historical Jesus. Failure to discover a mass of scientifically verifiable data allowing this photograph-like knowledge led to a reluctance to engage in serious study of the historical Jesus. Before the current widespread scholarly attention to Jesus would take place, the Gospels would cease to be approached simply with the analytical tools of source and form criticism. In this chapter we will treat developments in redaction criticism and genuine literary study of the Gospels.

Redaction Criticism

"Redactor" and "redaction" follow the German *Redakteur* and *Redaktion* and mean "editor" and "editing." Redaction criticism changed the focus from the context of the primitive church prior to the evangelists to the historical and sociological context of the evangelists and saw the evangelists as "redactors," that is, "editors," of traditional material.

Redaction Criticism and Form Criticism. Form and redaction criticism of the New Testament paralleled one another in their origin and development. Each of the disciplines was inaugurated, following the literary inactivity of a world war, by young scholars who were beginning their careers. Both methods were historically oriented. Form criticism gave attention to the history of the units that were transmitted orally in the early church and redaction criticism was concerned with the end of the historical process, the situation and theology of the evangelists and their churches, which can be ascertained by the editorial activity of the evangelists.

The relationship of form criticism and redaction criticism has led to the question of whether redaction criticism ought to be considered simply a further application of form criticism. The assumption of the earliest

form critics was that the form of the units coalesced out of the institutional life of the Christian communities. For Martin Dibelius, preaching was
the specific and all-inclusive setting for the formation of the tradition.
Rudolf Bultmann specified more carefully both the items of the tradition
and the settings. He placed apologetics, polemics, edification, discipline,
and scribal activity alongside preaching.[1] Rudolf Bultmann also maintained that the composition of the Gospels "involves nothing in principle
new, but only completes what was begun in the oral tradition."[2] Willi
Marxsen was responsible not only for the name "redaction criticism" but
also for the clear distinction between redaction criticism and form
criticism. Marxsen denied that the anti-individualistic sociological
orientation of the study of the tradition could be maintained in the study
of the Gospels as wholes. The redaction counteracts the fragmentation
that takes place in the anonymous transmission of material, and this
counteraction of redaction "cannot be explained without taking into
account an individual, an author personality who pursues a definite goal
with his work."[3]

Redaction critics after Marxsen did not agree unanimously with his
evaluation. Georg Strecker, for example, denied to the evangelist both an
individual dogmatic conception and individual creativity on the literary
level. The evangelists are exponents of their congregations, not authors
who want to compose literary works that express their individuality.[4] The
question of the relationship of form to redaction criticism and the nature
and role of the authors of the Gospels played a part in the transition from
redaction to literary criticism of the Gospels, with literary criticism
emphasizing conscious as well as unconscious use of literary conventions
by the evangelists.

Early Study of Matthew's Redaction. Günther Bornkamm, a student
of Rudolf Bultmann and professor at the University of Heidelberg,
published an article in 1948 on the account of the Stilling of the Storm

---

[1]Rudolf Bultmann, *History of the Synoptic Tradition,* trans. John Marsh (New
York: Harper; Oxford: Basil Blackwell, 1963) 60-61.

[2]Ibid., 321.

[3]Willi Marxsen, *Mark the Evangelist: Studies on the Redaction History of the
Gospel,* trans. James Boyce et al. (New York and Nashville: Abingdon Press,
1969) 18.

[4]Georg Strecker, *Der Weg der Gerechtigkeit: Untersuchung zur Theologie
des Matthaus* (Göttingen: Vandenhoeck & Ruprecht, 1962) 10.

in Matthew 8:23-27 that is credited with being the first work in the new method of study, which six years later would be given the title "redaction criticism" by Willi Marxsen. Bornkamm used source criticism and Bultmann's form-critical principles to make clear the evangelist's method of working. The redactional activity emphasized by Bornkamm was Matthew's reordering of the material. The nature miracle was taken out of the biographical context of Mark and placed by the evangelist-editor in a series in Matthew consisting primarily of healing miracles that are designed to show Jesus as Messiah of deed and parallel the presentation of Jesus as Messiah of the word in the Sermon on the Mount in Matthew 5–7. The two sayings of Jesus about discipleship that precede the miracle actually give the story its meaning:

> A scribe then approached and said, "Teacher, I will follow you wherever you go." And Jesus said to him, "Foxes have holes, and birds of the air have nests, but the Son of Man has nowhere to lay his head." Another of his disciples said to him, "Lord, first let me go and bury my father." But Jesus said to him, "Follow me, and let the dead bury their own dead." (Matt. 8:19-22)

Matthew interprets "the journey of the disciples with Jesus in the storm and the stilling of the storm with reference to discipleship, and that means with reference to the little ship of the Church."[5]

Bornkamm continued his investigation into the redactional activity of Matthew with a 1954 paper, "Matthew as Interpreter of the Words of the Lord," that was expanded and published in 1960 as "End-Expectation and Church in Matthew." The complete study sets out to examine Matthew's theological peculiarities and the theme of his Gospel and to show the extent to which the first evangelist is an interpreter of his tradition.[6]

In the analysis of Matthew's discourses that begins the work, Bornkamm uncovered a union of end-expectation and conception of the church that is peculiar to Matthew. The discourse of John the Baptist shows this unique union, particularly as it is related to the message of Jesus. By having John as well as Jesus preach the message "Repent, for

---

[5]Günther Bornkamm, "The Stilling of the Storm in Matthew," in *Tradition and Interpretation in Matthew*, by Günther Bornkamm, Gerhard Barth, and Heinz Joachim Held, trans. Percy Scott (Philadelphia: Westminster, 1963) 55.

[6]"End-Expectation and Church in Matthew," in *Tradition and Interpretation in Matthew*, 49.

the kingdom of heaven has come near" (Matt. 3:2 and 4:17), Matthew makes the Baptist into a preacher of the Christian congregation. John's call for repentance rejects the appeal of his hearers that they are the children of Abraham. Jesus' call (in 3:2 and in chapter 7, where false prophets replace the Pharisees and Sadducees) rejects the conception of the church held by the false prophets who appeal to their discipleship and charismatic miracles. The false prophets are not willing to admit that membership in the messianic community is decided according to the standard of bringing forth the "fruits of repentance" and doing the will of the heavenly father.

The understanding of the law is the link between the church and end-expectation in Matthew and is the key to Matthew's interpretation of the tradition. In this light, Matthew's indication that the law is binding down to the jot and tittle (Matt. 5:17-19) was seen by Bornkamm as having been given a representative place and a programmatic meaning by the evangelist. The passage is a clue to the situation of Matthew and his church in that it stems from a Jewish-Christian congregation and is directed against a tendency to abandon the law. Bornkamm confirmed the conclusion of G. D. Kilpatrick that the Jewish opposition in Matthew's Gospel is that of the Judaism between 70 and 135 CE, when Jewish sects and Christians were being accused of heresy and were excommunicated.[7] In Matthew, a Jewish-Christian congregation is pictured "which holds fast to the law and which has not yet broken away from union with Judaism but rather stands in sharp contrast to a doctrine and mission set free from the law (which Matthew would regard as lawless)"[8]

Early Study of Luke's Redaction. Redaction criticism is possible with Luke–Acts, according to Hans Conzelmann, because it is with the work of Luke that the distinction between the period of Jesus and the period of the church becomes fully conscious. In the first phase of the development of the tradition—up to Mark and Q—the problems and answers of the community are somewhat unreflectively projected back into reports of Jesus' life. In the second phase, the report (the kerygma) is not simply

---

[7]*Tradition and Interpretation in Matthew*, 22n.2.

[8]Ibid., 22. For a later view, see Bornkamm "Der Auferstandene und der Irdische: Mt 28, 16-20," in *Zeit und Geschichte: Dankesgabe an Rudolf Bultmann zum 80. Geburtstag*, ed. Erich Dinkler (Tübingen: Mohr-Siebeck, 1964).

passed down and received; the kerygma is itself the subject of reflection.[9] The theological reflection and the fundamental motif of Luke resulted, according to Conzelmann, from the delay of the parousia. This defined the Christology and ecclesiology of Luke and caused him to transform eschatology into a broad scheme of the history of salvation.

The view of eschatology as the key to Luke's reflection on the kerygma and salvation history as the result of Luke's reflection did not simply flow from a redaction-critical study of Luke–Acts. Earlier scholars had noted these matters.[10] Conzelmann's contribution was to show how Luke's editing of his sources may be related to the postulated historical and theological situation. Conzelmann's article of 1952, "Zur Lukas Analyse," summarized the purpose, method, and major results of his study on Luke–Acts. He utilized source and form criticism to deal with the composition, individuality, and purpose of the Gospel of Luke. His study showed that Luke's reaction to the delay of the parousia resulted in a reconstruction so radical that a timeless message was resounded and the length of the interim period no longer constituted a problem.

Conzelmann amplified and substantiated his interpretation of the work of Luke in *The Theology of Luke* (German *Die Mitte der Zeit*), and a typical picture of Conzelmann's method may be obtained by an examination of his treatment of "Luke's Eschatology." Mark contains evidence of a change of attitude toward eschatology, but this is an unconscious modification, and Mark himself retains the early expectation. With Luke, however, a new outline is provided: "A solution which will not demand further revision in the course of time."[11] At the beginning of the Gospel, this revision is evident in the elimination of the apocalyptic idea of a forerunner and the placing of John in the line of all the other prophets. Jesus, then, is understood not by reference to the eschatological idea of a forerunner but in light of the preparation for his coming in the whole

---

[9]Hans Conzelmann, *The Theology of St Luke*, trans. Geoffrey Buswell (New York: Harper & Brothers, 1960; original: [2]1957; [1]1954) 12.

[10]See H. von Baer, *Der Heilige Geist in den Lukasschriften* (Stuttgart: Kohlhammer, 1926) 108, 111-12; Bultmann, "The Transformation of the Idea of the Church in the History of Early Christianity," *Canadian Journal of Theology* 1 (1955); Philipp Vielhauer, "On the 'Paulinism' of Acts," in *Studies in Luke–Acts*, ed. Leander E. Keck and J. Louis Martyn (New York and Nashville: Abingdon Press, 1966).

[11]*The Theology of St. Luke*, 120.

period of the law and prophets.[12] The account of the rejection at Nazareth (4:16-30) gives evidence of the process of placing eschatology within the course of history. Jesus' statement that "today the scripture has been fulfilled in your hearing" is thought of as belonging to past history. It is "at that time," when Jesus was still living and active on earth, that the fulfillment that is described came about.[13]

A comparison of Luke 9:27 with Mark 9:1 shows how Luke interpreted the tradition so as to provide a permanent solution to the problem of the delay of the parousia.

Mark 9:1	Luke 9:27
And he said to them, "Truly I tell you, there are some standing here who will not taste death until they see that the kingdom of God has come with power."	[Then he said to them all] "But truly I tell you, there are some standing here who will not taste death before they see the kingdom of God."

Luke omits "come with power" because it is a realistic description of the parousia, and Luke wishes to replace the idea of the coming by a timeless concept of the kingdom. The reference to "those standing here" means "those who are standing by *at the time*," and "to see the kingdom" means the perception of the kingdom in the life of Jesus. From the life of Jesus we can see what the kingdom is like. But the time of the appearance of the kingdom is not disclosed. The coming of the kingdom, then, is proclaimed as a future fact. the nature of which can be seen now.[14]

Early Study of Mark's Redaction. Bornkamm and Conzelmann were not fully conscious of the fact that they were pioneering a new method of study. Willi Marxsen, however, was fully conscious of the novelty of the new approach and emphasized that the change of orientation from individual units to the completed Gospels makes of redaction criticism something different from form criticism and something not essentially dependent upon form criticism.[15]

Marxsen suggested that a redaction-critical study of Mark will follow two procedures: (1) a separation of tradition from redaction so that the composition of Mark may be illuminated, and (2) attention to the altered points of view of Matthew and Luke in order to get a clearer grasp of

---

[12]Ibid., 101.
[13]Ibid., 103.
[14]Ibid., 104.
[15]Marxsen, *Mark the Evangelist,* 22.

what is typically Marcan. This procedure was used by Marxsen in studies on John the Baptist, the geographical outline of Mark, the concept of "gospel," and Mark 13.

The key to Mark's composition in general and to the John the Baptist material in particular was seen by Marxsen as Mark's "backward composition."[16] The passion narrative is primary. To this Mark prefixes first of all the Jesus tradition and then the tradition of John the Baptist. The story of the Baptist, therefore, must be read with Jesus as the point of reference. The principle of backward composition governs not only the relationship of larger complexes to one another but also the relationship of the units within the larger complexes. Moreover, the same relationship that exists between Jesus and John the Baptist exists between John the Baptist and the Old Testament.

By means of analysis on the basis of backward composition, Marxsen showed the theological significance of John's location by Mark "in the wilderness" (Mark 1:4) and Jesus' appearance after John was "delivered up" (1:14 ASV; "arrested" RSV, NRSV). A "backward-directed prophecy" with the expression "in the wilderness" is prefaced by Mark to his Baptist tradition, and the tradition is adjusted to the prophecy by repeating "in the wilderness" in Mark 1:4. "In the wilderness," then, qualifies the Baptist as the one who fulfilled Old Testament prophecy. "Put in exaggerated form, the Baptist would still be the one who appears 'in the wilderness' even if he had never been there in all his life."[17] The historical concept of "delivered up" is also emptied of historical content. Mark prefixes the Jesus complex with the Baptist complex and records that Jesus made his first public appearance after John had been "delivered up" because the Baptist belongs to the topical "prehistory" of Jesus. The connection of John and Jesus is made not from a temporal but from a theological or Christological point of view[18]

Marxsen saw the geographical outline with the beginning in Galilee and the ending in Jerusalem as the result of Marcan redaction and a key to Mark's situation. The pre-Marcan passion narrative contained references that could have been used for an outline similar to that in the Gospel of John emphasizing Judea. But Mark composes an outline that emphasizes Galilee. The real stimulus for Mark's Galilean emphasis is a

---

[16]Ibid., 30-31.
[17]Ibid., 37-38.
[18]Ibid., 38-43.

community situation prevailing in the time of Mark himself. "To overstate the case, Mark does not intend to say: Jesus worked in Galilee, but rather: Where Jesus worked there is Galilee."[19] Mark's use of the term "Galilee," nevertheless, is seen by Marxsen as implying either the existence of a community in Galilee or movement toward Galilee. He believed that "the reason for the communities' sojourn in Galilee, or the reason for their journey to Galilee might be seen in the fact that the Parousia was expected there. This makes clear the problem of locale."[20]

Marxsen saw his study of Mark 13 as a validation of the hypothesis that Mark wrote with a view to the imminent parousia. Although the chapter results from the unification of various materials, Mark understood the chapter as a unity the meaning of which is to be deduced by Mark's connection of v. 2 to v. 3, which weaves the saying on the destruction of the temple into the discourse on last things. The destruction, then, is a part of the end event. Mark is the transformation of apocalyptic into eschatology. The several acts of apocalyptic eschatology are replaced with one last act, and "for Mark this act has already begun and . . . only the finale remains."[21]

The Shifting Sands of Redaction Criticism. Although redaction criticism seemed to be a rather simple and objective method, the practice of the method was not so simple. A distinction had to be made between the tradition and the redacted material, but this is not enough. The changes made in the sources do not necessarily reflect conscious theological decisions by the author. How can distinction be made between (1) the unconscious modifications resulting from the tradition and the community within which the evangelist works and (2) the conscious modification of the evangelist himself for theological purposes? When conscious redaction is presupposed, the meaning is not obvious from the redaction itself. Some larger historical and theological framework must be presupposed, accepted, or created by the critic in which the redaction can make sense. In general, redaction-critical studies immediately following the pioneers maintained their historical and theological presuppositions. But very quickly different presuppositions and conclusions appeared.

---

[19]Ibid., 93-94.
[20]Ibid., 107.
[21]Ibid., 189.

Studies in Matthew. Gerhard Barth and Heinz Joachim Held, students of Bornkamm at the University of Heidleberg, were the earliest successors of Bornkamm. In his attempt to situate the Gospel of Matthew, Barth sketched a picture of the antinomians who were opposed (along with the rabbinate) by Matthew. They held that "in the past the law and the prophets rightly held, but Christ has abolished the law and the prophets; since the coming of Christ their validity is ended."[22] The antinomians were not a Pauline group or in the area of Jewish Christianity at all. They must have been in the area of Hellenistic Christianity, even though gnostic influences are not present among them. Barth could not be more specific in his determination of the life setting of Matthew and his congregation, but he was convinced that the picture he had painted of the battlefront was important for an understanding of the Gospel of Matthew.[23]

For Held the meaning of Jesus for Matthew was shown by his collection of the miracle cycle of Matthew 8–9 and his placing of it into the framework of 4:17–11:16. Jesus is the one who fulfills Old Testament prophecy and is in particular God's servant who acts with authority, the Lord and helper of his congregation, and the one who brings the congregation to participate in the authority of her Lord.[24] The representation of the disciples as those of little faith (in those passages where Mark had spoken of unbelief or lack of understanding or inability) links the history of Jesus and his disciples with the later history of the church with its conflicts and challenges.[25]

Wolfgang Trilling, Georg Strecker, and Reinhart Hummel[26] came to views of the situation in Matthew's church that were in opposition to those of Bornkamm, Barth, and Held. Trilling did not deny the existence of Jewish-Christian tradition in Matthew, but he made a distinction

---

[22]Gerhard Barth, "Matthew's Understanding of the Law," in *Tradition and Interpretation in Matthew*, 159.

[23]Ibid., 159-64.

[24]Heinz Joachim Held, "Matthew as Interpreter of the Miracle Stories," in *Tradition and Interpretation in Matthew*, 246-75.

[25]Ibid., 275-96.

[26]Wolfgang Trilling, *Das wahre Israel: Studien zur Theologie des Matthausevangelium* (Leipzig: St. Benno-Verlag, 1950); Georg Strecker, *Der Weg der Gerechtigkeit: Untersuchung zur Theologie des Matthaus* (Göttingen: Vandenhoeck & Ruprecht, 1962); Reinhart Hummel, *Die Auseinandersetzung zwischen Kirche und Judentum im Matthäusevangelium* (Munich: Kaiser, 1963).

between Matthew's material and the final redaction. The Jewish-Christian traditions preserved in Matthew were not to end in a Gospel teaching a Jewish-Christian heresy; they were to be used in the development of a universal Christianity which cannot be called typically Jewish-Christian or typically Gentile-Christian.

Strecker explained the separatist Jewish-Christian and the universalist Gentile-Christian features in Matthew as did Trilling: the Jewish-Christian features are to be traced to the period of transmission and the Gentile-Christian features to the final redaction. The setting of the final redaction is Hellenistic-Jewish Christian.

Hummel determined Matthew's place in early Christianity by a redactional study of the passages in which a controversy with Judaism appears, and he did so on the assumption that the debates of Jesus with his Jewish opponents reflect the circumstances of Matthew's day as well as Matthew's theology. Hummel mediated between the view of Born-kamm and that of Trilling and Strecker. Matthew's church has actually not yet parted from the Jewish community; it has not yet been excluded from the society of Judaism. Nevertheless, Matthew's church is something fundamentally new compared with the Israelite national community.

Alongside Matthew's relationship to Judaism and to the law, salvation history, covenant, and Christology are themes that became important in later redactional study of Matthew. Rolf Walker[27] saw Matthew in terms of the history of salvation, which begins with Abraham and runs until the parousia. The situation of the author of Matthew is that of the last time, and from this perspective the evangelist composed a "life of Jesus," which is also an "acts of the apostles" in that the story of the post-Easter mission of the church is depicted in the story of Jesus.

For Kenzo Tagawa, "Matthew's undifferentiated community con-sciousness"[28] was the key to understanding the thought of the Gospel. The confusion between Israel and the church occurs because both of these are in Matthew's milieu. Insofar as the church is identified with Israel, the apostles are not to go beyond Israel (10:5). Insofar as the church is a

---

[27]Rolf Walker, *Die Heilsgeschichte im ersten Evangelium* (Göttingen: Vandenhoeck & Ruprecht, 1967); see also William G. Thompson, "A Historical Perspective in the Gospel of Matthew," *Journal of Biblical Literature* 93 (1974): 243-62.

[28]Kenzo Tagawa, "People and Community in the Gospel of Matthew," *New Testament Studies* 16 (1970): 149-62.

community distinct from the Jewish nation, the command to make disciples of all nations (28:19) makes sense.

According to Hubert Frankemölle,[29] Matthew's Gospel is an answer to the question of God's faithfulness, a question that arose because of Israel's rejection of Jesus as Messiah and the destruction of Jerusalem. To answer the question, Matthew employed covenant theology and developed a theology of God's activity in history. The church has taken the place of unfaithful Israel, and God, in the person of Jesus, has come to be with his own and to renew his covenant.

Jack Dean Kingsbury defined Matthew's purpose as Christological on the basis of Matthew's main threefold structure, which sets forth the person of Jesus Messiah (1:1–4:16); the proclamation of Jesus (4:17–16:20); and the suffering, death, and resurrection of Jesus Messiah (16:20–28:20). In a second organization, Matthew operated with a design of the history of salvation. He differentiates between the time of Israel and the time of Jesus, of which Matthew's own age is a subdivision.[30]

Studies in Luke. The view that Luke's work must be understood as a response to the problem of the delay of the parousia and as a theology of a history of salvation was quickly accepted as an "assured result" of Lucan studies. The framework provided by Conzelmann was a powerful way of understanding and presenting the material of Luke–Acts as a whole and of dealing with particular passages and themes in the books. Scholars immediately following Conzelmann followed his lead. Eduard Lohse applied Conzelmann's programmatic ideas in articles in 1953 and 1954.[31] The events in the Gospel are recounted to show what God has accomplished. For Luke, the life of Jesus is evidence of the faithfulness of God in regard to his people Israel. The work of Luke is also related to Old Testament historiography, particularly that of the Deuteronomist. Conzelmann had concluded that in Luke's development of his idea of

---

[29]Hubert Frankemölle, *Jahwebund und Kirche Christi* (Münster: Aschendorff, 1974).

[30]Jack Dean Kingsbury, *Matthew: Structure, Christology, Kingdom* (Philadelphia: Fortress, 1975).

[31]Eduard Lohse, "Die Bedeutung des Pfingstberichtes im Rahmen des lukanischen Geschichtswerkes," *Evangelische Theologie* 13 (1953): 422-36; "Lukas als Theologe der Heilsgeschichte," *Evangelische Theologie* 14 (1954): 256-75; and "Missionarisches Handeln Jesu nach dem Evangelium des Lukas," *Theologische Literaturzeitung* 10 (1954): 1-13.

redemptive history his attitude to history "represents something entirely new compared with that of Judaism."[32] In Lohse's view, however, Luke has joined the story of past salvation to his day, just as the Deuteronomist telescoped the past of Moses and the present of Israel.[33]

Ulrich Wilckens's study of the six missionary speeches in the first thirteen chapters of Acts[34] advanced the work of Conzelmann by the thesis that these speeches result from Luke's creative ability and theology. However, for the speeches of Paul in Lystra and Athens, Luke used a Hellenistic-Christian pattern that was known to him from the tradition. The difference in the form of the two types of sermons is due to Luke's theology. The mission to the Jews is reflected in the sermons to the Jews, which refer to their place in salvation history. When the Jews are dropped out of salvation history, the mission to the Gentiles is reflected in sermons that refer to their situation.

More than a quarter century after publication of Conzelmann's work, there was widespread agreement only "on the point that Conzelmann's synthesis is inadequate."[35] Günter Klein[36] found the Lucan emphasis upon apostolic succession to be related to the problem of gnostic heretics, and Charles H. Talbert[37] showed how Luke's work as a totality may be understood as a reaction to gnosticism. Hans-Werner Bartsch[38] declared that instead of a historicizing of eschatology, Luke urged constant readiness for the end. Gerhard Schneider,[39] following Jacques Dupont,[40]

---

[32]*The Theology of St. Luke*, 167.

[33]"Lukas als Theologe der Heilsgeschichte," 271n.60.

[34]Ulrich Wilckens, *Die Missionsreden der Apostelgeschichte: Form- und traditionsgeschichtliche Untersuchungen* (Neukirchen-Vluvn: Neukirchener Verlag, 1961).

[35]Charles Talbert, "Shifting Sands: The Recent Study of the Gospel of Luke," *Interpretation* 30 (1976): 395.

[36]Günter Klein, *Die zwölf Apostel: Ursprung und Gestalt einer Idee* (Göttingen: Vandenhoeck & Ruprecht, 1961).

[37]Charles Talbert, *Luke and the Gnostics* (Nashville and New York: Abingdon Press, 1966) and "The Redaction Critical Quest for Luke the Theologian," in *Jesus and Man's Hope*, Pittsburgh Festival on the Gospels 1970, 2 vols. (Pittsburgh: Pittsburgh Theological Seminary, 1970) 171-222.

[38]Hans-Werner Bartsch, *Wachet aber zu jeder Zeit! Entwurf einer Auslegung des Lukasevangeliums* (Hamburg-Bergstedt: Herbert Reich, 1963).

[39]Gerhard Schneider, *Parusiegleichnisse im Lukas-Evangelium* (Stuttgart:

found that in material unique to Luke there is an individualization of eschatology so that Luke is able to say that the kingdom is near for believers without contradicting his conception of the delay of the parousia. Luke anticipated the parousia as an event of immediate relevance for himself and his contemporaries, according to Eric Franklin.[41] The event that Franklin saw as central, however, is the ascension, and the value of Luke is that he was able to see the significance of continuing history without abandoning the traditional eschatology.

Luke's use of complementary, climactic, and antithetic parallelism convinced Helmut Flender[42] that Luke's work is more subtle than Conzelmann and other interpreters had discerned, and he found a kerygmatic emphasis within the historical aspects of Luke's work. William C. Robinson, saw a travel plan in the work of Luke that is the result of Luke's transformation of temporal eschatology into historical geography.[43] Karl Löning explained the salvation motif as a result of the apologetic nature of the work.[44] I. Howard Marshall defended the thesis that "Luke was primarily an evangelist or preacher, concerned to lead men to Christian belief on the basis of a reliable record of the historical facts."[45]

Studies in Mark. Although Marxsen established redaction criticism as a new study, his work did not meet with the same degree of critical acclaim as did Conzelmann's work on Luke and the work of Bornkamm, Barth, and Held on Matthew. Alfred Suhl continued the work of Marksen

---

Katholisches Biblewerk, 1975).

[40]Jacques Dupont, "L'apres-mort dans l'oeuvre de Luc," *Revue théologique de Louvain* 3 (1972): 3-21.

[41]Eric Franklin, *Christ the Lord: A Study in the Purpose and Theology of Luke-Acts* (Philadelphia: Westminster, 1975).

[42]Helmut Flender, *St Luke: Theologian of Redemptive History,* trans. Reginald H. Fuller and Ilse Fuller (London: SPCK; Philadelphia: Fortress, 1967).

[43]William C. Robinson, *Der Weg des Herrn: Studien zur Geschichte und Eschatologie im Lukas-Evangelium: Ein Gesprach mit Hans Conzelmann* (Hamburg-Bergstedt: Herbert Reich, 1964).

[44]Karl Löning, "Lukas—Theologe der von Gott geführten Heilsgeschichte," *Gestalt und Anspruch des Neuen Testaments,* ed. Josef Schreiner and Gerhard Dautzenberg (Würzburg: Echter Verlag, 1969; [2]1979) 200-28.

[45]I. Howard Marshall, *Luke: Historian and Theologian* (Exeter: Paternoster, 1970) 9.

in his study of Old Testament citations and allusions in Mark.[46] Suhl contrasted Mark's use of the Old Testament with the prophecy-and-fulfillment pattern of Matthew and Luke. This supports the view that Mark had a heightened expectation of the end and that the Gospel is to be understood as an address to Mark's church.

Johannes Schreiber[47] may be considered an adherent of Marxsen's method of backward composition and analysis in that he began with the account of the crucifixion, which was seen as the high point of the passion narrative. But Schreiber came to conclusions that were different from those of Marxsen. Mark taught that salvation and judgment are already included in the cross and, hence, the eschaton is present. Mark, then, is not concerned with anxious awaiting of the parousia, as Marxsen held. The parousia is for unbelievers to whom it will make clear the judgment and salvation already present for believers in the cross. Behind the Gospel of Mark, Schreiber saw a Gentile-Christian Hellenistic theology that is stamped with gnostic elements that determine Mark's concepts.

Immediately following the work of Marxsen, there developed "general scholarly agreement that henceforth Mark must be read as a theological book." But two decades after Marxsen, there was "a bewildering diversity of opinion as to the theological needs this gospel was designed to meet."[48] Quentin Quesnell interpreted Mark from Mark 6:52 and found that lack of comprehension, mystery, and the emphasis on bread were keys to Mark's message. The message is that the Christian faith is a mystery to be understood only through faith in the resurrection but that is symbolically expressed and experientially known in the celebration of the Eucharist.[49]

---

[46]Alfred Suhl, *Die Funktion der alttestamentlichen Zitate und Anspielungen im Markusevangelium* (Gütersloh: Mohn, 1965).

[47]Johannes Schreiber, "Die Christologie des Markusevangeliums: Beobachtungen zur Theologie und Komposition des zweiten Evangeliums," *Zeitschrift für Theologie und Kirche* 58 (1961): 154-83.

[48]Ralph P. Martin, "The Theology of Mark's Gospel," *Southwestern Journal of Theology* 21 (1978): 23.

[49]Quentin Quesnell, *The Mind of Mark: Interpretation and Method through the Exegesis of Mk 6,52*, Analecta biblica 38 (Rome: Pontifical Biblical Institute, 1969).

Theodore J. Weeden[50] suggested that Mark was confronting heretics who follow a "divine-man" theology by dramatizing the Christological dispute between Mark and his opponents in a historical drama, with Jesus serving as a surrogate for Mark and the disciples for the opponents of Mark.

Werner H. Kelber saw Mark as addressed to displaced Christians who were without hope after the fall of Jerusalem in 70. The fundamental purpose of the Gospel was to affirm the realization of the kingdom in Galilee. "This manifesto is truly gospel message for a people who had suffered the loss of the kingdom and were bereft of orientation in space and time. It reaffirms the Kingdom in a new spatiotemporal configuration."[51]

Howard Clark Kee[52] concluded that Mark was the product of an apocalyptic community just prior to the fall of Jerusalem. The Gospel was designed to serve as a guidebook for the community as it awaited God's vindication of Jesus as the triumphant Son of Man.

In the high point of redaction-critical studies, some scholars defended Mark as a "conservative" redactor. Jürgen Roloff declared that Mark "will not simply be a presentation of the risen lord in the historicized garb; it understands itself as a presentation of a past history to be contrasted fundamentally from the present."[53] Heine Simonsen saw the evangelist as standing in the midst of a living tradition that possessed authority for him and that he served through the formation of a Gospel. There is, then, continuity from Jesus' own view of his work through the process of tradition to the redaction of the Gospel.[54]

Rudolf Pesch's commentary on Mark was based on the thesis that Mark took a conservative attitude toward the material at his disposal,

---

[50]Theodore J. Weeden, *Mark—Traditions in Conflict* (Philadelphia: Fortress, 1971).

[51]Werner H. Kelber, *The Kingdom in Mark: A New Place and a New Time* (Philadelphia: Westminster, 1974) 139.

[52]Howard Clark Kee, *Community of the New Age: Studies in Mark's Gospel* (Philadelphia: Westminster, 1977; repr. with corrections: ROSE 6 [Macon GA: Mercer University Press, 1983]).

[53]Jürgen Roloff, "Das Markusevangelium als Geschichtsdarstellung," *Evangelische Theologie* 29 (1969): 73-93.

[54]Heine Simonsen, "Zur Frage der grundlegenden Problematik in form und redaktionsgeschichtlicher Evangelienforschung," *Studia theologica* 27 (1972): 22-23.

arranging traditional material for the instruction of his community in
Rome to convey the fundamentals of the gospel and the challenge of the
mission to the Gentiles.[55]

Methodological Problems and Movement Toward Literary Criticism.
In redactional studies it became increasingly clear that a dialectical relationship existed between detailed redactional studies and the understanding of the larger historical and theological context. The evangelists'
editorial activities could be used to explain different situations and theologies. Reliable principles and methods were needed to guide the discipline
and guard against purely idiosyncratic reconstructions. Some of the principles suggested included: comprehensiveness of redaction (all of the
verses that can be considered editorial must be used to determine the theology of an evangelist); composition as structure (the selection and
arrangement of the tradition suggests an evangelist's interest); the Gospel
genre (the genre of Greco-Roman biographies played a part in the work
of the evangelists); and coordination of the elements (the final outcome
is influenced by all of these elements but cannot be reduced to any one
element).[56]

Linguistic Challenges and Contributions to Redaction Studies. Not all
scholars agreed that continuity could be maintained between the oral and
written forms of the tradition, between form and redaction criticism.
Scholars suggested some higher-level theoretical perspectives to sort out
the question. These theoretical considerations played a part in the movement toward genuine literary approaches to the Gospels. Erhardt
Güttgemanns attempted to show that Bultmann's assumption of continuity
between the oral form and the written form of the tradition could not be

---

[55]Rudolf Pesch, *Das Markusevangelium.* I. Teil. *Einleitung und Kommentar
zu Kap. 1,1–8,26* (Freiburg, Basel, and Vienna: Herder, 1976) 12-13, 48-63.

[56]See Richard A. Edwards, "The Redaction of Luke," *Journal of Religion* 49
(1969): 392-405; Leander E. Keck, "Review of *John the Baptist in the Gospel
Tradition,*" *Union Seminary Quarterly Review* 24 (1968) 96; Kee, *Community of
the New Age,* 1-13; Jack Dean Kingsbury, *Matthew: Structure, Christology,
Kingdom* (Philadelphia: Fortress, 1975) 37; Norman Perrin, *What Is Redaction
Criticism?* (Philadelphia: Fortress, 1969) 66; Schreiber, "Die Christologie des
Markusevangeliums," 154-55; Charles Talbert, "Shifting Sands: The Recent
Study of the Gospel of Luke," *Interpretation* 30 (1976): 381-95; and Talbert,
What Is a Gospel? The Genre of the Canonical Gospels (Philadelphia: Fortress,
1977; repr.: ROSE 9 [Macon GA: Mercer University Press, 1985]).

maintained. The process of formation is a dialectical interlacing of collectively transmitted "material" and individual intentional "act." The result is that the "material" of the tradition is transformed into a new linguistic Gestalt ("form") and serves the meaning-structure of this new form with its meaning-horizon. The model that had been used in form criticism is thereby destroyed according to Güttgemans.[57]

Werner H. Kelber agreed with Güttgemanns that there was not a tendency in the oral tradition that resulted in the written Gospels, and he attempted to find a setting that would explain the creation of the new meaning-Gestalt. The "law of social identification"[58] and not verbal memory directed the oral tradition; many social interests resulted in many traditions. The written Gospel was seen by Kelber as a reduction of social interests to one and as "a crucial alternative to the oral way of being."[59] The written form resulted from the crisis mirrored in Mark 13. The event of 70 brought the primitive prophets' proclamation of the real presence of Christ in the logia more and more into disrepute. A crisis of trust developed, and the Gospel text was developed to set a new basis of trust and stability. "The text guaranteed as text a measure of permanence that was completely out of reach in the world of oral uncertainty."[60]

Hubert Frankemölle[61] sought to relate the tradition to the redaction by viewing the relationship of the evangelist to his church in terms of a model based on information theory and oriented toward human relationships. Such a model shows that the formation of tradition is a dialectical process involving the evangelist and his church. The religious practices and traditions of the evangelist and his church provide a repertoire of oral and written linguistic patterns for the process. In a model oriented toward human communication, the evangelist and the church are both seen as speakers and hearers, and the factors related to both are in continual flux. Hence, the Gospels (just as the New Testament letters) are to be seen as

---

[57]Erhardt Güttgemanns, *Candid Questions concerning Gospel Form Criticism* (Pittsburgh: Pickwick, 1979) 189.

[58]Werner H. Kelber, "Markus und die mündliche Tradition," *Linguistica Biblica* 45 (1979): 27.

[59]Ibid., 51.

[60]Ibid., 50.

[61]Hubert Frankemölle, "Evangelist und Gemeinde: Eine methodenkritische Besinnung (mit Beispielen aus dem Mattäusevangelium)," *Biblica* 60 (1979).

a "snapshot" out of a continuous linguistic communication between the evangelist and his church.

Gerd Theissen attempted to further (rather than destroy) classical form criticism by a structural approach to the miracle stories. Theissen asked if the individual units could have been taken up into a broader composition without the destruction of their narrative integrity. If so, form criticism is possible. "The solution rests in the fact that the small units were not only integrated in a totality external to them but that this totality was structured through them."[62] Theissen suggested that this mutuality is conceivable because of the existence of different levels of linguistic phenomena. With the distinction between potential form structure and realized or actualized structure (paralleling the Saussurean distinction between *langue* and *parole* and the Chomskyan distinction between competence and performance), Theissen was able to reconcile Bultmann's view to that of Marxsen and even that of Güttgemanns:

> Continuity reigns above all on the level of potential form structure. Each actualization of this form structure in concrete texts may be understood as a new creation. When one compares different actualizations as they follow one another, one can confirm either a further development or a recoinage.[63]

Theissen studied the miracle stories in terms of form (the synchronic moment), history (the diachronic moment), and function (the comprehensive structure of constraints and acts and intentions of social life). Theissen saw that the function (and *Sitz im Leben*) is not to be limited to typical narrative situations. A broader definition will include social constraints and anthropological data that help us understand why one seizes upon and utilizes particular literary forms.[64]

Klaus Berger agreed with Güttgemanns that the Gospel form does not result from the simple accumulation of smaller units, that analysis must proceed from the view that the Gospel text was a meaningful totality for the final redactor.[65] This does not mean that the individual units cannot

---

[62]Gerd Theissen, *Urchristliche Wundergeschichten: Ein Beitrag zur formgeschichtlichen Erforschung der Synoptischen Evangelien* (Gütersloh: Mohn, 1974) 211.

[63]Ibid., 227.

[64]Ibid., 12.

[65]Klaus Berger, *Exegese des Neuen Testaments: Neue Wege vom Text zur*

be analyzed linguistically and that their historical-sociological aspects cannot be clarified. Berger used the concept of "semantic field" to mediate between the individual units and the completed Gospels. "Texts are not enclosed systems. Semantic fields mediate between texts on the linguistic level. These semantic fields are 'intertextual,' that is, they do not exist isolated but only in a number of texts."[66]

An important insight of Berger had to do with the centrality of hermeneutics in form and redaction study. The origin and each later reception of a text is to be understood in terms of the same hermeneutic principles. The formation of tradition and understanding are inextricably related. Considering origin and reception as coparticipants results in a vision of the unification of the linguistic process in linguistic forms and semantic fields and the unification of essential significance of interest and the fundamentally sociological dimensions of the linguistic process.[67]

Plainly the objectifying historical presuppositions and methods of source and form criticism with which redaction criticism began were being challenged by the very practice of redaction criticism. As far back as 1969, Norman Perrin emphasized not only that redaction criticism must go beyond redaction in the limited sense to include the arrangement of the material and narrative development but also that the "whole range of creative activities which we can detect in an evangelist" ought to be used in determining the theology of the evangelist.[68] Attention to the product of the author as "literature" inaugurated a phase of Gospel study that emphasizes the "text of the gospel as a coherent text with its own internal dynamics."[69] The view of the Gospels as literary products to be studied in light of such factors as plot and character yields a system that requires a rethinking of the presuppositions of form and redaction criticism and their possible coordination with a genuine literary perspective. Can the material of the Gospels be studied with form, redactional, *and* literary-critical presuppositions and methods? Do literary approaches offer a way of reconciling the "necessary" truths of theology and the "contingent" and "fallible" truths of history?

Auslegung (Heidelberg: Quelle & Meyer, 1977) 64-65.

[66]Ibid., 166.

[67]Ibid., 268-69.

[68]Perrin, *What Is Redaction Criticism?* 66.

[69]Norman Perrin, "The Interpretation of the Gospel of Mark," *Interpretation* 30 (1976): 120.

Literary Criticism of the Gospels

The philosophical and religious context of the early church constrained the reading of the Gospels. Conventions of reading in the early church allowed attention to the "literal" level, levels beyond the literal, and the life of readers (individuals and groups). With the critical approaches warranted by the world of the Enlightenment, the reference was taken to be history, at first the history recounted in the text (to be discounted or supported by critical study) and later the historical context of the formation of the tradition or of the final composition of the Gospels. With literary approaches there has been a return to a variety of concerns comparable to the concerns of the early church.

Precritical, Critical, and Literary Reading Compared. Precritical Reading of the Gospels. In the reading of the Gospels in the precritical period, no distinction was made between the world depicted and the real historical world. Indeed, the Bible as a whole was seen as referring to the whole of historical reality. In the Bible and in the early church, biblical stories were seen as referring directly to specific temporal events and indirectly (as figures or types) to later stories and events. But the biblical world extended to the present, to the world of the reader of any age. Readers saw their own actions and feelings and the events of their world as figures of the biblical world and so were able to fit themselves into the biblical world.

The power of a precritical realistic reading extending from the Old Testament to the readers' day depended in part upon the fact that the world depicted in the Bible and the real historical world was not the ultimate reality. Old Testament individuals and events were types of New Testament individuals and events, but the deepest meaning is not the historical in any sense. The Passover lamb may be a type that is made clear in the sacrifice of Christ. But both of these refer to a heavenly sacrifice for the sins of every conceivable form of being.

Critical Reading of the Gospels. With the Enlightenment, the historicity of literary and other cultural phenomena replaced the framework of the theological conceptualization of the ancient and medieval world. The realistic feature of biblical narrative was related consciously to historical reference. The role of the biblical stories was to enable readers to uncover the historical sequence of events to which they referred. Undermined was the correlation between the world of the reader and the biblical world, made possible when both were seen as expressions of the preexisting divine world. This diminished the potentiality of the narratives to allow readers to make sense of themselves in relation to the world of the narrative in a somewhat direction fashion.

Subordination of Literary Qualities. When literary qualities of the Gospels were noted and commented on in both the precritical and critical periods, they were subordinated to dogmatic or historical interests and they were not appreciated because they were not within the "truth" of contemporary thinking. In the period of the ancient and medieval church, Augustine noted the literary qualities of the Fourth Gospel (in comparison with the Synoptics). The divine nature of the Lord was set forth by the writer "in such a way as he believed to be adequate to men's needs and notions."[70] Augustine, of course, sees no tension between the dogmatic nature of the Gospel of John, the author's creative formulation of materials, and the facticity of the story. The writer of the Gospel "is like one who has drunk in the secret of His divinity more richly and somehow more familiarly than others, as if he drew it from the very bosom of his Lord on which it was his wont to recline when He sat at meat."[71]

Because of the historical focus of critical biblical study in the nineteenth century, the observations of David Friedrich Strauss concerning the poetic or "mythical" nature of Gospel material did not lead to genuine literary appreciation, and the successors of Strauss have been as blinkered in their approach. Instead of myth's being valued as a literary category, myth has been seen as something to eliminate—by outright suppression or by theological interpretation. Or it has been defined as "historical" in some sense.

Beginnings of Literary Study. Concern with genuine literary matters began to surface in the 1960s and 1970s and became commonplace in the 1980s. The literary turn was prepared for in the attempt of Rudolf Bultmann and proponents of the "New Hermeneutic" to prolong the text hermeneutically by attention to its linguistic dimensions. Preoccupation with existential categories and the lack of interaction with genuine literary criticism hindered the task. In his 1964 publication, *The Language of the Gospel*, Amos Wilder advocated a move that takes advantage of literary insights. He expounds the New Testament as "language event" in terms of literary form with the conviction that "behind the particular New

---

[70]*On the Harmony of the Gospels* 1.4.7.
[71]Ibid.

Testament forms lies a particular life-experience and a language-shaping faith." Wilder explicitly criticizes Bultmann's restriction of meaning to existential concepts. The view that the New Testament "tells us about ourselves, not about 'things' and the way they are and the way they happen," according to Wilder, results in a disparagement of "the whole story of man and salvation as the Bible presents it."[72] The literary criticism appropriate for New Testament study is not one that remains confined to forms and conventions. There is reference in the text, but the reference is not the same as that in conventional study of the Gospels. Students of the New Testament can learn about its literary language and reference from students of poetry: "this kind of report of reality—as in a work of art—is more subtle and complex and concrete than in the case of a discursive statement, and therefore more adequate to the matter in hand and to things of importance."[73]

The Gospels and Literary Conventions and Strategies

The development of literary approaches to the Gospels has resulted in the recognition that the Gospels serve a variety of functions. The perception of the role and function of the Gospels influences the strategies that are followed in reading and interpretation.

A Compass for Criticism: "Internal" and "External" Relationships. The dynamic coexistence of different sorts of relationships in literature helps to explain the different references and perspectives in literary criticism. Some of these relationships are internal, to be sought within the literary work of art itself. But some are external, imposed by linguistic and literary relationships in general and/or by perspectives taken by readers and critics.

One set of relationships in literature is comparable to the syntactic relationships on the level of sentence. These syntagmatic relationships exist within discourse and enable linguistic and literary elements to have meaning as they are combined or chained together in a linear sequence. In Gospel narrative readers must discern syntagmatic relationships between words and sentences in order to follow the plot of units of the Gospels (parables, miracle stories, and so on) and readers must discern

---

[72]Amos N. Wilder, *The Language of the Gospel: Early Christian Rhetoric* (New York: Harper, 1964) 133.

[73]Ibid.

syntagmatic relationships between even larger units in order to follow the plot of the Gospels as completed wholes.

Relationships outside of discourse are necessary for making sense of the combinations within discourse. These may be called "associative" or "paradigmatic" (terms borrowed from linguistics). The topic, reference, literary category, and function of the literary unit are not built up simply from below by words and sentences and their combination. Formal, semantic, and other categories outside discourse are imposed upon and complete the syntagmatic structures of discourse.

Interdependence and Variety of relationships. In the episode of Jesus and the disciples crossing the lake in Mark 8, Jesus told the disciples, "Watch out—beware of the yeast of the Pharisees and the yeast of Herod" (Mark 8:15). The disciples recognized a syntactic and semantic unity; they made sense of the sentence by judging that Jesus' statement was to be taken literally and that he was speaking about bread—the bread that the disciples failed to bring with them. Readers know more than the disciples knew and they know the topic is not bread—not bread in the simple literal sense of the disciples.

At the level of every literary unit some topic must be discerned. Then, at the level of the total literary work, a comprehensive organizing principle or idea must be formulated in order for the identification of topics and relationships throughout the work, and, therefore, for the meaning of the work as a whole. The topic of the subordinate unit and the idea of the work as a whole must be consistent with the literary data, but the interplay of literal, figurative, and often paradoxical meanings of words and other units makes the literary data susceptible to a variety of meanings. The same word, expression, or entire text can signify two or more distinct references and express and elicit different attitudes or feelings.

More than topics and ideas are involved in literary appreciation. The contrast between the discernment of the readers and the intellectual and spiritual density of the disciples has an ironic function in Mark 8. This irony is characteristic of the Gospel of Mark. The knowing readers come to feel superior to the simple disciples as readers share the point of view of the evangelist. The ironic function and the discernment of topics are related. As readers discern different levels of meaning in Mark, they may see that the irony of Mark 8 is ambiguous, that what the disciples think is the topic is closer to the truth than readers initially realize. Readers may eventually discern that bread (at a symbolic level) is indeed the theme (or at least one of the ways that the theme of the Gospel may be expressed).

The Role and Function of the Gospels as Literature. A literary approach to the Gospels in not designed to reduce the Gospel text to dogma and history but neither is it designed to reduce the text to a nexus of linguistic and literary data. What references and/or functions of Gospel texts are conceivable and satisfying in literary study? (Nonliterary references and functions are not ruled out, of course.) Is there a function of Gospel texts comparable to the function of literary texts—a function that is faithful to the nature of the Gospels and that remains in a dialectical relationship to dogmatic and historical references? The Gospels may be viewed in terms of the discovery and creation of a world that sustains intellectual, spiritual, and emotional vitality, a world that is a divine gift and not simply the consequence of human quest and achievement. When the reference of the text is seen as a world of grace and truth, narrow dogmatic and historical references are relativized, no longer seen as the primary goal of study. This world-creating or world-revealing function of the Gospels is comparable to the way art and poetry function in enabling readers to create worlds, to come to know who they are and where they come from and are going, and to better understand their place in life and relation to nature and their fellows.

Form and Structure. Form is most often used to describe the principle of organization of a work. Attention has been given primarily to mechanic form, the shape that is imposed externally, much as a mold imposes a shape on wet clay. (Organic form, on the contrary, is concerned with the shape that develops from within, like a growing plant.) At times the principle of organization is seen in terms of chronology. Each of the Gospels contains a passion narrative preceded by accounts of Jesus' words and deeds. In Mark and Matthew a distinction is made between an early ministry in Galilee and a later mission and passion in Jerusalem. Luke makes this distinction, but in addition has a lengthy travel narrative connecting the two phases.

At times the different sorts of content has been the basis of structuring. Matthew has narrative and discourse material alternating in such a way that five "books" can be discerned, each consisting of a section of narrative and a section of discourse. This pentateuchal structuring is supported by the similarity of the conclusions of each of the five sections of discourse, something like "Now when Jesus had finished saying these things . . . " (Matt. 7:28; 11:1; 13:53; 19:1; and 26:1). But a threefold structure is seen when 4:17 and 16:21 are taken as dividing marks. Each of these verses contains the words "From that time [on] Jesus began . . . " with an infinitive and a summary of the content to follow. Other structures are dependent upon readers observing relationships between earlier and later sections.

The threefold chronological pattern of Luke has been modified by attention to references to Jerusalem that appear at turns in the story. The conclusion of an initial section (Luke 1:5–3:38) indicates that Jerusalem is the site of Jesus' final temptation. A second section (4:1–9:50) concludes with Jesus "setting his face" to go to Jerusalem (9:51). The travel narrative as a whole is movement toward Jerusalem and can be divided into 9:51–13:35 (the beginning of the journey) and 14:1–19:27 (the conclusion of the journey). The final section (19:28–24:53) tells of the reign of Jesus in Jerusalem by means of crucifixion and resurrection.

Mark can be perceived as a story of Jesus' ministry in and around Galilee followed by a journey to Jerusalem and Jesus' activities there. But it can be read as a passion narrative, prefaced by a series of controversies that lead up to the passion. It can also be read as three successive and progressively worsening stages in the story of the relations between Jesus and his disciples (1:16–8:26; 8:27–14:9; and 14:10–16:8).

The Gospel of John can be divided mechanically into prologue, book of signs, and book of passion. When weight is given to organic form, the Fourth Gospel may be compared with a musical fugue, with a theme announced and developed to a point, after which other themes are introduced and interwoven with the earlier themes. The themes that appear are introduced in the prologue.

Plot. Plot or narrative unity of the Gospels is related to but is not the same as form and structure. In some measure, the concept of "story" mediates form and plot, for story normally refers to the synopsis of the temporal order of events in a narrative. In summarizing a work, we say that something happened, then something else, then something else, and so on. Plot goes beyond the chronological ordering and accounts for the relationships between the events and the organization of the events for the particular effect created. Luke–Acts provides directions for ordering the Gospel that are easily seen when a literary perspective is assumed. Readers are invited to read the Gospel in light of the perspective of Acts. Prologues tie the two works together, as do events in Acts that parallel those in the Gospel. Jerusalem is central in both works, with the Gospel moving toward Jerusalem and the book of Acts moving away from

Jerusalem. There is a clear correlation between events predicted by characters in the Gospel and their fulfillment in Acts. Readers are prepared for this correlation between Luke and Acts by correlation within each of the writings. Jesus' declaration that a prophet is not acceptable in his own country is followed immediately by his own townspeople's rejection (Luke 4:16-30), and Agabus's prediction of Paul's suffering (Acts 21:10-14) comes true immediately (Acts 21:30-35). Just as Jesus' commission in Acts 1:8 guides the reader for the reading of the book of Acts, the prophecy of Simeon in Luke 2:34 prepares the reader for understanding the Gospel as the story of the prophet Jesus who created a division among the people in his ministry.

The beginnings and endings of the Gospels are important from a literary perspective. The prologue of the Gospel of John prepares the reader for the entire Gospel. The infancy stories of Matthew and Luke serve the same function for those Gospels. Mark is unique in that it lacks a full-blown prologue, contains a problematic ending, and fails to establish a clear and unambiguous set of connections among and between the episodes. The critical and imaginative competence and skill of readers are stretched in discerning the plot of Mark.

Character. Characters are necessary for the actions that move the story along, but actions help define characters, so there is a dialectical relationship between plot and character in the Gospels. In the Gospels, characters are portrayed—their moral, emotional, and volitional qualities are expressed—in what they say and do as well as in what is said of them. Of primary interest in literary study is the way that convincing portraits of Jesus, God, and figures around Jesus are fashioned within the totality of the Gospel and how those portrayed persons are related to the rest of the story.

The Gospels differ widely in the way they utilize literary means to present portraits of Jesus (and other characterizations follow from the presentation of Jesus). John and Mark are at opposite poles. The Gospel of John utilizes a prologue, lengthy discourses of Jesus and a prayer to his father, a series of signs, testimony of independent witnesses, and explicit statements of the narrator to present an unambiguous picture of the messiahship and divine sonship of Jesus. In Mark, there is no prologue, but the opening says that Jesus is the Christ, the son of God. Yet, what seems to be so obvious at the beginning becomes problematic. Jesus is not Messiah in the traditional sense. What is revealed in the literary strategies is as confusing for the reader as Jesus' disclosure is to the disciples within the story.

God is a character in a literary sense in the Gospels. In the Gospel of John, God is characterized by Jesus. He is the one who sent Jesus. In Luke there is a process of "deconstruction" at work in the tension between "revolutionary" and "conservative" aspects of Luke's God. The purpose of God is universal salvation, and the story of Luke–Acts is a "dialogue between God and a recalcitrant humanity"[74] with God overrruling as well as ruling. But Luke–Acts proclaims God's faithfulness to Israel. The revolutionary and conservative aspects of the characterization of God creates a tension that is not clearly resolved in the story.

Narrative World and Rhetoric. The narrative worlds of the Gospels are important. The world may be considered a "poetic" (not a "fictional") world in that the writers craft a unified sequence and introduce characters and tell the readers (directly and indirectly) how those characters are to be considered, and so on. But in a real sense, the world (or the values of the world) is profoundly true for the authors. So true, that the Gospels are attempts to lead readers to affirm or reaffirm belief in such a world. The Gospels may, then, be called narrative rhetoric, and a literary approach will give attention to the means utilized in the Gospels to appeal to the reader.

Authors and Narrators. Literary criticism of the Gospels is concerned with authorship in quite a different fashion than is historical criticism. What sort of author is it who is leading readers to affirm belief? What can be discovered from the work itself? This "author" is called the "implied author" in literary criticism and is to be distinguished from the real author who can be given a name and address. The narrator is also a literary figure. Literary criticism distinguishes between first and third person narrators and (with third-person narrators) between the omniscient and limited point of view. The omniscient narrator may be intrusive or nonintrusive. The narrators of the Gospels are third person, omniscient, and intrusive. Gospel narrators know what needs to be known about persons and events, even having access to the characters' feelings, motives, and thoughts. The narrators not only tell the story, they

---

[74]Robert C. Tannehill, *The Gospel according to Luke*, vol. 1 of *The Narrative Unity of Luke-Acts: A Literary Interpretation* (Philadelphia: Fortress Press, 1986) 3.

introduce the story, provide explanations, translate terms, tell us what is known or not known by characters, and express judgments directly and indirectly. Readers are influenced by the nature of the narrator. There is a correlation between the dependability of the narrator and the more ultimate trustworthiness and trust that are being manifested and elicited.

Reader Response Criticism. Reader-response criticism views literature in terms of readers and their values, attitudes, and responses. The nature and role of the reader varies in the different forms of reader-response criticism, but in all forms there is a movement away from the view of interpretation as the determination by an autonomous reader of the meaning of an autonomous text. In one form (reader-reception criticism) an attempt is made to situate a literary work within the cultural context of its production and then explore the shifting relations between this context and the changing contexts of historical readers. Another form (aesthetic-response criticism) emphasizes the process by which a reader actualizes a text. A text is marked by gaps that the reader must complete and blanks that the reader must fill in. Psychological approaches to the reader emphasize the stages of development of individual readers or the role played by the "psychological set" of readers.

The community influences the attention given by the reader and the kind of "actualization" made by the reader. To some extent, then, criticism involves the determination of the perspective from which reading will proceed and becomes a matter of persuasion as well as a matter of demonstration. Interest in and appreciation of "interpretative communities" in literary study may provide appreciation for and insight into the way different religious communities read the Gospels. Roman Catholics, mainline Protestants, and Evangelicals are inevitably constrained by histories of interpretation, traditions, and contemporary communities of faith. Meaning must always have some locale.

Literary approaches to the Gospels complement conventional approaches. They may enable readers to rediscover value and meaning in the Gospels that have become problematic with approaches that distance texts for purposes of critical examination. The assumptions and strategies of literary criticism allow readers to interact with texts in critical and creative modes and fashions.

Redaction and Literary Criticism and Lives of Jesus

The fact that Jesus is a character in the Gospels, depicted in different ways in different Gospels, and that the depiction of Jesus both in the

Gospels and in later presentations is related to the life of believers does not mean that Jesus was not a historical figure. Scholars may move, then, from their discovery and creation of Jesus as a literary figure to the historical figure of Jesus. But is this figure any more objectively real than the literary figure?

Contemporary studies of the historical Jesus seem to take different perspectives. Some are eager to find objective academic means of historical rediscovery of the historical Jesus and denigrate methods that are not purely objective. Others seek objective methods while acknowledging the impossibility of a purely objective quest. The awareness of the impossibility of a purely objective quest increases their attempts to engage in such a quest. Traditionally oriented scholars seek to clothe their reconstructions of Jesus within the context of first-century Judaism with intelligibility that is recognizable by both the academy and the church.

Chapter 7, below, deals with major contemporary scholarly treatments of Jesus that reflect these activities and concludes with a discussion of the church's investment in the critical study of Jesus. But this attempt to mediate or transcend the different perspectives demands some appreciation of broader philosophical and hermeneutical arguments and approaches to truth. Chapters 4 and 5 provide a discussion of these philosophical and hermeneutical approaches.

Chapter 4

Philosophical Constraints
for Jesus Study

At the height of human pride in intellectual achievement, scholars distinguished a precritical (pre-Enlightenment) epoch from a critical or Enlightenment epoch, and they viewed developments from the precritical to the critical as progress from ignorance and superstition to increasingly more perfect knowledge about the world of nature and the human world. Intellectual achievement influenced scholarly reconstruction of the life of Jesus, not only directing specific attempts to recover the historical figure of Jesus but also generating the confidence that objective historical research could achieve such a goal.

Today, scholars append a "postcritical" epoch to the precritical and the critical epochs. This postcritical epoch does not call into question the genuine intellectual and material progress and gains of critical approaches. It does, however, caution us about human pride. It views the critical Enlightenment approaches as overreaching themselves, as claiming for themselves more than they could reasonably have been expected to deliver. The history of human knowledge looks a little different from a contemporary postcritical perspective. To some extent this history looks like a continuous reformulation of a set of basic presuppositions about what humans know and how they know.

In this chapter we will take advantage of our customary practice of viewing cultural data in a periodic fashion. We will begin with the classical period, move to Enlightenment developments, and conclude with our contemporary epoch. We will view our contemporary epoch as one that relativizes intellectual achievement, recognizing that intellectual and theoretical aspects of life are bounded by and completed by human experience, by praxis and community. The debate between idealism and realism in the classical period is viewed as a form of the theory/praxis (modernism/postmodernism) dichotomy of our present time. The transformation of this dichotomy will be traced in philosophy and theology, providing perspectives and tools for our present struggle with questions of what we know and how we know.

Classical and Medieval Views of Reality

Plato (ca. 428–348/347 BCE) and Aristotle (384–322 BCE) were the classical philosophers whose views on the nature of reality (ontology) became primary in philosophy and theology. They agreed that philosophy seeks truth, but they disagreed on the reality that is captured by philosophical truth. Plato saw forms and universals as being objectively real— before things. The particular historical thing is seen through the lens of the Idea. For Aristotle, however, the real was not the universal beyond things; the real was the universal in things. The schema for interpretation was the particular historical thing. These differences became important in philosophy and theology in general and in interpretation in particular.[1] How can any reliable truth be established if reality is founded on the historical, the changing, the ephemeral? Why should and how can any concern be focused on he historical, on historicality in general, if what is real is not directly founded on the historical?

In different epochs idealism in some form was satisfying as the overarching paradigm and the historical and contingent were reduced in some way to that paradigm. Human activity was often devalued in favor of transhuman perspectives. The concept of God in the early church, for example, resulted in large measure from this idealistic Platonic perspective. And human activity was limited to passive response to divine omnipotence, omniscience, and omnipresence.

In other epochs, the realistic Aristotelian paradigm in some form was satisfying. What is really real is what transpires in the world. But how does one make sense of natural and human data and experiences apart from some transcending or overarching reality and schema?[2]

The classical perspectives of Plato and Aristotle became exclusive alternatives, and two major epistemological approaches developed, one

---

[1] In *Thought, Action, and Passion* (Chicago: University of Chicago Press, 1954) 115-18, Richard McKeon discusses the way different views of the relationship between art and what art represents results in different ways of conceiving and discussing art.

[2] In his introduction to *The Critical Tradition: Classic Texts and Contemporary Trends* (New York: St. Martin's Press, 1989) 12-14, David H. Richter (editor) uses McKeon's scheme and discusses different maps of criticism growing out of different presuppositions.

holding that universal ideas are innate (Plato) and the other that universal ideas are obtained through the senses (Aristotle). In different transformations these ideas influenced both pre-Enlightenment and Enlightenment thought. They became part of the furniture of the mind. When Western philosophy became linked with the church and the Jewish and Christian traditions and philosophy became the means for understanding and expressing the faith, the different philosophical paradigms expressed themselves in theology. The Platonic tradition was dominant for the first millennium after which the Aristotelian tradition became dominant. The Platonic position was reflected by Augustine (354–430) and Augustine's influence explains domination of this tradition for one thousand years. Although knowledge stems from them, our sensations do not teach us truth. It is something in us that is purely intelligible, necessary, motionless, and eternal that teaches us truth. This is divine illumination.

In the thirteenth century, the philosophical tradition of Aristotle succeeded that of Plato. As Augustine became the means for Plato entering the mainstream of Western thought, so Thomas Aquinas (1225–1274) is responsible for making the philosophy of Aristotle the speculative framework of thinking systematically about reality. In his *Summa theologica* Thomas synthesized the rational human wisdom of Aristotle with the divine truths of the Christian tradition. The method of Aristotle became the method of scholasticism. It was a project of reflection based on assumptions about the nature of authoritative texts, the nature of reason, and the grounds of rational pedagogy. The procedure was the posing of a question, the citing of evidence (Scripture, the opinions of the Fathers, philosophical arguments), the resolution of the problem through rational argument, and the defense of the position by responses to contrary opinions.

The Influence of Descartes and Locke

The marriage of theology and philosophy resulted in the domination of dogmatic systems. More than religious thought and biblical study were affected; the entire culture—including government—was subservient to this comprehensive dogmatic system. The epoch that facilitated movement away from this dogmatic system is known as the Enlightenment. The work of René Descartes (1596–1650) and John Locke (1632–1704) prepared the way. These two may be seen as recapitulating in the area of epistemology the work of Plato and Aristotle in ontology.

René Descartes. The scholastic tradition of the time of Descartes emphasized logic and a respect for antiquity. Knowledge was acquired through definition, division, and argument. This deductive system was based on scripture and tradition. Scripture and tradition provided unquestioned and secure premises that allowed simple and certain conclusions to be reached logically and, therefore, immediately. The movement from a deductive system to an empirical system in theology involved treating Scripture and tradition as data to be handled according to the acceptable scientific assumptions and methods. Results are at best probable and the path from data to interpretation is long and difficult. But the same must be said for all areas of knowledge.

Descartes's new way of thinking based on mathematics obviated the scholastic tradition of theology, but it sought the simplicity and certainty of that deductive tradition. The roots for Descartes's thought go back to the philosophical thought of Augustine and the mathematical thought of Galileo. Augustine differentiated between knowledge of corporeal things gained through the bodily senses and knowledge of incorporeal things gained through the mind's knowledge of itself.[3] This influenced Descartes's separation of the realm of mind as "thinking thing" from the realm of matter as "extended thing." Galileo's approach to nature involved a distinction between primary qualities (the constant characteristics of the experienced world, such as form and magnitude) and secondary qualities (the subjective effects of these primary characteristics on our senses). Descartes was interested in employing Galileo's new way of using mathematics as a tool to relate to the sensible world conclusions that had been drawn theoretically. In the accomplishment of this task, the reality of the empirical world was reduced to the formal relations of extended bodies. Empirical objects, then, are subordinate to space that is a reality detached from such objects. Through these formal and spacial relations, the mind apprehends universal and necessary truths.

The work of Descartes was an implicit challenge to the authority of tradition; it was finally an appeal to look for truth only in the reason of a thinking individual. The Cartesian method demands that we accept as true only what is presented "clearly and distinctly" to our mind. No room for doubt should be left. Hence, judgment should be suspended in all matters where the slightest doubt is possible. This suspension of doubt includes the truths of common sense. Sense perception cannot be accepted

---

[3]*De Trinitate* 9.3.3.

as giving indubitable knowledge, since it cannot be determined a priori that we are not dreaming or being deceived by a malicious demon. The very act of doubting, and the thinking that is involved in that doubting, however, cannot be doubted, according to Descartes. This is the foundation: I think, therefore I, the thinker, must exist. The basis of knowledge is summarized in the famous formula "Cogito ergo sum." Descartes's position may be termed "epistemological idealism" in that he stressed innate ideas over against the thesis that ideas derive from the senses.

The dualism of Descartes created questions in terms of perception, questions that have been answered in idealist and positivist directions. But perhaps most important was his elevation of the thinking ego and creation of the instrumental reason in the triumph of the human spirit over nature. Thomas F. Torrance summarized the significance of Descartes for later theology:

> So far as Descartes himself was concerned, his profound faith in God and the central and necessary place for God in his whole system of thought, curbed the presumption of his reason, restraining it from trying to transcend its own limits and from trying to limit the possible or the real to the humanly conceivable. But when skepticism, poised upon the certainty of the self-understanding, replaced his methodological doubt, and God as the creative ground of objective intelligibility in the universe began to disappear out of the picture, rationalism and materialism entrenched themselves in European culture. The age of the autocratic reason, what Kant was later to call heautonomy, set in.[4]

John Locke. John Locke opposed what had become the "received doctrine" that humans "have native ideas, and original characters, stamped upon their minds in their very first being" and defended the proposition that "all ideas come from sensation or reflection." External material things are the objects of sensation, and the operations of our minds (perception, thinking, doubting, believing, and so on) are the objects of "internal sense" or reflection. External objects are known only as they are represented by ideas in the mind. A distinction is made between ideas of objects and qualities of objects that cause ideas. The idea is the immedi-

---

[4]Thomas F. Torrance, *Transformation & Convergence in the Frame of Knowledge: Exploration in the Interrelations of Scientific and Theological Enterprise* (Grand Rapids MI: Eerdmans, 1984) 11.

ate object of perception, thought, or understanding. The power that produces the idea is the quality of the object.[5]

John Locke's epistemology developed against the background of the
very practical question of the authority of the civil magistrate to regulate
matters of religious worship. After the restoration of Charles II to the
throne of England in 1660, Locke had defended the right of the state to
determine "indifferent" matters of religious worship. This authority was
needed to maintain religious and political peace. By 1667, Locke had
changed his position and defended religious toleration. Religious opinions
were not to be imposed. The basis for this opinion was epistemological:
since the magistrate has no more certain knowledge than anyone else, the
magistrate has no authority to impose religious opinions.[6]

Locke's essay *Concerning Human Understanding* (1690) confronts
issues of epistemology directly, but with religion and politics still in the
background. He charged that proponents of innate ideas use that theory
to impose their opinions on others as infallible and to govern by
demanding unquestioning faith in their judgments. In this essay, Locke
attempted to find a place in his epistemology for the possibility of
deducing moral principles and norms. In an earlier work entitled *Essays
on the Law of Nature*, Locke had indicated that humans can gain clear
and true ideas of the concepts of morality in the same way they do those
of mathematics. He returned to this theme in his 1690 essay. "Simple"
ideas are developed "passively" through sensation and reflection, but
"complex" ideas are gained "actively" through the combination of different kinds of simple ideas. These "mixed modes" are generally related to
the sphere of human action—especially thought, movement, and power.
They form the conceptuality for the norms of laws and morality. It is true
that the "mixed modes" do not have a relationship with an immediate
reality. They have no other reality than what they have in the minds of
humans. Nevertheless they are real. Nothing more is required to make this
kind of ideas real but that they be framed in such a way they have a
possibility of existing. Locke concluded:

> Upon this ground it is, that I am bold to think, that *Morality is capable
> of Demonstration*, as well as Mathematicks: Since the precise real
> Essence of the Things moral Words stand for, may be perfectly known;

---

[5]*Essay Concerning Human Understanding*, 2.1.1-2.
[6]*An Essay Concerning Toleration* (1687) and *A Letter on Toleration* (1689)

as so the Congruity, or Incongruity of the Things themselves be certainly discovered, in which consists perfect Knowledge[7]

The fact that Locke's epistemological approach to external material things is not applicable to moral questions moves the discussion to the role of revelation. All knowledge stops on the one hand at the limits of the physical world that can be grasped by the senses and on the other hand at the limits of systems that can be constructed from the "mixed modes." Human knowledge, therefore, is limited. In Locke's day, the concept of revelation was a concept to be taken seriously—in light of the dogmatic background and also in light of the philosophical problem of knowledge. The premises of scripture and tradition had not yet become mere data to be treated scientifically. In his work *Concerning Human Understanding*, Locke spoke of the relationship between "faith" and "reason." Important principles were given in relation to the concept of revelation. One principle has to do with revelation and communication.

Communication of revelation (as ideas) requires some framework of conceivable experience and conceptuality. Ideas that others have not already had (by sensation or reflection) would be quite incomprehensible, and therefore incapable of communication. Another principle has to do with the relationship of revelation to data that can be discovered by reason or to ideas naturally at our disposal. Natural or reasonable knowledge could also be communicated by revelation, but "in all things of this kind, there is little need or use of revelation, God having furnished us with natural and surer means to arrive at the knowledge of them."[8] Revelation, therefore, is not needed in the cases of things that rest on clear perception, the correspondence of ideas, or the deduction of reason. Even if God should reveal something directly, certainty of this cannot be greater than the knowledge that it is a revelation from God. An epistemological principle results: "Whether it be a divine revelation, or no, reason must judge; which can never permit the mind to reject a greater evidence

---

[7] *Essays on the Law of Nature*, 3.11.16: cited in Henning Graf Reventlow, *The Authority of the Bible and the Rise of the Modern World*, trans. John Bowden (London: SCM Press, 1984; Philadelphia: Fortress Press, 1985) 254. Reventlow shows that Locke runs into considerably difficulties in carry out this program. The examples purported to illustrate the possibility of demonstrating morality are either very commonplace or are taken from the traditional law of nature. A large number of them like the love commandment come from scripture.

[8] *An Essay Concerning Human Understanding* 4.18.4.

to embrace what is less evident, nor allow it to entertain probability in opposition to knowledge and certainty."[9]

Locke did refer to specific items of faith about which revelation informs us and not reason. And yet, it is on the basis of reason that we must judge what is "clear revelation." "There can be no evidence that any traditional revelation is of divine original, in the words we receive it, and in the sense we understand it, so clear and so certain, as that of the principles of reason."[10]

Locke did not exclude revelation. He attempted to correlate revelation and reason in a *reasonable* fashion. In *The Reasonableness of Christianity*, Locke returned to authority, the authority of the New Testament and the teachings of Jesus. The impossibility of an approach through a theoretical epistemology caused Locke to return to authority. In principle and practice, human reason is hindered by all kinds of circumstances and is not able to press forward to a comprehensively based morality. Human reason, then, is directed toward the "law of grace" that is contained in the message of Jesus. Even here, however, there is a dialectical relationship between reason and faith: "It is at least a surer and shorter way, to the apprehensions of the vulgar, and mass of mankind, that one manifestly sent from God, and coming with visible authority from him, should, as a King and lawmaker, tell them their duties, and require their obedience, than leave it to the long, and sometimes intricate deductions of reason, to be made out to them."[11]

The limitations of reason *and* the necessity of reason were discussed by Locke in a treatment of the interpretation of the writings of the Old and New Testaments. The biblical writings have the same deficiencies as all writings, they share in the "imperfections of language." Locke questioned, however, whether the deficiency is in language or in understanding.

> When . . . I began to examine the extent and certainty of our knowledge, I found it had so near a connection with words, that, unless their force and manner of signification were first well observed, there could be very

---

[9]Ibid. 4.18.10.

[10]Ibid. 4.18.10.

[11]*The Reasonableness of Christianity as Delivered in the Scriptures* 241.2; *The Reasonableness of Christianity, with A Discourse of Miracles, and part of A Third Letter Concerning Toleration*, edited, abridged, and introduced by I. T. Ramsey (Stanford CA: Stanford University Press, 1958) 60-61.

little said clearly and pertinently concerning knowledge: which being conversant about truth, had constantly to do with propositions. And though it terminated in things, yet it was for the most part so much by the intervention of words, that they seemed scarce separable from our general knowledge. At least they interpose themselves so much between our understandings, and the truth which it would contemplate and apprehend, that, like the medium through which visible objects pass, the obscurity and disorder do not seldom cast a mist before our eyes, and impose upon our understandings.[12]

The history of interpretation of the Bible provides proof of the fact that "the signification of words in all languages" depends very much on "the thoughts, notions, and ideas of him that uses them." Because of the imperfections of language even the will of God as clothed in words is "liable to that doubt and uncertainty which unavoidably attends that sort of conveyance." Humankind, therefore, must turn to the light of reason and the precepts of natural religion. These precepts "are plain, and very intelligible to all mankind, and seldom to be controverted." From natural religion mankind can derive plainly and without fail all that is necessary to know about God and the obedience owed God.[13]

The Enlightenment in France

The ideas of Descartes and Locke were used in a struggle against systems that appealed to traditional modes of authority, modes that involved theology and the church. We tend to view the Enlightenment in either an uncritically positive or an uncritically negative way. In both cases, unlimited confidence in human reason is emphasized. The sketch of the Enlightenment in this volume will show its occupation with the limits of human cognitive powers and its kinship to the postmodern view.

The Enlightenment is considered primarily a French development because in France the ideas of Descartes and Locke were first taken and applied as weapons against church and state. Dialogue in philosophy, theology, and biblical study did not take place in France because intellectual leaders there were interested in social and religious criticism for the purpose of change. They were more ideological than philosophical, more devoted to appropriating ideas for their own purposes than to weighing those ideas. Whatever ideas were at hand were used as weapons against

---

[12]*An Essay Concerning Human Understanding* 3.9.21.
[13]Ibid. 3.9.22-23.

church and state and in arguments among themselves. The dominant position of the Roman Catholic church and the lack of a Protestant understanding of scripture that could be accommodated to Enlightenment ideas contributed to the lack of dialogue and caused the Enlightenment in France to be opposed not only to specific practices but to the church in principle.

The Enlightenment in Great Britain

Deism. In Britain, the Enlightenment did involve a dialogue that included theology and religion. There, the Enlightenment was associated with the movement known as deism. The term *deism* refers most specifically to belief in a single god and religious practices based on natural reason rather than supernatural revelation. The deist, then, was to be differentiated from the atheist. But the deist was also differentiated from the orthodox Christian who held fast to the supernatural, to authority, and to tradition.

A number of influential seventeenth- and eighteenth-century thinkers claimed for themselves the title of "Christian deist" because they accepted both the Christian religion based on revelation and a deistic religion based on natural reason. This deistic religion was consistent with Christianity but independent of any revealed authority. Christian deists often accepted revelation because it could be made to accord with natural or rational religion. Allegorical readings of scripture were offered to secure such agreement. Moreover, even the deist who recognized no revelation often avoided or even disavowed any denigration of Christian scriptures, expressing admiration for the way the truths of natural religion were offered in the scriptures. From a later perspective when distinctions between the natural and supernatural, between reason and tradition, lose their sharpness, where greater tolerance of opinion within Christian society lessened the need for a term to chastise independent thinkers, and where there was an increasing tendency of rationalists to become simple unbelievers rather than settle for compromise, the term itself fell into disuse.

Descartes and Locke were not deists. But their ideas were not incompatible with the movement. Descartes provided a psychological argument for God. For Descartes, the very presence of the idea of God as a perfect being was proof of the actual existence of this perfect being. Since our mind perceives that it is not perfect itself, it could not have fabricated the idea of a perfect being (a more perfect thing cannot be produced by a less perfect thing). The function of God in the construction of Descartes is to assure reliability of human knowledge. Since God is perfect, he cannot deceive. We can, therefore, rely on our commonsense belief in the reality of the material world and on our intellectual intuition. The material world, however, is conceived of by Descartes in a deterministic or a mechanistic fashion. All processes are explained by the laws of mechanics. Even though God is needed to sustain the universe just as he is needed to create it, the philosophy of Descartes made God absent in the world and useless in interpreting the world.

John Locke and George Berkeley. Locke's epistemology was a foundation for eighteenth-century deism, but Locke himself denied that his religious opinions were influenced by or the same as the deists. Indeed, the *Reasonableness of Christianity* can be seen as directed against the deists.[14] Developments in Britain that were eventually to play a part in developments in Germany and in major movements in theology and biblical studies, nevertheless, may be seen most clearly in relation to John Locke's empiricism. The position of Locke was a nuanced position allowing distinctions not only between ideas themselves and the qualities of objects causing ideas but also between original (or primary) qualities and secondary qualities. Original or primary qualities are those inseparable from the object. A grain of wheat, for example, has solidarity, extension, figure, and mobility no matter how small it may be. Secondary qualities are those that are not in the objects themselves but are in the powers to produce various sensations by means of the primary qualities.

Locke's position (known as representative realism or British empiricism) was challenged by George Berkeley (1685–1753) who questioned the distinction between primary qualities and secondary qualities (between real substance and appearances). If the objective or primary qualities of experience are accorded the status of the real, and secondary qualities merely subjective, how can we ever know the primary at all? Berkeley's philosophy is an example of subjective idealism. He held that our visual perception of the world is not of any substantial "thing" but rather of shapes and colors. On the basis of that visual perception, we project "physical substance" into the picture. Reality is a perception on the part of a perceiver. All we know are perceived qualities.

---

[14]See John C. Higgins-Biddle, "John Locke," in *The Encyclopedia of Religion*, 16 vols., ed. Mircea Eliade et al. (New York: Macmillan, 1987) 9:4-5.

David Hume. Berkeley's ideas formed the basis for David Hume's radical skepticism. Hume (1711–1776) is conventionally seen from the modern perspective that assumes that epistemological problems can be settled and a certain and secure foundation established for knowledge. Hume, then, is the foil for the work of Kant and the restructuring of the problem of knowledge. From the postmodern perspective that does not seek a foundation that can be universally quantified, Hume may be considered a forerunner. Hume acknowledged that it seems evident "that men are carried, by a natural instinct or prepossession, to repose faith in their senses; and that, without any reasoning, or even almost before the use of reason, we always suppose an external universe, which depends not on our perception, but would exist, though we and every sensible creature were absent or annihilated." It also seems evident that men always suppose "the very images, presented by the senses, to be the external objects, and never entertain any suspicion, that the one are nothing but representations of the other." This "universal and primary opinion of all men" is destroyed by the philosophy that teaches that "nothing can ever be present to the mind but an image or perception, and that the senses are only the inlets, through which these images are conveyed, without being able to produce any immediate intercourse betweens the mind and the object."

The new system of philosophy is embarrassed, however, because it is unable to prove that "the perceptions of the mind must be caused by external objects . . . and could not arise either from the energy of the mind itself, or from the suggestion of some invisible and unknown spirit, or from some other cause still more unknown to us." The question whether perceptions of the senses are produced by external objects must be determined by experience. But the mind has never anything present to it but the perceptions and cannot possibly reach any experience of the connection of perceptions with objects. "The supposition of such a connection is, therefore, without any foundation in reasoning."[15]

"Excessive skepticism," however, *is* challenged by experience. The skeptic "must acknowledge, if he will acknowledge anything, that all human life must perish, were his principles universally and steadily to prevail. All discourse, all action would immediately cease; and men remain in a total lethargy, till the necessities of nature, unsatisfied, put an

---

[15]Hume, *Enquiry Concerning Human Understanding* 12.1.

end to their miserable existence." Individuals "must act and reason and believe; though they are not able, by their most diligent inquiry, to satisfy themselves concerning the foundation of these operations, or to remove the objections, which may be raised against them." Nevertheless, excessive skepticism may be of advantage in the development of a mitigated skepticism. One species of such skepticism involves "a degree of doubt, and caution, and modesty, which, in all kinds of scrutiny and decision, ought forever to accompany a just reasoner." Another species of mitigated skepticism is "the limitation of our inquiries to such subjects as are best adapted to the narrow capacity of human understanding."[16]

Hume's finely nuanced distinctions between such things as imagination and judgment, abstract reason and experimental reason, and general and particular facts are applicable to theology in general and to biblical studies in particular as those studies become empirical sciences. Hume contrasted the two capacities of imagination and judgment. Judgment "confines itself to common life, and to such subjects as fall under daily practice and experience." Beyond that, imagination reigns.

As illustration of matters beyond the scope of judgment Hume cites determinations we may form "with regard to the origin of worlds, and the situation of nature, from, and to eternity." How can we satisfy ourselves concerning such matters when "we cannot give a satisfactory reason, why we believe after a thousand experiments, that a stone will fall, or fire burn?" "Those who have a propensity to philosophy, will still continue their researches; because they reflect, that, besides the immediate pleasure, attending such an occupation, philosophical decisions are nothing but the reflections of common life, methodized and corrected. But they will never be tempted to go beyond common life, so long as they consider the imperfection of those faculties which they employ, their narrow reach, and their inaccurate operations." In contrast to judgment, imagination is "naturally sublime, delighted with whatever is remote and extraordinary, and running, without control, into the most distant parts of space and time in order to avoid the objects, which custom has rendered too familiar to it."[17]

Hume distinguished not only between imagination and judgment but also between the judgment of *abstract reasoning* concerning quantity and number and judgment of *experimental reasoning* concerning matters of

---

[16]Ibid. 12.2-3.
[17]Ibid. 12.3.

fact and existence. The proper subjects of abstract science and inquiry, in the view of Hume, are quantity and number. "As the component parts of quantity and number are entirely similar, their relations become intricate and involved; and nothing can be more curious, as well as useful, than to trace, by a variety of mediums, their equality or inequality, through their different appearances." Attempts to "extend this most perfect species of knowledge beyond these boundaries are mere sophistry and illusion." Hume challenged the idea that conceivability and lack of contradiction establishes matters of fact and existence. This was a thesis emphasized at that time particularly by Christian Wolff in Germany. "That the cube root of 64 is equal to the half of 10, is a false proposition, and can never be distinctly conceived. But that Caesar, or the angel Gabriel, or any being never existed, may be a false proposition, but still is perfectly conceivable, and implies no contradiction." Ideas other than quantity and number "are clearly distinct and different from each other [and] we can never advance farther, by our utmost scrutiny, than to observe this diversity, and, by an obvious reflection, pronounce one thing not to be another." Inquires into fact and existence differ from inquiry into quantity and number in that fact and existence are "evidently incapable of demonstration." In the area of fact and existence, argument is made from cause and effect. These arguments are based entirely on experience.

Hume was not denigrating experience, rather he was arguing against the use of a priori reasoning in the establishment of anything outside quantity and number.

> If we reason a priori, anything may appear able to produce anything. The falling of a pebble may, for aught we know, extinguish the sun; or the wish of a man control the planets in their orbits. It is only experience, which teaches us the nature and bounds of cause and effect, and enables us to infer the existence of one object from that of another.[18]

Hume did allow for general facts as well as particular facts. The sciences (including such disciplines as politics, natural philosophy, physics, and chemistry) deal with general facts. Disciplines such as history, chronology, geography, and astronomy deal with particular facts. Divinity or theology has a foundation in reason to the extent that it is supported by experience, and it deals with both particular and general facts. "But its best and most solid foundation is *faith* and divine

---

[18]Ibid.

revelation." Matters that are the object of taste and sentiment and not reason (morals and beauty, for example) may be transformed into objects of reasoning and inquiry. When we reason concerning some matter of taste or sentiment or attempt to fix a new standard, new facts are being developed that become the object of reasoning and inquiry. Hume concluded:

> When we run over libraries, persuaded of these principles, what havoc must we make? If we take in our hand any volume; of divinity or school metaphysics, for instance; let us ask, *Does it contain any abstract reasoning concerning quantity or number?* No. *Does it contain any experimental reasoning concerning matter of fact and existence?* No. Commit it then to the flames: for it can contain nothing but sophistry and illusion.[19]

The Enlightenment in Germany

The work of Hume may be considered a foil for the contributions of Kant, but Kant's contributions were made in the context of the German Enlightenment that was slower in coming and more moderate than in France or England. The same social, political, economic, and intellectual conditions that were intolerable in France and England were tolerated in Germany for a time because Germany had been exhausted by the Thirty Years War. When the Enlightenment did come to Germany, moreover, it was moderate. The first stage of the German Enlightenment, in fact, has been called "Scholastic Rationalism," "Enlightened Scholasticism," or even "Pietist Enlightenment."

Leibniz. The work of Gottfried Wilhelm von Leibniz (1646–1716) and Christian Wolff (1679–1754) exemplify the early stage of Germany's form of the Enlightenment. Leibniz was a rationalist who supported the concept of innate ideas. In *New Essays Concerning Human Understanding* he cites the axiom directed against innate ideas, "that there is nothing in the soul which does not come from the senses." He then declared that the soul itself and its affections must be exempted from this axiom. "Now the soul comprises being, substance, unity, identity, cause, perception, reason, and many other notions which the senses cannot give."[20]

By means of a "middle way" Leibniz came to terms with movements in modern science *and* held to teleological explanation of physical phe-

---

[19]Ibid.
[20]Leibniz, *New Essays Concerning Human Understanding*, 2.1.

nomena, that is, he embraced both "efficient causes" and "final causes." Leibniz was dealing with a theme that has become important in post-modern scientific and philosophical thought, the limitations of Enlightenment rationality in itself, the inability of a science to explain and rationalize itself from within itself. His solution, of course, utilizes arguments available in his day, but the problem he dealt with is a contemporary problem.

Consistent with modern science, Leibniz accepted systematic mathematical order, the hypothetical status of explanations of phenomena, and the role of observation and experimentation in the testing of hypotheses and the empirical filling in of mathematical form. The principle of efficient causes, then, was the basis for the scientific explanations of physical phenomena. What produced the "middle way" was Leibniz's acceptance of the usefulness and necessity of teleological explanations of physical phenomena. Leibniz held that explanation of nature is incomplete when only the laws by which events can be demonstrated to occur are stated. The laws themselves must be explained in terms of causes that lie outside the complex of nature or the series of natural events—final causes. Laws of nature must be explained in terms of their causes.

The "middle way" allows for the study of the world in two ways. As a phenomenal realm, everything is to be explained according to causes discovered in experience. As a noumenal realm, however, the world is to be explained by the reasons God had in creating the world. These two explanations of the world are not incompatible. Each is the same world looked at in a different way.

The "middle way" is the way between the extremes of the scholastics and natural philosophers and the mechanists or reformed philosophers. The scholastics and natural philosophers are right to see the world (under the architectonic aspect) as a world of wisdom, grace, and final causes. But they err in attributing final causes to specific phenomena and believing that they have explained a phenomenon by showing that it benefits humankind and, therefore, is designed for the purposes of humankind. The mechanists are incorrect in their total denial of final causes. This is metaphysically wrong; mechanical principles cannot be explained mechanically. Moreover, the way of efficient causes cannot go far without dependence on regulative or heuristic considerations related to the way of final causes. Neither the method of efficient causes nor the method of final causes can be used perfectly.

According to Lewis White Beck the most perfect method for Leibniz "would be a 'demonstration' of contingent truths of fact, beginning with a priori knowledge of the internal constitution of bodies attained by a contemplation of God and leading to mechanical laws derived from teleological premises."[21] In *The Monadology*, Leibniz emphasized the harmony that exists between efficient and final causes, between "the physical realm of nature and the moral realm of grace, that is to say, between God considered as the architect of the mechanism of the world and God considered as the monarch of the divine city of spirits." This is not a static harmony, for "this harmony brings it about that things progress of themselves toward grace along natural lines."[22] Leibniz' considered view is that "absolute method" is to be saved for a better life. Nevertheless (in opposition to Locke who gave up the search for real essences and satisfied himself with nominal essences), Leibniz held to the ideal of a knowledge resulting from a knowledge of real essences.

Christian Wolff. Christian Wolff (1679–1754) was a transmitter and a modernizer of the tradition of Leibniz. It was against "the Leibniz-Wolffian philosophy" that the more radical form of the German Enlightenment represented by Lessing and Kant revolted. Philosophy for Wolff had the *goal* of knowledge of why things must be as they are. Why are things possible (if they are)? Why are things actual (if they are)? Wolff emphasized repeatedly that there are two ways of knowing: experience and reason. Historical knowledge (empirical sense experience) is the source of knowledge of existence. What things are actual is learned historically by experience. But if they are actual, they must be possible. Why are they possible? This questions leads beyond experience. The *method* of philosophy with the goal of discerning possibility is logical or mathematical in form—but a scholastic type of mathematics with analysis and synthesis that involve an array of definitions and syllogisms. Wolff would begin with experience and with historical knowledge. But experience is not always trustworthy. By means of analysis, replacement of unclear ideas with clear and distinct ideas, and abstraction, simple and trustworthy ideas may be uncovered. These may be combined into defini-

---

[21]Lewis White Beck, *Early German Philosophy: Kant and His Predecessors* (Cambridge MA: Harvard University Press, 1969) 231.

[22]Leibnitz, *Monadology*, 87-88.

tions and then by means of syllogisms movement may be made back to the starting point in historical experience.[23]

Wolff tacitly assumed that a priori knowledge in the logical sense, that is, knowledge expressed in the conclusion of a valid syllogism, had value lacking in an unproved "historical" proposition. Possibility (and being) is defined by the potentiality of being thought. Thinkability defines knowledge and being. Epistemological criteria of knowledge are identified with ontological criteria of possibility and real existence. Analytic thought offers a sufficient condition for asserting extralogical or extramental being. The system of logic followed by Wolff equated "possible" with "nonself-contradiction." For Wolff, propositions could be established by an appeal to their nonself-contradiction. A thing is logically possible if its predicates (attributes) are not contradictory. There is a parallel relationship (if not identity) between a concept of a thing and the thing's essence or possibility. Whatever can be defined is possible, and whatever is possible can be defined or have a corresponding concept. From a later position, it was seen that thinkability does not establish possibility. Analytic thought alone is not sufficient for asserted extramental being. A logical distinction was made between analytic and synthetic judgments and an epistemological distinction between a priori and a posteriore knowledge.[24]

Wolff was the reigning philosopher during the beginning of critical historical study of the New Testament. Samuel Reimarus in particular was influenced by Wolff's idea that for a particular revelation to be actual and valid it must not only be internally consistent but must also be necessary, that is, contain knowledge not attainable by ordinary means. Wolff was important in his time, according to Lewis White Beck, because his philosophy

> was the first comprehensive system to be published in German and was until 1750 either the source of most of the intellectual life or the target of attack by the few who stood with the Pietism for the past or who were preparing the way for a new philosophy and the end of the intellectual dogmatism of the Enlightenment. . . .

---

[23]See selections from Wolff's *Reasonable Thoughts on God, the World, the Soul of Man, and All Things in General* (commonly called *The German Metaphysics* and first published in 1719) in *Eighteenth-century Philosophy*, ed. Lewis White Beck (New York: Free Press, 1966) 217-22.

[24]See Beck, *Early German Philosophy*, 263-66.

. . . Wolff is the best German representative of a general movement of thought toward deism, utilitarianism, and free thought that was sweeping over Europe as a whole, though he seems in many respects to belong to the century before Locke and Diderot."[25]

Gotthold Ephraim Lessing. When Wolff's influence declined, the empiricism of Locke penetrated Germany and a part of Leibniz's philosophy previously ignored rose to the surface. This was the dynamic, evolutionary aspect of Leibniz's thought. In his treatment of the monad, Leibniz spoke of continuity in development from indistinct consciousness to full consciousness of things, as historical and empirical knowledge is brought into the light of reason by means of knowledge of causes. By a theory of continuous development, Leibniz was able to introduce a historical dimension into the religious conflicts of his time. The world appears in various ways to different beings; none is wholly right or wholly wrong. This idea of Leibniz was reintroduced by Lessing in his own work.

Another idea shared by Leibniz and Lessing is that truths of fact cannot be raised to the level of truths of reason.[26] The insight that truths of fact cannot be raised to truths of reason is relevant for theology. A rational theology cannot be founded on a historical record, accurate or not. And though the historical record be false, a rational theology can still be true. Lessing's appropriation of ideas of Leibniz brought him to the conclusion that revelation is a stage in the education of humanity. Revelation is valid within limits and leads toward reason or enlightenment.

Lessing wanted to maintain a moving line rather than to collapse the distinction between revelation and reason. He did not want to see faith squeezed in a corner or reason frozen with the dogmas and rationalities of his own day. The conception of a moving line of division between the truths of faith and the truths of reason implies a dynamic and unfinished character of theology and rationalism and suggests an appropriate modesty—for faith and reason.

In *The Education of the Human Race*, Lessing intellectualized revelation (as Kant accused Leibniz of the error of intellectualizing the senses)[27] by seeing a distinction between historical, empirical revelation and a more perfect reason emerging from it in the course of history and development.

---

[25]Beck, *Early German Philosophy*, 261, 274.
[26]Beck, *Eighteenth Century Philosophy*, 223-24; *Early German Philosophy*, 348, 350.
[27]Beck, *Early German Philosophy*, 351.

He speculated that what was once given only historically, in revelation and during the childhood of humankind, might later be understood rationally—as reason has developed another sense as it were. At that later time the historical evidence (even if authentic) will no longer be sufficient or necessary.

Revelation and education were seen by Lessing as analogous. Revelation is to the whole human race what education is to the individual human being. Education gives individuals nothing that individuals could not have gotten themselves but it is given more quickly and easily. Just as education is dependent upon the developing powers of the child, revelation takes place progressively in an order determined by the capacity of the people who are to receive it. Revelation, then, is not simply a static once-for-all body of doctrine; later revelation supersedes the earlier, but nothing essential in the earlier revelation is lost. The literal truth of the earlier revelation or the vehicle of the revelation may be given up, but truth is not lost. Lessing cites various biblical accounts: "creation in the image of growing day, the origin of evil in the story of the forbidden tree, the source of the variety of languages in the story of the tower of Babel." These contain abstract truths "which could scarcely be passed over, in allegories and instructive single circumstances, which were narrated as actual occurrences." The truth of the fall of humankind is preserved even if the forbidden fruit is not literally the occasion.[28]

Different theological strategies could claim the work of Lessing as their foundation. Lessing's counsel to maintain the dividing line between faith and reason could be claimed by orthodox theologians in order to preserve and defend the mysteries of the faith from rational and historical criticism. Rationalists could justify an attempt to cross the line and refute dogma, for Lessing takes an intellectual position that severely relativized revelation and dogma. The work of Lessing could mean that while disputes between the rationalists and irrationalists go on, Christians should find themselves within theological truths above rational argument. Those who see him advising Christians to find theological truth within themselves see Lessing as the leading eighteenth-century forerunner of existential theology. But Lessing can be seen from today's perspective as supporting the postmodern emphasis on the necessity of the local and the timely instead of the general, abstract, and timeless. The famous state-

---

[28]Lessing, *The Education of the Human Race*, thesis 48.

ment of Lessing usually quoted for its rhetoric may today be emphasized for its deep philosophical and theological truth:

> If God were holding all the truth that exists in his right hand and in his left just the one ever-active urge to find the truth, even if attached to it were the condition that I should always and forever be going astray, and said to me, "Choose!", I should humbly fall upon his left hand and say, "Father, give! Pure truth is for thee alone."[29]

Mathematical and Mechanical Models in Science and Philosophy. The developments in philosophy discussed to this point must be seen not only from the perspective of scholasticism (conventionally seen as a limiting influence) but also from the perspective of the science of the time (which may be seen as both a liberating and a limiting influence). One model of science (dominant in the seventeenth century and seen in the work of Descartes) was that of mathematics. Mathematical techniques (deduction from axioms according to fixed rules, tests of internal consistency, a priori methods, and so on) were confidently applied to philosophy because of their unprecedented success in the natural sciences. The mechanical model in science and philosophy (dominant in the eighteenth century) was different. Nature was a cosmos in which there was harmony. Humans were objects in nature just as trees and stones. Not only the sphere of the mind but also the realms of social and political relations were susceptible to this science. Philosophers such as Locke, Hume, and Berkeley (influenced by the mechanical model) saw that a science of the mind parallels natural science. General laws must be formulated on the basis of observation (both "inner" and "outer") and experience (when necessary) and conclusions deduced from such laws. "To every genuine question there were many false answers, and only one true one; once discovered it was final—it remained for ever true; all that was needed was a reliable method of discovery."[30]

Rationalists and empiricists in philosophy as well as natural scientists believed that "the truth was one single, harmonious body of knowledge; that all previous systems—religions, cosmologies, mythologies—were but so many different roads, some longer or wider, some more twisted and darker, to the same rational goal; that all the sciences and all the faiths, the most fanatical superstitions and the most savage customs, when

---

[29]*Gesammelte Schriften*, 13:24: cited in Beck, *Early German Philosophy*, 350.
[30]Isaiah Berlin, "Introduction," *The Age of Enlightenment: The 18th Century Philosophers*, ed. Isaiah Berlin (New York: New American Library, 1956) 16.

'cleansed' of their irrational elements by the advanced of civilization, can be harmonized in the final true philosophy which could solve all theoretical and practical problems for all men everywhere for all time."[31] The eighteenth century, according to Sir Isaiah Berlin, "is perhaps the last period in the history of Western Europe when human omniscience was thought to be an attainable goal."[32]

Immanuel Kant. Kant brought an end to the attempt to make philosophy a natural science. Kant shifted the center of philosophical inquiry to an examination of the concepts and categories in terms of which we think and reason, frames of reference and systems of relations. Kant's mature thoughts were a consequence of his "recollection" of Hume that interrupted his "dogmatic slumber."[33] Hume had asked what right reason had to think that something can be constituted in a way so that if that thing is posited something else must be posited (causation). Hume concluded that it was not a legitimate right and concept but a convenience that subsumed certain representations under the law of association. It erroneously turned a habit into an objective necessity resulting from rational insight.

If no intrinsic and necessary relationship exists between observed factors, important aspects of scientific knowledge are called into question. If components of scientific knowledge such as substance, relation, and causality are not reached by sense experience and cannot be used in inductive operations from phenomena, how can thought proceed beyond immediately apprehended particulars? Kant saw that a new foundation is necessary, one in which theoretical factors not derived from observation play a part along with phenomenal data.

Kant may be understood as expanding the simple relationship between the subject (the knower) and the object (what is known) to a three-way relationship: the object, the empirical subject (the individual existing in time and space), and the transcendent subject. The empirical subject makes sense of the object by means of omnipresent transcendental rules ("transcendental apperception"). The matter of knowledge is not supplied by Kant's transcendental rules or principles, only the form. If I say, "Last week's rain caused the grass to grow," the form of the judgment and pattern of causality, and so on, are supplied by the mind. The factual data are supplied by sensation. Whether it rained and whether the

---

[31]Ibid., 28.
[32]Ibid., 14.
[33]*Prolegomena*, 8: cited in Beck, *Early German Philosophy*, 465.

rain caused the grass to grow are not matters for a priori reason, but for empirical verification.

Kant came to his insight by generalizing the conclusion of Hume concerning causation. He found that the concept of the connection of cause and effect was only one of a group of concepts used by the understanding to connect things a priori. Kant devised a terminology and made a number of distinctions allowing him to solve the problem raised by Hume and generalized by Kant. Distinctions between the uses of reason and understanding were sharpened. Reason has to do with the faculty of inference. The content of reason are the concepts of the understanding or the ideas generated by pure reason beyond the limits of experience. A priori and a posteriori reasoning are distinguished: "A posteriori" means derived from experience while "a priori" means independent of experience. Understanding has to do with judgments about experience using pure concepts or rules that do not have their basis in reason. Analytic and synthetic judgments are distinguished. An analytic judgment is one whose predicates (attributes) are thought of as identical with all or part of the concept of the subject (object). Such judgments are logical, often involving implicit tautologies. A synthetic judgment has to do with schemata that allow perceptions or concepts to fit into a particular context instead of existing as a random rhapsody of perceptions. The schema of causality, for example, is "the succession of representations, insofar as that succession is subject to a rule."[34] Synthetic judgments known a priori form the principles of a metaphysics of experience.

Both empiricism and rationalism—as they had developed to the time of Kant—were challenged. This is because for Kant the questions of philosophy are neither questions for which there is a clear empirical method of investigation nor questions that can be answered by deduction from self-evident axioms. From the perspective of the argument between the empiricists and rationalists, Immanuel Kant is to be seen as attempting to reconcile empiricism and rationalism by his view that ideas are derived from the senses *and* from reason. Ideas deriving from the senses are the a priori elements of cognition; those deriving from reason are they a posteriori elements of cognition. Both are equally indispensable for human knowledge. Kant's compromise resulted in the distinguishing of reality itself from its appearance. It is the appearance of reality that is the

---

[34]*Critique of Pure Reason*, A 144 = B 183: cited in Beck, *Early German Philosophy*, 480.

object of sensation. The appearances are called "phenomena" of the things in themselves. In *Critique of Pure Reason*, Kant stated the thesis in the form of an inquiry:

> Now the question arises whether there are not also antecedent concepts *a priori*, forming conditions under which alone something can be, if not seen, yet thought as an object in general; for in that case all empirical knowledge of objects would necessarily conform to such concepts, it being impossible that anything should become an object of experience without them. All experience contains, besides the intuition of the senses by which something is given, a concept also of the object, which is given in intuition as a phenomena. Such concepts of objects in general therefore must form conditions *a priori* of all knowledge produced by experience, and the objective validity of the categories, as being such concepts *a priori*, rests on this very fact that by them alone, so far as the form of thought is concerned, experience becomes possible. If by them only it is possible to think any object of experience it follows that they refer by necessity and *a priori* to all objects of experience.[35]

The domain of knowledge is limited to the world of phenomena. Nevertheless, we have *a priori* ideas about supersensible reality—ideas that cannot be proved true or false. This inability to demonstrate the truth or falsity of an idea distinguishes phenomena from noumena, for knowledge is inseparable from the power of demonstrating truth or falsity.

The inability to prove or disprove objects of faith does not establish them as true or false. It establishes them as matters of faith. Although matters of faith cannot be demonstrated as true, however, they are subject to reason. Practical reason has the ability to rule over the admissibility of matters of faith. In *The Critique of Practical Reason*, Kant examined the rational facility concerned with human conduct. The basic postulate of practical reason has to do with the rationality of the world. It is impossible to find out whether this world is rational or irrational, but if it is rational there must be a God who assures the harmony of moral and natural good. The postulate of natural reason that is sometimes known as the moral proof of the existence of God holds that the ideal of the complete good can be fulfilled only by God in another world.

The medieval world had separated the natural order from a supernatural order. Kant did not follow this distinction; rather he distinguished

---

[35]*Critique of Pure Reason*, A 92-94 = B 125-27; in Beck, ed., *Eighteenth Century Philosophy*, 255-56.

between phenomena and noumena. The transcendental noumenal world cannot be known as can the phenomenal world nor can theoretical reason achieve knowledge of this noumenal world. Yet the noumenal world is functionally imminent for moral life, and moral precepts that belong to the noumenal world can be realized in the phenomenal world.

The epistemology of Kant may be seen as a transformation of the idealist/realist (rationalist/empiricist) debate going back to Plato and Aristotle. But it may be seen historically as the apex of Enlightenment rationalism and the point of departure for later scientific, philosophical, and theological formulations. From the side of empiricism (which would eliminate the noumenal world of Kant) August Comte, John Stuart Mill, and logical positivism are important. And from the side of rationalism (and metaphysics) Hegel and the phenomenological tradition are important.

Thomas F. Torrance indicates a twofold effect of Kant's reconstruction of the foundation of knowledge:

> By tracing the theoretic components of knowledge to the structures of the mind which are independent of experience, and therefore not modifiable through experience, Kant built into the foundation of knowledge a disastrous ingredient of necessity or determinism. Since it is now the human understanding in its unchanging and uniform structures which becomes the centre of absolute rest, in accordance with which all knowledge of the universe is formalised, scientific concepts inevitably acquire a finally static and necessary character. Moreover, by grounding these theoretical factors in the human mind through which it shapes, regulates and controls everything we apprehend, Kant gave powerful philosophic form to the concept of the active, creative reason, and thus contributed in a massive way to the formation of the way in which modern people have tended to think.[36]

The Modern and Postmodern Worlds

The "modern" world is a result of developments from Descartes to Kant.[37] In an insightful introduction to postmodern biblical criticism,

---

[36]Torrance, *Transformation & Convergence in the Frame of Knowledge*, 37.

[37]The major elements of the modern world are delineated by Langdon Gilkey in his summary of the creation of this world:

This "world" began to develop powerfully in the seventeenth century with the exploration of the whole earth, the rise of science, the appearance of mechanical

A. K. M. Adam provides a postmodern perspective for viewing Enlightenment developments: "Postmodern critics characteristically problematize *legitimation*, the means by which claims about truth or justice or reality are validated or rejected."[38] Following Cornel West, Adam distinguishes three related ways of understanding postmodern's challenge, as antifoundationalism, antitotalizing, and demystifying.

> Postmodernism is antifoundational in that it resolutely refuses to posit any one premise as the privileged and unassailable starting point for establishing claims to truth. It is antitotalizing because postmodern discourse suspects that any theory that claims to account for everything is suppressing counterexamples, or is applying warped criteria so that it can include recalcitrant cases. Postmodernism is also demystifying; it attends to claims that certain assumptions are "natural" and tries to show that these are in fact ideological projections.[39]

Foundational, totalizing, and mystifying approaches are not limited to the Enlightenment rationality. The precritical approach of theology that accepted without question and argued from the premises of scripture and tradition may be seen as foundational, totalizing, and mystifying. Contemporary postmodernism and Enlightenment modernism may, nevertheless, be appreciated most fully in comparison with each other. How do the modern approaches of the Enlightenment exemplify foundational, totalizing, and mystifying understandings of reality and truth?

The Modern World. The major overriding characteristic of the Enlightenment and of the modern world was confidence in reason and progress. The Enlightenment was the age of *reason*. As we have seen, Descartes set the tone for later developments that were essentially refinements of the principle of doubt and the supremacy of reason. The

---

technology and so industry, and the slow development of democratic, liberal, and capitalistic ideals. This rapidly expanded and transformed culture became full blown by the eighteenth century; and it has in ever-new forms dominated not only the West ever since but also, until 1945, the rest of the world. . . . The intellectual and moral heart of the Enlightenment was rationalist and humanist; it believed in the identity of nature and reason and in the autonomy of the rational and moral human being. It was, on the whole, antitraditional, antimetaphysical, and antireligious.
Gilkey, *Through the Tempest: Theological Voyages in a Pluralistic Culture*, ed. Jeff B. Pool (Minneapolis: Fortress, 1991) 4.

[38]A. K. M. Adam, *What Is Postmodern Biblical Criticism?*, Guides to Biblical Scholarship (Minneapolis: Fortress Press, 1995) 5.

[39]Ibid.

authority of ancient sources was repudiated, and the shackles of theological and metaphysical dogma and speculation were loosed to make way for the emancipated human reason. Descartes's rational and deductive method was complemented by an empirical and inductive scientific method. Although the rational and empirical methods competed and no one ultimately eliminated the other, the preeminence of reason became unassailable in the modern world. The belief that all problems are in principle solvable was part and parcel of the rationalism of the Enlightenment. No problems and questions could permanently remain unsolved and unanswered, so belief in progress was explicit. Belief in progress in general and not just in scientific progress was a mark of the modern world. (When belief in progress is seen as a substitute for belief in purpose, human activity may be substituted for transcendence.) The idea of progress accompanied by the idea that development was an inevitable process that would work "naturally" in every culture expressed itself in Western programs of development.

The concept of direct mechanistic causality in which a specific cause determines a specific effect was a guiding assumption of the scientific rationalistic agenda and led to a view of the task of knowledge as the reduction of the object of study to its elements and simplest relationships. Fundamentals and basic laws were sought. The subject-object distinction and the compartmentalization of knowledge were part and parcel of the scientific rationalistic search for fundamentals. Humans distanced themselves from their natural environment in order to examine that natural world from the point of view of scientific objectivity. In examining the natural world, scientific divisions were made, and these divisions of the natural world were assigned priority over the whole. Human beings also became objects of analysis and were subjected to scientific methods of study modeled on the natural sciences. As with the natural sciences, human beings were seen from different perspectives (philosophy, sociology, biology, anthropology, and so on).

The simple linear model of causation in which a simple action always leads to the same predictable result provided an argument for a static view as matter is driven by a mechanical force in a totally determined manner. Not only was the direct impingement of a transcendent world repudiated in this approach, also repudiated was the principle of purpose or teleology. The questions of by whom and for what purpose the world came into being were excluded methodologically at first and then philosophically. This elimination of purpose in scientific study became a characteristic of the human sciences as well as the natural sciences. Human experiences lost their mystery as they were reduced to scientific biological and sociological processes.

The factual, neutral, and value-free nature of knowledge is implied in the mechanistic model and the subject-object dichotomy. This factual nature of knowledge made all else opinion or belief, a matter of preference. The correspondence view of knowledge became dominant. A belief is true when there is a fact that corresponds to it. When there is no corresponding fact, the belief is false.

As humans were emancipated from the dogma of the church and from transcendent forces, they became autonomous individuals. Prior to the modern world, individuality was recognized, but this individuality was subordinated to society and in religion to the church and to God. With the modern world, the individual was free, autonomous, infinitely perfectible, and equal to all others. This freedom, seen not as deriving from religion and/or God or from society but from "nature," calls for exalting humankind above not only God and the church but above society.

The background for the development of Enlightenment rationality was Western Christendom, and many Enlightenment scholars attempted to maintain religious perspectives alongside rational and empirical assumptions and procedures. From the eighteenth century on, however, a serious split developed. The split was implicit in Augustine's differentiation between knowledge of empirical data (gained through the bodily senses) and knowledge of nonempirical data (gained through the mind's knowledge of itself). But the split became clearer with Kant's basic epistemological distinction between knowledge of phenomena and understanding of noumenal realities. Developments after Kant may be seen as the challenge of accommodating transcendence in any traditional sense whatsoever. The epistemological distinction tends to become an ontological dualism. Phenomenal reality becomes distinct from noumenal reality. And then the noumenal world of Kant disappears. Such things as purposes, meanings, and intrinsic and normative values become problematic.

The Postmodern World. Scholars today speak of a basic shift from a critical paradigm to a postcritical paradigm. In the critical paradigm, the problem of the relationship between empirical knowledge and rational understanding was never really settled. Perhaps at this point the modern characteristic of mystifying/demystifying assumes importance. Adam points out that "appeals to abstract universal entities are mystifications of more concrete, worldly reasons"[40] The precritical theological system in which scripture and tradition provide unquestioned premises may be conceived of as involved in a process of mystification. Enlightenment rationality has demystified this theological enterprise. But, according to Adam, "when modern rationalist demystifiers appeal to 'reason,' without specifying what sort of reason they mean, they are mystifying their own debt to one particular tradition of reasoned inquiry. They cover the particularity of their intellectual position by treating reason as if it were a natural universal category."[41] From a postcritical or a postmodern perspective, Enlightenment rationality is not invalidated but it is seen as limited, instrumental, and penultimate. The problematizing of rationality leads to alterations in all of the other characteristics of the Enlightenment. One of the interesting problems in getting a grasp on the contemporary situation is that judgments upon Enlightenment rationality are made in part by means of such rationality and share the limitations of the rationality being judged. A postmodern paradigm is in tension with a modern paradigm. Since one of the aspects of postmodernism in science in general is acknowledgment of the limitations of reason, metalevel reflection of postmodern (postempiricist) philosophy of science "excludes the possibility of arriving at a complete and coherent theoretical articulation of 'the new paradigm,' as though it could be a monastic metatheoretical absolute, deductively or inductively articulating rationality fully."[42]

One way of beginning to appreciate the challenge of postmodernism is to give attention to contemporary mathematical and scientific theories that oppose the sort of scientific approach that employs a linear model of inductive understanding. The work of Alfred Tarski makes clear that any particular system in itself is incomplete (or inconsistent). When the question of verifiable truth is at stake, objects to which a particular sentence refer cannot include the sentence itself. In order to talk about this language, therefore, another language is needed. The language talked about would be the "object language," and the language used for talking about the object language would be the "metalanguage." We must recognize that the metalanguage of one level becomes the object language on

---

[40]Ibid., 11.

[41]Ibid., 14.

[42]Matthew L. Lamb, "The Dialectics of Theory and Praxis within Paradigm Analysis," in *Paradigm Change in Theology*, ed. Hans Kung and David Tracy, trans. Margaret Kohl (New York: Crossroad, 1991) 85.

a higher level.[43] An Archimedean point from which the total hierarchy of truths can be reached is impossible. Alternatives from the perspective of conventional logic, then, are objectivity and incompleteness (moving beyond one level but never arriving at the ultimate system) or completeness and inconsistency (remaining in one system).

Any delineation of aspects of a postmodern paradigm must acknowledge that the charges of attempts at foundationalism, totalization, and mystifying may be leveled against the project. "Postmodern criticism cannot accept any system of knowledge as absolute or foundational; it cannot accept the premise that some body of knowledge, or subject of knowledge, constitutes a unified totality; and it cannot accept mystifying claims that any intellectual discourse is disinterested or pure."[44] The description of postmodernism provided in this volume is not disinterested or pure. Indeed, it seeks a starting point for a study of Jesus, a reading of the Bible, and for contemporary theological thought that is satisfying to contemporary readers.

One aspect of a postcritical or postmodern paradigm is the awareness that paradigms exist, that different worldviews provide the lens through which we see everything. In order to appreciate the impact of this awareness we are being forced to think on a metacritical level. We must think about thinking and knowing, but not from the perspective that we can arrive at the certainty provided either by revelation or Enlightenment rationality. This metacritical thinking involves not just more and different thoughts on the critical, but thoughts that order the "laws" on the first order of generality. The ideal of objectivity has been replaced with the concept of perspective. Objectivity is an illusion, but total subjectivity is not the only alternative. Perspective is a more useful concept. Perspective involves a view from a particular focus with the idea that *what we see is affected by where we look from*. No one focus of observation ever gives a complete picture, so the concept of reality itself is altered when movement is made from objective to perspective. A shift is made from the "absolute" truth to a plurality of kinds of knowing and from the "right" method toward a multiplicity of methods.[45]

---

[43]Alfred Tarski," The Semantic Conception of Truth," in *Readings in Philosophical Analysis*, ed. Herbert Feigl and Wilfrid Sellars, Century Philosophy series (New York: Appleton-Century-Crofts, 1949) 60.

[44]Adam, *What Is Postmodern Biblical Criticism?* 15.

[45]Peter Schwartz and James A. Ogilvy, *The Emergent Paradigm: Changing Patterns of Thought and Belief*, Values and Lifestyles Program report no. 7 (Menlo Park CA: SRI

From the contemporary perspective, "openness" and "interaction" are the nature of things. The world is composed of diverse interacting things, which in principle cannot be separated from each other and from their interactive environment. The simple linear model of causation in which a simple action always leads to the same predictable result is replaced with a concept of mutual causality. We not only have the negative feedback of cybernetics ("if A causes B, then B provides a feedback signal to A such that A changes in a way to reduce or limit the magnitude of B") but also positive feedback ("the feedback signal from B affects A in a fashion such that A tends to increase B"). The new vision is a sort of symbiosis. Elements evolve and change together, affecting each other in such way as to make the distinction between cause and effect meaningless.[46]

The diversity, openness, complexity, mutual causality, and indeterminacy of a postcritical or postmodern paradigm are ingredients for qualitative change, while the mechanistic paradigm is more or less static, viewing matter as driven by a mechanical force in a totally determined manner. Change may be understood in a postmodern paradigm in terms of the reorganization of a set of mutually dependent variables in a way that is beyond the constraints of the mechanistic model. Peter Schwartz and James Ogilvy speak of an overall change of pattern "from reality as a machine toward reality as a conscious organism." Machines are relatively simple mechanical instruments, but conscious beings are very complex and unpredictable. *The world we see is like the human beings we are.*

This move toward humanization is an important move. Instead of reducing human beings to older models of the natural sciences, the sciences are being reinvisioned from the perspective of the human world. Foundations for knowledge are being sought that are more basic than the scientific theories and procedures of any one or all of the sciences, foundations are sought in human relationships and actions.

Postmodernism and Benign Skepticism

The contingent and unpredictable life-world and explanatory scientific and philosophical system seem to be diametrically opposed. They seem to cancel each other out, so how can they coexist and contribute to some

---

International, 1979) 15.
[46]Ibid., 14.

interactive whole? They are indeed opposed as explanatory systems have
been developed and refined on this side of the Enlightenment—at least
one reading of the Enlightenment. The modern mentality that cannot
abide skepticism is the result of a certain telling of the story of the
Enlightenment. In that telling, according to Stephen Toulmin, humanity
in the seventeenth century "set aside all doubts and ambiguities about its
capacity to achieve its goals here on Earth, and in historical time, rather
than deferring human fulfillment to an Afterlife in Eternity—that was
what made the project of Modernity 'rational'—and this optimism led to
major advances not just in natural science but in moral, political, and
social thought as well."[47]

The story as seen from the end of the twentieth century and the
beginning of the twenty-first century is more ambiguous. Toulmin
declares that "in choosing as the goals of Modernity an intellectual and
practical agenda that set aside the tolerant, skeptical attitude of the
sixteenth-century humanists, and focussed on the seventeenth-century
pursuit of mathematical exactitude and logical rigor, intellectual certainty
and moral purity, Europe set itself on a cultural and political road that has
led both to its most striking technical successes and to its deepest human
failures."[48]

Two phases of the development of the modern world and modern
culture are distinguished by Toulmin. The first phase was literary or
humanistic and involved "respect for the rational possibilities of human
experience" and "a delicate feeling for the *limits* of human experience."[49]
In theology or philosophy during this first phase of development, "you
may (with due intellectual modesty) adopt as personal working positions
the ideas of your inherited culture; but you cannot deny others the right
to adopt different working positions for themselves, let alone pretend that
your experience 'proves' the truth of one such set of opinions, and the
necessary falsity of all the others."[50] What was offered by sixteenth-
century humanists was not proof or repetition of particular philosophical
positions but rather "a new way of understanding human life and motifs."
Sixteenth century humanists "like Socrates long ago, and Wittgenstein in

---

[47]Stephen Toulmin, *Cosmopolis: The Hidden Agenda of Modernity* (New York: Free
Press, 1990) ix.
[48]Ibid., x.
[49]Ibid., 27.
[50]Ibid., 29.

our own time, . . . taught readers to recognize how philosophical theories overreached the limits of human rationality."[51]

The second phase of development of modernity was scientific and philosophical. "After 1600, the focus of intellectual attention turned away from the humane preoccupations of late 16th century, and moved in directions more rigorous or even dogmatic, than those the Renaissance writers pursued."[52] Toulmin suggests that the birth of modern philosophy and the exact sciences involved not simply a forward movement from the sixteenth century but also a rejection of the values of the earlier humanistic scholars. To a certain extent, then, the birth of modern philosophy and the exact sciences involves something of an actual counter-Renaissance. In philosophy, Toulmin affirms, scholars were "committed to questions of abstract, universal theory, to the exclusion of . . . concrete issues. There is a shift from a style of philosophy that keeps equally in view issues of local, timebound practice, and universal, timeless theory, to one that accepts matters of universal, timeless theory as being entitled to an exclusive place on the agenda of 'philosophy.' "[53]

Toulmin points out four different kinds of practical knowledge in which seventeenth-century philosophers set aside the longstanding preoccupations of Renaissance humanism. These were the oral, the particular, the local, and the timely.

1. *From oral to written.* Before 1700, questions of argumentation (the "external" conditions on which arguments were convincing to hearers) and questions of logic (the "internal" steps followed in establishment of "truth") were legitimate parts of philosophy. For modern philosophy, the rhetorical questions are no longer considered, only the rational merit of arguments.[54]

2. *From the particular to the universal.* Case analyses (like those in American case law) were handled by philosophers and moral theologians in the Middle Ages and the Renaissance. In the seventeenth century, moral philosophers made ethics a field for general abstract theory, and since that time philosophers have assumed that the "good" and the "just" are timeless universal principles.

---

[51]Ibid., 99.
[52]Ibid., 23.
[53]Ibid., 24.
[54]Ibid., 30-31.

3. *From the local to the general*. Sixteenth-century humanists found valuable sources in materials in which geometrical methods of analysis have little power—ethnography, geography, and history. With Descartes, philosophical understanding has to do with abstract, general ideas and principles and not with accumulated experience of particular individuals and cases. The abstract principles allow particulars to be connected together.

4. *From the timely to the timeless*. For sixteenth-century scholars, questions about "timeliness" were important. "For Descartes and his successors, timely questions were no concern of philosophy: instead, their aim was to bring to light permanent structures underlying all the changeable phenomena of nature."[55]

Toulmin indicates that our present need is "to reappropriate the wisdom of the sixteenth-century humanists, and develop a point of view that combines the abstract rigor and exactitude of the seventeenth-century 'new philosophy' with a practical concern for human life in its concrete detail. Only so can we counter the current widespread disillusion with the agenda of Modernity, and salvage what is still humanly important in its projects."[56]

Important heroes in the retelling of the story of philosophy are the early humanists who were content with a lack of certainty. Acknowledgment of the impossibility of the ideal of Enlightenment certainty may then result in a positive (instead of a nihilistic) "skepticism." This sort of skepticism would acknowledge that questions are always asked and answered in terms dependent upon historical and social contexts. It would have a toleration for other contexts with their questions and answers. It would even question the level of validity of one's own answers in one's own context and not be disabled by such questioning.

The philosophical horizon is helpful in understanding the parameters of Jesus study—dogmatic and critical, theological and historical, modern and postmodern. We are able to appreciate the contributions made by Jesus study in epochs other than our own as well as the contribution of contemporary scholars who embrace different intellectual traditions. In the task of recovering Jesus today, the plethora of approaches is both disabling and enabling. When confronted with the different (and seemingly incompatible) approaches, a reader who seeks Enlightenment-type certain-

---

[55]Ibid., 34.
[56]Ibid., xi.

ty is surely disabled. This intellectual challenge may cause such readers to continue down one academic road following a more-or-less positivistic agenda and ignore postmodern challenges to this agenda. But readers who are relieved of the demand for final, complete, and objective truth may proceed with the postcritical quest. This is not the same as the precritical quest. This quest may be intellectually, emotionally, and spiritually satisfying as the critical agenda is modified to include not only the individualistic rational tools of the Enlightenment but the larger social and cultural contexts, and relationships and practices within which truth takes place.

Chapter 5

Hermeneutical Possibilities in Jesus Studies

Chapter 4 outlined (1) the inability to establish the idealism of Plato or the realism of Aristotle (in their original forms or in their transformations) as single foundations for and methods of arriving at truth and (2) the value of maintaining both approaches in the framework of local and ad hoc knowledge with a benign skepticism about human achievement of final rational truth. This chapter emphasizes the possibilities of meaning and truth that exist within such contemporary postmodern epistemological presuppositions. The hermeneutical vision offered is designed to support the extension or prolongation of the meanings of the Gospels' text into the lives of contemporary readers along with the meanings of the historical event refracted in the text. Present-day experience of something akin to "revelation" is advocated. A reader-oriented literary or poetic approach is the means of this experience, an approach that gives proper attention to scientific *and* artistic elements and methods, with the focus being upon both the text *and* the subject as the creators of meaning and truth that is possible and appropriate at particular times and places. This chapter does not simply recount the major moves in the hermeneutical tradition; it examines these moves from the perspective of what they offer for a reader-oriented literary approach. The periodization in this treatment is not designed to show that scholars have moved from ignorance to knowledge. The arrangement is a convenient way to show relationships between individuals and ideas and to provide options for the present day. The hermeneutical tradition provides a myriad of suggestions as to the reference or truth of literary texts beyond the superficial reference and as to the way from the text to the reference.

At the outset the illusory nature of our modern Enlightenment agenda must be admitted and celebrated. The goal of discovering some ultimate foundation for meaning that guides the process of interpretation of texts is similar to the goal of arriving at a comprehensive scheme giving full account of all of the elements involved in interpretation and a full account of all the ways these elements are related. Both of these goals may be seen in the hermeneutical tradition, but both are illusions. At one particular time and place, within a particular community with definite agendas, a foundation or particular nexus of relationships appears to be ultimate. Satisfying meaning is found. But then the foundation or connection is seen to be partial or incomplete. A helpful hypothesis is that all of the various accounts of reference and methods appropriate for those references have validity. Instead of concluding that there is no meaning and no method, we may conclude that there are many references and meanings—as many meanings as humans need and can conceive. These meanings, and methods designed to discover and create those meanings, are not reducible to one ultimate comprehensive meaning and method. In our day, in our communities, with our needs and resources, we find references and meanings that are satisfying. There is continuity and discontinuity between these references, meanings, and methods. We may exhaust the potentiality of meaning possible with one approach and find other approaches that are satisfying.

The analogy between the way we utilize the various approaches in making sense of texts and the way our bodies digest food is instructive. When we consider the text as a piece of food we are eating we can appreciate the necessity of different stages of reception or digestion. At one stage of interaction between nerve receptors, acids, and enzymes, some portion of the food is digested. But some portion remains undigested—but digestible at another stage.[1] The analogy is imperfect, of course, because the process of digestion is an orderly unidirectional process, while the process of interpretation is not so orderly and directional. Also the same elements in a literary text may operate at different "stages," may enter into the development of different systems in which that element is assimilated. The food digested at one stage is used up and not available for later stages, but the text that provides insight within a source-critical scheme may also fit into form-critical and redactional organizations. But that text can enter into schemes giving attention to the existential needs and possibilities of readers and to values that transcend but give additional force to existential meanings.

---

[1]See Juri Lotman, *The Structure of the Artistic Text* (Ann Arbor: University of Michigan Press, 1977) 58, for a development of this analogy.

Before examining the hermeneutical tradition beginning with Schleiermacher to gain insight into references and methods (beyond the method of reducing the function of the text to the scientific transmission of specific constant information), the literary tradition onto which hermeneutics can be grafted is sketched. And after the mining of the hermeneutical tradition, a reader-oriented literary hermeneutics is outlined.

Hermeneutics and Literary Questions of Knowledge and Truth

The classical period offers major paradigms for literary study as well as for developments in philosophy and theology, for the question of reality and knowledge is directly related to the question of artistic creativity and interpretation. For Plato, the artist (including the writer) makes a copy of the material world that is itself a copy of the eternal world of Ideas. Art is, then, an inferior activity compared to artisanship (the making of useful objects), not only because copies are involved but also because the artist needs only the knowledge of the appearance of things. A variant upon this view is that of Plotinus (a Neoplatonic philosopher of the third century CE). Plotinus saw the artist as imitating the Ideas as they were embodied in the material world. A statue of Zeus, then, is not a copy of a flesh and blood human being but a representative of power—what the concepts of power and majesty might look like if those concepts could be visible. In the dialectical approach of Plato and Plotinus, the forms of expression or of art objects are imitations of separate and eternal forms. In analysis the structures of the world of matter are related analogically to the world of Ideas. The analysis of art, then, may have to do with the recollection and direct experience of forms. This would constitute the highest knowledge, virtue, and beauty. Experiences of art, however, may have to do with enthusiasm, inspiration, imagination, and madness as the vision of forms possesses the mind.

For Aristotle the artist captures in language not Ideas or copies of Ideas but the general principles of human action. Aristotle did not believe in an eternal world of Ideas but rather saw everything as involved in process, growth, and change. Artists, then, are not merely copying; they are imitating human action. In the artistic work, the accidental and the incidental are eliminated, and action is unified into a plot and beautified with expressive language. Moreover, the artistic work has the capacity of commanding the emotions, and through a complex imitation it can cleanse the individual and serve the state. (Plato was fearful of the corrupting power of the artistic work because of its distance from the truth.) The problematic method of Aristotle was a method of inquiry distinguishing questions according to the different disciplines in which questions are specified and solved. Art is only one discipline, and the problems of such disciplines as rhetoric, history, and philosophy are different from those of art. In art, as indicated earlier, the form is related to human action as the object of imitation. The problems of art have to do with the best use of parts in the construction of wholes that are artful and different in each of the various forms of art. Analysis demonstrates the role of parts in the artistic unity and the unifying effect of form. The tragedy, for example, is an organic whole in which the various parts are brought together into a unity of structure with the resources of character and thought by means of language and linguistic devices.

Along with Plato and Aristotle, two other classical views must be noted. The Sophists held that opinion alone—not truth—is possible. In this tradition, art is not conceived of as imitation of Ideas or of human action but as a skill. Humankind is the measure of all things for the Sophists, and the natural ability of humans may be developed by art. The operational approach of the Sophists gives attention to the form provided by words and the manner of expression. Orator, historian, poet, and philosopher are comparable in the way they treat problems of form or expression. Analysis deals with content, form, and the relationships between content and form. "Content is treated by the commonplaces designed to give the marks of sublime or beautiful thoughts or to identify the thought in poetry with common thoughts expressed either with uncommon wit or in the language of the ordinary man, while style is treated according to standards of what is appropriate—lofty, mean, or medium—or by analysis of figures, tropes, and larger forms of verbal organization."[2] For Democritus (ca. 460–370 CE), on the other hand, all things—the world and all that occurs in it, natural and artificial—result from the modification in shape and arrangement of eternal atoms of which all things are composed. Change is the movement and redistribution of atoms in the void. Art operates in the same way, by the modification in shape and arrangement of material objects. In the logistic approach of Democritus, the problems of art focus on the relation of knowledge to emotion and of nature to appearance. The analysis of art has to do with

---

[2]Richard McKeon, *Thought, Action, and Passion* (Chicago: University of Chicago Press, 1954) 116.

psychological insight into the perception of pleasure and its accompaniments or with the analysis of structures of the material of art as causes of pleasure.[3]

Hermeneutics understood in the broadest sense of interpretation is concerned with all of these approaches and the correlation of these approaches. Richard McKeon emphasized that these approaches cannot be separated:

> There is an important sense in which all these varieties of theories are engaged in the treatment of the same problems, described roughly as a problem of art. It is obvious that the analysis in which "form" and content are taken as basic [the operational approach] will find some place to treat transcendent values [the dialectical approach], organic unities [the problematic approach], and pleasures [the logistic approach], as consequences of style and what is expressed. Eternal ideas likewise are embodied in language that is organized in unities, and, however adumbrated, they cause pleasure and pain; indeed in the dialectical examination of the actual world pleasure and pain may take precedence as immediate signs of ultimate values, as they do in Plato's *Laws*. Plots, which are the soul of tragedy, are constructed by use of language as matter; they attain beauty in their organization and order; and they cause a "proper" pleasure peculiar to that art form, so that the analysis of drama affords data for the discrimination of kinds of emotions even though the occurrence of emotion or pleasure is not a mark by which to distinguish a work of art. Finally, experienced pleasure is expressed in media, heightened by artful organizations; and, so conceived, pleasure is the unique sign of value.[4]

In the history of literary criticism, however, each of these approaches may be seen as dominating a particular epoch. M. H. Abrams (*The Mirror and the Lamp*, 1953) saw the history and practice of criticism in terms of the dominance of one of the four elements comparable with the classical perspective. Abrams entitled the four elements as the work, the artist, the universal imitated in the work, and the audience. Present-day approaches may be located in this schema.

The type of criticism most characteristic of the classical age was mimetic criticism that viewed the literary work as an imitation (mimesis) of the world and human life. Plato and Aristotle illustrate mimetic

---

[3]Ibid., 116-17.

[4]Ibid., 117. In his introduction to *The Critical Tradition: Classic Texts and Contemporary Trends* (New York: St. Martin's Press) 12-14, David H. Richter shows the relationship of McKeon's scheme to other maps of criticism.

criticism even though the different views of the object of imitation results in different strategies of analysis. (This critical view is characteristic of contemporary theories of literary realism, and Marxist critics in particular view literature as a reflection of reality). The second type in the schema of Abrams was the rhetorical (comparable to the operational approach of the Sophists). Abrams saw this type of criticism as dominant from the poet Horace (first century BCE) through the eighteenth century. This emphasized the effect of the work on the audience, including both pleasure and instruction. Recent revival of rhetorical criticism recapitulates rhetorical (or pragmatic) criticism's emphasis on the strategies used by an artist in engaging and influencing the response of readers.

Theories of expressive criticism (Romanticism, comparable to the logistic approach of Democritus) proliferated during the late eighteenth and most of the nineteenth centuries. These theories define the literary work in terms of the operation of the artist's imagination on his or her perception. Contemporary psychologically oriented critics retain concerns of expressive criticism, looking in the work for indications of the particular temperament and experiences of the author. The fourth type (Formalism/New Criticism, comparable in some measure to Aristotle's analysis of tragedy) developed around the beginning of the twentieth century and became dominant in the mid twentieth century. In these formal theories, however, the literary work became its own world which transcends the facts of composition, the imitated universe, the nature and character of the author, and the effect on the audience. (Reader-oriented theories and practices have taken their place in literary criticism in the final decades of the twentieth century. These theories and practices will be discussed later in this chapter as complementing nineteenth- and twentieth-century developments in hermeneutics.)

The modern hermeneutical tradition began in conjunction with the movement of Romanticism in literary criticism with its distrust of the severely cerebral rationalism of the Enlightenment. Major factors included: (1) the completion and general acceptance of the worldview emphasizing rational argument and reflection; (2) the adoption of the historical-critical approach to the Bible by biblical scholars (supplementing the earlier philological achievements); and (3) the questions about the conditions for the possibility of knowledge introduced by Kant.

Hermeneutics asked the question: How can a historical text (a text that originates in a particular historical context) be unfolded beyond the historical flux? (This is a form of the question: How is the historically constrained meaning of historical criticism related to the "necessary" truth of theology?) To answer the question, hermeneutics transformed the question of interpretation into the question of knowledge ("How do we know?") and the question of being ("What is the mode of being of that being who only exists through understanding?").

The question of the real and the ideal are raised in hermeneutics, then, in terms of language and human existence. Language and being are treated in terms of both the particular and the general, language as a tool is related to language as a transcendent social system and human existence is related to being in general. A realist perspective would make the tool of language, on the one hand, and human existence, on the other hand, the really real, with anything beyond being a generalization or abstraction founded on the particular. An idealist perspective would make the particularities of language and historical development only form and formal change, reflecting the primordial Idea that is really real. Hermeneutics ties the different levels together. Language in hermeneutics, then, involves meaning of words and sentences and meaning on existential, theological, and even ontological levels. Clearly it is not merely the material, physical side of language (the sound, the letters on a page, and so forth) that accomplishes these levels of meaning. But the material aspect of language is involved. The material of language is a means to the meaning that the author intends to communicate in the text, meanings implicit in the meaning of the author, and to the various higher levels of meaning that impinge upon the author and reader.

Language for New Testament hermeneutics came to be seen as involving the reader or hearer in such a way that the result of reading or hearing is to be thought of as an event in the present. Although reading is not merely the deciphering of an ancient text, the ancient text is necessary for the "language event" in the present day. The goal of hermeneutics, then, must be differentiated from the goal of historical interpretation on the one hand and the goal of theological, religious, or homiletic application on the other hand. Its focus is the relationship or the application of the New Testament to the present day, even to the point where the text facilitates present-day "language-event." But it is also concerned that the event in the present be related to the original text and author and not merely to the reader or hearer in the present situation.

Insights from both the structuralist and phenomenological traditions may be helpful for appreciation for the concept of language and meaning being developed in hermeneutics. The structuralist distinction between *langue* and *parole* and structuralism's emphasis that meaning is a consequence of a nexus (structure or *Zusammenhang*) of relationships rather than the result of one foundational pillar may illuminate the hermeneutical concept of language as existing on different levels with the interdependence of these levels (with their various elements) in the hermeneutical task. Ferdinand de Saussure (1857–1913) is the key scholar in the movement from the historical linguistics of the nineteenth century to the linguistics of the twentieth century, and *langue* and *parole* were the two aspects of language in Saussure's analysis. *Parole* is the actual concrete act of speaking of an individual. This is the effect of language directly available to the linguist because it is a social activity that exists in a given situation. *Langue*, on the other hand, is the *language system* behind parole. *Langue* is the totality of a language deducible only from an examination of the experiences and memories of all the language users. Saussure felt strongly that *langue* is not simply an abstraction, that the characteristics of *langue* are actually present in the brain.[5] Meaning, for Saussure, is the result of different sorts of relationships—between objects and ideas and the language referring to the objects and ideas and between the sequence of signs in actual discourse (syntagmatic relationships) and the associations that these signs have outside of discourse (paradigmatic relationships).

Edmund Husserl (1859–1938) and the phenomenological tradition were concerned with the essential structures at the foundation of human experience. They took issue with the separation of subject from object (with the subject being a naturalized and mathematized object) and with Kant's view that what we are aware of is mere appearance and objects as things-in-themselves are utterly unknowable. Their slogan, "To the things themselves," indicates the determination to turn away from philosophical theories and concepts toward the intuition and description of phenomena

---

[5]Ferdinand de Saussure, *Cours de Linguistique General*, published by Charles Bally and Albert Sechehaye, with the collaboration of Albert Riedlienger, 3rd ed. (Paris: Payot, 1949) 23-39. Another way of beginning to appreciate the different levels of language and the interdependence of the factors associated with these levels is through the concept of "form" or "genre." The concept of genre may help to tie meaning in historically oriented biblical study to meaning in theologically oriented study. The form critics of the Gospels gave attention to the sociological and historical situation out of which the different units arose while students of narrative in the structural tradition gave attention to the higher-level rules or conventions of narrative. See Edgar McKnight, *Meaning in Texts: The Historical Shaping of a Narrative Hermeneutics* (Philadelphia: Fortress Press, 1978), for a discussion of structuralism in general and the structural study of narrative in particular.

and thereby to break the tyranny of philosophical traditions and sciences that isolated subjects from objects. "Intentionally" is the way of describing how consciousness or experience constitutes phenomena. "Intentionally" refers to the property of all consciousness as consciousness of something. Objects are objects of consciousness and consciousness is always consciousness of objects. This is a critique of idealism (placing thought prior to being) and realism (placing being prior to thought). We could use the terms "immediacy" or "experience" rather than "consciousness" to indicate the nonreflective or disclosive nature of the experience of phenomena. The subject in itself—apart from the experience of phenomena—is an abstraction that emerges through reflection. Idealism and realism are not thereby denied; they are relativized, falsified only as isms.[6] The idealism/realism dichotomy is not finally eliminated. Husserl, for example, proposed that in the intuition of essences, the particular, actual given datum could be eliminated in a move to the plane of "pure possibility." Others in the phenomenological tradition emphasize that historical phenomena have a kind of priority, that particular phenomena should be seen as source of our constitution and judgment and not solely as constituted by us.

Friedrich Schleiermacher

With Friedrich Daniel Ernst Schleiermacher (1768–1834) the decisive move took place from a hermeneutics of inquiry to a hermeneutics of understanding. The hermeneutics of inquiry is concerned with the formulation of criteria for understanding the biblical text in relation to a context that is already presupposed. It may include the Roman Catholic context in which the church with its tradition and magisterium is the focus, the context of the reformers in which specific theological perspectives give control, or the antisupernaturalist context that emphasizes study proceeding independently of all theological and dogmatic considerations. With the historical-critical approach, the context that gives control is history.

---

[6]One writer uses the expression "pure experience" to describe what is involved. "In Pure Experience, known intuitively rather than reflectively, there are neither subjects nor objects. There is only experiencing. Since there are no subjects, there is no experiencer prior to experiencing; neither is experiencing produced by an experiencer. . . . Neither the subject nor the object is absolutized at the expense of the other, for both are accounted for as coaspectual features derived from experience" Harold H. Oliver, *Relatedness: Essays in Metaphysics and Theology* (Macon GA: Mercer University press, 1984) 52-53.

Schleiermacher made the preconditions for understanding in itself the object of study. This was not a study to be conducted as a purely rational enterprise for intellectual purposes. Schleiermacher's understanding of religion as the feeling of absolute dependence distinct from knowing and doing was correlated with his hermeneutics. This immediate prereflective self-consciousness, or the feeling of absolute dependence, is not simply a consciousness of a reciprocal relationship between self and world, a dependence upon world. It is consciousness of self and world together as absolutely dependent. The consciousness of being absolutely dependent is a consciousness of God. In his work in theology, Schleiermacher made religious consciousness primary. The task of the theologian is to develop the conceptions of God and the world that are implied in the religious consciousness and that are representative of that consciousness. Christian faith cannot be reduced to the acceptance of certain doctrinal ideas or adoption of certain patterns of moral conduct. What is involved is a trusting and experiential relationship with God.

Schleiermacher's concept of religion did not mean that he was anti-critical. In fact, his understanding of religion made possible a critical approach to the biblical text at least theoretically uncontrolled by dogmatic conclusions. Johann Salomo Semler (1725–1791), the "father of historical criticism" of the Bible and an influence upon Schleiermacher's hermeneutics, had suggested a dialectical relationship between historical investigation and knowledge and theological insight and knowledge. His stress on historical study (knowledge and use of the biblical languages and the historical circumstances of biblical writings) grew out of his conviction that intelligent persons have the duty to judge the content of biblical books to determine what is divine and worthy of the highest being and what is not worthy. Semler made a distinction between the biblical text as a historical record and the biblical text as theological object, between contents of biblical books that are permanently useful and aspects of those biblical books that are only accidental, and between "holy scripture" and "the word of God." But historical study is necessary in each case to distinguish between the Holy Scriptures and the Word of God.[7] Robert Morgan points out that "once Christian beliefs were grounded experientially in the believer's religious consciousness, it

---

[7]Werner Georg Kümmel, *The New Testament: The History of the Investigation of its Problems* (New York and Nashville, Abingdon Press, 1972) 62-73.

was possible to describe the biblical religion historically or phenomeno-logically, and at the same time identify with it religiously."[8]

In his hermeneutics, Schleiermacher followed and transcended lines set in place by scholars of the eighteenth and early nineteenth centuries who distinguished hermeneutics from theology and historical-oriented hermeneutics from existential-oriented hermeneutics.[9] The hermeneutics of Schleiermacher may be summarized in seven interdependent arguments.[10] The first four relate thinking, speaking, and the social and personal aspects of language.

(1) Hermeneutics is philosophical because it is part of the art of thinking. Because it presupposes shared experiences and language, thinking is not merely an individual phenomenon. Speaking is the "outer side" of thinking.

(2) Thinking entails both general and particular aspects—the general includes inherited concepts and shared conventions of language and

---

[8]Robert Morgan with John Barton, *Biblical Interpretation* (Oxford: Oxford University Press, 1988) 32. Morgan applauds the reorientation of much modern theology since Schleiermacher towards reflection on religion and human experience. This enables biblical scholarship and Christian theological speaking of God. "Biblical scholars can study the human religion disclosed in these texts by whatever historical, literary, and social science methods are available, without either asserting or denying the believers' claims that their tradition mediates a knowledge of God" (32-33).

[9]Johann August Ernesti (1707–1781) and Johann Salomo Semler (1725–1791) are generally regarded as the fathers of general biblical hermeneutics. Ernesti distinguished between general hermeneutics and theology. Hermeneutics deals with the historical situation of the text, the author's intention, and the author's use of the language of the day. Theology (the understanding of the content or the truth of a text) is distinguished from hermeneutics. Semler saw hermeneutics as embracing both meaning and truth—but he insisted that the task proceed independently of dogmatic considerations. He provided a rationale for serious study of the Bible as both historical record and theological object.

Friedrich Wolf (1759–1824) and Friedrich Ast (1778–1841) dealt with classical literature and made distinctions concerning levels and goals of understanding that are significant. Wolf distinguished between linguistic knowledge, historical reconstruction, and critical evaluation. Ast (ten years younger than Schleiermacher), published his *Hermeneutik und Kritik* (*Hermeneutics and Criticism*) in 1808. His aim was to enable classical literature to become more than a timeless or static scholastic study and to become significant as living reality for later generations. Ast was expressing the romantic conviction that life and the human spirit are fuller than their verbal and artistic expressions. For Ast, then, the historical and linguistic study must be accompanied by a "spiritual" or intuitive vision of the author's creation in the context of the author's values and individuality and the spirit of the author's age.

[10]In *New Horizons in Hermeneutics: The Theory and Practice of Transforming Biblical Reading* (Grand Rapids MI: Zondervan, 1992) 216-26, Anthony Thiselton has discussed these arguments in great detail.

speech; the particular grows out of the distinctive individuality of an author.

(3) Grammatical hermeneutics (concerned with language) may be contrasted with psychological hermeneutics (concerned with the expressions of thought of persons). They are equal and interdependent. The nature of the text and the concerns of the interpreter influence the relative importance of the grammatical and psychological sides of interpretation.

(4) Neither grammatical nor psychological interpretation is able to achieve a final or complete result. Schleiermacher declared that since complete knowledge is impossible in both cases, "it is necessary to move back and forth between the grammatical and psychological sides, and no rules can stipulate exactly how to do this."[11]

The final three arguments explore the cyclical nature of interpretation involving the interdependent relationship between parts and the whole, the comparative (critical) and the divinatory, and the author's intention and the contribution of the reader.

(5) Complete knowledge involves an apparent circle with each part understood in terms of the whole and the whole understood in terms of the parts.

(6) This circular process moves not only between the grammatical and psychological and the general and the particular, but also between the divinatory and the comparative. He associates the divinatory (the creative and intuitive capacity) with the feminine: "Divinatory knowledge is the feminine strength in knowing people: comparative knowledge, the masculine . . . the divinatory is based on the assumption that each person is not only a unique individual in his own right, but that he has a receptivity to the uniqueness of every other person."[12]

(7) The meaning of a text is rooted in its original historical situation and determined by its historical and linguistic context; but the contemporary interpreter has the capacity of grasping the meaning of a text better than its author. The interpreter is able to gather data of which the author was only dimly conscious because a work is never able fully and completely to embody the creative spirit behind it. Every feature that might contribute to the author's work—the author's will, competence, and performance in the work—is to be examined. Since interpreters are able

---

[11]F. D. E. Schleiermacher, *Hermeneutics: The Handwritten Manuscripts*, ed. H. Kimmerle (Missoula MT: Scholars Press, 1977) 100.
[12]Ibid., 150.

to read things into a text because of their own bias, successive readings must be made, but these readings will increase knowledge of the material itself and hence increase understanding. The possibility of misunderstanding and the plurality of attempts at understanding give rise to hermeneutics and make it an art.

Wilhelm Dilthey

The beginning point for Dilthey (1833–1911) was the hermeneutics of Schleiermacher and the task of understanding "better than the author understood himself." Roy J. Howard summarizes the importance of Dilthey for hermeneutics in relation to Schleiermacher:

> He accepted Schleiermacher's insight that the problem of hermeneutics was fundamentally an epistemological one and hence belonged to philosophy rather than to philology. He also accepted . . . demarcation of the field of knowledge into the areas of the natural sciences, where explanation-theory was the metaphilosophical task, and of the cultural sciences, where understanding-theory was needed. He set himself the task of composing the latter. History, as the most conspicuous record of life and mind, was the proper place to begin. Writings, as the primary objective datum for the historian, became the focus of reflection. Philosophical hermeneutics, then, would be a metatheory of the understanding of life-experiences as they are given in linguistic expression.[13]

In "The Imagination of the Poet: Buildingblocks for a Poetics" (referred to in this chapter as *Poetics*)[14] Dilthey pointed out the kinship of poetics to hermeneutics and indicated that Schleiermacher raised hermeneutics to the level of an aesthetic form of observation. Schleiermacher saw all interpretation of literature as dependent upon understanding, but understanding is not to be separated from production. It is in the relationship between understanding and production that rules of interpretation can be defined on the basis of universal human nature shared by the interpreter and the author. The hermeneutics of Dilthey emphasized understanding that allows us to move from the effect of the expression to the cause of lived experience and even to share or relive the experience of another person. The task of hermeneutics, "to understand better than

---

[13]Roy J. Howard, *Three Faces of Hermeneutics: An Introduction to Current Theories of Understanding* (Berkeley: University of California Press, 1982) 22.

[14]*Die Einbildungskraft des Dichters: Bausteine für eine Poetik, Gesammelte Schriften* VI, 5th ed. (Göttingen: Vandenhoeck und Ruprecht, 1968) 124.

the author understood himself," is an art. The process, Dilthey says, is one of "divination." Only through inner affinity and sympathy can it come close to perfection. In fact, the process of hermeneutics goes beyond the limits of logical reflection, beyond the explicit consciousness even of the original author of a work. The interpreter operates with the same creative possibilities of the author and can, by means of the expression of that author, move beyond the author. In the notes published after his death, Dilthey affirmed that "in the sense of an unconscious structure that is effective in the organization of the work and is understood from this inner form, an idea is really present (not an abstract thought) of which the poet need not be, and indeed will never be, completely conscious. The interpreter lifts it out and that perhaps is the greatest victory of hermeneutics."[15] A theoretical universality of interpretation was found by Dilthey in face of the finite historical nature of man and understanding by giving attention to poetics or to the creative nature of humankind. Language and meaning (ranging from denotation of individual terms to life itself) are held together in creative tension in a comprehensive systematic approach that centered in the human's mental structure. This mental structure was a continuously developing system integrating and equilibrating various stages of inner and outer development.

Peter Krausser has traced chronologically the development of Dilthey's criticism of historical reason and he finds the theory of a unified and unifying mental structure as the core of Dilthey's work.[16] In development of his ideas, the relationship of the dynamic fundamentally unified system was seen more and more as purposeful by Dilthey. This development was no doubt influenced by the work of Husserl. Indeed, Paul Ricoeur declares that the "concept of intentionality and of the identical character of the intentional object allowed Dilthey to reinforce his concept of psychic structures through the Husserlian notion of meaning."[17]

Dilthey's system of hermeneutics can be compared with that of Schleiermacher. In Dilthey there was a broad conceptualization of language and literature involving human creativity as universal and historical reality; the text as an expression of historical experiences and

---

[15]*Gesammelte Schriften* V, 335.

[16]Krausser, *Kritik der endlichen Vernunft: Wilhelm Diltheys Revolution der allgemeinen Wissenschafts- und Handlungstheorie* (Frankfurt: Suhrkamp Verlag, 1968) 210.

[17]Paul Ricoeur, "The Task of Hermeneutics," *Philosophy Today* 17 (1973): 118.

the structure of the mind; meaning as reference to things in the world, meaning as reference in terms of the course of life, meaning that belongs to life, and meaning as life itself. There are levels of creativity, text, and meaning; and there are relationships among these levels and the elements of the various levels. A major difference between Dilthey and Schleiermacher is that Dilthey did not, as Schleiermacher, ground human life and the world in God as the whole. He purposed to begin with no a priori, not even a philosophy of history, but from the "standpoint of life," and epistemology becomes an empirical study. Life, experience, and history were the focus of Dilthey, not some universal that is presupposed and that cannot be developed out of lived experience. Schleiermacher's philosophical presupposition, in Dilthey's perspective, was such that historical development is only formal change, that what happens in the history of an individual shows what the individual was in the beginning. Dilthey was not interested in any timeless principle embodied in humankind but in humankind's social and historical situation.

The particular social and historical situation, however, has meaning beyond the local, not because it is related to a timeless Idea, but because it is related to past and future meanings. In memory, with which we can see the past flow of life, we grasp the meaning of a moment of the past. It is meaningful because in that moment a commitment for the future took place, or the plan for future life was secured, or the realization of such a plan was hindered, or the engagement of the individual's own being in humanity occurred. The moment has meaning in the relation of past and future, individual existence and humanity. Since meaning depends upon the relation of the parts to the whole, our grasp of meaning constantly changes, and meaning must await the end of history. Dilthey used analogies to try to express his concept of meaning, and in the analogies he gave some insight into the use of the concept of meaning for hermeneutics. "As words have a meaning by which they point to something, or sentences have a meaning, which we construe, so the coherence of the parts of life can be construed to the defined-undefined meaning of the parts."

> Meaning is the special kind of relationship that in life the parts of life have to the whole. This meaning we recognize as the meaning of words in a sentence, in recollections and possibilities of the future. The essence of the meaning references is in the relationships that the form of a course

of life contains in the course of time on the ground of the structure of life under the constraints of the environment.[18]

For Dilthey, meaning is not ultimately an intellectual relationship; it is not simply a rational process. "Meaning is obtained from life itself." But if one would point to a structure as the meaning of a total life as it is given out of the meaning of the parts, "the poetic work speaks forth the meaning of life by means of the free creation of the structure of meaning."[19] In his *Poetics*, Dilthey applied psychological insights to artistic life and activity. His view of artistic creation is much more interesting than a simplistic stimulus-response view. The total structure of the inner life that alters and gives form to perceptions, representations, and circumstances operates as a unity but Dilthey distinguished different classes of creative processes: cognitive, volitional, and affective. In *Poetics* Dilthey was most concerned with the analysis of the affective area, of feelings. He declared that the perceptions and images that come from the outside are inspired, colored, and invigorated by "feelings." Dilthey saw the area of feeling as forming a continuum from those feelings that have physical causes with no mental representations to those which spring from a contemplative uniting of mental representation and not from a physical cause or even from the content of the mental representation. After setting up a model to relate the external material for literary creation and the structure of the mind, Dilthey deduced laws of aesthetic effect and creation and discusses ways that representations transform themselves beyond the limit of the real.[20]

In the *Poetics*, Dilthey introduced the concept of the "type" to explain how a literary work communicates to a reader. The essential nature of a work is its "type" or its "typical." "The characters and situations presented to us in a poem, and the feeling-response evoked by them in us, are *typical* of a segment of possible human experience, and of its value or significance for us. By contemplation of the type, our acquaintance with what it represents is widened, and our power to see its true significance is heightened."[21]

In the final part of the *Poetics*, Dilthey treated the specific poetic technique that can be built on psychological foundations. Norms of

---

[18]*Gesammelte Schriften* VII, 233-34.
[19]Ibid., 240.
[20]*Poetics*, 154-63.
[21]Ibid., 185-88. We would relate Dilthey's discussion of the type to studies on genre.

technique should be derived from human nature itself not from metaphysical presuppositions. Dilthey, however, did not make the error of concentrating wholly on the unconscious creativity as the Romantics did. The poetics that Dilthey supported must involve rational understanding with involuntary creativity, it must "open both doors of its experience as wide as possible so that no thought of fact or experience is excluded!" Dilthey concluded the *Poetics* with applications of the psychological foundation of poetics for artist and critic. Of relevance for reader-oriented literary study (and related to his earlier discussion of the typical) is Dilthey's treatment of the creation of epic poetry, drama, and the novel. He indicated that before actual composition, a structuring stands before the eyes of the poet. Tradition has called this structure "myth" or "fable." In this fable or plot, characters and actions are united as two sides of the same fact. This plot is not an attempt to represent reality; the element contained in the nexus are those that are effective, the elements that are dead insofar as feeling is concerned being eliminated. From this plot, comes the detailed composition involving elements from the experience of the author.[22]

Dilthey continued to see a relationship between poetics and hermeneutics throughout his life. His *Poetics* was published in 1887. A sequel to this work, "The Three Epochs of Modern Aesthetics and Its Present Task," published in 1892, maintained continuity with the basic ideas in the work of 1887. Even after publications in hermeneutics, Dilthey continued to be concerned with poetics in itself. Until his death in 1911, he maintained notebooks in which he gave his plans for the reworking and expansion of the text of *Poetics* into a full-sized book.[23] In his notes, Dilthey indicated that he would use a terminology in his new work that moved away from the orientation toward the feeling and hedonistic satisfaction toward one favoring experience and meaningfulness, but this represents no absolute turn from an explanation of poetic creativity on the basis of psychology and the use of this in hermeneutics. Indeed, the notes indicate that he planned to utilize his work on structural or developmental psychology in the projected work, and in the notes there is a fragment on

---

[22]Ibid., 219-26.

[23]*Gesammelte Schriften* VI, the same volume containing *Poetics* and *Three Epochs*, contains notes concerning the projected revision from two different periods of Dilthey's life.

structural psychology that was to form a part of the work.[24] The literary tradition that gave attention to the work itself (American New Criticism and European Text-Intrinsic Criticism) did not find Dilthey's wedding of poetics and hermeneutics instructive. But a reader-oriented literary hermeneutics interested in literature as a "happening of meaningfulness" will benefit from Dilthey's insights.

Dilthey's attention to a transcending (nonidealistic) reality, beyond individual historical experiences, may be compared with Schleiermacher's attempt to ground a consciousness of God in the consciousness of absolute dependence. In the *Poetics*, Dilthey related the meaning he sees as obtained from life itself to religion. He indicated that since "religion has lost the support of metaphysical arguments for the existence of God and the soul," for many people a comprehension of "the meaning of life" is available only in art and poetry. Poetry has the difficult task of finding form to express "an immense content." The core of meaning that is expressed by the poet is the same for all times. In this sense, the great poets possess something eternal. Humankind, on the other hand, is a historical being. "When the social order and the meaning of life change, the poets of past ages no longer move us as they once did. This is true today. We await the poet who will speak to us as we suffer, eat and drink, and wrestle with life."[25]

Martin Heidegger

When Heidegger (1889–1976) is examined in the light of the comprehensive vision of Dilthey suggested in his outline for a revised *Poetics*, it may be argued that Heidegger dealt with all the major elements with which Dilthey dealt: the creativity of the author, the text, and meaning. He dealt with all of these on the one level of life or Being. In his treatment he extended and amplified the concern of Dilthey with meaning as life. Heidegger's estimation of the philosophical importance of Dilthey gave a focus to the work of Heidegger, for Dilthey's importance, in Heidegger's opinion, was "in the fact that in all this [in his attempts to understand the experiences of life in their structural and developmental

---

[24]*Gesammelte Schriften* VI, 317-19. The editor of *Gesammelte Schriften* in a preface to vol. 5, declared that poetics along with the theory of history were the general bases for Dilthey's ideas of life and the understanding of life and that he continued an active interest in poetics throughout his life (ix).

[25]*Poetics*, 237, 240, 241.

inner connections] he was, above all, on his way toward the question of 'life.' "[26]

Heidegger correctly saw that for Dilthey the logic of the humane sciences was not the central concern as is so often asserted. While he did research on the humane sciences in distinction to the natural sciences and wrote on the history of the humane sciences, Dilthey was primarily concerned with a psychology in which the "whole fact of humankind" could be presented. All the areas of study permeate and intersect in the goal of understanding life philosophically and of securing a hermeneutical foundation for this understanding of life in terms of life itself. Humankind as the object of the humane sciences, and, especially the root of the sciences, is central, for everything centers in the way that humankind is.[27]

Heidegger, however, was only indirectly concerned with humankind—as a means of questioning Being. "Understanding of Being belongs to the kind of Being which the entity called *Dasein* possesses."[28] The problem of fundamental ontology can be solved as *Dasein* is explicated. Heidegger saw anthropological, psychological, and biological questions as questions to be handled subsequent to the existential questions. Yet, Heidegger sounds much like Dilthey when he speaks of a "totality of *Dasein*'s structural whole" that is built upon the Being of *Dasein* and which gives access to the Being of *Dasein*. This is a unity that is not defined by the elements in its structure, by deduction from an idea of humankind, nor even by "our immanent perception of Experiences."[29]

In many ways the conceptualization of Dilthey can be seen in Heidegger with the important exception that Heidegger is concerned primarily with the creative aspects of humankind to show the real nature of *Dasein*'s expression of itself, the communication of "the existential possibilities of one's state of mind" that amounts to a "disclosing of existence."[30] Dilthey saw the text as an expression of the historical experiences of humankind and the structures of the mind. Heidegger, of course, saw the text in some fashion as a human product, but he was not concerned with the biological or psychological nature of the text.

---

[26]Martin Heidegger, *Being and Time*, trans. John Macquarrie and Edward Robinson (Oxford: Basil Blackwell, 1973) 46. Page numbers refer to original German text.

[27]Ibid., 398.

[28]Ibid., 16.

[29]Ibid., 181-82.

[30]Ibid., 162.

Heidegger was concerned with the "ontological locus" of the phenomenon of language in "*Dasein*'s state of Being."[31]

Dilthey conceived of a continuity of meaning from the smallest elements of language to life itself. Heidegger extended the meaning of life to Being. "In 'poetical' discourse, the communication of the existential possibilities of one's state of mind can become an aim in itself and this amounts to a disclosing of existence."[32] After *Being and Time*, the questioning of *Dasein* for the sake of Being was no longer the procedure. Rather, Being, in poetic terms to be sure, was the absolute. Language, moreover, in some sense was the equivalent of Being. *Dasein* was no longer the locus of discourse. Being itself was the explanation for language and the essence of language was Being's self expression. Being was the creative explanation, Being was the text, Being was the meaning.

In the essay on "Language" in *Poetry, Language, Thought* (*Unterwegs zur Sprache*) Heidegger said that the speaking of language should be sought in what is spoken purely, and he declared that "what is spoken purely is the poem." The basis of this assertion was not given in theoretical terms at all. The basis is experience. We may assert that "what is spoken purely is the poem" if "we succeed in hearing in a poem something that is spoken purely." While Heidegger in his interpretation overturned the "current view" of language that saw speech as "the activation of the organs for sounding and hearing" and "the audible expression and communication of human feelings" that are accompanied by thoughts, he did not wish to state in theoretical terms "a new view of language." "What is important is learning to live in the speaking of language." The human's speaking, indeed, is a response of hearing, so the way that the human learns "to live in the speaking of language" is to "examine constantly whether and to what extent we are capable of what genuinely belongs to responding."[33]

Rudolf Bultmann and the New Hermeneutic

Bultmann's work is related to Dilthey and Heidegger. Rudolf Bultmann (1884–1976) made Dilthey's name known in New Testament studies through his use of the insight that genuine comprehension of

---

[31]Ibid., 166.

[32]Ibid., 162.

[33]*Poetry, Language, Thought*, trans. Albert Hofstadter (New York: Harper, 1971) 194, 192, 210.

poetry and art as well as works of philosophy and religion is "oriented
. . . to the *inquiry into the understanding of one particular existence in
history.*"[34] "Dilthey," Bultmann indicated, "maintained that the 'basis of
human nature as a whole' is a condition for the possibility of understanding." Bultmann defined this further by saying that a condition for
exposition is the fact that the expositor and author live as humans in the
same historical world, in which "human being" occurs as a "being" in an
environment, in understanding intercourse with objects and our fellows.[35]
But Bultmann limited his use of Dilthey because of his view that
Dilthey's basic concepts were no longer tenable. He saw that Dilthey was
caught up in the "ultimately aesthetic approach of romanticism."[36]
Bultmann wished to emphasize not feelings but the understanding arising
from the possibilities of human being that are revealed in a work.
Although his poetic hermeneutics was not appropriated by Bultmann,
Dilthey's concept of the poetic nature of the structure of the mind helps
us understand how Bultmann was able to move from the text to the
subject matter of human understanding of itself.

Hans Jonas, a student of Heidegger and Bultmann, presented the
argument. The need for moving from language back to meaning,
according to Jonas, "derives from an unavoidable fundamental structure
of the mind as such." "The innermost nature of the mind" is that it is
"symbolistic," that is, "it interprets itself in objective formulae and
symbols."

> In order to come to itself, it [the mind] necessarily takes this detour via
> the symbol, in whose enticing jungle of problems it tends to lose itself,
> far from the origin preserved symbolically in it, taking the substitute as
> ultimate. Only in a long procedure of working back, after an exhausting
> completion of that detour, is a demythologized consciousness able
> terminologically to approach directly the original phenomena hidden in
> this camouflage. . . . [37]

---

[34]Rudolf Bultmann, "The Problem of Hermeneutics," in *Essays Philosophical and
Theological*, trans. C. G. Greig, Library of Philosophy and Theology (London: SCM
Press; New York: Macmillan, 1955) 248.

[35]Ibid., 243, 256.

[36]Ibid., 250-51.

[37]Hans Jonas, *Augustin und das paulinische Freiheitsproblem* (Göttingen: Vanden-
hoeck & Ruprecht, 1930) 67. The translation is based on that in James M. Robinson,
"Hermeneutics since Barth," in *The New Hermeneutic*, ed. James M. Robinson and John
B. Cobb, Jr., vol. 2 of New Frontiers in Theology (New York: Harper & Row, 1964) 36.

The phenomenon that is hidden in the camouflage of language is the way the human understands itself in the world. Bultmann's task then was more related to the work of Heidegger than to the work of Dilthey, but Bultmann did not question language for Being nor did he analyze *Dasein* for philosophical ends. He saw his task as interpretation, scientific interpretation. He distinguished between scientific interpretation and "paying simple heed to what the New Testament says," for which philosophical analysis is not necessary. He wished "to make Scripture itself speak as a power, which has something to say to the present, to present-day existence," not simply "to read the biblical writing as a compendium of dogmatic pronouncements, or as 'sources' for the reconstruction of a section of past history, or to study a religious phenomenon or the nature of religion in general, or to know the psychological course and theoretical objectivization of religious experiences."[38]

Bultmann answered the objection to his program that states that the subject of the New Testament is God by asserting that an "*existentiell* knowledge about God" is to be found in human existence "in the form of the inquiry about 'happiness,' 'salvation,' the meaning of the world and of history, and in the inquiry into the real nature of each person's particular 'being.' " "Inquiry into the reality of human existence," then, is inquiry about God and the manifestation of God."[39]

Bultmann's view of the Bible and the Word of God, of the church and proclamation, influenced his choice of the level of interpretation of the New Testament. Although he recognized the possibility and legitimacy of using the Scriptures for historical and aesthetic purposes, the Bible, as Word of God, is to be interpreted so that it speaks as Word, for only in this way is faith and new understanding possible. To speak as Word to modern man is to speak in terms of human existence. "I think I may take for granted that the right question to frame with regard to the Bible—at any rate within the Church—is the question of human existence." Two reasons are given for this assumption: (1) "I am driven to that by the urge to inquire existentially about my own existence," (2) "the Church's proclamation refers me to the Scriptures as the place where I shall hear things about my own existence which vitally concern me."[40]

---

[38]"The Problem of Hermeneutics," 258-59.
[39]Ibid., 257, 259.
[40]"Bultmann Replies to His Critics," *Kerygma and Myth: A Theological Debate* [I], ed. Hans Werner Bartsch, trans. Reginald H. Fuller, Harper Torchbooks (New York:

The "New Hermeneutic" is the name given to a movement associated with students of Bultmann, especially Ernst Fuchs and Gerhard Ebeling, which changed the hermeneutical dialectic from language (or myth) versus understanding of existence to language versus language-event. The language which the New Hermeneutic saw as the key to the task of theology is not merely the creation of humankind. "Language," Fuchs declared, "consists not only in a statement of meaning that is heard. Language is indeed not merely discourse. Language is rather primarily a sign or a letting be, a meaning in the active sense." He affirmed that "where meaning is, there is also language." But the meaning of something is "only an abbreviation of language."[41]

Fuchs seems to be utilizing the concepts of the later Heidegger, while at the same time maintaining continuity with insights in *Being and Time*. Like Heidegger in *Being and Time*, Fuchs saw understanding as an *existentiale*.[42] Heidegger had postulated that language is related to a superior and prior "discourse" that is an *existentiale* equiprimordial with state of mind and understanding. This allows humankind or *Dasein* to be questioned for existence or Being. After *Being and Time*, "language" assumed a more central position, displacing or incorporating state of mind, understanding, and discourse. Also, as discourse and understanding were equiprimordial for Heidegger, so language and understanding for Fuchs belonged together in an inseparable way.[43] Being and language are related not only in that Being is the condition of language but also in that language warrants Being. "Being is the ground of language," and "without Being language is groundless, absurd, imaginary, glossolalia, indeed impossible." But at the same time, language is "earlier" than its ground, earlier than Being, and "without language Being is also nothing." Although speech is not Being, only in speech is Being spoken out; so in language we must question for Being.[44] Being is not God. Being is not a "something" but a "how" that forms room for all beings, although beings are not created by Being and all beings as a totality are not equated with Being. Being is not reality although it is the possibility of

Harper & Row, 1961) 191-92.

[41]Ernst Fuchs, *Marburger Hermeneutik*, Hermeneutische Untersuchungen zur Theologie 9 (Tübingen: J.C.B. Mohr, 1968) 177-78.

[42]Ernst Fuchs, *Zum Hermeneutischen Problem in der Theologie: Die existentiale Interpretation*, vol. 1 of his *Gesammelte Aufsätze* (Tübingen: J.C.B. Mohr, 1965; c1960).

[43]*Marburger Hermeneutik*, 239.

[44]*Zum Hermeneutischen Problem in der Theologie*, 128.

responsiveness to an "ultimate" that is also "the first," the human itself in the case of human beings.[45]

The translation of the language-event in biblical texts is what is important. The translator must form the room the text sought to form when the Spirit spoke in it. The content and form of the translation must unite to allow the life of the text to appear. Proclamation is the true translation of the text, not because the New Testament text was necessarily originally proclamation, but because of the nature of the Word itself.[46]

Gerhard Ebeling began his contribution to the New Hermeneutic with a proposal for a new understanding of church history as "the history of the interpretation of Holy Scripture," and he continued by recasting theology as a whole in terms of hermeneutics. Dogmatics, says Ebeling, "resting on the exposition of Scripture and the history of theology, . . . has the task of bringing the church's teaching into contact and discussion with contemporary principles of thought, there to submit it to critical sifting and present it in its fuller inner coherence."[47] Ebeling would redeem the insight of the Reformers into the Word event with the help of contemporary hermeneutical sophistication. The aim of hermeneutical interpretation "cannot . . . be anything other than the removal of the obstacle which prevents the Word from mediating understanding itself."[48]

Ebeling saw Holy Scripture, "the testimony to the provisional and the conclusive proclamation of God," as "*the* absolute source of present proclamation" and "the authoritative text of theology." The historical-critical method itself leads to dogmatics and beyond the text of historical study. "Criticism is an element of integration in the effort to understand the text." But the ultimate purpose of the historical-critical method is "the interpreter's self-criticism in view of all of the conceivable possibilities of deceiving himself as to the aim of the biblical text," and "the question which is ultimately appropriate to the biblical text is, how it affects the conscience." The biblical text, then, is not the Word of God in the strict sense. The proclamation is God's Word. "Insofar as the proclamation is

[45]Ibid., 124-25, 128.

[46]Ernst Fuchs, *Studies of the Historical Jesus*, trans, Andrew Scobie, Studies in Biblical Theology 42 (London: SCM Press; Naperville IL: Allenson, 1964) 192-96.

[47]*Word and Faith*, trans. James W. Leitch (London: SCM Press, 1963; Philadelphia: Fortress Press, 1964) 27.

[48]"God and Word," in *The Interpretation of Texts*, vol. 1 of *Hermeneutical Inquiry* (2 vols.), ed. David E. Klemm, AAR Studies in Religion 43-44 (Atlanta: Scholars Press, 1986) 212.

dependent on the text, the exposition therefore serves toward the text proving itself a Bible text, i.e., becoming the source of God's Word."[49]

The New Hermeneutic of Fuchs and Ebeling may be criticized for advocating a new sort of dogmatic interpretation. The ecclesiastical context for their work is obvious. Werner G. Jeanroud says that the theological readings of the scriptures by Fuchs and Ebeling were "not open-ended endeavours motivated by a search for a new and always better understanding of what the biblical texts have to say about God, anthropology, and eschatology, but attempts to stabilize particular sets of traditional theological interpretations of the Bible."[50] A. C. Thiselton, on the other hand, criticized Fuchs for ignoring the function of language on the purely cognitive level. But he used the work of J. L. Austin (1911–1960) to support Fuchs' concept of language and language-event. In the language-event of Fuchs and the performative utterance of Austin, "the issuing of the utterance is the performing of an action." Thiselton suggested that the work of the later Wittgenstein may help to bridge the gap between the function of language on the purely cognitive level and the function of language on the deeper level, the function of "exposing or reorienting attitudes and presuppositions."[51] Wittgenstein's later doctrine, seen by Thiselton as supporting Fuchs's hermeneutic of faith, was that there are no objective points of support outside human thought and speech. Wittgenstein's change in attitude to factual discourse involves a move to anthropocentrism that parallels Dilthey's relating of anthropology and the literary expression, poetics, and hermeneutics.[52]

The ordinary language analysis of Austin and Wittgenstein and the New Hermeneutic moved beyond the function of language as conveying information. In the early 1970s, Paul Ricoeur delineated the conditions of the functioning of language that are uncovered by ordinary language analysis and that are "not provisory defects or diseases" to be eliminated

---

[49]*Word and Faith*, 427, 428, 429.

[50]Werner G. Jeanrond, "After Hermeneutics: The Relationship between Theological and Biblical Studies," *The Open Text: New Directions for Biblical Studies?*, ed. Francis Watson (London: SCM Press, 1993) 92.

[51]A. C. Thiselton, "The Parables as Language-Event: Some Comments on Fuchs's Hermeneutics in the Light of Linguistic Philosophy," *Scottish Journal of Theology* 23 (1970): 466. See Ludwig Wittgenstein, *Philosophical Investigations*, trans. G. E. M. Anscombe, 2nd ed. (Oxford: Blackwell, 1958; [1]1953) ¶¶108, 316-94.

[52]See David Francis Pears, *Wittgenstein*, Modern Masters series (London: Fontana/Collins, 1971) 168-86, for a discussion of the mediation of Wittgenstein's positivistic and antipositivistic tendencies in the "true center" of humankind.

by the reformation of language but are rather conditions that are "permanent and fruitful." These are the variability of semantic values, the sensitivity of semantic values to contexts, and the irreducibly polysemous character of lexical terms. On the basis of the work of Austin and Wittgenstein, Ricoeur judged ordinary language "to be a kind of conservatory for expressions which have preserved the highest descriptive power as regards human experience . . . " and he stated his conviction that hermeneutics would benefit from an inquiry into the functioning of ordinary language. "The whole problem of text-interpretation could be renewed by the recognition of its roots in the functioning of ordinary language itself."[53]

Hans-Georg Gadamer

The work of Hans-Georg Gadamer (b. 1900) is helpful for envisioning the relationship of readers to historical texts in general and readers' interaction with the Jesus tradition in particular—an original event in the life of Jesus and its imaginative historical construal and the eventful actualization of the literary text by contemporary readers. The correspondence version of truth is related to the participatory version of truth.

Wilhelm von Humboldt's (1767–1835) view of language as an unbordered creative power of thought and speech making unlimited use of limited materials was used by Gadamer to develop a hermeneutics giving attention to historical consciousness and expanding hermeneutical options beyond the "Romanticism" of Schleiermacher and Dilthey, the existentialism of Heidegger and Bultmann, and the dogmatics of Fuchs and Ebeling. Humboldt had said that the learning of a foreign language must be the winning of a new standpoint in a person's worldview but that this achievement is not complete because one carries to the foreign language one's own worldview. Gadamer saw the carrying of one's worldview to a language not as a limitation but as the means of the power of the hermeneutical experience.

Gadamer accepted Heidegger's temporal analysis of *Dasein* as demonstrating that understanding is the way of being of *Dasein* itself. The meanings that appear in human existence are structures with a past and a future. The essence of human existence (the disclosure of these struc-

---

[53]"From Existentialism to the Philosophy of Language," *Philosophy Today* 17 (1973): 95-96.

tures of meaning), then, is temporality. The correspondence of sentences with reality assumes a justified shape against the horizon of a temporal ontological ground. Understanding is "never subjective behavior toward a given object, but towards its effective history—the history of its influence; in other words, understanding belongs to the being of that which is understood."[54] The semantic version of truth as an attribute of sentences (true or false) rests upon an ontological version of truth, the experience that is the original impetus toward the assertion resulting from the act of consciousness. The thesis of *Truth and Method* was that "the element of effective-history is operative in all understanding of tradition." This is true even where the methodology of the modern historical sciences has been adopted, a methodology that "makes what has grown historically and has been transmitted historically an object to be established like an experimental finding—as if tradition were as alien and, from the human point of view, as unintelligible, as an object of physics."[55]

Historically realized consciousness (*Wirkungsgeschichtliches Bewusstein*) is the consciousness of being acted upon by history so that this action upon us is not objectified but is part of the historical phenomenon itself. In "The Continuity of History and the Moment of Existence," Gadamer explained what he meant by the assertion that "all our historical understanding is defined through a historically realized consciousness":

> We cannot lift ourselves out of the event and, so to say, confront it with the result that the past might become an object for us. If we think in this way we come much too late to receive the real experience of history. We are not only a part of this forward moving chain . . . but we also have the possibility of understanding that moment in the past which comes to us and transmits itself to us. I call this the historically realized consciousness [*wirkungsgeschichtliches Bewusstein*] because I wish to say, on the one hand, that our consciousness is defined by the effective working of history, that is, defined through an active element that does not allow our consciousness to be free in the sense of a confrontation with the past. On the other hand, I intend to say that it is possible for the consciousness of this action to be created in us—so that everything past which comes into our experience constrains us to become prepared with it to take over its truth in a certain way upon ourselves.[56]

---

[54]Hans-Georg Gadamer, *Truth and Method*, trans. Garrett Barden and John Cumming (New York: Seabury, 1975) xix.

[55]Ibid., xxi.

[56]"Die Kontinuität der Geschichte und der Augenblick der Existenz," *Kline Schriften* 1

The application of the theory of historically realized consciousness was made by Gadamer in three areas of hermeneutics: aesthetics, history, and language. In each case the debate is between a method that studies an object and an experience of participation. In each area there is a legitimate application of criticism, but with criticism there is an experience of being grasped, being carried by tradition, participating with the creators of discourse. The work of art allows a "world" to be encountered, but because of the nature of the work this is not a foreign universe in which we are transformed in time and moment. We do not question the work with our methods *or* merely see in the work what we bring; we come to the work participating in the same structure of being that is the basis for our understanding of what was intended in the work. The principles that Gadamer gave for art in general are true also for literature and the understanding of literature. A text, as word, is not basically a mere instrument or sign of something. That a text is the object of interpretation means that it presents a question to the interpreter. To understand the text is to understand the question of the text. Whoever wishes to understand the text must see it as the answer to the question. But the interpreter does not come as an empty vessel; the interpreter comes with a horizon of meaning that is broadened so as to become fused with that of the text. The possibility of a fusion of horizons is based on the grounding of text and interpreter in being.

The reconstruction of the text historically and philologically in itself is not the work of hermeneutics, yet "the reconstruction of the conditions in which a work that has come down to us from the past fulfilled its original purposes is undoubtedly an important aid to its understanding." The result of the operation, however, is not the meaning of the work. Gadamer declared that the reconstruction of the original circumstances is a weak beginning in light of the historical nature of our being.[57]

The hermeneutical experience has to do with tradition; it is tradition that is to come to experience. However, tradition is not simply an event that humans recognize through experience and learn to master. The intimate "I"-"you" relationship was used by Gadamer to explain his position. Experience speaks as an intimate friend (a "you" [*Du*]). One must experience tradition as one experiences an intimate friend, not as

---

(Tübingen: J.C.B. Mohr, 1967) 158.
[57]*Truth and Method*, 148-49.

one experiences an object. The tradition must be experienced as a friend who has something to say. The means of understanding is the content of tradition, to be sure, but "all meaning is related to the 'I' . . . all the meaning of what is handed down to us finds its concretion, in which it is understood, in its relation to the understanding 'I'—and not in the reconstruction of an 'I' of the original meaning." Gadamer found mediation of the two poles—tradition and the "I"—in language. Tradition brings itself to language and human consciousness is linguistic. In this mediation, human consciousness is not dissolved. Indeed, Gadamer emphasized this when he strongly asserted that "there is no possible consciousness . . . in which the 'object' that is handed down would appear in the light of eternity. Every assimilation of tradition is historically different: which does not mean that every one represents only an imperfect understanding of it. Rather, every one is the experience of a 'view' of the object itself."[58]

Gadamer's specific contributions may be seen not only in light of the problem of radical historical finitude that was seen in Dilthey's work and the problem of language and understanding seen in Heidegger, Bultmann, and the New Hermeneutic but also in light of the contemporary wide-ranging critique of critical foundations for disciplines in the natural as well as the social sciences. Different views of Gadamer—and different hermeneutical programs claiming his contribution—are possible. From the perspective of Enlightenment rationality, Gadamer may be seen as a postmodernist who surrenders completely the notion of objectivity. But he may be seen as a radical modernist who expands the understanding of rationality itself.[59] European scholars are able to accommodate Gadamer to theories of communicative action within the legacy of transcendental idealism. The turn to the subject, then, is immediately objectivized in

---

[58]Ibid., 430.

[59]In an essay entitled "On the Scope and Function of Hermeneutical Reflection," Gadamer answers the charge that he has blind trust in the self-purifying nature of the process of interpretation in his evaluation of Habermas's emancipatory consciousness as reflective of a hermeneutically false consciousness and in his indication of the need for a "more universal hermeneutical reflection." Gadamer says that "the basically emancipatory consciousness must have in mind the dissolution of all authority, all obedience. This means that unconsciously the ultimate guiding image of emancipatory reflection in the social sciences must be an anarchistic utopia. Such an image, however, seems to me to reflect a hermeneutically false consciousness, the antidote for which can only be a more universal hermeneutical reflection." In *Philosophical Hermeneutics*, trans. and ed. David E. Linge (Berkeley, Los Angeles, and London: University of California Press, 1976) 42.

terms of Kant's "conditions of possibility" or other forms of philosophical objectivism. American scholars display greater flexibility. In the natural sciences, for example, they are "more inclined to understand the rationality operative . . . as disciplinary matrices where intersubjective communities of investigators pose questions to nature by means of the observational procedures of experimental measurements."[60]

Regardless of the perspective from which Gadamer is viewed, he is seen as moving the hermeneutical discussion more decisively to a meta-critical level. At a precritical level, readers read texts and are not consciously engaged in interpretation. Readers are mastered by texts. At a critical level, readers reverse the procedure. They master texts. Texts become the objects of inquiry of the critic. Metacritical evaluation is criticism of criticism, evaluation of the critics' program of evaluation. At this level the deepest challenge of hermeneutics arises. At the critical level criteria are used that are acceptable to the critic's community. At the metacritical level, the question of criteria seems to be tied to the aims and interests of those involved. An important question is how to move back to the sorts of operation of the text in the life of readers that was possible on the precritical level after consciousness of theoretical metacritical issues.

Paul Ricoeur

How does an Enlightenment consciousness, a self concerned with the sort of explanation of concern to the natural sciences (and with that sort of explanation of understanding!), move to the sort of experiencing understanding in terms of specific texts? Can we engender in our contemporary post-Enlightenment world an interaction of the imagination with reflective and critical modes of knowing—a relationship between explanation and understanding or hermeneutical interpretation? Paul Ricoeur (b. 1913) offers help in his understanding of the reference of literary texts:

---

[60]Matthew L. Lamb, "The Dialectics of Theory and Praxis within Paradigm Analysis," in *Paradigm Change in Theology: A Symposium for the Future*, ed. Hans Küng and David Tracy, trans. Margaret Kohl (New York: Crossroad, 1991; 1989) 74. The pragmatic tradition of C. S. Peirce and Josiah Royce has influenced hermeneutics in America, and in America a sociopragmatic hermeneutics has developed (in contrast to the sociocritical hermeneutics of the continent).

I do not hesitate to say: [literary texts are] about a world, which is the world of the work. For us, the world is the totality of references opened up by texts . . . the nonsituational references . . . which offer themselves as possible modes of being, as possible symbolic dimensions of our being-in-the-world.[61]

The dichotomy between explanation and hermeneutical interpretation and appropriation is transposed in Ricoeur's hermeneutical tradition into the relationship between one's own worldview and the worldview offered or disclosed in the literary text and its tradition. Wilhelm von Humboldt's view of the learning of a foreign language as the winning of a new standpoint in a person's worldview and awareness that this achievement is mixed because one carries to the foreign language one's own world-view, may be taken not only as the encapsulation of the work of Gadamer but also as the basic program of Ricoeur.

Instead of a hermeneutical circle consisting of the subjectivity of reader and the subjectivity of author or a hermeneutical circle consisting of the subjectivity of reader imposing the reader's self in the reading process, Ricoeur sees the circle consisting of the mode of being of the reader (beyond the knowledge the reader possesses) and the mode opened up and disclosed by the text as the world of the work. Ricoeur does not simply abandon earlier hermeneutical perspectives (perspectives that he himself shared at points); he transforms them and incorporates them in later perspectives. An early phenomenological approach sought to extract the essential meanings of structures of purpose, motive, and so forth from lived experience. Hermeneutics came to be the interpretation of symbol. In his two volumes *Fallible Man* and *The Symbolism of Evil*, Ricoeur saw that purpose, motive, and ability can be spoken of in direct language, but evil must be spoken of indirectly in metaphors such as estrangement, errancy, burden, and bondage; these symbols are embedded in mythical narratives that tell the story of how evil began. Hermeneutics for Ricoeur at that time had to do with the interpretation of symbolic or indirect language. Symbolism and hermeneutics were defined in terms of each other, and hermeneutics was identified with the art of deciphering indirect meanings.[62]

---

[61]Paul Ricoeur, *Hermeneutics and the Human Sciences: Essays on Language, Action, and Interpretation*, ed. and intro. by John B. Thompson (Cambridge: Cambridge University Press, 1981) 177.

[62]"From Existentialism to the Philosophy of Language," *Philosophy Today* 17 (1973):

A broader view of hermeneutics came when Ricoeur considered psychological perspectives. Psychoanalysis reduces symbols, explaining them as the results of unconscious factors. Ricoeur's problem of uniting psychological approaches with an approach seeking to recover the original meaning of the symbol broadened his view of hermeneutics. Ricoeur did not give up his earlier definition of hermeneutics as the general theory of symbolic language, but he introduced into the theory the polarity between the reduction of symbol to unconscious factors and the recovery of an original meaning of the symbol.[63] The psychoanalytic revolution as embraced by Ricoeur requires a hermeneutics of suspicion because it had shown that the ego is not master in its own house. Suspicion, however, is not the final answer. It is subject to the task of retrieval.

In his later writings, the creative power of language came to be emphasized. Hermeneutics, from this perspective, has the task of bringing "back to discourse the written text, if not as spoken discourse, at least as speech-act actualized in the act of reading." The object of hermeneutics, then, is not the text but "the text as discourse or discourse as the text." Discourse was defined by Ricoeur as "the actualization of language in a speech-act based on a kind of unit irreducible to the constituents of language as 'code.'" But discourse is not unrelated to language as "code." The concept of "work" was used to relate the discourse as text to language. Discourse appears as a work because of modes of discourse or literary genres which impose a form upon discourse.

> The concept of work must be taken literally. It implies the extension to discourse of categories proper to the world of production and labor. To impose a form upon a material, to subject a production to specific codes, to produce those unique configurations which assimilate a work to an individual and which we call style, these are ways of considering language as a material to be worked and formed. They are ways in which discourse becomes the object of a praxis and a technique.[64]

Literary genres, as Ricoeur sees them, are means of production, but they also function in communication to: (1) provide a common ground of understanding and of interpretation because of the contrast between the traditional genre and the novel message; (2) preserve the message from distortion because of the autonomy of the form; and (3) secure the

---

91.

[63]Ibid., 92.
[64]"Biblical Hermeneutics," *Semeia* 4 (1975): 66-68.

survival of the meaning after the disappearance of its primitive *Sitz im Leben*. The form or genre, then, may start the process of " 'decontextualization' which opens the message to fresh reinterpretation according to new contexts of discourse and of life." The form, then, not only establishes communication and preserves the message from distortion but it also opens the text to a history of interpretation.[65]

Hermeneutics uses the dialectics of discourse and work for the reconstitution of message or discourse. Hermeneutics identifies the message through the codes (the modes of discourse) that generate it as a work of discourse. In the hermeneutical decontextualization, a redefinition of author, audience, and situation take place. This makes it possible for a work "to transcend its psychosociological conditions of production and to be open to an unlimited series of readings, themselves situated within different sociocultural contexts."[66] This decontextualization or distanciation of the text, however, affects the reference. When discourse becomes a text "the structure of the work alters the reference to the point of making it entirely problematic." In oral discourse, the reference is determined by the situation of discourse that furnishes the reference. In literature, where reference is abolished because concrete conditions for the act of pointing something out do not exist, reference to the given world is abolished. "The language seems to glorify itself without depending on the referential function of ordinary discourse." Ricoeur, however, is not willing to abolish the role of reference. The abolition of "first order reference" in poetic literature is "the condition of possibility for the liberation of a second order of reference which reaches the world not only at the level of manipulative objects, but at the level Husserl designated by the expression *Lebenswelt* and Heidegger by 'being-in-the-world.' "[67]

Ricoeur sees interpretation no longer as the search for persons and psychological intentions hidden behind the text but as the explication of a sort of being-in-the-world unfolded in front of the text. The metaphorical process (not simply rhetoric) reinterprets reality by abolishing the literal reference and illuminating the "life-world" and "nonmanipulable being-in-the-world." Metaphor, then, "includes new information"; it "says something new about reality. . . . the metaphorical interpretation gives

---

[65]Ibid., 71

[66]"The Hermeneutical Function of Distanciation," *Philosophy Today* 17 (1973): 139, 133.

[67]Ibid., 140.

rise to a reinterpretation of reality itself, in spite of, and thanks to, the abolition of the reference which corresponds to the literal interpretation of the statement."[68]

In the work of Ricoeur we are brought to the same sort of question faced in Heidegger, how one makes the transition from the language of existence to the language of being. For Ricoeur the question is the reference of the biblical text, the reference that governs not only the process of the hermeneutics of retrieval and reconstruction but that also governs the hermeneutics of suspicion. In the essay "Biblical Hermeneutics," Ricoeur deals with the redescription of biblical language: "What it redescribes is human experience. In this sense we must say that the ultimate referent of the parables, proverbs, and eschatological sayings is not the Kingdom of God but human reality in its wholeness."[69] Is it possible for us to conceive of the coincidence of God and God's rule and human reality in its wholeness? Do these two simply illuminate each other or do they coincide? With the self no longer conceived of as an autonomous naturalized mathematized entity but as existing essentially in relationship with objects and other selves, the question about knowledge and reference going back to Plato and Aristotle are changed. The idealism/realism dichotomy is transformed. Of course, we conceive of objects (not only in the natural world but also in the human world) as existing independently of their being actualized or concretized by subjects. And we conceive of subjects existing independently of objects.

But these ways of conceiving (necessary for ordinary life and scientific inquiry, including literary study) are abstractions from the primary experience. When the essential role of relationship of subject and object is appreciated in the definition of self, the question arises if this relationship is not also essential for understanding the sacred. That is, can we not conceive of the sacred as existing essentially in terms of relationship, in terms of the impingement of the sacred upon the mundane. The definition of the sacred in Platonic terms may have served to guard the idea of the Christian God from being contaminated by ideas of lesser deities in the ancient world. But it also altered the biblical representation of God as being actively involved in this world.

Can we conceive of revelation of the divine being involved in the creative or metaphorical activity of readers. Elsewhere I have suggested

---

[68]"Biblical Hermeneutics," 87, 80, 84.
[69]Ibid., 127.

that the experience of the reader in the actualization of biblical texts may be seen as an experience of ultimacy. This experience does not bypass the historical and contingent; indeed, the historical and contingent are vital aspects of the experience. It is not a reduction of the divine to the text. It is not a deification of pure experience. It grows out of the recognition that *for us* in our pilgrimage, revelation occurs in our imagining and imaginative constructs.[70]

The Contemporary Theoretical Context

In the contemporary context, different hermeneutical assumptions are possible. No one worldview has become so universal in its intellectual and emotional appeal that it has become a "given" and directs unconsciously the way that we think and act. One assumption would essentially ignore the entire history of hermeneutics. It would avoid theoretical questions or attempt to give an intellectual basis for an approach that ignores historical consciousness. E. D. Hirsch, Jr. represents this position. His purpose in *Validity in Interpretation* is to show that meaning is to be separated from the historical being of the reader. The determinacy of meaning is a result of the author's will because verbal meaning is what the author has willed to convey by a particular sequence of linguistic signs.[71]

Within the hermeneutic tradition, which takes historical consciousness seriously, scholars like Jürgen Habermas and Karl-Otto Apel attempt to maintain a critical (or metacritical) approach by critical (or metacritical) approaches to Enlightenment rationalism while moving away from Enlightenment ideals of timeless certainty. These scholars do not deny that truth always and of necessity exceeds method, but they posit some kind of provisional notion of the universal that is then used as basis for a metacriticism that is able to acknowledge and contain the relativity of Enlightenment rationalism. Paul Ricoeur has contrasted the work of the Frankfurt philosopher Jürgen Habermas with the work of Gadamer.

---

[70]See Edgar V. McKnight, *Postmodern Use of the Bible: The Emergence of Reader-Oriented Criticism* (Nashville: Abingdon, 1988) 266.

[71]E. D. (Eric Donald) Hirsch, *Validity in Interpretation* (New Haven CT: Yale University Press, 1967) 3, 67. Elliott E. Johnson has defended the work of Hirsch as a theoretical model for biblical interpretation in *Expository Hermeneutics: An Introduction* (Grand Rapids MI: Academie, 1990) 54-69. See Edgar V. McKnight, *The Bible and the Reader: An Introduction to Literary Criticism* (Philadelphia: Fortress Press, 1985) 94-100, for a fuller discussion and criticism of the work of Hirsch.

Gadamer's pathway of hermeneutics reflects an "ascending" pathway that ignores the methodological status of the human sciences to such an extent that they have no role in the discovery of truth. Habermas's approach, in contrast, constitutes a "descending" pathway that involves the sciences and leads toward an epistemology of methods.[72]

Habermas has provided different ways of conceiving of a metacritical perspective from which critical activities of the human subject may be understood. In *Knowledge and Human Interests*, Habermas distinguished between three different levels of cognitive interests: technical, practical, and emancipatory. "The approach of the empirical-analytic sciences incorporates a *technical* cognitive interest; that of the historical-hermeneutical sciences incorporates a *practical* one; the approach of critically oriented sciences incorporates the *emancipatory* cognitive interest. . . . "[73] The technical level is the level seeking freedom from the resistance and capriciousness of nature. Here there is a human interest satisfied by science's supplying us with food, shelter, and so on. The practical level seeks freedom to be in contact with the past and one's contemporaries. The interest here is in access to meanings and opinions that can form the basis for cooperative effort.

Technical, empirical, or positivistic knowledge, then, is only one type of knowledge. This knowledge answers only instrumental interests and is related in a dialectical fashion to the "practical" knowledge involving interests of interpersonal understanding and social cooperation. Habermas finds a place for a metacriticism, a transcendental critique. The "interest" governing this transcendental critique is emancipatory. That is, it combines social theory and practice in a way to provide liberation "from dependence on hypostatized powers. Self-reflection is determined by an *emancipatory cognitive interest*."[74]

The question as to how engagement in specific social struggles can be identified with universal conditions of knowledge remained a problem in *Knowledge and Human Interests*, and in *The Theory of Communicative Action*, Habermas developed a linguistic-behavioral paradigm to attempt to transform the question. The interpersonal understanding and cooperative behavior of the life world demands a standpoint that transcends the

---

[72]"History and Hermeneutics," *Journal of Philosophy* 73 (1976): 683-95.
[73]Jurgen Habermas, *Knowledge and Human Interests*, trans. Jeremy J. Shapiro, 2nd ed. (London: Heinemann Educational, 1978) 308.
[74]Ibid., 310.

contextual-behavioral features. Remaining at the level of life world, we are under the illusion that language conveys only its surface meaning, that language is transparent. This is a hermeneutic of innocence. A more comprehensive system of language and social practice provides a frame or dimension for ideology and social critique.[75]

The conceptualization provided by Habermas is one that correlates the various levels and sorts of study and knowledge. Roy J. Howard suggests that the three areas of interest uncovered by Habermas ("appropriation by work, communication, and the practice of critique") characterize any particular society. The emancipatory interest of critical hermeneutics is the main one because of its capacity to include the other two in its research. Howard's summary shows both the power and remaining challenge of Habermas' conceptualization:

> The natural sciences methodologically exclude the subjective level of interest from their work, and they are right to do so. . . . The historico-philological sciences aim at the elucidation of a past or foreign interest. They, too, are right to discount the interests of the researcher himself. . . . Only a philosophy anchored in the social sciences can have a methodology that can contain and reflect back the interests of the researcher himself. Only this approach would, in short, have the power of self-reflection. Since, as Marx showed, there is no such thing as interest-free . . . knowledge, the critical need now is to find a method of knowledge whereby the governing interests can be exposed, held to account, and corrected in the interests of truth, justice, and freedom.[76]

Karl-Otto Apel, like Habermas, seeks to expand and not to undermine traditional epistemology. Before Habermas's *The Theory of Communicative Action*, Apel had expounded a three-dimensional conceptualization involving "scientistics," "hermeneutics," and "the critique of ideology." The first two correspond to the familiar "explanation" and "understanding." Apel finds these two complementary, with empirical data constituted in the context of particular "language games." The critique of ideology is the part of Apel's conceptualization dealing with emancipation from ideological impediments to understanding. In this part of his work Apel seeks to enlarge Kant's transcendental question about preconditions for the possibility of knowledge. Defining his philosophy as "transcendental-

---

[75]Jurgen Habermas, *The Theory of Communicative Action: The Critique of Functionalist Reason*, 2 vols. (Cambridge: Polity Press, 1984 and 1987).

[76]*Three Faces of Hermeneutics*, 119.

pragmatic philosophy," Apel will, like Kant, understand the necessary conditions of rational subjectivity as such. In opposition to Kant, Apel holds that subjectivity as such is not solitary but is necessarily intersubjective with an essential relationship to others. Validation has to do with communities of conversation. A claim to validity includes the claim that reasons can be given that command the assent of others. The claim to validity, then, is an offer to communicate and argue. Hermeneutical rationality, the capacity to understand the thoughts of other subjects is presupposed by scientific and practical reason.[77]

Apel, then, seeks a transcendental dimension that is not merely contextually internal to particular societies but will allow a critique of particular societies. Apel here is dependent upon a hypothesis of universal commensurability whereby languages are intertranslatable and "language games" overlap, merge, fall apart, and reintegrate. The historically constituted life form of a given society (language) is "not only the normatively binding 'institution of institutions,' . . . it is also the 'meta-institution' of all dogmatically established institutions. As a *meta*institution, it represents the instance of criticism for all unreflected social norms, and . . . it does not abandon the individual persons to their merely subjective reasoning."[78]

Wolfhart Pannenberg finds a modified version of Hegel's philosophy of history useful for development of a unitary theory of knowledge and a universal foundation for knowledge that transcends particular and contingent expressions of knowledge. Pannenberg acknowledges human historical finitude and the hermeneutical dimensions of understanding involved in knowledge. But, as E. Frank Tupper summarizes his work, Pannenberg finds it essential "to develop a conception of universal history which . . . would preserve the finitude of human experience, the openness of the future, and the intrinsic validity of the particular."[79]

---

[77]"Types of Rationality Today: The Continuum of Reason between Science and Ethics," *Rationality Today*, Proceedings of the International Symposium on Rationality Today Held at the University of Ottawa, October 27-30, 1977, ed. Theodore F. Geraets (Ottawa: Ottawa University Press, 1979) 315.

[78]Karl-Otto Apel, *Toward a Transformation of Philosophy*, trans. Glyn Adey and David Fisby, foreword by Pol Vandevelde, Marquette Studies in Philosophy 20 (Milwaukee: Marquette University Press, 1998) 119.

[79]E. Frank Tupper, *The Theology of Wolfhart Pannenberg* (Philadelphia: Westminster, 1973) 121.

For Pannenberg, paralleling Hegel, God reveals God's self indirectly in the whole of historical reality as the reality that destines everything for God's future. Pannenberg rejects a personalistic interventionist view of a direct revelation of God's self in history as he indicates that it is history itself as a whole that is God's revelation. For an insight into how revelation can occur since it is history in its totality that is revelation, Pannenberg uses the Jewish expectation of God's ending of history in a final judgment and the resurrection of Jesus Christ:

> It is only in the course of this history brought about by Jahweh that this tribal God proves himself to be the one true God. This proof will be made in the strict and ultimate sense only at the end of all history. However, in the fate of Jesus, the end of history is experienced in advance as an anticipation.[80]

For Pannenberg the key is the future that is still hidden from the world but already revealed in Jesus. "Pannenberg poses a conception of universal history wherein the end of history, which gathers history into a whole, is only known provisionally: the eschatological activity and destiny of Jesus of Nazareth constitutes the prolepsis of the *eschaton* wherein the meaning of the entirety of history is anticipated."[81] Biblical exegesis must move to the question of how the biblical texts have conceived of the self-disclosure in history of God as the all-determining reality, what this idea achieved historically in the biblical period toward the mastery of reality, and the normative nature of this biblical concept of faith for later epochs of Christianity.[82]

---

[80]*Revelation as History*, ed. Wolfhart Pannenberg with Rolf Rendtorff, Trutz Rendtorff, and Ulrich Wilkens, trans. David Granskou (New York: Macmillan, 1968) 134.

[81]Tupper, *The Theology of Wolfhart Pannenberg*, 121.

[82]A move is possible that parallels the efforts of E. D. Hirsch, Jr. at the skeptical pole. It has been characterized by one of its most able advocates as the transformation of hermeneutics from a way of knowing to a way of coping (Richard Rorty, *Philosophy and the Mirror of Nature* [corr. repr.: Princeton: Princeton University Press, 1980; ¹1979] 356). Epistemological skepticism may be turned into ontology. A universal claim would then be made not only for the absence of a means of achieving knowledge on a level transcending particular social groups but also for the absence of any such level of knowledge. Anthony Thiselton has compared the attitude of scholars such as Rorty and scholars such as Habermas and Apel by showing that they represent different reactions to the loss of the ideal of "some absolutized foundationalism outside time, place, and history." Rorty places a priority on "historical contingency and contextualism," while his opponents see a "positive dialectical relation between contextual contingency and ongoing metacritical exploration and testing in the form of an open system." The problem is the "possibility of such a system in which neither contingent life-world nor explanatory system has the

Reader-Oriented Literary Approaches

At the same time that continental scholars in the hermeneutical tradition were attempting to correlate explanation, understanding, and metacriticism, a move was being made by American scholars to transform biblical study in general and hermeneutics in particular into a form of literary criticism, more particularly a form of reading understood in terms of literary conventions. Reader-oriented literary criticism (rather than a philosophical metacriticism) changes the perspective taken in regard to the philosophical and theological assumptions discussed to this point. But popular assumptions concerning literary criticism and literary meanings have problematized appreciation and uses of literary approaches in biblical studies in general and in biblical hermeneutics in particular.

Formal theories of literary criticism (including American New Criticism) became dominant in the mid-twentieth century. Reader-oriented theories developed against the background of formal theories in which the literary work became its own world that transcended the facts of composition, the imitated universe, the nature and character of the author, and the effect on the audience. From the perspective of New Criticism, the literary text is "closed." The text is autonomous and is not to be contaminated by extrinsic factors, such as history. But the ideal reader is also "closed" or autonomous. The variability of readers' responses, therefore, was viewed negatively in New Criticism. "Subjective" and "idiosyncratic" responses of readers were suspect and to be discounted.

When one move is made in the conceptualization of the composition of the literary work, the new-critical dogma may be affirmed and transcended—the inclusion of the reader as an indispensable ingredient in literature. By the 1960s in America, New Criticism was being reconceptualized. Edgar Lohner reacted to the intrinsic method of New Criticism from within the new-critical tradition. He asked: "How can a critic communicate, in terms that are universally valid, the result of an act of comprehension which can be realized only individually and subjectively?" Lohner reconciled the claims for the autonomy of the literary work with claims for the cognitive value of the work by a definition of the ontological status of a work of art that includes the reader. He affirmed

---

last word, but contribute to some interactive whole" (*New Horizons in Hermeneutics*, 401).

that "the literary work of art exists essentially within the triad of poet, work, and reader" and that the literary work of art "forever remains essentially dependent upon its comprehension by a reader." Because the work of art includes the reader, criticism must ask about the mind of the reader and about the nature of the act resulting in the literary work of art and the process of understanding.[83]

As reader-oriented theories and practices influenced American literary criticism and biblical criticism beginning in the middle of the century, earlier European developments were transported to America and became important. In these earlier developments methods of correlating history, the literary text, and the reader had been explored. In the late 1920s, long before reader-oriented approaches in America transformed the new-critical paradigm, Russian formalism as a whole had integrated the formalist view of a literary work with history and with individual literary response. The formalist view of the literary work as an organized whole influenced the way scholars such as Jurij Tanjanov and Jan Mukarovsky related culture and the individual to the literary work. Tynjanov viewed literature as a system standing in correlation with other systems that define literature. Literature in general and specific works of literature, therefore, are influenced by changes in culture. The individual was first seen by Tynjanov and Mukarovsky as defined by culture, but Mukarovsky eventually shifted attention from impersonal cultural codes to human beings as the subject and ultimate source of aesthetic interaction. The individual is then seen as the crucial aspect of aesthetic interaction. The reader is no longer an irrelevant individual superimposing private associations upon a social meaning but an active force who is indispensable to meaning from the beginning.[84]

The phenomenological tradition conceives of the literary work of art in such a way as to emphasize the role of the reader. In the phenomenological approach of Roman Ingarden, the work of art itself was distinguished from the work as an aesthetic object that is constituted or concretized through the intentional act of reading. The complexity of a

---

[83]Edgar Lohner, "The Intrinsic Method: Some Reconsiderations," *The Disciplines of Criticism: Essays in Literary Theory, Interpretation, and History,* ed. Peter Demetz, Thomas Greene, and Lowry Nelson, Jr. (New Haven CT and London: Yale University Press, 1968) 168, 170.

[84]See McKnight, *The Bible and the Reader: An Introduction to Literary Criticism* (Philadelphia: Fortress Press, 1985) 17-25, for a discussion of the work of Tynjanov and Mukarovsky.

literary work and its apprehension is such that the reader cannot give himself or herself equally to all of the components of the total apprehension. Only a few of the multiplicity of experienced and interwoven acts become central. The rest are only coexperienced. This means that there is constant change with regard to which component acts are central at any particular moment. The same literary work is apprehended, then, in various changing "aspects."[85]

Wolfgang Iser emphasized the process by which a reader actualizes a text. The work of Iser is to be seen in the hermeneutical tradition but more directly in the phenomenological tradition of Ingarden. Iser is concerned with the formulation of "a theory of aesthetic response" that "has its roots in the text."[86] Iser makes the "gaps" and completion of "gaps" by the reader a central factor in literary communication. A text is seen as a system of processes whereby language is broken up and reconstituted. The place where language is broken and reconstituted is marked by gaps which the reader must complete and blanks which the reader must fill in. Communication begins when the reader fills in the blanks and bridges the gaps.

Reader-response approaches see the result of reading not only in terms of interpretation or the specification of meaning but in terms of an effect upon the reader. This is visualized in different ways. Jonathan Culler, for example, suggests that the process of reading shows the reader the problems of the reader's condition as maker and reader of signs, and this is the meaning of the work.[87] Iser sees the process of reading as the coming together of text and imagination. It is an experience of continual modification closely akin to our experience in life. Because of the nature of the process the "reality" of the experience of reading illuminates the basic pattern of real experiences.[88] Georges Poulet emphasizes the achievement of self-transcendence in reading. In reading, the object of the reader's thought is the thought of another. Yet it is the reader who is the subject in the act of reading. The subject exists in the work. In reading

---

[85]See ibid., 26-36, for a discussion of the work of Ingarden.

[86]Wolfgang Iser, *The Act of Reading: A Theory of Aesthetic Response* (London: Routledge & Kegan Paul; Baltimore: Johns Hopkins University Press, 1978) x.

[87]"Literary Competence," in *Reader-Response Criticism: From Formalism to Post-Structuralism*, ed. Jane P. Tompkins (Baltimore: Johns Hopkins University Press, 1980) 116-17.

[88]"The Reading Process: A Phenomenological Approach," in *Reader-Response Criticism: From Formalism to Post-Structuralism*, 56.

there is a movement beyond the objective elements of a work with the purpose (or at least result) of criticism's elevation "to the apprehension of a subjectivity without objectivity."[89]

The practice of deconstruction is perhaps the practice that is most radical in its involvement of the reader. Its beginnings may be seen with Roland Barthes's emphasis upon the reader and the possibilities the text offers readers to arrive at satisfying plural meanings. In debate with French structuralists' attempt to find an abstract or deep-level structure that explains the surface-level narrative, Barthes declared that the task of seeing "all the world's stories . . . within a single structure" is not only an exhausting task, "it is also an ultimately undesirable task, for the text thereby loses its difference." The structure of the text is such that it involves the reader in a process of analysis without a final synthesis or end. The text is like a group of threads braided together to form a core. The material for the textual braid is a group of codes, existing in a linear and in a nonlinear relationship. The code of actions is the familiar linear sequence that moves the story along. The hermeneutic code gives the dynamics of the text a paradoxical nature by arresting the enigma and keeping it open. The code of actions and the hermeneutic code operate together on the linear level within the constraints of time, but other codes establish connections that are permutable and reversable. The aim of decoding for Barthes is not the determination of a final denotation. Just as there is no narrative structure, grammar, or logic that serves as the final base of the text, there is no final denotation. Reading does not result in a final synthesis of the codes.[90]

The work of Jacques Derrida takes advantage of the openness of the text to allow readers to make their mark on the text. Derrida's deconstructive approach to literature is concerned with the examination of the desire for master—the mastery of knowledge through language and the mastery of meaning through interpretation—and the subversion of that desire through the very nature of language itself. The logic and language that form the resources of an author cannot be dominated absolutely by an author. The author uses them by being governed by them. A deconstructive reader seeks to discover relationships between what the author

---

[89]"Criticism and the Experience of Interiority," in *Reader-Response Criticism: From Formalism to Post-Structuralism*, 46-47.

[90]Roland Barthes, *S/Z*, trans. Richard Miller (London: Jonathan Cape, 1975) 3, 92.

commands and what the author does not command of the patterns of language used by the author.[91]

In a statement reminiscent of Roland Barthes, Derrida says that the text

> always reserves a surprise for the anatomy or physiology of a critique which might think it had mastered its game, surveying all its threads at once, thus deceiving itself into wishing to look at the text without touching it, without putting its hand to the "object," without venturing to add to it.[92]

Gary Phillips has shown the continuing importance of the text and conventional readings for the practice of deconstruction. Readers show their indebtedness in a hands-on, face-to-face encounter with the text in which the independence of the text is affirmed. Key to deconstruction is

> the recognition that readers are fundamentally indebted to texts and that texts preserve an independence over against readers and any interest they may bring to their reading . . . Readers show respect for the alterity of the text by writing upon it, by applying a "countersignature" to the text. In this way readers supplement and thereby affirm their indebtedness as well as the independence of the text every time they "sign on."[93]

Phillips emphasizes that the Other of the text (what lies beyond the text, the event that escapes human control) "interrupts the critical effort to limit the potential of texts to mean in different ways" and that "the Other is never reducible to a particular meaning. Deconstructive reading points to the rigorous encounter with the Other that somehow 'precedes', 'lies beyond' or 'intersects' the text and the significance it produces."[94] For deconstruction to enable this encounter with the Other, however, it must first of all disclose what the text says as a sign-signal in its reference to the world. Derrida emphasized the conventional reading of a text as "an indispensable guard rail" or "safeguard."[95] Traditional

---

[91]Jacques Derrida, *Of Grammatology*, trans. Gayatri Chakravorty Spivak (Baltimore: Johns Hopkins University Press, 1976) 158).

[92]Jacques Derrida, *Positions*, trans. and annotated by Alan Bass (Chicago: University of Chicago Press, 1981; orig. 1972) 71.

[93]"The Ethics of Reading Deconstructively, or Speaking Face to Face," in *The New Literary Criticism and the New Testament*, ed. Edgar V. McKnight and Elizabeth Struthers Malbon (Sheffield: Sheffield Academic Press; Valley Forge PA: Trinity Press International, 1994) 284.

[94]Ibid., 186-87.

[95]Jacques Derrida, *Limited Inc.* (Evanston IL: Northwestern University Press, 1988)

reading, then, is necessary for deconstruction: "To recognize and respect all its classical exigencies is not easy and requires all the instruments of traditional criticism. Without this recognition and this respect, critical production would risk developing in any direction at all and authorize itself to say almost anything"[96]

Conclusion

In the hermeneutical tradition we have seen a critique of a scientific correspondence (or semantic) view of truth, a move beyond a limited tautological level of truth to levels where the text is read as founded upon or referring in some fashion or another to contingent human experience *and* to transcendent levels that impinge upon human existence. When we move beyond the tautological system of truth, however, we are at sea and must discover and create systems that allow us to make sense that is satisfying. Toward the end of *Symbolism of Evil*, Recoeur asks how we are able to get beyond the "circle of hermeneutics." Ricoeur says that this is possible by "transforming it into a *wager*." He says that he wagers that he will have a better understanding of humans and of all beings "if I follow the *indication* of symbolic thought. That wager then becomes the task of *verifying* my wager and saturating it, so to speak, with intelligibility."[97] The same sort of process is involved in the formulation of a theoretical or metacritical system within which references and methods are postulated and sense is made.

The hermeneutical tradition provides some resources for formulation of a theoretical model and for use of different approaches within the model. A beginning point might be the insight that life in all of its manifestations is not finally divided into completely unrelated parts. There is a relationship between all of the different ways that we view the reference of cultural works in general and literary texts in particular

---

141.
[96]*Of Grammatology*, 158, See Phillips, 289.
[97]Paul Ricoeur, *The Symbolism of Evil*, trans. Emerson Buchanan (Boston: Beacon Press, 1967) 355. In "Metaphor and the Central Problem of Hermeneutics" (in Ricoeur, *Hermeneutics and the Human Sciences: Essays on Language, Action, and Interpretation*, ed., trans., and intro. by John B. Thompson [Cambridge: Cambridge University Press, 1981] 175.) Ricoeur affirms that understanding a text at the level of its articulation of sense and understanding a metaphorical statement are alike. In both cases "the construction takes the form of a wager or guess." He says that while there are no rules for making good guesses, there are methods for validating our guesses.

(between the different "language games" we use to make sense). When we remain in one system, verifying meaning and truth within the framework of that system, the meaning we discover and create is actually related to meaning in other systems. The meaning we find is valid, but it becomes richer and fuller in relation to other truths and meanings.

Schleiermacher's movement back and forth from such things as language in general and the language of the author of the literary text, the parts of a work and the whole of a work, the critical and the affective, and the intention of the author and the intention of the reader may be a model. Meaning or meaningfulness is experienced in a prereflective moment in a unified fashion. It is explicated in reflection in terms of different critical assumptions and methods (different language games). Different critical and noncritical moves may enable us to come closer to the prereflective unified understanding so that we are able to recover meanings that escape even the author. A comprehensive model for understanding and interpretation based on the model of Schleiermacher is not built up simply from objective-type systems and levels of meaning. Such systems play their part but cannot be allowed to become the gate-keeper to all truth. Praxis will be coordinated with theory, so the community within which truth and meaning is sought is important and will be acknowledged in a comprehensive model. The dynamic literary and theological competence of the community and individuals in the community means that the system will be dynamic and capable of change in the process of life. A hermeneutical approach, then, does not present a last word in terms of textual meaning or in terms of relationship between the life world and transcending explanatory systems. Contingent life world is a given as is a transcendent (metacritical) standpoint that is in dynamic correlation with the contingent life world.

Believers are provided resources for understanding their faith, correlating this understanding with systems that map the biblical text onto the life world, and experiencing a transcendent Word in actualizing the biblical text. In a prereflexive experience of the world of things and of human being, we experience the sacred, as the sacred and the life-world are a unity. In the reflexive moment of mapping the biblical text onto the life-world, we implicitly deal with the sacred. We need not identify the sacred with human historical experiences and thereby reduce the sacred to the life-world in order to affirm the sacrality of historical experience. In the mapping of the biblical text onto the sacred, we need not reduce (or enlarge) the sacred to the transcendent ideal world so that the historical is irrelevant, with its truth being its ideality and not its reality. God's being in the world in relation to persons and things is an essential part of the definition of God. In the reflexive (and secondary) movement we may utilize the "language of beings" to serve as a model for a "language of Being."

In our day, with the introduction of literary resources for understanding both Bible and theology we may find poetic or literary resources helpful, bypassing some of the hermeneutical thicket. The question is, then: How can we imagine the activity of God, the Kingdom of God? The conceptualization of ultimacy is then the result of the imaginative work of readers "in front of" the text. But we need not despair of any loss in the turn to the literary. The believer is no less able to claim a relationship of the imaginative construction to reality than is the historian or social scientist who attribute reality to their abstractions. The poetic construction of the divine is, in fact, a more satisfying conceptualization of God than that in more dogmatic views. Deity is viewed not as God is in God's self nor as the unmoved mover, nor as other forms in which God is some static force essentially unrelated to world and humans. God—as well as humans and world—is defined in terms of dynamic relationship.

Chapter 6

The Precritical Horizon
and the Original Quest

This chapter and the following chapter attempt to account for the critical reception of the Jesus tradition. They do more than give an account of the so-called three quests of the historical Jesus. They look at the stories behind those quests, the philosophical, theological, historical, and literary stories that not only make sense of the quests but allow us to enter into a contemporary quest. They also deal with the question of the proper stance for the church if it wishes to remain in touch with contemporary critical approaches *and* with the Jesus of the Christian tradition.

The Precritical Horizon for Jesus Study

Harmonizing: The Fourth Gospel as Template. A cursory glance at the Gospels could lead to the conclusion that it is a fairly easy task to write a full and accurate account of the life and teaching of Jesus. After all, there are four accounts in the New Testament. Two of the accounts (Matthew and John) bear the names of disciples who had been with Jesus and who (it is thought) doubtless gave complete, accurate reports of their experiences. Even the other two Gospels, according to tradition, are directly dependent upon earlier reports (Mark dependent upon Peter and Luke upon Paul). The task is simply to arrange the materials of the Gospels into a unified story, a "harmony." The Christian also brings to the reading of the Gospels a concept of Jesus from religious tradition; the church's proclamation of Jesus Christ as Lord and the carefully developed doctrines of the church naturally influence the concept of Jesus gained in a reading of the Gospels.

The task (assuming the authorship of the Gospels by eyewitnesses and the authority of the church) is to organize the material of the Gospels into one harmonious account and to paraphrase, explain, and apply the materials for the benefit of the faithful. This was basically the method of the ancients. The title of one of the most important harmonies, that by the Reformed theologian Andreas Osiander (1498–1552) in the sixteenth century, describes the method used: *Greek and Latin Gospel Harmony in Four Books, in Which the Gospel Story Is Combined according to the Four Evangelists in Such a Way that No Word of Any One of Them Is Omitted, No Foreign Word Added, the Order of None of Them Is Disturbed, and Nothing Is Displaced, in Which, However, the Whole Is Marked by Letters and Signs Which Permit One to See at a First Glance the Points Peculiar to Each Evangelist, Those Which He Has in Common with the Others, and with Which of Them.*[1]

The harmonizing of the Gospels and the interpretation of the resultant story of Jesus in prose, poetry, and drama continued into the eighteenth and nineteenth centuries—and continue among many Christians today— and the values of such an approach must not be ignored. Although there are values that derive from the precritical approach to the Gospels and the life of Jesus, it is impossible for a student who is acquainted with the true nature of the Gospels and their witness to Jesus Christ to follow this method. The Gospels are not simple biographies of Jesus written for historical purposes by the original disciples of Jesus; rather, they are religious writings produced a generation after the earthly Jesus to serve the life and faith of the early church. Critical methods have been developed for moving through the tradition of the Gospels to the earthly Jesus, but the precritical understandings form the horizon against which those critical methods were developed and used.

One result of the harmonizing method was to make the Fourth Gospel the template for the Jesus tradition. The synoptic material can more easily be inserted in at least a superficial way into the outline of the Fourth Gospel than vice versa. As we have seen, the Gospels contain both materials that are theological in nature and materials that are historical in nature. Scholars today have concluded that the Fourth Gospel is more of a theological interpretation of the nature of Jesus as the Word of God than it is a source of historical data. When the outline of the Fourth Gospel with its theological interpretation is made the basic pattern, the his-

---

[1]*Harmoniae Euangelicae libri IIII graece et latine: in quibus Euangelica historia ex quatuor euangelistis ita in unum est contexta, ut nullius uerbu[m] ullum omissum, nihil alienum immixtum, nullius ordo turbatus, nihil non suo loco positum: omnia uero literis & notis ita distincta sint, ut quid cuiusq[ue] euangelistae proprium, quid cum aliis, & cum quibus commune sit, primo statim aspectu deprehendere queas. Item annotationum liber unus elenchus harmoniae* (Basel, 1537).

torical data of the synoptic Gospels tends to be overpowered by the theological.

The methods of biblical interpretation in the precritical period essentially reinforced theological uses of the Gospels that relativized attention to the historicity of Jesus. In fact, in the earliest period no distinction was made between the Bible and theology. (With such a distinction, theology is seen as a second-order discourse depending upon a prior critical understanding of scripture.) There was a direct application of Bible reading to theology and practice. The terminology reflects the relationship between the Bible and theology. Terms such as "Sacred Scripture," "Scared Knowledge," and "Divine Pages" were used in place of "Theology."[2] Augustine's (354–430) treatise on biblical interpretation was called "On Christian Doctrine." When Peter Abelard (1079–1142) used the term "theology" as the title of a work on Christian dogma in its entirety, the modern use of the term was established.

Irenaeus: History, Allegory, and Typology. Biblical interpretation and theological reading of the Bible (to whatever extent they can be distinguished in the early period) were one in that they began with a Christology from above (the preexistent Word) and interpreted the earthly Jesus in terms of the Christ of faith. Explication of the different patterns of such Christological interpretation began with Irenaeus of Lyon (ca. 130–ca. 200) who was forced to give attention to the question of the interpretation of the Bible by movements in Gnosticism. The Gnostics denied or devalued the Hebrew scriptures and the creator God of those scriptures and separated the Messiah from the Christian God. In Irenaeus' refutation of the Gnostics, we see methods that examine scripture in light of (1) the temporal context of that scripture, (2) later historical contexts (as type), and (3) a higher rational or intelligible order of immutable reality (as allegory).

A central issue for Irenaeus and orthodox Christianity was the authenticity and meaning of the Hebrew scriptures. All three methods maintain the value of the Hebrew Scriptures. Irenaeus indicates, first of all, that the Hebrew scriptures have value in their own right. The Jews, declares Irenaeus in *Against Heresies* 4.15.1, had "a law, a course of discipline, and a prophecy of future things." "Law" refers to the "natural" law that remains in force for Christians. "Course of discipline" refers to the

---

[2]Yves Congar, "Theology: Christian Theology," *The Encyclopedia of Religion*, 16 vols., ed. Mircea Eliade et al. (New York: Macmillan, 1987) 14:455.

Mosaic law and practices required by that law. "Prophecy" indicates in part instruction appropriate for the Jews. But prophecy also involves significance beyond instruction to the Jews, a significance gained through a view of scripture as the story of human progress from creation to redemption and the accompanying typological method of interpretation. Irenaeus's idea of salvation history focused on the story of the incarnate Word of God active in creation and in the history of Israel. Jesus was the Word of God incarnate. The incarnation involves Jesus' virgin birth; his life of obedience; his death, resurrection, and ascension; and his coming at the end of the ages.[3]

Irenaeus also used another method, an allegorical method that distinguishes between the perceptible order of sense appearance and a higher level of reality. When Moses constructed the tabernacle according to the pattern shown on the mountain, for example, he not only foreshadowed Christ, he was instructing the people as well "calling them to the things of primary importance by means of those which were secondary; that is, to things that are real, by means of those that are typical; and by things temporal, to eternal; and by the carnal to the spiritual; and by the earthly to the heavenly."[4]

The struggle of the early church in Christology was to maintain a relationship between Jesus Christ and God the Father in light of a Platonic view of God as omnipotent, omnipresent, and omniscient. Irenaeus was able to maintain the human and the divine in Jesus by means of a view of humankind with the potentiality of growing toward God. He took the story in Genesis of the creation of humans in the image and likeness of God to mean not that Adam and Eve were created perfect, but that they were created with the potentiality of growing toward God (this potentiality was the "image") with the goal of achieving the glory of closeness (this was the "likeness"). The first attempt to create humans in the image and likeness of God failed, but in Christ God succeeded. In the case of Christ, Irenaeus said that "the Word . . . having become united with the ancient substance of Adam's formation, rendered man living and perfect,

---

[3]See Rowan A. Greer, "The Christian Bible and Its Interpretation," in James L. Kugel and Rowan A. Greer, *Early Biblical Interpretation* (Philadelphia: Westminster Press, 1986) 156, 171-74.

[4]*Against Heresies* 4.14.3. See Greer, "The Christian Bible and Its Interpretation," 173.

receptive of the perfect Father, in order that as in the natural [Adam] we all were dead, so in the spiritual we may all be made alive."[5]

Origen and the Alexandrians. In the work of Origen of Alexandria (ca. 185–ca. 254) and Theodore of Mopsuestia in Antioch (ca. 350–ca. 428) and their successors we see the conscious elaboration of methods of Irenaeus (allegory and typology) that are opposed to each other, Origen and the Alexandrians elaborating an allegorical method and Theodore and the Antiochenes elaborating a typological method. Origen made a fundamental distinction between the letter and the spirit, between the obvious narrative meaning of the biblical text and a mysterious spiritual meaning. This distinction correlates with the Platonic distinction between the intelligible order and the perceptible order. Both narrative meaning and spiritual meaning are to be found in most passages of scripture. The impossibility of discerning narrative meaning in certain passages, however (anthropomorphic expressions referring to God, for example), demands spiritual meaning. Rowan A. Greer points out that Origen's method does not in fact reject typology because Origen retains the teleological character of the Christian story. The end is to be distinguished from the beginning that it resembles. The pattern of the heavenly tabernacle revealed to Moses on the Mount, for example, corresponds to earthly tabernacles (the one in the wilderness, the temple in Jerusalem). But the "shadow" of the temple points forward in a typological fashion to the "image" of the church. This "image" is in its turn a type of the true tabernacle that signifies the ultimate destiny of the rational beings.[6]

Origen's Christology began with the divine Wisdom understood not abstractly or impersonally but as a living personal being (hypostasis). This Wisdom is eternally generated by God. That is, God the Father never existed without generating this Wisdom. Christ, then, is coeternal with the Father. This Wisdom is also called the Word as she interprets the secrets of the mind. Origin was not a docetist for he stressed that Jesus had a human soul that had always been united with the Word (for Origen, all creatures had immortal souls. That is, they will live forever in the future as they have lived forever in the past). Origen's famous simile of iron heated in a fire shows how the human soul is divine in its actions:

---

[5]*Against Heresies* 5.1.3. See John Macquarrie, *Jesus Christ in Modern Thought* (London: SCM Press, 1990) 153-55.

[6]Greer, "The Christian Bible and Its Interpretation," 180.

If . . . a mass of iron be kept constantly in the fire, receiving the heat through all its pores and veins, and the fire being continuous and the iron never removed from it, it becomes wholly converted into the latter. . . . In this way, then, that soul which, like an iron in the fire, has been perpetually placed in the Word, and perpetually in the Wisdom, and perpetually in God, is God in all that it does, feels, and understands.[7]

Theodore and the Antiochenes. The approach of Origen and the Alexandrians may be described as a "descending" Christology. Theodore and the Antiochenes were concerned that Origen's allegorical approach would abolish the significance of the historical events recorded in scripture and that the "descending Christology" would abolish the true and complete humanity of Jesus. Theodore adhered to the idea of two different and successive historical dispensations or ages. The "contemporary needs" of the two different ages must be considered in interpretation. This historical view limited not only the allegorical reading but also the typological reading of the Old Testament as referring to Christ. The Hebrew scriptures know nothing of the Trinity, for example. Predictions of Christ in the Hebrew scriptures are practically eliminated. Only four of the psalms predict Christ; psalms traditionally thought of as predicting Christ merely used words that Christians find appropriate to the story of Christ. In the Prophets, moreover, no predictions of Christ are found, save Malachi's revival of David's prediction of Christ. Although Theodore takes most seriously the different historical situations of the two ages and emphasizes that the old dispensation fulfills a "contemporary need," he does see the old dispensation as establishing a type of the new dispensation "since it has a certain resemblance to it" and supplies "indications" of it. Typological use of the Hebrew scriptures, then, is recognized but it extends and does not replace the historical or narrative meaning. The narrative meaning is to be extended only when the text itself is metaphorical or when a typological interpretation is required.

Just as the rational and human in the scriptures were emphasized by Antioch so were the rational and human in Jesus. But the difference between the Antiochenes and the Alexandrians may be seen as one of emphasis rather than an essential conflict. R. V. Sellers indicates that the Alexandrians, "ever impressed by the thought that man's deification is the end of the work of Christ," saw in the incarnation "the elevation of our

---

[7]Origen *De Principiis* 2.6.6. See Macquarrie, *Jesus Christ in Modern Thought*, 156.

nature to the conditions of the divine life in the Person of the Logos."
The Antiochenes, emphasizing "the fundamental difference between the
uncreated and the created nature" saw in the incarnation "a Divine self-
emptying which operates only so far as human limitations will allow."[8]
The principle of the two natures played a part in the exegesis of the
Antiochenes. Sellers cites words of Theodoret, Bishop of Antioch, as a
rule followed by earlier and later Antiochenes: "We 'contemplate two
natures' in the Lord Christ, and 'apply to each its own properties'; we
ascribe the words of humiliation as to Man *hos anthropo*, and as to God
hos Theo, the God-befitting words of exaltation."[9] To the Godhead belong
the miracles and whatever is God-befitting; to the Man, belong the birth,
growth, suffering, and death. In exegesis the question is faced whether a
particular text, particularly a saying of Jesus, has to do with the divine or
with the human hypostasis.

Augustine and Aquinas. In the thirteenth century the tools for
speculation on the constitution of Christ changed from earlier logical
systems to the metaphysical system of Thomas Aquinas (1224/5–1274).
It was this dogmatic system of Scholasticism with its understanding of
revelation and reason against which the Enlightenment reacted. The
system of Scholasticism may be contrasted with the system of Augustine
of Hippo (354–430) that had reigned for a millennium. Augustine, of
course, followed Platonic or Neoplatonic thought and Thomas fitted the
prevailing Platonic-Augustinian ideas into a new system stamped by an
Aristotelian orientation.

The contrast between Augustine and Thomas may become clearer by
distinguishing the perspectives Augustine and Thomas had as to things.
For Augustine, things are considered in relation to God. To know things
is to know them in reference to God. For Thomas, things had their own
nature that did not consist of their reference to God. The approach of
Augustine is neatly formulated in the well-known phrases "understand
that you may believe" and "believe that you may understand."[10] St.
Thomas valued human reason in itself and saw human reason as capable
of securing a genuine knowledge of the world and the nature of things.

---

[8]R. V. Sellers, "The Antiochian School: Logos-anthropos Christology," in *The
Theology of Christ: Commentary: Readings in Christology*, ed. Ralph J. Tapia (New York:
Bruce Publishing Co., 1971) 123. Excerpted from R. V. Sellers, *The Council of
Chalcedon: A Historical and Doctrinal Survey* (London: S.P.C.K., 1953) 158-81.
   [9]Sellers, "The Antiochian School: Logos-anthropos Christology," 126.
   [10]*Sermons* 43.9.

To be sure, for Thomas the attainments of reason alone are finally inadequate. Revelation supplements reason. But the truths of revelation are not contrary to reason. Reason itself, moreover, can show the inadequacy of objections to the truths of revelation. Congar portrays the theological enterprise as seen by St. Thomas:

> To sum up, theology, as St. Thomas understood and practiced it, appears to us as a rational and scientific consideration of the revealed datum, striving to procure for the believing human spirit a certain understanding of the datum. It is, if you will, a scientifically elaborated copy of the faith. What objects of simply adherence the faith delivers, theology develops in a line of humanly constructed knowledge, seeking the reason for facts; in short, reconstructing and elaborating in the forms of human science the data received by faith from the science of God Who created all things. Thus through his spirit directed by faith, man arrives at a strictly *human* understanding of the mysteries, utilizing their connection or their harmony with his world of natural knowledge. He must radiate the revealed doctrine by his human psychology replete with all its legitimate and authentic acquisitions which, after all, are also a gift of God.[11]

The *Summa theologica* of Thomas illustrates the method of Scholasticism. A question was posed, the evidence cited (scripture, the opinions of the Fathers, philosophical arguments), the problem resolved through rational argument, and responses made to contrary opinions. In the *Summa*, St. Thomas studies the three "opinions" concerning the incarnation (the assumption of human nature by the Word, the "composite person," and the Word clothed with humanity) and shows that the first and third are heresies and the second is the true teaching of the Catholic faith. The key for St. Thomas's compromise between a view of the pure becoming of humankind and a view of the annihilation of the divine in the human was the view that "the Word descended into the human by taking the human to himself." Everything that must be attributed to Christ in accord with his condition as human is an *effective consequence* of the union of persons. "[T]he mystery of the Incarnation is considered as a condescension of the fullness of the godhead into human nature rather than as the promotion of human nature, already existing, as it were, to the godhead. Therefore in the man Christ there was perfection of spiritual life

---

[11]Yves M.-J. Congar, *A History of Theology* (Garden City NY: Doubleday, 1968) 102-103.

from the very beginning."[12] Following the delineation of the union of persons in the *Summa*, St.Thomas deals with the conditions in which the incarnation was realized—the theological problems of the life of Jesus from his conception through his ascension and the study of the Mother of God and of redemption.[13]

With the Reformers came a reaction to the speculations of the Scholastics. Philip Melanchthon (1497–1560) gave classic expression to this reaction: "The mysteries of the Godhead are not so much to be investigated as adored. It is useless to labor long on the high doctrines of God, his unity and trinity, the mystery of creation, the mode of incarnation. . . . To know Christ is to know his benefits, not to contemplate his natures and the modes of his incarnation."[14] John Macquarrie cites Melanchthon and then remarks, "This is true if one is preaching, but it is hardly a recipe for theology, and both Luther and Melanchthon soon went back to the Scholasticism which they professed to despise."[15] The ages-long classical Christology and the Scholastics' method of doing theology, therefore, was the immediate background for the new age of the Enlightenment in general and the approach to the life of Jesus in particular.

Reimarus and Lessing

Reimarus. The first phase of the critical study of the historical Jesus took place during and immediately following the Enlightenment. It is common to sketch the first phase as movement from Samuel Reimarus (1694–1768) to Albert Schweitzer (1875–1965). The scholars of this phase of this study worked against the vital horizon of Christian conviction that the New Testament was a faithful (even divinely inspired) account of the life and teaching of Jesus and that Jesus was the God-Man defined at Chalcedon in the fifth century. Albert Schweitzer characterizes the study in the first phase in this way:

> It set out in quest of the historical Jesus, believing that when it had found him it could bring him straight into our time as a Teacher and Saviour. It loosed the bands by which He had been riveted for centuries to the

---

[12]*Summa* 3a.34.1.1.
[13]*Summa* 3a.27-59.
[14]*Loci Communes*, ed. G. L. Plitt and Th. Kolde (Erlangen: A. Deichert, 1890) 60.
[15]John Macquarrie, *Jesus Christ in Modern Thought*, 171.

stony rocks of ecclesiastical doctrine, and rejoiced to see life and movement coming into the figure once more. . . .

Of course, Schweitzer continued with the declaration: "But He does not
stay; He passes by our time, and returns to His own."[16]

The rather positive characterization by Schweitzer of the agenda of
the initial critical quest is not valid for all scholars in the first period.
Reimarus, for example, portrayed Jesus as an unsuccessful would-be
reformer of the first century and Reimarus wanted to keep Jesus in that
context. His aim was to show that Christianity rested on historical
distortion. The quest began with Reimarus, therefore, as an anti-Christian
movement, with the agenda to show that Christian faith (as conceived by
Reimarus) could not be based on the real Jesus. In the initial quest, then,
some scholars began with the question of historicity and saw the whole
of Christianity toppled on the basis of historical questions. Other scholars
saw historical study as a way of recovering what had been lost to
Enlightenment rationality. Another group of scholars separated the
question of the significance of Jesus from the question of the historicity
of the Gospels and supported some form of Christological affirmation in
spite of historical problems.

The reigning philosopher in the time of Reimarus was Christian
Wolff (1679–1754), a transmitter and modernizer of the ideas of Gottfried
Wilhelm Leibniz (1646–1716) who forged a "middle way" between the
Scholastics and Reformed philosophers. It was against the Leibniz-
Wolffian philosophy that the more radical form of the German Enlightenment revolted. Wolff applied his philosophical ideas to the question of
revelation. For Wolff, possibility and necessity were keys for testing
reason. Revelation is not ruled out of the realm of possibility by
philosophy, but possibility does not mean actuality. For a particular
revelation to be actual it must be internally consistent and it must be
necessary—that is, it must contain knowledge not attainable by natural
means. On the basis of both of these criteria of Wolff, Reimarus judged
that the Gospels' presentation of Jesus Christ are falsified as revelation.[17]

---

[16]Albert Schweitzer, *The Quest of the Historical Jesus: A Critical Study of Its
Progress from Reimarus to Wrede*, trans. William Montgomery (repr.: New York:
Macmillan, 1968; =1910) 399.

[17]Reimarus is best known today for his position that revelation is displaced by reason.
That position was worked out in his secret writing entitled *Apologie oder Schutzschrift
für die vernunftigen Verehrer Gottes*. The entire work has never been published, but
enough of it has either been published or summarized for an idea of the whole to be

Natural reasons may be given for the story of Jesus, that is, that what Jesus taught about repentance and the kingdom of God comes from Judaism and that what the apostles taught is to be understood in natural terms as is their success in the missionary enterprise.

So revelation is not necessary, but it is really the criterion of freedom from internal contradictions that is used most effectively by Reimarus. The contradictions between the intention of Jesus and his disciples, the contradictions between the evidence for the resurrection in the different Gospels, contradictions between what was said about the parousia of Jesus and what actually happened, all of these invalidate the essentials of Christian teaching. Reimarus reconstructed Jesus as a pious Jew dedicated to the task of calling Israel to repent in light of the establishment of God's kingdom on earth. Jesus became obsessed with the idea that he could force God's hand through death as a martyr, but he died disillusioned with the God who had forsaken him. The Gospels, then, are not historical accounts but result from the ingenuity and duplicity of the disciples who proclaimed (for their own benefit) that Jesus had been raised from the dead and would return to establish the kingdom of God.

Reimarus concluded that the historical figure of Jesus must be understood in a nonsupernatural fashion and that the Gospels contain intentional fraud. Matthew's story of the guard at Jesus' tomb (28:11-15), according to Reimarus, serves to answer Jewish claims that the body of Jesus had indeed been stolen by the disciples. Reimarus suggested that the historical reality is that the disciples stole the body of Jesus because they had enjoyed being in the limelight with Jesus and did not relish the prospect of returning to working for their living and to face mockery after following a lost leader. Moreover, the disciples revised the record of the teachings of Jesus to make it appear that Jesus viewed himself as a suffering messiah who would be raised on the third day. The body of Jesus was stolen so that the disciples could claim that what Jesus had foretold had taken place. Some Old Testament texts were twisted to support the case of the disciples and the warning added that the world

---

gained. G. E. Lessing published seven fragments between 1774 and 1778 in 1850, Wilheim Kolse began publishing parts of the work in Niedner's *Zeitschrift für die historische Theologie*. Then in 1861–1862 David Friedrich Strauss summarized the entire work, gave a critical appraisal of it, and prefaced it with a biographical sketch of Reimarus (*Hermann Samuel Reimarus und seine Schutzschrift für die vernünftigen Verhrer Gottes*).

was to end shortly and that those who did not accept the message would burn in hell.

Reimarus's antireligious prejudices must not blind us to some important insights that have continued to influence the study of the historical Jesus. He distinguished between the historical value of the Synoptics and the theological interpretation of the Fourth Gospel. He recognized that the life of Jesus had undergone significant interpretation by his followers and that Christology was largely a process following the death of Jesus. Although he did not stress the apocalyptic aspect of the historical Jesus, he saw that Jesus was an apocalyptic visionary who entertained hopes of a future kingdom of God.

Lessing. The work of Reimarus was not published in his lifetime. It was published by the German critic and dramatist Gotthold Ephraim Lessing (1729–1781) who used the work of Reimarus to make his own position known. Of course, the reaction of orthodoxy was to attempt to refute Reimarus on the basis of revealed dogma and the denial of the rational approach. J. S. Semler refuted Reimarus from the point of view of moderate orthodoxy.[18] Lessing, however, responded in a different direction, by a division of the question of historical truth and rational truth and by the introduction of a historical dimension into the very concept of revelation (and not merely into its content) without denying its validity altogether. In fact, Lessing agreed with Reimarus that it is impossible to deny contradictions in the Gospels, for example, in the accounts of the resurrection. He showed, however, that contradictions among what were taken to be eyewitness accounts of the resurrection are consistent with eyewitness reports of other events. The obscurities and contradictions stressed by Reimarus point to the historically conditioned character of the Gospels and not to fraud.

Lessing denied, moreover, that the factual inaccuracies of the Bible constitute an argument against its divine inspiration. The certainty of Christianity does not depend on the infallibility of the Bible. Even if the Bible were infallible, it could not support Christian theology, because no eternal or necessary truth can be based upon any contingent historical truth. Historical truth and necessary truth are radically different. First of all, alleged historical truths are never certain. But, then, if they were certain, if one knew with absolute certainty some historical truth, that

---

[18]Semler was a left-wing Wolffian who saw revelation as historically conditioned, God accommodating God's self to the local condition of the recipients of revelation.

truth would still be contingent or accidental. It would lack the universality that the true rationalist seeks. Lessing spoke of an "ugly ditch" separating accidental historical truths from necessary truths.

Although Lessing relativized history so that Reimarus's questioning of the facticity of the Gospels became irrelevant, he valued history as a process for the realization of religious truth. Revelation, then, is seen not as the miraculous communication of absolute truth at a particular moment in history. Revelation is contingent. It involves the production of different degrees of insight in different historical communities—a degree of insight sufficient for that community and expressed in terms of that community. Revelation is also seen as existing in a dialectical relationship with reason. A ditch remains not only between historical truth and necessary truth but also between faith and reason—but it is a moving line. In the course of human progress, both revelation and reason develop, with revelation submitting to reason, but with reason developing under the guidance of revelation.

Kant, Schleiermacher, and Strauss

Kant and Schleiermacher. The Christology of Immanuel Kant (1724–1804) parallels that of Lessing and is usually taken as the best example of a rationalist Christology. A timeless essence of Christianity is isolated and identified with natural or rational religion. In *Religion within the Limits of Reason Alone*, Kant offers a moral interpretation of Christian dogmas. The dogma of original sin, for example, has to do with the innate propensity of humans to do evil. Kant sees this as a propensity that is related to the very nature of humankind. (This emphasis of Kant distinguishes him from Lessing who was an optimist.) The incarnation of God in Christ, for Kant, is the manifestation of moral ideal. The realization of this ideal in this world can be called an incarnation of God. Jesus Christ is an instance or an example of the ideal of moral perfection. Nevertheless, the archetype of moral life cannot be identified with Jesus Christ alone. Kant rejects the claim that revelation is capable of discovering or authenticated supernatural truths inaccessible to human intelligence; but he also rejects the view that revelation is unrelated to the discovery of religious truths. Kant is important for his reordering of the medieval world's separation of the natural order from a supernatural order. Instead of this distinction, Kant distinguished between phenomena and noumena. The transcendent noumenal world cannot be known as can the phenomenal world, nor can theoretical reason achieve knowledge of this world.

Yet the noumenal world is functionally imminent for moral life, and moral precepts that belong to the noumenal world can be realized in the phenomenal world.

With Friedrich Daniel Ernst Schleiermacher (1768–1834), the historical and religious were divided in a way to do justice to both. Schleiermacher emphasized feeling and imagination, attributes of humanity highlighted by the Romantics, in opposition to the arid intellectualism and moralism of the Enlightment. Instead of presupposing that religion was a system of factual beliefs and debating over the questions of which beliefs are essential to religion, whether these beliefs are defensible rationally, and whether they have the beneficial consequences attributed to them, Schleiermacher declared that religion has a sphere of its own. Religion can maintain this sphere only by renouncing claims on anything that belongs either to knowledge or to morality. Religion is a sense and taste for the infinite, the underlying unity or wholeness of the perceptual world. This unity reveals itself to feeling; it is not present to the senses like an object. When reflected upon, this feeling generates the idea of God. The individual imagination then moves that idea either toward a theistic supreme being outside the world or toward a pantheistic ALL. Christian beliefs, then, are grounded experientially in the religious consciousness of the believer. The believer may identify with the biblical religion religiously. But believers and nonbelievers alike are able to study the particular human religion disclosed in biblical texts by historical, literary, sociological, and other methods. This human reality of religion disclosed by scholarship may or may not mediate the reality acknowledged by believers. This ultimate, nonempirical reality is acknowledged by believers on the basis of their participation in religious community. Rational procedures cannot settle the question of God. The question, nonetheless, is left open and believers are allowed to affirm it on other grounds.

Schleiermacher's approach to the problem is exemplary and may have consequences for scholars today, but for actual historical study of Jesus his work is faulted primarily for his dependence on the Gospel of John. His *Life of Jesus*, in fact, presented a Jesus consistent with Schleiermacher's analysis of the essence of religious experience as a sense of utter dependence on God. In Jesus this dependence was uniquely developed. Schleiermacher used the Gospel of John as a historical outline of Jesus' life into which he placed Synoptic material.

Strauss. David Friedrich Strauss (1808–1874) may be seen as consolidating what Reimarus began in that he exposed contradictions and lack of historical substance in the Gospels. But he faulted Reimarus for his harsh view of Christianity as a deception. Strauss saw the nineteenth century as producing a balance between the unnecessarily harsh view of the eighteenth century and the uncritical view of previous centuries. The Hegelian dialect is noted by Strauss whereby history moves from thesis to antithesis to synthesis in a way that earlier ideas are absorbed into later ideas with the inadequacies of the earlier ideas corrected and refined.[19] Prior to the eighteenth century, the Christian religion could not be understood critically. Christians were too deeply enmeshed in the practice of their religion to understand it. A critical understanding resulted from the eighteenth century's reaction to its expanded historical and geographical perspective and its attempt to do justice to world religions. One way to do justice was to see all religions (including Judaism and Christianity) as products of human deception. This harsh view was held by Reimarus, in part, because of the prevailing assumption of the historical character of the biblical accounts. The rational either-or position of the eighteenth century concluded that the apostles were either telling the truth or lying in their proclamation that their master had been put to death and had gone forth living from the tomb on the third day, and Reimarus had effectively called into question the literal truth of at least some of the material in the Gospels. A broader ground for the harsh view was the fact that in the eighteenth century, reason prevailed and the imagination was scorned. Therefore, the eighteenth century "scorned religion, whose father is spirit and whose mother is imagination."[20]

In the beginning of the nineteenth century the rationalism of the eighteenth was renounced in an unproductive fashion by a Romantic excess. The Hegelian dialectic of taking things up into a higher unity was not followed even by the theological pupils of Hegel who followed him most closely. The task called for a dialectical continuation and completion

---

[19]Strauss presented his own views in light of historical developments in his essay on Reimarus. See his "Hermann Samuel Reimarus and His Apology," in *Reimarus: Fragments,* ed. Charles H. Talbert, Lives of Jesus series (Philadelphia: Fortress Press, 1970) 44-57. The correlation of the various ideas in a nonfoundational systemic approach is not the same as the Hegelian scheme, but some of Strauss's criticisms of the limitations of the eighteenth and early nineteenth centuries are pertinent in a nonfoundationalist approach.

[20]Ibid., 51.

of the eighteenth century and not a rejection of it. When Reimarus said that "Christianity is not a divine revelation but a human deception," Strauss declared, "we know today, of course, that this an error and that Christianity is not a deception. But is it for that reason a divine revelation in the sense that the church thinks? Has Reimarus's statement been completely negated?"[21] The conclusion of Strauss is clear, the "No" of Reimarus to the historical facticity of the Gospels remains a "No." The theology of Strauss's day was too willing to forget the "No" of Reimarus. "Because Moses certainly was not a charlatan, he is once more a miracle worker in theology's view; because no support can be found for accusing Jesus' disciples of stealing a corpse, theology thinks itself able to proclaim anew his resurrection as a supernatural event."[22]

The "Yes" that affirms and goes beyond the "No" of Reimarus also goes beyond the "Yes" Reimarus was able to muster. In an early edition of his *Life of Jesus* Strauss salvaged an underlying truth of the Christian faith by use of the philosophy of Hegel. Christianity, then, becomes a representation of the general truth concerning transformation of life by the Absolute Spirit. In the first edition of his *Life of Jesus*, Strauss gave attention to Jesus as a historical figure who was a disciple of John the Baptist. Jesus conducted a ministry in Galilee, came to regard himself as Messiah, called disciples, traveled to Jerusalem with plans of his kingdom, had premonitions of his death and predicted his second coming as Son of Man, and was crucified. In the third edition, Strauss omitted the apocalyptic element in Jesus' message and recast Jesus as a man with an intense consciousness of the Divine (in line with the translation of the truth of Christianity in Hegelian terms). An important constant was an understanding of the Gospels as the result of the use by the early Christian community of Messianic myths or legends to make sense of Jesus.

The position of Strauss is that in the affirmation of the Christian writers we do not have fraud; rather we have the imagination of the followers of Christ. "[T]he imagination of his followers, aroused in their deepest spirit, presented their master revived, for they could not possibly think of him as dead."[23] Strauss does not hesitate to use the term "delusion" to describe the ideas of the disciples that Jesus arose and appeared to them or their belief that he would soon return in the clouds

---

[21]Ibid., 55.
[22]Ibid.
[23]Ibid., 52.

of heaven. Nevertheless, it was "a delusion that contained a great deal of truth." From the perspective of Strauss, "the true and important thing was not the visible, but the invisible; not the earthly, but the heavenly; not the flesh, but the spirit."[24] Strauss declares that a truth can be revealed "at first in an unsuitable form; if you will, within the husk of a delusion, where it nonetheless may possess the value and the effectiveness of a truth."[25] It was this sort of truth that has "transformed the history of world." This truth

> first became mankind's common property in the form of a belief in Jesus' resurrection. And what sweeping consequences lay in this knowledge! As a result, in the Greek world there had to be a rupture of the beautiful accord between spiritual and sensual; spirit was not proved an independent force as long as it did not maintain itself in opposition to the sensual, in pain and castigation, in the insignificant and ugly. The unshakable, proud edifice of the Roman Empire must fall, the church outgrow the state, the pope outgrow the emperor in order to make mankind aware that in the long run no material power, strong as it might be, could resist the strength of conviction, of ideas. The belief in Jesus' resurrection contained all that in a germ, as if in abbreviated form or in a cipher, while the presentiment that the principle of Christianity was ordained to be the introduction of a new order in the world lay in the hope of his speedy return to establish his kingdom.[26]

Strauss used the expression "evangelical myths," to speak of stories that express early Christian ideas of Christ. He used negative and positive criteria to identify what is mythic in the Gospels. Myth contradicts physical or physiological laws of cause and effect, is inconsistent with itself, or contradicts other biblical accounts. From a positive perspective, if the idea expressed in the narrative is in accordance with the ideas of Christ found in Christian circles, the narrative can be regarded as a consequence of those ideas. The narrative may be seen as a result of the activity of early Christians to express their Christology. The methodology of Strauss resulted in the conclusion that the vast majority of the Gospel material is myth. The material is so permeated with Christian views that it cannot be regarded as solid history.

---

[24]Ibid., 53.
[25]Ibid., 53.
[26]Ibid., 53.

Reimarus himself prepared for the mythical interpretation of biblical narratives. He did this when he spoke of "oral tradition as the medium in which so many a story enjoyed a long existence and underwent frequent modifications before being set down in writing."[27] Strauss also gleans from Reimarus insights into the development of biblical materials that partially contradict Reimarus's harsh judgment of fraud: When Reimarus

> called to our attention how each of these writings was intended originally for a restricted circle and only slowly became known to larger groups, how they owned their acceptance to very accidental factors, and that only much later a general agreement was reached about the canon of the New Testament, he opened a wide prospect for a free historical criticism of the documents of the New Testament.[28]

The Liberal Quest of New Testament Scholars

New Testament scholars following Reimarus in the eighteenth century and Strauss in the nineteenth century had to choose between three different sets of alternatives. The first set of alternatives was either an uncritical supernatural approach to the study of Jesus or a strictly critical and historical approach. The poetic approach of Strauss was not a religious or a critical possibility in that epoch. It took some time to arrive at the conclusion, but the choice was clear: a strictly historical approach. The second set had to do with the question of sources—either the Fourth Gospel or the Synoptics. The Synoptics was the clear choice—from a strictly historical perspective. The third set was a non-eschatological Jesus or a thoroughly eschatological Jesus. These questions are most important in the story of the liberal quest for the historical Jesus as it is traced among New Testament scholars who had essentially become historians. This story may be traced in Schweitzer's *The Quest of the Historical Jesus: A Critical Study of its Progress from Reimarus to Wrede.*

The story behind the quest delves into the historical questions of sources and expectations of the end time. Some of these questions include: Can history be related to meaning? Can the Enlightenment split of history from meaning be overcome? How can the theistic worldview and spiritual history presupposed if Christ is to have the meaning claimed by the church be reclaimed or transformed? The Christological story

---

[27]Ibid., 56.
[28]Ibid., 57.

behind the quest for the historical Jesus may be traced in John Macquarrie, *Jesus Christ in Modern Thought*.

Schweitzer traced the liberal quest for the historical Jesus following the work of Strauss, showing the debate that resulted with the lack of confidence in the Fourth Gospel as a historical source and the stages of development and use of the Marcan hypothesis in the study of Jesus. (Schweitzer of course concluded his story with his own view of sources that fits his view of a throughly eschatological Jesus.) Schweitzer spoke of a victory of the liberal questers that involved a victory of the "Marcan hypothesis." It was a victory not of the Marcan hypothesis pure and simple, but of the Marcan hypothesis "as psychologically interpreted by a liberal theology."[29]

Schweitzer contrasted the work of Christian Hermann Weisse (1801–1866) with the liberal questers, particularly with the work of Heinrich Julius Holzmann (1832–1910), in order to make his point. Weisse admired Strauss and may be seen as the direct continuator of Strauss. His aim was to discover some thread of general connection in the Gospel narratives that would represent a historically certain element in the life of Jesus and serve as an effective standard by which to determine the extent of myth in the Gospels. Weisse came to the conclusion that Mark was the earliest Gospel. The Gospel of Mark is not the work of an eyewitness or even of one who had had an opportunity to question eyewitnesses thoroughly and carefully. Yet the writer was guided by a just recollection of the general course of the life of Jesus. The work of Weisse was not nearly as developed as the liberal works that followed in the 1860s and that became the standard view.

Schweitzer distinguished between the view of Weisse and the later view of liberal scholars in terms of the Marcan hypothesis: Weisse was skeptical about the details in Mark, but the new Marcan hypothesis was so confident that it based conclusions even upon incidental remarks. For Weisse there were no distinct periods of success and failure in the ministry of Jesus, but the new Marcan hypothesis confidentially affirms a distinction between periods of success and failure. The earlier hypothesis specifically denied that outward circumstances influenced the resolve of Jesus to die, but according to the new view, Jesus entered on the path of suffering because of the opposition of the people and the impossibility of carrying out his mission any other way. The Jesus of Weisse com-

---

[29]Schweitzer, *The Quest of the Historical Jesus*, 204.

pleted his development at the time of his appearance, but the Jesus of the
new interpretation of Mark continued to develop during his public
ministry.[30]

Holzmann, the teacher of Albert Schweitzer to whom Schweitzer's
1901 volume on Jesus was dedicated, was the scholar responsible for the
new Marcan hypothesis:

> Holtzmann read into this Gospel [the Gospel of Mark] that Jesus had
> endeavored in Galilee to found the Kingdom of God in an ideal sense;
> that He concealed his consciousness of being the Messiah, which was
> constantly growing more assured, until His followers should have attained
> by inner enlightenment to a higher view of the Kingdom of God and of
> the Messiah; that almost at the end of His Galilean ministry He declared
> Himself to them as the Messiah at Caesarea Philippi; that on the same
> occasion He at once began to picture to them a suffering Messiah, whose
> lineaments gradually became more and more distinct in His mind amid
> the growing opposition which He encountered, until finally, He communi-
> cated to his disciples his decision to put the Messianic cause to the test
> in the capital, and that they followed him thither and saw how his fate
> fulfilled itself.[31]

The view of Holtzmann was the characteristic view of the 1860s and
continued up until the time of Schweitzer himself. It was one that rejected
eschatology. In this regard the view of the liberal questers and the view
of Weisse were one. Jesus wished to found an inward kingdom of
repentance and made messianic claims only in the spiritual sense. He did
not seek superhuman glory, rather it was his purpose to bear the sin of
the whole people, and he experienced baptism as a humble member of the
community of Israel. When he came to clear consciousness of his
vocation, his teachings consisted of a constant struggle to rid his disciples
of their theocratic hopes and to transform their traditional messianic ideas.
When he responded to Simon's hailing him as the Messiah, that flesh and
blood has not revealed it to Simon, he meant that Simon had at that
moment overcome false Messianic ideas and recognized in Jesus the
ethical and spiritual deliverer of Israel.[32]

---

[30]Ibid., 204-205.

[31]Ibid., 203.

[32]Ibid., 205. Schweitzer quotes from Weisse, Holzmann, Daniel Schenkel, and Karl
Heinrich Weizsäcker in this passage.

Schweitzer saw the lives of Jesus written from the 1860s to his own day as illustrating the danger that scholars would offer "a Jesus who was too small, because we had forced Him into conformity with our human standards and human psychology."[33] He, of course, saw this danger from his eschatological perspective, a perspective that benefited from the Marcan hypothesis but took seriously the world-denying sayings of Jesus, viewing them in the light of Jesus' understanding of himself as Messiah. To see that the Jesus of liberal scholarship is too small, Schweitzer said from his perspective at the end of the century,

> one need only read the Lives of Jesus written since the 'sixties and notice what they have made of the great imperious sayings of the Lord, how they have weakened down His imperative world—contemning demands upon individuals, that He might not come into conflict with our ethical ideals, and might tune His denial of the world to our acceptance of it. Many of the greatest sayings are found lying in a corner like explosive shells from which the charges have been removed. No small portion of elemental religious power needed to be drawn off from His sayings to prevent them from conflicting with our system of religious world-acceptance. We have made Jesus hold another language with our time from that which He really held.[34]

Liberal Christologies

Liberal theologians, as liberal New Testament historians, gave attention to the question of sources and drew portraits of Jesus that used the two-source theory and made the concrete historical features of Christianity essential. They are among those chastised by Schweitzer for presenting a Jesus who is too small, but liberal Protestant theologians viewed their study of the historical Jesus as a continuation of the ideals of the Reformation. As the Reformers had freed Protestantism from the dogmas of the Medieval church, liberal Protestant theologians would continue this back to the New Testament. The liberal portraits of Jesus focused on Jesus' moral teachings, asking what we can learn from Jesus about the ordering of human life in this world. Albrecht Ritschl (1822–1889), Wilhelm Herrmann (1846–1922), and Adolf Harnack (1850–1931)

---

[33]Ibid., 400.
[34]Ibid., 400.

provide resources to supplement the story Schweitzer provided of liberal New Testament scholars.

Ritschl. Ritschl was an early exponent of the liberal view of Jesus Christ, and his view of the relationship of the historical Jesus to his contemporary lordship is important for those who are concerned with present-day revelation on the basis of the biblical text and the historical experience that is expressed in and available in some fashion in the biblical text. Ritschl, as a good Lutheran, presented his ideas in terms of justification, reflecting the opinion of Melanchthon that to know Christ is to know his benefits. Justification sets the believer in a new relationship with God but this justification is related to the religious community founded by Christ, the final realization of which is the kingdom of God. It is the significance of Christ for our lives as experienced in justification that we confess when we confess Christ's divinity. But there is a dialectical relationship between the Christian experience of salvation in the community and the historical witness to Jesus in the tradition.

> If the Godhead of Christ, or His lordship over the world in His present state of exaltation, is to be a postulate of the Christian faith, an integral part of the Christian view of the world, then it must be demonstrated to us in Christ's influence upon ourselves. But every form of influence exerted by Christ must find its criterion in the historical figure presented by His life. Therefore the Godhead or universal lordship of Christ must be apprehended in definite features of His historical life, as an attribute of His existence in time. For what Christ is in virtue of His eternal destiny, and what the influence is which He exerts on us because of His exaltation to God, would be wholly beyond our ken if we did not also experience the effects of the same in His historical existence in time. Unless the conception of His present lordship receives its content from the definite characteristics of His historical activity, then it is either a meaningless formula or the occasion for all kinds of extravagance. If, on the other hand, we are to hold fast our faith that Christ is at this moment Lord over the community of the Kingdom of God, and is working toward the gradual subjection of the world to this its true end, then lordship over the world must be recognizable as already a conspicuous feature of Christ's historical life.[35]

---

[35]Albrecht Ritschl, *The Christian Doctrine of Justification and Reconciliation* (Clifton NJ: Clifton Book Publishers, 1966) 406. See John Macquarrie, *Jesus Christ in Modern Thought*, 252-58.

Ritschl does not develop this idea by means of historical study of the Gospels. Rather he deals with it in terms of the different Reformation systems of theology. He contrasts the Lutheran doctrine that maintains that "through the incarnation of the Divine Word, or through the union of the Divine with the human nature, the latter becomes endowed with all the Divine attributes" with the Reformed doctrine that maintains that "the Divine Word, in order to become man, gave up the fulness of His Divine attributes, more especially those relations in which, as Creator and Lord, He stands to the world." Ritschl says that the Reformed doctrine faithfully follows the historical picture. To be faithful to the historical picture, the Lutheran doctrine must be supplemented by the statement that "the Incarnate Word of God during His earthly life regularly refrained from the manifestation of His Divine attributes."[36] Ritschl may be helpful if his discussion is extended beyond the dogmatic framework in which his statements are embedded. He wishes to affirm the possibility of attributing the predication of Godhead to the historical life of Jesus—a position that goes even beyond the Reformed doctrine. The Reformed doctrine does "certainly remains true to those human and temporal limits within which it perceives the life of Jesus to have been lived." But as it does so, "it compels us to refuse the predicate of Godhead to the historical life of Christ."[37] Ritschl makes light of the system that acknowledges a Divine nature that stands behind the human person of Jesus but occupies only a vague relation to it. Attention is concentrated in that case on the man Jesus as mediator without any effort to find an indication of his Godhead in his human life on earth. Ritschl bids us "learn the meaning of Christ's Godhead in Christ our Redeemer." According to Ritchel, Jesus has the right to be understood in the light of His own individuality. When the thought of God is not suspended the individuality of Jesus will be seen as that of the religious man and thereafter of the prophet and founder of a religion. Ritschl concludes that it is in the historical life of Jesus, in carrying out his purpose to redeem humankind and reveal to humankind the love of God, that the Godhead of Jesus Christ is revealed:

> Jesus is the bearer of the perfect spiritual religion, which consists in mutual fellowship with God, the Author of the world and its final goal. In the idea of God as the final goal of all things lies the reason why Jesus

---

[36]Ritschl, *The Christian Doctrine of Justification and Reconciliation*, 407.
[37]Ibid., 408.

recognizes as binding upon Himself for God's sake the widest conceivable aim of moral effort, namely, the union of mankind through love; while in the idea of God as the Author of the world lies the reason why Jesus for His own personal life repudiates every motive that is individual, worldly, and therefore less than Divine. But inasmuch as Jesus desired His own attitude to God to be shared by the rest of mankind, He laid upon His disciples, as their aim also, the union of mankind through love, or, in other words the realisation of the Kingdom of God; and through His own personal freedom in relation to the world, He led His disciples, in accepting their view of the world from Him, to the assured conviction that human life is of more worth than all the world. By making the aim of His own life the aim of mankind, who are to be called into the fellowship of His community, He is before all else the founder of a religion and the Redeemer of men from the dominion of the world.[38]

In moving to a definition of God emphasizing love rather than omniscience, omnipotence, and omnipresence, Ritschl is able to view Jesus as a revelation of the Divine. As John Macquarrie notes, however, the importance which Ritschl attaches to the historical Jesus and to historical knowledge about Jesus is not matched with study of the historical Jesus.[39] Theological prolegomena to such a study is provided by the liberal schema of the unification of humankind by love.

Herrmann. Wilhelm Herrmann also repudiates metaphysics, but he sees a practical motivation in the metaphysical quest—the need of humans to gain an orientation for their lives in this world. Religion, not metaphysics, is the answer, religion expressed in concrete faith. Herrmann's reverential attachment to the person of Jesus accompanied his repudiation of metaphysics and emphasis on moral values. From one perspective, the basis for faith is subjective, the power of Jesus' personality. But Herrmann did claim that he found objective grounds in the facts of history and ethics: "The Christian's consciousness that God communes with him rests on *two objective facts, the first of which is the historical fact of the Person of Jesus.* This fact is an element in our own personal reality. . . . *The second objective ground* of the Christian's consciousness that God communes with him is *that we hear within ourselves the constant demand that we do right.* . . . Here we grasp an

---

[38]Ibid., 414.
[39]Macquarrie, *Jesus Christ in Modern Thought*, 255.

objective fact which must be held to be valid in any historical study of life"[40]

Herrmann sees the actual human historical relationships in which we stand as providing the possibilities for coming to God. "It is only out of life in history that God can come to meet us. In proportion as what is essential in our historical environment becomes an element of our consciousness are we led into the presence of those facts which can reveal God to us."[41] When we simply endure our relations with others—instead of entering into and enjoying that relationship—the personality within us to which God would reveal God's self remains dead and we cannot see the facts through which God can reveal God's self to us. "Hence the Christian religion is inseparable from those moral activities in which we become conscious of personal fellowship and its laws, and take our part in the same. It is only when we share these moral activities that we first begin to live in that world in which we can become aware of our God."[42]

Within this sort of historical environment and within the historical movement where the Christian stands, the revelation of God may be discovered on the basis of the testimony of earlier Christians who have experienced such revelation. Herrmann acknowledged that "we should have no certain knowledge of Jesus if the New Testament did not tell us about him" and that "narratives by others contribute in all cases not a little to the picture we form for ourselves of historical reality."[43] But he is insistent that the content of these narratives may become a fact for us as we experience revelation. In the Christian fellowship we become acquainted with the external matter concerning Jesus in the transmission of the tradition. But in that same Christian fellowship "we are also led into His presence and receive a picture of His inner life."[44] This picture of Jesus' inner life is preserved by those who experienced the emancipating influence of that fact upon themselves. In the Christian fellowship, we see the effects of that inner life and our eyes are opened to its reality "so that we may thereby experience the same effect."[45] "He who has found the inner life of Jesus through the mediation of others, in so far as he has

---

[40]Wilhelm Herrmann, *The Communion of the Christian with God: A Discussion in Agreement with the View of Luther* (London: Williams and Norgate, 1895) 102-103.
[41]Ibid., 55.
[42]Ibid.
[43]Ibid., 56-57.
[44]Ibid., 60-61.
[45]Ibid., 61.

really found it, has become free even of that mediation. He is so set free by the significance which the inner life of the man Jesus has for him who has beheld it. If we have experienced His power over us, we need no longer look for the testimony of others to enable us to hold fast to His life as a real thing. We start indeed from the records, but do not grasp the fact they bring us until the enrichment of our inner life makes us aware that we have touched the Living One."[46]

Herrmann's emphasis upon the inner life of Jesus that is active in the world as we read the New Testament narrative in the Christian community is different from the story of Jesus being born of a virgin as the Son of God, performing miracles, being raised from the dead, and ascending to the Father. "These things, received with childlike simplicity, may certainly draw men's attention to Jesus and give them an impulse to seek Him for themselves; but we certainty have not in these statements that Person of Jesus Himself which is able to redeem us."[47] When we present those doctrines and narratives as the main thing in which people ought to believe in order to find the redeemer, we delude them. In fact, "such statements are a great hindrance to men today, for the majority can no longer accept these things with childlike simplicity. The most that can happen is that assent may be wrung from them in anxiety for their soul's welfare, and in terror excited by a violent sermon."[48] We may legitimately preach that

> those men who found the way to God through Jesus did actual believe such marvelous things concerning Him. Let us by all means have this testimony of the disciples earnestly made known; but for this very reason, if we are seeking the same redemption which they found, we are not to take it for granted that everything which influenced the disciples, and was beyond all doubt real to them, must influence us in exactly the same way. If we do expect this, then the very testimony of the disciples will prevent us from seeing that which is to us, in our present position, the accessible and sure basis of salvation.[49]

What can overpower us and lift us up is a reality in our own experience that is beyond all doubt to ourselves as we are today. Herrmann asks the question: "And what is thus real?" He answers: "First,

---

[46]Ibid., 61-62.
[47]Ibid., 66.
[48]Ibid.
[49]Ibid., 66-67.

the testimony of the disciples concerning the power and glory of Jesus. It is a fact that they did testify thus, and this ought to point us to Jesus Himself, and warn us why we are powerless to give such a testimony. But then, secondly, another reality is the inner life of Jesus, which rises up before us as a real power that is active in the world whenever we read the testimony of the disciples. In this we have Jesus Himself as the ground of our salvation."[50]

Herrmann discusses the value of historical criticism. Historical work on the New Testament has value for faith. "In the first place it shows us how small a foundation those writings afford for a historical account in the modern sense of the term, hence it shatters certain false props of faith, and that is a great gain." Herrmann's view will be seen later in the work of Rudolf Bultmann, but with both the question remains of the relationship of some "absolute truth" to historical research. Nevertheless, Herrmann emphasized that "the Christian who imagines that the reliability of the records as historical documents gives certainty to his faith, is duly startled from his false repose by the work of the historian, which ought to make it clear to such a man that the possession of Christianity cannot be obtained so cheaply as he thinks." Historical work is valued by Herrmann in the second place because it is

> constantly constructing afresh, with every new modification, whatever results can be obtained from the records. By this means the Christian believer is constantly called upon to compare afresh that portrait of Jesus which he carries within himself as absolute truth, with the relative truth obtained by historical research. And this helps us directly to increasing knowledge of the inexhaustible treasures of the inner life of Christ, and to growing acquaintance with the ways of His sovereignty over the real world."[51]

Herrmann does not define the inner life of Jesus that brings "absolute truth." He describes it and its effect upon humankind. "We feel that He first reveals to us what personal, spiritual life is, and He makes us feel how starved and perplexed is our own inner life. If the portrait of Jesus tells us these things, then we need not insist on knowing it in the exact historical sense: we can accept that portrait as the historical effect of a Person who is all-powerful in His sway over us, but whose personality

---

[50]Ibid., 67.
[51]Ibid., 64.

we cannot describe with historical exactness."[52] Herrmann compares the experience with Jesus and our capacity to express this in human language with the confidence that we come to have in humans: "If a man wins our confidence, we find that the immediate impression which his personality makes upon us has far more in it for us than all we might say to others in justification of our trust. The more powerfully the personal impression lays hold of us, the greater is the contrast between our powers of description and the impression which the memory retains. But when the way is pointed out to us, then we can construct for ourselves the picture of Jesus' inner life from the gospels."[53] When we see the fact of the inner life of Jesus that is present before our own souls, we become aware of God. "We find out how God works, for we actually experience God making us feel, by the spiritual power of Jesus, who He is, what is His will, and what are His purposes with us."[54]

When we try to express this reality we constantly fall into the use of conceptions that contradict each other and cannot be combined in one definite and consistent picture. "God takes away our self-confidence, and yet creates within us an invincible courage; He destroys our joy in life, and yet makes us blessed; He slays us, and yet makes alive; He lets us find rest, and yet fills us with unrest; He takes away the burden of a wasted life, and yet makes human life much more serious than it is without Him. God gives us a new existence that is complete and well rounded; yet what we find therein is always turning into a longing for a true life, and into desire to be renewed in spirit."[55] If Herrman defines the inner life of the man Jesus, it is in his description of the effect:

> But we are only raised to such life amid new reality when that fact remains present to us which alone can tell us the depths of our moral need, and then can raise us to the experience of divine life. We affirm that this fact is the inner life of the Man Jesus, and yet we cannot prove it. How could we, since everyone must experience *for himself* that the spiritual power of Jesus destroys his confidence in self, and creates in him a trust in God, so making him a new creature? All we can do is to show how a man becomes inwardly changed, when he does find and

---

[52]Ibid., 90-91.
[53]Ibid., 91.
[54]Ibid., 92.
[55]Ibid.

understand the communion of God with his soul in the influence of Jesus upon him.[56]

The "historical fact of the person of Jesus" that is grasped "as an element in our own personal reality" is not historical research or the results of historical research. It is the "inner life" of Jesus, the power of which is known through the New Testament. According to Herrmann, the New Testament makes an impression on us as it did on the first disciples. The term "impression" here is more than superficial impression. It refers to a forcible imprint, like the striking of a coin in a mint. The New Testament is the means for experiencing the "inner life" of Jesus because it expresses the experience of Jesus' disciples, which is experience of the sacred. Two important insights may be noted at this point, one illuminated by the Kantian philosophical and theological context of Herrmann's day, the other illuminated by contemporary literary insights into the Bible.

Herrmann does not honor the chasm between the conditional empirical sphere of history and the unconditioned. The unconditioned is objectifiable within history. God, then, is not consigned to the position of a transcendent postulate. But the reality experienced, the nature of the knowledge and certainty of the reality, is situated on a different level than the conventional intellectual categories. It is on the level of personal relationship. Validation is in terms of specific spiritual reactions in personal encounter with religious realities that have been impressed upon biblical texts.

The idea that the biblical text is able to mediate the experience of the sacred in such a fashion that those experiencing the sacred have a certainty that transcends rational historical-critical study calls for a method of study different from those available to Herrmann. The method does involve the rational—it is not merely a mystical experience (one of the three major sections of *The Communion of the Christian with God* is devoted to a challenge to the mystical approach to Christianity). It involves the testimony of the disciples and the experience of the Christian fellowship, but it demands personal experience. It involves the construction of a portrait of Jesus (not a scientific historical-critical reconstruction) that is faithful to the experience of the sacred in Jesus. The overcoming of the gap between the transcendent and the historical in the

---

[56]Ibid., 98.

interaction with the biblical text must be discussed in the contemporary epoch in light of literary resources. The critical tools of the literary tradition may be used in conjunction with historical and theological resources to reconceptualize the vision of Herrmann.

Harnack. Adolf Harnack (1850–1931) is the scholar in whom the liberal antimetaphysical or historical tendencies reached a logical conclusion. The title of Harnack's lectures at the University of Berlin, "The Essence of Christianity," shows us what he was about in his historical work and indicates a problem—how to speak of an "essence" and to hold onto a nonmetaphysical particularity. According to Harnack, Christianity is a way of life—not primarily a system of doctrine. This way of life deteriorated into a system when Christianity established itself in the Hellenistic world. But through historical study the essence can be regained. The lectures are divided into two major parts: (1) the Gospel and (2) the Gospel and history. Both of these are necessary to answer the question "What Is Christianity?", for a complete answer demands attention to Jesus himself, his earliest disciples, and all the later products of the spirit of Christianity.

> It is true that Christianity has had its classical epoch; nay more, it had a founder who himself was what he taught—to steep ourselves in him is still the chief matter; but to restrict ourselves to him means to take a point of view too low for his significance. Individual religious life was what he wanted to kindle and what he did kindle; it is, as we shall see, his peculiar greatness to have led men to God, so they may thenceforth live their own life with Him. How, then, can we be silent about the history of the Gospel if we wish to know what he was?[57]

Harnack's view of the sources reflects the view of liberal New Testament scholarship. The Fourth Gospel cannot be taken as a historical document in the ordinary sense of the word, and while the synoptic Gospels are credible as historical documents, "they were not written with the simple object of giving the facts as they were; they are books composed for the work of evangelization. Their purpose is to awaken a belief in Jesus Christ's person and mission; and the purpose is served by the description of his deeds and discourses, as well as by the references to the Old Testament."[58] Mark was the earliest Gospel and provides the

---

[57]Adolf Harnack, *What Is Christianity?*, intro. by Rudolf Bultmann, trans. Thomas Bailey Saunders, Harper Torchbooks TB 17 (New York: Harper & Row, 1957) 11.
[58]Ibid., 20.

basis for the geographical and historical framework found in the synoptic Gospels. But Matthew and Luke also used another source. Harnack, however, is aware of the fact that the synoptic Gospels "leave a very great deal to be desired, and even when judged by a more human standard they suffer from not a few imperfections."[59]

Harnack is conservative in his judgments about the reliability of the Gospels. He notes that they do not exhibit "rude additions" from a later age but they do reflect "here and there, the circumstances in which the primitive Christian community was placed and the experiences which it afterwards underwent."[60] Harnack notes, however, that "people nowadays . . . put such constructions on the text more readily than is necessary."[61] He also feels that the conviction that Old Testament prophecy was fulfilled in Jesus had a "disturbing effect" on tradition. Also, "in some of the narratives the miraculous element is obviously intensified," even though the view of Strauss that the Gospels contained a very deal that is mythical "has not been borne out."[62] Harnack's overall judgment is that "none of these disturbing elements affect the heart of the narrative; not a few of them easily lend themselves to correction, partly by a comparison of the Gospels one with another, partly through the sound judgment that is matured by historical study."[63]

The Gospels are not sufficient to serve as a source for a "biography" in spite of their historical value. They are weighty from the perspective of Harnack because they give information on three important points:

> In the first place, they offer us a plain picture of Jesus' teaching, in regard both to its main features and to its individual application; in the second place, they tell us how his life issued in the service of his vocation; and in the third place, they describe to us the impression which he made upon his disciples, and which they transmitted.[64]

Harnack does not see any evidence in the Gospels of a "stormy crisis" or "breach with his past." He indicates that we discover no "signs of inner revolutions" or the "scars of any terrible conflict." He is in agreement with Weisse on this question. "Everything seems to pour from him

---

[59]Ibid., 23.
[60]Ibid.
[61]Ibid.
[62]Ibid.
[63]Ibid., 24.
[64]Ibid., 31.

naturally, as though it could not do otherwise, like a spring from the depths of the earth, clear and unchecked in its flow."[65] He acknowledges that the life of Jesus did not lack in deep emotion, temptation, or doubt. But he is convinced that it was impossible that the life of Jesus was spent in inner conflict.

Harnack gives three heads under which the totality of the teachings of Jesus can be seen. "Firstly, the kingdom of God and its coming. Secondly, God the Father and the infinite value of human soul. Thirdly, the higher righteousness and the commandment of love."[66] He indicates that each one of them is "of such a nature as to contain the whole" so that the teaching of Jesus is exhibited in its entirety under any one of them. The nature of the kingdom of God is basic for understanding the totality of Jesus' teaching. Harnack indicated that Jesus' message of the kingdom ranges from the teaching of the kingdom as a purely future event (with the kingdom itself being the external rule of God) to the view of the kingdom as something inward (something that is already present and making its entrance at that moment). Harnack's conviction is that the external view of the kingdom was a result of the influence of the Judaism of Jesus' day and that the idea of the kingdom as something inward was the basic contribution of Jesus himself:

> There can be no doubt about the fact that the idea of the two kingdoms, of God and of the devil, and their conflicts, and of that last conflict of some future time when the devil, long since cast out of heaven, will be also defeated on earth, was an idea which Jesus simply shared with his contemporaries. He did not start it, but he grew up in it and he retained it. The other view, however, that the kingdom of God "cometh not with observation," that it is already here, was his own.[67]

Harnack acknowledged that in Jesus' day the two views did not clash, but he declared that it was difficult to reconcile in Harnack's time those divergent views of the kingdom. He felt that it was important not to seek to reconcile the different views but to distinguish between what is traditional and what is peculiar (between "kernel" and "husk") in Jesus' message of the kingdom of God. The most striking testimony of Jesus' understanding of the kingdom as an internal and present reality is constituted by the parables. In the parables, "the kingdom of God comes

---

[65]Ibid., 32, 33.
[66]Ibid., 51.
[67]Ibid., 54.

by coming to the individual, by entering into his soul and laying hold of it. True, the kingdom of God is the rule of God; but it is the rule of the holy God in the hearts of individuals; *it is God himself in his power.*"[68] From the point of view of the parables, "everything that is dramatic in the external and historical sense has vanished; and gone, too, are all the external hopes for the future . . . it is not a question of angels and devils, thrones and principalities, but of God and the soul, the soul and its God."[69]

Albert Schweitzer

The history of the first phase of Jesus research came to a climax at the turn of the century against the background of nineteenth-century liberal scholarship. Johannes Weiss (1863–1914) and Albert Schweitzer (1875–1965) are the scholars whose work has the reputation for calling into question the quest for the historical Jesus. Weiss and Schweitzer saw the historical work of the liberal scholars as bad historical research because it was not thoroughgoing enough. Throughgoing historical study uncovers a kingdom of God in direct opposition to that of Ritschl and his followers. The external future rule of God was not "husk," it was "kernel." Jesus' kingdom involved apocalyptic eschatological expectations. Weiss showed that Jesus' teaching about the kingdom was eschatological and Schweitzer showed that eschatology was the key to the course of life of Jesus.

In light of contemporary debate over the eschatological views of Jesus, it is instructive to review Schweitzer's conclusions. In August 1901, he wrote a preface to a treatise entitled "The Lord's Supper in Connection with the Life of Jesus and History of Early Christianity."[70] In

---

[68]Ibid., 56.

[69]Ibid. Martin Kähler's work must be considered as a way of avoiding two equally invalid ways of conceiving of Jesus Christ—the way of classical Christology and the way of liberal historical study. Kähler's alternative is Kerygma: "It is as Kerygma, as a deliverance of the divine commission to his heralds, that the ancient word of scripture acquires its significance in the church." Kähler, *The So-Called Historical Jesus and the Historic Biblical Christ*, foreword by Paul Tillich, trans. Carl E. Braaten, Seminar Editions (Philadelphia: Fortress Press, 1964) 131.

[70]*Das Abendmahl im Zusammenhang mit dem Leben Jesu und der Geshchichte des Urchristentums.* The second part of this treatise was issued independently as *Das Messianitats und Leidensgeheimnis. Eine Skizze des Lebens Jesu* ("The Secrets of Jesus Messiahship and Passion: A Sketch of the Life of Jesus"). Subsequently, a translation was published as *The Mystery of the Kingdom of God. The Secret of Jesus' Messiahship and*

that preface, Schweitzer dealt with several interrelated matters centering in the secret of Jesus' messiahship. The key to understanding the life of Jesus, Schweitzer suggested, is the fact that Jesus took himself to be the Messiah but did not feel obliged to make this a factor in his public ministry.

> Only that conception is historical which makes it intelligible how Jesus could take himself to be the Messiah without finding himself obliged to make this consciousness of his tell as a factor in his public ministry for the Kingdom of God,—rather, how he was actually compelled to make the messianic dignity of his person a secret! Why was his messiahship a secret of Jesus? To explain this means to understand his life.[71]

Implicit in the framing of this question is the understanding of the synoptic Gospels not as artful redaction of tradition but as accurate transmission of tradition.

> For the Synoptic question especially, the new conception of the life of Jesus is of great importance. From this point of view the composition of the Synoptists appears much simpler and clearer. The artificial redaction with which scholars have felt themselves compelled to operate is very much reduced. The Sermon on the Mount, the commission to the Twelve, and the eulogy of the Baptist are not "composite speeches," but were for the most part delivered as they have been handed down to us. Also the form of the prophecy of the Passion and the Resurrection is not to be ascribed to the early Church, but Jesus did actually speak to his Disciples in these words about his future. This very simplification of the literary problem and the fact that the credibility of the Gospel tradition is thereby enhanced is of great weight for the new interpretation of the life of Jesus.[72]

In his "Summary of the Life of Jesus," Schweitzer makes clear that the "Life of Jesus" was very short. He began his ministry at "the season

---

Passion, trans. with intro. by Walter Lowrie (London: A. & C. Black; New York: Dodd, Mead, and Co., 1914).

A translation of the first part of Schweitzer's 1901 treatise was finally published in 1982: The Problem of the Lord's Supper according to the Scholarly Research of the Nineteenth Century and the Historical Accounts, vol. 1 of The Lord's Supper in Relationship to the Life of Jesus and the History of the Early Church, trans. A. J. Mattill, Jr., ed. with intro. by John Reumann (Macon GA: Mercer University Press, 1982).

[71]Schweitzer, The Mystery of the Kingdom of God. The Secret of Jesus' Messiahship and Passion, trans. Walter Lowrie (repr.: New York: Macmillan, 1950) ix.

[72]Ibid., x.

of the summer seed sowing" and he ended his ministry on "the cross at Easter of the following year." This brief ministry was divided into three periods. The first was a period of public ministry and lasted from seedtime to harvest. The second period was the autumn and winter when Jesus was alone in Gentile territory with his disciples. The third period was the time of his second public ministry, a ministry in Jerusalem.

The beginning took place when Jesus was going up to Jerusalem for Passover. He came in contact with John the Baptist, was baptized by John, and became aware that he was the one whom God destined to be the Messiah. Following his baptism, Jesus, as John before him, proclaimed the near approach of the kingdom. He did not proclaim himself as a Messiah—that remained a secret to be revealed only at the dawning of the new aeon—but the secret controlled all of his preaching. The proclamation of Jesus involved repentance and ethical content, but behind this ethical preaching of Jesus loomed the secret of the kingdom of God.

> That which, as performed by the individual, constitutes moral renewal in preparation for the Kingdom, signifies, as accomplished by the community, a fact through which the realization of the Kingdom in a supernatural way will be hastened. Thus individual and social ethics blend in the great secret. As the plentiful harvest, by God's wonderful working, follows mysteriously upon the sowing, so comes also the Kingdom of God, by reason of man's moral renewal, but substantially without his assistance.[73]

Signs and wonders were involved. For the people they served to confirm the preaching of the nearness of the kingdom. The signs and wonders condemned those who did not now believe that the time is at hand, "for they plainly attest that the power of ungodliness is coming to an end."[74] Behind the signs and wonders, for Jesus, was the awareness of messiahship. The Pharisees ascribed to the signs the power of Satan, but Jesus knew that by his acts "he binds the power of ungodliness, as one falls upon a strong man and renders him harmless before attempting to rob him of his possessions. Wherefore, in sending out his Apostles, he gives them, together with the charge to preach, authority over unclean spirits. They are to deal the last blow."[75]

An important element in the preaching of the kingdom was the "intimation of the pre-Messianic affliction." This was not simply the

---

[73]Ibid., 161-62.
[74]Ibid., 162.
[75]Ibid., 162-63.

suffering of Messiah, it was the suffering of believers who were proving themselves the elect of the kingdom in their steadfast resistance to the final attack of the power of the world. The afflictions signify not only a probation but also an atonement. "It is foreordained in the messianic drama, because God requires of the adherents of the Kingdom a satisfaction for their transgressions in this aeon."[76] Schweitzer adds the fact that God is almighty and in God's omnipotence God determines the question of membership in the kingdom. Also, the necessity of the final affliction is relative because God can abrogate it.[77]

During the initial period of public ministry Jesus remained on the northern shore of the Sea of Galilee. Chorazin, Bethsaida, and Capernaum were the major centers of his activity. From this area he did make an excursion across the lake to the region of the Decapolis and a journey to Nazareth. In spite of the lack of success in this initial period, Jesus recognized that the time was near. Jesus sent forth his apostles as he and his disciples were returning to Nazareth, for he now recognized it was harvest time, the time of success. Jesus' sending out of the twelve was the last effort for bringing about the kingdom. As the disciples returned and announced to him their success, reporting the power they had over the evil spirits, it signified to Jesus that all was ready. He expected the dawn of the kingdom in the most immediate future. In fact, it had seemed to him that the kingdom would come even before the twelve returned. He had told them that the appearing of the Son of Man would overtake them before they had gone through the cities of Israel.

At the conclusion of the first period of public ministry, Jesus saw that his work was done. He and his disciples entered a boat and sailed along the coast toward the north. The multitude, however, followed after them along the shore and surprised them when they landed upon a lonely beach. Jesus celebrated with the crowd in anticipation of the messianic feast. Neither the crowd nor the disciples understood the significance of the meal because they did not know his secret. After the meal, he sent the crowd away and ordered the disciples to skirt the coast as they traveled to Bethsaida. He himself went to the mountain to pray and then followed along the shore on foot. The morning after the supper by the seashore, he collected the crowd and the disciples at Bethsaida and warned them to stand by him and not to deny him in the humiliation. Six days later he

---

[76]Ibid., 163.
[77]Ibid., 163-64.

went with the twelve to the mountain where he had prayed and there he was revealed to the three as the Messiah. On the way home he forbade them to say anything about it until he would be revealed at the resurrection in the glory of the Son of Man.

The kingdom expected in the near future failed to make its appearance.

> This first eschatological delay and postponement was momentous for the fate of the Gospel tradition, inasmuch as now all the events related to the mission of the Twelve became unintelligible, because all consciousness was lost of the fact that the most intense eschatological expectation then inspired Jesus and his following. Hence it is that precisely this period is confused and obscure in the accounts, and all the more so because several incidents remained enigmatical to those even who had a part in the experience. Thus the sacramental Supper by the seashore became in the tradition a "miraculous feeding," in a sense totally different from that which Jesus had in mind.[78]

In the second period of the ministry, the retreat with his disciples, Jesus came to an understanding about two messianic facts: the execution of John the Baptist by the secular authority before the Messianic time had dawned and the failure of the kingdom to appear although the tokens of its dawning were present.

> The secret is made known to him through the Scripture: God brings the Kingdom about *without the general Affliction*. He whom God has destined to reign in glory accomplishes it upon himself by being tried as a malefactor and condemned. Wherefore the others go free: he makes the atonement for them. What though they believe that God punishes him, though they become offended in him who preached unto them righteousness,—when after his Passion the glory dawns, then shall they see that he has suffered for them.[79]

When the time came for the Passover pilgrimage, Jesus set out with his disciples for Jerusalem. Before they left the north, he asked the disciples about whom the people took him to be. Peter, mindful of the revelation on the mountain, said: "Thou art the Son of God." Jesus then informed them of his secret.

---

[78]Ibid., 167.
[79]Ibid., 168.

Yes, he it is who shall be revealed as Son of Man at the Resurrection.
But before that, it is decreed that he must be delivered to the high priests
and elders to be condemned and put to death. God so wills it. For this
cause they are going up to Jerusalem.[80]

The journey to Jerusalem, then, was "the funeral march to victory."
It was within the secret of the passion that the secret of the kingdom lay
concealed. With the arrival in Jewish territory, the second period of Jesus'
public ministry began. Jesus was again surrounded by the people. He was
thronged by the multitudes expectant of the kingdom. Schweitzer
concludes his summary of the life of Jesus recounting the passion story
from the perspective of Jesus' secret. He describes the last supper:

> In the neighborhood of death Jesus draws himself up to the same
> triumphant stature as in the days by the seaside,—for with death comes
> the Kingdom. On that occasion he had celebrated with the believers a
> mystic feast as an anticipation of the messianic banquet; so now he rises
> at the end of the last earthly supper and distributes to the Disciples
> hallowed food and drink, intimating to them with a solemn voice that this
> is the last earthly meal, for they are soon to be united at the banquet in
> the Father's Kingdom.[81]

"The hearing of witnesses is merely a pretense," according to
Schweitzer.

> After they have gone the High Priest puts directly the question about
> messiahship. "I am," said Jesus, referring them at the same time to the
> hour when he shall appear as Son of Man on the clouds of heaven
> surrounded by the angels. Therefore he was found guilty of blasphemy
> and condemned to death.
> On the afternoon of the fourteen of Nisan, as they ate the Paschal
> lamb at even, he uttered a loud cry and died.[82]

In a postscript, Schweitzer acknowledged that the judgments passed
upon his realistic account of the life of Jesus would be diverse. He
declared, however, that critics should not find fault with the aim of the
book: "to depict the figure of Jesus in its overwhelming heroic greatness
and to impress it upon the modern age and upon the modern theology."
His final paragraph related Schweitzer's work to Schweitzer's world:

---

[80]Ibid., 169.
[81]Ibid., 172.
[82]Ibid., 173.

We must go back to the point where we can feel again the heroic in Jesus. Before that mysterious Person, who, in the form of his time, knew that he was creating upon the foundation of his life and death a moral world *which bears his name*, we must be forced to lay our faces in the dust, without daring even to wish to understand his nature. Only then can the heroic in our Christianity and in our *Weltanschauung* be again revived.[83]

Schweitzer's *Quest of the Historical Jesus*, published in 1906 (English translation, 1910), was designed to vindicate Schweitzer's conclusions on eschatology, views that had been published in 1901 but had received little attention, but the book was quickly taken to be the definitive history of the study of the historical Jesus and to show that the recovery of the historical Jesus was impossible. In his comprehensive and magisterial volume entitled *Jesus Christ in Modern Thought*, John Macquarrie declared that "the enterprise of bringing to view the plain unvarnished historical Jesus was shown to be so highly problematical that any so-called 'new quests' for the historical Jesus have been much chastened compared with the earlier ones."[84] This prepares us for a chastened second quest of the historical Jesus and for a set of third quests that challenges Macquarrie's judgment.

---

[83]Ibid., 174.
[84]Macquarrie, *Jesus Christ in Modern Thought*, 276.

Chapter 7

From Bultmann
to Crossan and Wright

During the nineteenth century, scholars used the results of Gospel research to attempt a reconstruction of the life of Jesus. The possibility of such a work was presupposed; only the correct procedure needed to be found and followed. From the beginning of the twentieth century, however, two basically different approaches were followed. One group of scholars, represented by C. H. Dodd, T. W. Manson, and Vincent Taylor, continued the original quest. They rejected the possibility of a complete "biography," but they did feel that a "life" of Jesus with a broad chronology was possible. Another group, influenced more strongly by form critics in general and by Rudolf Bultmann in particular, gave up the quest in a conventional sense. They concluded that the nature of the only real sources for the life of Jesus—the synoptic Gospels—makes a biography impossible.

The community that was most influential in the formation of the tradition was not concerned with a biography as such and did not transmit a connected, chronological, geographical outline of developments in the life of Jesus. It transmitted individual sayings and narratives. According to Dibelius and Bultmann, the originators of New Testament form criticism, the individual units do not go back to Jesus. The church formulated them for its purposes! We do not delete "additions" here and there and get back to a primitive form from Jesus' day; we get back to the form that originated in the church. However, both Dibelius and Bultmann wrote books on Jesus, books that begin with similar presuppositions regarding the formation of the tradition and yet arrive at diverse positions as to how the tradition can be used in a life of Jesus.

This chapter deals with books on Jesus by Dibelius and Bultmann, the post-Bultmannian abortive renewal of the quest, the current explosion of books on Jesus (including a return to a non-Bultmannian quest), and the investment of the church in the critical study of the historical Jesus.

The Jesus Books of Dibelius and Bultmann

Martin Dibelius was a conservative form critic and published a book on Jesus in 1939 that was written on the basis of his earlier work in form criticism.[1] Dibelius saw that a distinction was to be made insofar as historical reliability is concerned on the basis of the form of the units. The passion story is unique in the tradition and the general outline of the passion story is viewed by Dibelius as trustworthy. Paradigms (sermonic examples) are the most historical of the three forms of narrative material (tales [or miracle stories] and myths and legends being the other two) because, like the passion narrative, they arose earliest among the eyewitnesses who could control and correct the tradition. Their place in the life of the church also assures their relative trustworthiness, for they arose in connection with preaching, and "the nearer a narrative stands to the sermon the less it is questionable, or likely to have been changed by romantic, legendary, or literary influences."[2] The tales and legends are less historical than paradigms because of their very nature, but they are not devoid of historical value. Only when a non-Christian story is the probable origin of a Christian tale is the historical reliability of the narrative really brought into question. Even legends must not be ruled out as possible vehicles of history, for legends too may contain some historical content.

In general, Dibelius was confident of the trustworthiness of the sayings. In various ways, he said, "we can see that Jesus' sayings were handed down with great fidelity, thanks to the unencumbered memory of his unspoiled followers and to their reverence for their Master's word."[3] Dibelius concluded that in general the sayings of Jesus may be relied upon as historical, yet he warned that the historian would do well to look at the tradition as a whole and not build too much upon an individual saying if it does not cohere with the rest of the tradition.

According to Dibelius, then, the narratives and sayings may be used with proper critical care in a study of Jesus. This he proceeded to do in

---

[1]Dibelius, *Jesus*, trans. Charles B. Hedrick and Frederick C. Grant (Philadelphia: Westminster Press, 1949).

[2]Dibelius, *From Tradition to Gospel*, trans. Bertram Lee Woolf (New York: Charles Scribner's Sons, 1934) 61.

[3]*Jesus*, 25.

his book as he discussed Jesus' particular historical and religious background and examined the general features of the movement among the
masses led by Jesus, a Galilean prophet and holy man. In the rest of the
book, Dibelius dealt with Jesus' teaching concerning himself and his relationship to God, Jesus' basic principles for life in the kingdom, the forces
that opposed Jesus and brought about his death, and the witness of the
church to his resurrection. Dibelius's use of form criticism in a study of
Jesus resulted in a rather full and confident presentation of the earthly
Jesus.

Bultmann's analysis of the Gospel tradition, along with his other
theological and historical presuppositions, gave a particular slant to his
views on reconstructing a history of the earthly Jesus. He was skeptical
about the possibility of historical research into the life of Jesus and
seriously doubted the legitimacy of such a study. Bultmann's view of the
nature of the *narrative* tradition made him skeptical of its historicity. Of
course, he did not doubt that Jesus lived and did many of the *kinds of
works* attributed to him in the tradition. But he was skeptical about the
report of any specific activity being a historical report and was quite sure
that the narrative material in the tradition cannot give us insight into the
life and personality of Jesus.

> I do indeed think that we can now know almost nothing concerning the
> life and personality of Jesus, since the early Christian sources show no
> interest in either, are moreover fragmentary and often legendary; and
> other sources about Jesus do not exist.[4]

Bultmann gave assurance that

> the doubt as to whether Jesus really existed is unfounded and not worth
> refutation. No sane person can doubt that Jesus stands as founder behind
> the historical movement whose first distinct stage is represented by the
> oldest Palestinian community. But how far that community preserved an
> objectively true picture of him and his message is another question.[5]

Bultmann was not as skeptical of the sayings as he was of the narratives. "Little as we know of his life and personality, we know enough of
his *message* to make for ourselves a consistent picture."[6] Yet the sayings

---

[4]Bultmann, *Jesus and the Word*, new ed., trans. Louise Pettibone Smith and Erminie
Huntress Lantero (New York: Charles Scribner's Sons, 1958; [1]1934; orig. 1926) 8.
[5]Ibid., 13.
[6]Ibid., 12.

in the tradition as well as the narratives go back to the Christian community that both passed on actual sayings of Jesus and placed its own teachings on the lips of Jesus. How is it possible to distinguish between the actual teachings of Jesus and those teachings that were put into his mouth by the church or modified by the church? The knowledge that the synoptic Gospels were composed in Greek within the Hellenistic community, while Jesus and the oldest Christian group lived in Palestine and spoke Aramaic, helps in the process. "Everything in the synoptics which for reasons of language or content can have originated only in Hellenistic Christianity must be excluded as a source for the teaching of Jesus."[7] It cannot be supposed that all of the material thus retained goes back to Jesus, however, for there was an Aramaic-speaking Palestinian church after the time of Jesus.

So, within the Palestinian material different layers must be distinguished. Whatever materials show the specific interest of the church or reveal characteristics of later development must be rejected as secondary. An oldest layer is thus determined, although it can be determined with only relative exactness. Even this oldest layer *may* not go back to Jesus. "Naturally we have no absolute assurance that the exact words of this oldest layer were really spoken by Jesus. There is a possibility that the contents of this oldest layer are also the result of a complicated historical process which we can no longer trace."[8]

Bultmann's work on Jesus, therefore, was really a treatment of the message of Jesus, and "Jesus" here, according to Bultmann, actually refers to the complex of ideas in the oldest layer of the Synoptic tradition. Bultmann said, "By the tradition Jesus is named as bearer of the message; according to overwhelming probability he really was." But Bultmann suggested that "whoever prefers to put the name of 'Jesus' always in quotation marks and let it stand as an abbreviation for the historical phenomenon with which we are concerned, is free to do so."[9]

Bultmann concluded that a quest of the historical Jesus as carried out in the nineteenth century was impossible because of the nature of the sources. But just as important in bringing scholars to give up what remained of the original quest was Bultmann's judgment that such a quest was unnecessary and indeed illegitimate since the object of Christian faith

---

[7]Ibid., 13.
[8]Ibid.
[9]Ibid., 14.

is not the historical Jesus. Interest in the historical Jesus was taken by Bultmann to be an illegitimate clinging to this-worldly props for faith, a desire for an objective verification of faith. The real Christ event, however, is the church's proclamation. We cannot and must not use the "proclamation" as a "source" to reconstruct the "historic Jesus" with his "messianic consciousness," his "inwardness," or his "heroic character." This is the "Christ according to the flesh" who belongs to the past. "It is not the historic Christ who is the Lord, but Jesus Christ as he is encountered in the proclamation."[10]

In his treatment of the parables, Bultmann gave a criterion that was designed to enable us to judge that a saying is authentic. "We can only count on possessing a genuine similitude of Jesus where, on the one hand, expression is given to the contrast between Jewish morality and piety and the distinctive eschatological temper which characterized the preaching of Jesus; and where on the other hand we find no specifically Christian features."[11] This may be stated positively in a form that was found useful by all students of the earthly Jesus: we may be sure that sayings attributed to Jesus are authentic when they differ from contemporary Judaism or from the proclamation of the church. This criterion of dissimilarity or distinctiveness is, of course, a criterion that leads to minimal rather than to maximal results. Jesus could have used much from the Old Testament and the Judaism of his day, and much of the teaching useful to the early church could well have come from Jesus himself.

The Post-Bultmannian Quest and the Contemporary Scene

The Post-Bultmannian Quest. By the mid-twentieth century, a "new quest" of the historical Jesus developed among the disciples of Bultmann. If a date can be given for the beginning of this new quest it is 20 October 1953, when Ernst Käsemann gave a lecture on "The Problem of the Historical Jesus" at a reunion of students of Bultmann. Käsemann acknowledged that the Gospels were not written to give mere historical information about Jesus. The New Testament presents Jesus as the Lord of the believing community, "not as he was in himself, not as an isolated

---

[10]Bultmannn expressed this opinion in 1929 in an essay on "The Significance of the Historical Jesus for the Theology of Paul," reprinted in *Glauben und Verstehen* I, 2nd ed. (Tübingen: J.C.B. Mohr, 1954) 208.

[11]Bultmann, *History of the Synoptic Tradition*, trans. John Marsh (New York: Harper & Row, 1963) 205.

individual." Käsemann even questioned whether the formula "the historical Jesus" is appropriate or legitimate, because "it is almost bound to awaken and nourish the illusion of a possible and satisfying reproduction of his life story."[12]

The fact that the New Testament is not concerned merely with Jesus as an isolated individual but as Lord of the community, however, does not permit the question about the Jesus of history to be ignored. Käsemann raised the very question raised by Ritschl when Ritschl declared that "the Godhead or universal lordship of Christ must be apprehended in definite features of His historical life, as an attribute of His existence in time." Primitive Christianity itself, according to Käsemann, was not minded to

> allow myth to take the place of history nor a heavenly being to take the place of the Man of Nazareth. . . . Primitive Christianity is obviously of the opinion that the earthly Jesus cannot be understood otherwise than from the far side of Easter, that is, in his majesty as Lord of the community and that, conversely, the event of Easter cannot be adequately comprehended if it is looked at apart from the earthly Jesus.[13]

Likewise, the fact that the materials of the tradition do not give enough information to weave "the fabric of a history in which cause and effect could be determined in detail"[14] should not lead to a complete lack of interest in the earthly Jesus. Ignoring the earthly Jesus indicates a failure to take seriously the primitive Christian concern with the identity between the exalted and humiliated Lord and overlooks the fact that "there are still pieces of the Synoptic tradition which the historian has to acknowledge as authentic if he wishes to remain an historian at all."[15] The concern of Käsemann in his address was "to show that, out of the obscurity of the life story of Jesus, certain characteristic traits in his preaching stand out in relatively sharp relief, and that primitive Christianity united its own message with these."[16]

The theological *necessity* of a new quest, then, grew out of the proclamation of the church itself. The Gospel is not just the story of the

---

[12]Ernst Käsemann, *Essays on New Testament Themes*, trans. W. J. Montague (London: SCM Press, 1964) 23.
[13]Ibid., 25.
[14]Ibid., 45.
[15]Ibid., 46.
[16]Ibid.

earthly Jesus. but it is not just the proclamation of a mythological—preexistent and exalted—Lord. James M. Robinson said:

> It is this concern of the *kerygma* [proclamation] for the historicity of Jesus which necessitates a new quest. For how can the indispensable historicity of Jesus be affirmed, while at the same time maintaining the irrelevance of what a historical encounter with him would mean, once this has become a real possibility due to the rise of modern historiography? . . . [A position maintaining the irrelevancy of the results of the quest] cannot fail to lead to the conclusion that the Jesus of the *kerygma* could equally well be only a myth, for one has in fact declared the meaning of his historical person irrelevant.[17]

Other students of Bultmann followed the lead of Käsemann. Ernst Fuchs concentrated upon Jesus' message as evidenced in his action. Jesus' conduct as a whole gives evidence of who he is. His conduct and teaching imply an understanding of his relation to God. This implicit understanding becomes explicit in the kerygma of the church.[18] Gerhard Ebeling asked, "Who shall forbid us to ask the question concerning the historic Jesus? This defeatism has no justification . . . either as regards the state of the actual historical sources available to us or in relation to the possibility of historical understanding in general."[19] Günther Born-kamm pressed the question:

> How could faith of all things be content with mere tradition, even though it be that contained in the Gospels? It must break through it and seek behind it to see the thing itself. . . . But it cannot be seriously maintained that the Gospels and their tradition do not allow enquiry after the historical Jesus. Not only do they allow, they demand this effort.[20]

The method followed in the post-Bultmannian quest was a modified form of the skeptical method of Bultmann. The work of the source critics was accepted: Mark was the earliest Gospel and was used by Matthew and Luke along with another source (Q) that is basically a sayings source earlier than Mark. Matthew and Luke each also had a unique source or

---

[17]James M. Robinson, *A New Quest of the Historical Jesus*, Studies in Biblical Theology 25 (London: SCM Press, 1959) 88.

[18]Ernst Fuchs, *Studies of the Historical Jesus*, trans. Andrew Scobie (London: SCM Press, 1964) 11-31.

[19]*Zeitschrift für Theologie und Kirche*, additional number (1959): 20.

[20]Bornkamm, *Jesus of Nazareth*, trans. Irene McLuskey and Fraser Mcluskey with James M. Robinson (London: Hodder and Stoughton; New York: Harper & Brothers, 1960) 9, 22.

sources. But the material now written in the Gospels existed earlier in independent units and the overall framework in which the units now exist is a creation of the Gospel writers. The oral tradition passed through or was created by the church as it developed from an Aramaic-speaking Palestinian community.

Source criticism must first be applied to the unit of tradition. When a unit occurs in all three Synoptic Gospels, Mark is to be taken as the earliest written form of that unit, and attention may be limited to Mark's version of the tradition. When a unit of the tradition occurs in Q, the unit may be carried back even further. But it is necessary to reconstruct the original Q form from the later forms in Matthew and Luke. At times the Matthean form of the Q unit is more original and at times the Lukan form is more original. The tendencies of the two Gospel writers must be considered as the more original form of Q is determined. It is incorrect, however, to assume that a unit in Mark and/or Q is necessarily more primitive than a unit in the material unique to Matthew or to Luke since all of the material passed successively through Palestinian and Hellenistic stages. Source criticism, then, may assist in determining the earliest written form of a unit. Source criticism may also assist in a limited way in verifying the historicity of tradition. Since the sources may be regarded as relatively independent, when the content of a unit is repeated in two or more sources, the possible authenticity of the tradition may be regarded as being increased.

Once the unit has been studied from the perspective of the written sources, form criticism in its strictest sense is applied to the unit of tradition. The history of the tradition must be traced to determine the earliest form of the unit. Sayings of Jesus, for example, passed succes-sively through the Palestinian church, the Jewish Hellenistic church, and into the Gentile Hellenistic church. Additions and modifications of the later church must be seen and deleted. The tendencies in the transmission of the material must be discounted. The test of multiple attestation found helpful in a study of the sources helps here also, for when a teaching or purportedly historical fact occurs in more than one form the possible authenticity of that teaching or fact is increased. If, for example, a piece of factual information occurs in a paradigm, parable, and isolated saying, it may be assumed that the fact was not created for the forms but existed before the forms were created.

Since it cannot be assumed that the earliest form of the unit of tradition that has been studied with the methods of source and form criticism is authentic, a distinction must be made between authentic and inauthentic material. The criterion of dissimilarity or distinctiveness was found to be essential in the determination of authentic material. Students of the new quest judged that it was safer to follow the skeptical methodology than to accept everything that was in doubt. Reginald Fuller said that "on some points Jesus could have agreed with the post-Easter church" and that "Jesus might also have quoted or used with approval Rabbinic teaching." Yet, this skeptical method provided a safer course than the principle of accepting whatever tradition may be doubtful. "It may result in a reduction of the available historical data, but at least it should be reliable enough as far as it goes; and actually it turns out that it does go far enough for our purposes."[21]

Another criterion, a criterion of consistency or coherence, was suggested to compensate for the negative aspect of the criterion of dissimilarity or distinctiveness. Bultmann's criterion of distinctiveness helps with the tradition comparable with the teachings of contemporary Judaism and the early church; but what of the material that cannot be so tested? The criterion of coherence suggested that material that cannot be tested by the criterion of distinctiveness be judged as authentic if it "will fit reasonably well into the eschatologically based demand for repentance that was characteristic of Jesus' message, and . . . will reflect or fit into the conditions (social, political, ecclesiastical, linguistic, etc.) prevailing during the earthly ministry of Jesus, rather than (or, in some cases, as well as) conditions which obtained in the postresurrection church."[22]

An early new-quest treatment of Jesus was given by Günther Bornkamm. It is instructive to compare Bornkamm's work with Bultmann's *Jesus and the Word* that had appeared thirty years earlier. Bultmann confined his presentation to Jesus' "word" and even here he confessed that "Jesus" means the message of the oldest layer of the Synoptic tradition which may not be the message of the earthly Jesus— although Bultmann believed that it was. Bornkamm acknowledged that it was impossible to attempt critically a detailed description of the course of Jesus' life biographically and psychologically. But he declared that in the tradition "the person and work of Jesus, in their unmistakable

---

[21]Reginald H. Fuller, *The New Testament in Current Study* (New York: Scribner's, 1962) 33.

[22]Charles Edwin Carlston, "A *Positive* Criterion of Authenticity?" *Biblical Research* 7 (1962): 34.

uniqueness and distinctiveness, are shown forth with an originality which again and again far exceeds and disarms even all believing understandings and interpretations. Understood in this way, the primitive tradition of Jesus is brim full of history."[23] Hence Bornkamm, after a discussion of the relationship between faith and history in the Gospels and the cultural and religious environment of Jesus, offered a chapter in which he tried "to compile the main historically indisputable traits, and to present the rough outlines of Jesus' person and history."[24]

Although "the childhood and adolescence of Jesus are obscure for us from the historical point of view," Bornkamm asserted that "the home of Jesus is the semipagan, despised Galilee. His native town is Nazareth. His family certainly belonged to the Jewish part of the population which, since the times of the Maccabees had reattached themselves to the temple cult in Jerusalem and the legal practices of Judaism." He was the son of Joseph the carpenter. Mary was his mother and we know the names of his brothers. Jesus' mother tongue was the Aramaic of Galilee, and the scene of his ministry was small towns like Bethsaida, Chorazin, and Capernaum.[25]

Jesus' baptism by John is "one of the most certainly verified occurrences of his life." We cannot say how long Jesus' ministry lasted, but "we learn a great deal about his preaching, the conflict with his opponents, his healing and the additional help he granted the suffering, and the powerful influence which went forth from him. The people flock to him. Disciples follow him, but his enemies also arise and increase." The tradition allows us to see that "the last decisive turning point in his life is the resolution to go to Jerusalem with his disciples in order to confront the people there with his message in face of the coming kingdom of God. At the end of this road is his death on the cross." Bornkamm declared that "these meagre, indisputable facts comprise a very great deal. There is little enough in this enumeration, and yet it contains most important information about the life story of Jesus and its stages."[26]

---

[23] *Jesus of Nazareth*, 26.

[24] Ibid., 53.

[25] Ibid., 53-54.

[26] Ibid., 54-55. In addition to the one chapter consisting of a personality sketch of Jesus, Bornkamm devotes one chapter each to a discussion of Jesus' disciples and Jesus' journey to Jerusalem resulting in suffering and death. The remainder of the book is given to the teaching of Jesus.

Rudolf Bultmann responded to the new questers in a paper read before the Heidelberg Academy of Sciences on 25 July 1959. He declared that he had not denied the continuity between Jesus and the kerygma. The continuity is between the historical Jesus and the primitive proclamation, not between the historical Jesus and the Christ. "The Christ of the kerygma is not a historical figure which could enjoy continuity with the historical Jesus. The kerygma which proclaims him is a historical phenomenon, however. Therefore it is only the continuity between the kerygma and the historical Jesus which is involved."[27] The kerygma presupposes the historical Jesus; without the historical Jesus there would be no kerygma. But, Bultmann said, the kerygma only presupposes the fact that Jesus was, and it is not interested in the content and character of Jesus' history. The use of historical research to legitimize the kerygma is a denial of the nature of the kerygma.

Bultmann's disinclination to enter into the new quest did not halt the project completely. However, the reservations expressed by Bultmann influenced the work of other scholars. A careful distinction was made between the various kinds of information in the New Testament, and care was taken in describing the exact significance of the historical knowledge of Jesus. This discussion is important in the new context for the study of Jesus. James M. Robinson, for example, had declared that modern historiography mediates an existential encounter with Jesus, an encounter also mediated by the kerygma.[28] Although the historical Jesus does not prove that the kerygma is true, Robinson said, the historical Jesus does confront us with "action and a self which, like the exorcisms, may be understood either as God's Spirit (Mark 3:29; Matt. 12:28), or Beelzebub (Mark 3:22), or insanity (Mark 3:21). The historical Jesus confronts us with existential decision, just as the kerygma does."[29] After Bultmann's 1959 statement, however, Robinson reformulated his position and dropped much of the emphasis on an encounter with the historical Jesus through modern historiography. Christians are to proclaim not the historical Jesus but the kerygma, but it is also important to implement the claim of the kerygma to be proclaiming a risen Lord who is identified with the earthly

---

[27]Rudolf Bultmann, "The Primitive Christian Kerygma and the Historical Jesus," in *The Historical Jesus and the Kerygmatic Christ: Essays on the New Quest of the Historical Jesus*, trans. and ed. by Carl E. Braaten and Roy A. Harrisville (New York: Abingdon, 1964) 18.

[28]*A New Quest*, 90.

[29]Ibid., 77.

Jesus by participating in the present critical historical study of Jesus. According to Robinson's later formulation, the historical study of Jesus is not of the basic task of preaching but in our situation it is necessary for the well-being and improvement of preaching.[30]

Norman Perrin, a scholar who came to the quest as a student of T. W. Manson and Joachim Jeremias, found it helpful, following Bultmann, to distinguish between three different kinds of knowledge: historical knowledge, historic knowledge, and faith knowledge. Historical knowledge is the objective factual knowledge concerning the earthly Jesus. Historic knowledge is historical knowledge that becomes significant to us in our present situation. Faith knowledge is "knowledge of Jesus of Nazareth which is significant only in the context of specifically Christian faith, that is, knowledge of him of a kind dependent upon the acknowledgment of him as Lord and Christ."[31]

The historical knowledge that we can gain from the Gospels cannot mediate an existential encounter with Jesus, but it is significant to faith. "In a tradition which 'believes in Jesus,' historical knowledge can be a source for the necessary content of faith . . . without thereby becoming the main source of that content."[32] The main source, of course, is the proclamation of the church, "a proclamation arising out of a Christian experience of the risen Lord." Knowledge of the historical Jesus can also "act negatively as a check on false or inappropriate faith-images, or aspects of a faith-image." Because the claim of the Christian church is that the risen Lord is none other than the earthly Jesus, "we may and we must use such historical knowledge of Jesus as we possess to test the validity of the claim of any given form of the Church's proclamation to be *Christian* proclamation."[33] Perrin also declared that historical knowledge of the teaching of Jesus is relevant for modern Christians. If a modern believer responding to the proclamation of the church stands in a relation to God parallel to the ancient disciple who responded to the proclamation of the earthly Jesus, then the teaching of Jesus to the disciple is also applicable to the modern believer. Of course, the practical problems remain of

---

[30]"The Recent Debate on the New Quest," *Journal of Bible and Religion* 30 (1962): 207.

[31]Norman Perrin, *Rediscovering the Teaching of Jesus* (New York: Harper & Row, 1967) 236.

[32]Ibid., 244.

[33]Ibid., 247-48.

crossing the barrier of two thousand years and a quite different world-view. But Jesus' teachings are important for Christian faith and life.

The Contemporary Scene. As we move into the contemporary period, it is difficult to discern the story behind the multiplicity of lives of Jesus, much less to examine these lives within the space allotted in this book. The subtitle of this chapter ("from Bultmann to Wright and Crossan") indicates the author's perspective. "Bultmann" indicates that for a half century Rudolf Bultmann and his school dominated the field of New Testament study in general and the approach to the life of Jesus in particular. "Wright and Crossan" refer to particular individuals who are important in the current quest, but the two names indicate that no one person has assumed the mantle of Rudolf Bultmann. In place of the two names, dozens of names could be substituted.

In the present epoch, all the options in the history of Jesus research are once more available. The different reconstructions of Jesus may be seen as resulting from different decisions concerning the following: sources to be considered (canonical sources only versus all Jesus tradition in the first three centuries); the integrity of the canonical Gospels (the Gospels as honest versus the Gospels as frauds); the historical dependability of the Markan narrative (Mark as reflective of history verses Mark as fiction), the theoretical foundation for constructing a life of Jesus (study of Jesus founded on individual units certified as authentic versus study founded on a priori hypotheses); the cultural context of the historical Jesus (Judaism versus Hellenism as the background for Jesus); the focus of the formation of the Jesus tradition (Jesus versus the church as the focus), the question of apocalyptic eschatology (Jesus as an apocalyptist versus Jesus as a moral reformer or cynical teacher); the priority of sayings or acts (the sayings of the tradition versus the deeds as more central for reconstructing Jesus).

Each of these themes has had numerous books and essays devoted to them, and most of the questions answered in a finely nuanced fashion that allows elements of both parts of the opposition to be maintained. The most interesting theories, of course, are those that attempt to defend one of the poles in the dichotomy and exclude the other and/or to defend a thesis that is original or marginal in some sense. The two groups that are most visible today are the "Jesus Seminar" (which revives the new quest in the tradition of Bultmann and his disciples) and "Third Questers" (who return to the basic agenda of Albert Schweitzer to maintain a non-Bultmannian quest).

The Jesus Seminar and Dominic Crossan

The Jesus Seminar. The Jesus seminar, beginning with concern for what the historical Jesus actually said and did, has developed a broad range of interests. It became known—even infamous—because of its work on a red-letter edition of the Gospels, that is, an attempt to determine what words attributed to Jesus were actually spoken by the historical Jesus. A scholarly agenda and a parallel popular agenda are evident in this task. The scholarly agenda grows out of the recognition that not everything attributed to Jesus in the Gospels was spoken by Jesus. Some materials are reflections of the convictions of the early church. The parallel agenda is seen in the plan to construct a red-letter edition of the Gospels. Red-letter editions are popular among Christians who approach the Gospels uncritically with the assumption that everything in red, everything attributed to Jesus in the Gospels, go back in fact to Jesus himself. Both of these agendas can be understood and appreciated by the fact that the founder of the Seminar is Robert W. Funk. Funk is a New Testament scholar who is director of the Westar Institute now of Santa Rosa, California. He taught for three decades in colleges, universities, and seminaries, writing important books in New Testament studies. He served as executive secretary and president of the Society for Biblical Literature and as director of Scholars Press. He is well known among his colleagues as a person with imagination and entrepreneurial instincts.

In *Honest to Jesus*, written between the public reports on evaluation of words ascribed to Jesus and acts attributed to Jesus, Funk described how the Jesus Seminar came into being and how it operates. In the mid-1980s, Funk wrote thirty colleagues, asking them to join him in collecting and analyzing all words and deeds attributed to Jesus up to 300 CE. Funk was surprised that no critical list of Jesus materials that could be used as the basis for a picture of Jesus had been drawn up and he felt that a group of scholars could come to some consensus about which items probably echo or mirror the life of Jesus and which belong to subsequent stages of the Jesus tradition. These original fellows were asked to invite other colleagues to join the project, and eventually about two hundred fellows and associates became part of the seminar.

Two practices in particular have been commented on in reviews of the work of the seminar—the method of voting and the public reporting of the results of the work of the seminar. The fact that textual critics responsible for creating critical texts of the Greek New Testament could come to some consensus about which text to print and which texts to consign to variants in the notes encouraged Funk to think that scholars could do the same with the Jesus tradition. The committees of textual critics used a voting procedure to determine consensus opinion, but apparently some of the members of the seminar were not so sure that they wanted to follow that procedure. Funk reports:

> We agreed at the outset, although reluctantly, to come to some decision, however tentatively and belated, however provisional, this side of the millennium. So we adopted the simple expedient of voting to see whether a consensus existed among us and, if so, what its magnitude might be. We employed our now notorious colored beads for voting purposes.[34]

The following definitions of the four colors were adopted by the seminar for the *sayings* of Jesus. Red—"Jesus said it or something very close to it." Pink—"Jesus probably said something like it, although his words have suffered in transmission." Gray—"These are not his words, but the ideas are close to his own." Black—"Jesus did not say it; the words represent the Christian community or a later point of view."

For the *acts* of Jesus, the colors indicated the following. Red—"The report is historically reliable." Pink—"The report is probably reliable." Gray—"The report is possible but unreliable; it lacks supporting evidence." Black—"The report is improbable; it is not congruent with verifiable evidence, and may well be fictive."[35]

The practice of public reports was of a piece with the purpose of the Westar Institute under whose umbrella the Jesus Seminar operates. The institute was "formed to bring the best in high scholarship—the best we can enlist—to bear on the religious issues that matter in our time, and to do so within earshot of literate readers. We have not asked ourselves to popularize or 'write down' to our readers but to say the profoundest things we have to say in plain English."[36] "In this enterprise," says Funk, "We are mounting a frontal assault on a pervasive religious illiteracy that blinds and intimidates, even those, or perhaps especially those, in positions of authority in the church and in our society."[37]

---

[34]Robert W. Funk, *Honest to Jesus: Jesus for a New Millennium* (San Francisco: HarperSanFrancisco, 1996) 8.

[35]Ibid.

[36]Ibid., 6.

[37]Ibid., 6-7.

The early work of the Jesus Seminar may be considered a continuation of the work of the new quest by disciples of Bultmann. The criteria for authentication discussed earlier in this chapter were a part of the academic heritage of the scholars involved—as of liberal New Testament scholarship in America in general. The tradition of the scholars gave allegiance to careful, critical, objective scholarship that arrived at "assured results" that were beyond question in the academy. The seminar did not begin with wide-ranging original hypotheses about Jesus that would guide discussion of the Jesus tradition. It was the project itself that was original and experimental. As the seminar members worked together on specific texts, conventional ideas about the historical Jesus and about the formation and transmission of the Jesus tradition were modified by new theories.

In a certain sense the work of the seminar has been directed at two different levels at the same time. At an implicit level is the development of a particular view of Jesus and the early church; the explicit task, of course was the work with the detailed list of sayings of Jesus. Hypotheses about Jesus and the early church affect the way that particular sayings are evaluated, but particular sayings influence the view of Jesus and the early church. An important criticism of the Jesus Seminar has been with regard to its attempt to deal with the *sayings* of Jesus in isolation from the *deeds* of Jesus. E. P. Sanders has been most critical of the results of analysis of the saying materials. He declares that "analysis of the sayings material does not succeed in giving us a picture of Jesus which is convincing and which answers historically important questions."[38]

The Parables of Jesus: Red Letter Edition was published by the Jesus Seminar in 1988. It shows continuity with scholarship on the parables and presents a picture of Jesus that is consistent with the parables seen as authentic. The sayings in the Gospel of John are excluded, not only because John contains no parables of Jesus but also because the fellows agreed that it contains no words of the historical Jesus. The fellows of the seminar agree that the two pictures painted by John and the synoptic Gospels cannot both be historically accurate. In the synoptic Gospels, Jesus speaks in brief sayings and in parables. His sayings are sometimes embedded in a short dialogue with disciples or opponents. In John, by contrast, Jesus speaks in lengthy discourses or monologues, or in

---

[38]E. P. Sanders, *Jesus and Judaism* (Philadelphia: Fortress Press; London: SCM Press, 1985) 133.

elaborate dialogues prompted by some deed Jesus has performed. The fellows of the seminar were unable to find a single saying in the Gospel of John that could with certainty be traced back to the historical Jesus. One saying in John (John 4:44) might have originated with Jesus, but this saying has synoptic parallels. The words attributed to Jesus in the Fourth Gospel are the creation of the evangelist for the most part and reflect the developed language of John's Christian community.

The parables constitute the major source of authentic sayings of Jesus. The fellows of the Jesus Seminar agree with earlier scholars of the parables that in broad structural outline the parables survived the later process of transmission very well. But at the same time the process of reinterpretation by the church is so obvious and so much at variance with the original thrust of the parables that the original form and thrust of the parables can be reconstructed with some ease. The fellows specified the characteristics of the parables of Jesus that scholarship had agreed upon, characteristics that give evidence that the parables go back to Jesus.

The parables of the synoptic Gospels, especially of Matthew and Luke, must be supplemented by other sources of the sayings of Jesus, especially the *Gospel of Thomas*. (The *Gospel of Thomas* is the name of a document discovered in this century in Egypt containing a series of sayings of Jesus.) However, the same care must be taken in determining which of these sayings in the *Gospel of Thomas* go back to Jesus as we take in determining in which of the parables of Matthew and Luke go back to Jesus. The *Parables of Jesus* indicates that most fellows hold that *Thomas* is a valuable witness to the parables and sayings of Jesus, sometimes giving a more original version of a saying or parable than the Synoptic Gospels. Most fellows hold that "Thomas is an independent witness to the Jesus tradition and is not dependent on the synoptic Gospels."[39] In fact, of the sayings unique to *Thomas*, none were voted red by the seminar and only two pink.

The results of the work of the Jesus Seminar on the parables can be evaluated in different ways. From the perspective of an uncritical observer, an observer who assumes that everything attributed to Jesus in the Gospels goes back to Jesus, the results are troublesome. There is no saying of Jesus judged by 100 percent of the fellows as undoubtedly coming from Jesus himself. In the red-letter edition of the parables of

---

[39]Robert W. Funk, Bernard Brandon Scott, and James R. Butts, *The Parables of Jesus: Red Letter Edition* (Sonoma CA: Polebridge Press, 1988) 11.

Jesus, sixty parables or variations of parables are treated, and no one of the parables is judged by 100 percent of the fellows to come from Jesus. Fourteen of the parables, indeed, were given no red votes by members of the seminar. But from the perspective of a very severe set of criteria, the results are also amazing. From the perspective of someone who thinks that everything that Jesus is quoted as saying comes from the early church, the results are astounding. Taking the red and pink vote together, representing what Jesus said or what Jesus probably said, only seventeen of the sixty parables or variations are given less than fifty percent of the vote. That is, fifty percent or more of the fellows judge that forty-three of the sixty sayings attributed to Jesus in the synoptic Gospels very probably come from Jesus himself.

On what basis did the fellows vote red or black? Rudolf Bultmann's criterion of dissimilarity was designed to sift out problematic sayings. To be sure that a saying comes from Jesus, it must be a saying that the church would not have formulated and a saying that would not have been found in contemporary Judaism. The use of this criterion is obvious in consideration of the parable of the tenants in the versions in Matthew, Mark, and Luke. These versions receive no red votes (it should be noted, however, that they received black votes from only twenty-seven percent of the fellows). Sixty-four percent of the fellows gave them gray votes. Why is there some question? The fellows judge that the versions in Matthew, Mark, and Luke have been reworked to form an allegory of the history of salvation, culminating in the rejection and death of Jesus. The landlord is God who establishes a vineyard and leases it out to tenant farmers. He sends his servants (the prophets) to collect the rent, but they treat the servants shamefully. Finally he sends his beloved son. The Christian conviction that God has vindicated his son by raising him from the dead is obvious. Interestingly enough, there is a version of the parable of the tenants found in the *Gospel of Thomas* that does not have the allegorical traits. The fellows of the seminar conclude, therefore, that the version in *Thomas* is closer to the original version, and thirteen percent gave it a red vote while sixty-four percent gave it a pink vote.

Which of the parables are overwhelmingly supported by red or pink votes? The saying of Jesus on leaven and the parables of the good Samaritan, the vineyard laborers, the dishonest steward, the prodigal son, the lost coin, the treasure, the unmerciful servant, mustard seed, unjust judge, lost sheep, the pearl, and the feast are among those at the very top in terms of red and pink votes. The saying of Jesus in Matthew

13:33b—"The kingdom of heaven is like yeast that a women took and mixed in with three measures of flour until all of it was leavened"— received ninety percent red or pink votes, and therefore, was judged by the vast majority of the members of the seminar to come from Jesus himself. The fellows judge that

> the parable of the Leaven transmits the voice of Jesus as clearly as any ancient written record can. . . . Jesus employs the image of the leaven in a highly provocative way. In Passover observance, Judaism regarded leaven as a symbol of corruption, while unleaven stood for what was holy. The Leaven provides a surprising reversal of expectations—leaven representing the kingdom of God—a strategy Fellows believe to be typical of Jesus.[40]

In terms of the good Samaritan, Jesus Seminar fellows judge that the technique and the content are typical of Jesus. "The Samaritan breaks down social and ethnic barriers by serving as the friend and savior of the anonymous Jew who was waylaid on a dangerous road."[41] A story with a Samaritan hero would have shocked a Jewish audience. The parable of the dishonest steward is seen as "typical of Jesus' authentic parables."[42] The master in the story commends the steward's dishonesty. This is a shocking story that has embarrassed Christendom from the beginning. Such shocking elements are typical of the authentic parables of Jesus.

The Jesus who is reconstructed in the process of determining which of the sayings of Jesus are authentic is a Galilean sage, not an eschatological prophet expecting history to come to an end in his own time. In *Honest to Jesus*, Funk declared that "the Fellows of the seminar were a bit surprised at their own discovery."[43] When members of the seminar were polled in 1985 on their opinions as to whether Jesus expected the end of the world in his generation, only a little over half rejected the conventional apocalyptic consensus. By 1986 three-fourths replied no. The same sort of dilemma acknowledged by the liberal scholars of the last century (such as Harnack) have faced and continue to face the Jesus Seminar and other scholars. The New Testament has apocalyptic and nonapocalyptic materials. The nineteenth-century liberal scholars chose a nonapocalyptic kingdom (explaining the apocalyptic as a nonessential

---

[40]Ibid., 29.
[41]Ibid., 31.
[42]Ibid., 32.
[43]*Honest to Jesus*, 145.

remainder of the Jewish world of Jesus) while Schweitzer chose an apocalyptic kingdom (explaining the moral teachings of Jesus as an integral part of his view of the coming of the kingdom). Some larger historical, theological, or literary framework must be posited to make sense of the coexistence of the different sorts of traditions in the Gospels. Funk provides what he calls "the best explanation" for a discrepancy between "what Jesus said and what his disciples said he said":

> Many of his followers were originally followers of John the Baptist; John was an eschatological prophet, to judge by the sayings attributed to him in Q; after Jesus died, his disciples, who had not understood his sophisticated notion of time, reverted to what they had learned from John and assigned that same point of view to Jesus.[44]

Dominic Crossan. The actual work of the Jesus Seminar shows that historical results in Jesus research are never certain; they are judgments made at particular times and places by individuals and groups on the basis of their experiences, knowledge, and ability to correlate diverse materials. The consensus arrived at by members of the seminar ought not be translated into unanimity, much less final truth. The different portraits developed by members of the Jesus Seminar show differences of temperament and judgment.

Dominic Crossan is important in the recent revival of scholarly interest in the life of Jesus because he combines historical, literary, and theological or religious interest and competence. He recognizes the limitations of historical method but this recognition leads him to attempt to be more exact in terms of method rather than to abandon historical method. He also sees the activity of the evangelists not as an illegitimate falsification of the Jesus tradition, but as a hermeneutical process that is a pattern for current believers. Above all, perhaps, is his appreciation of the literary nature of the Gospels and his own literary skill in telling the story of Jesus. His books on the historical Jesus are read not only for their scholarly achievement but also for their accessibility and pleasure.

Crossan provides important frameworks or schemata not only for uncovering "authentic" Jesus tradition but also for appreciating the processes by which those traditions were developed and used as the basis for new creations. He speaks of three major layers of the Jesus tradition. One layer is that of retention, "recording at least the essential core of

---

[44]Ibid., 145-46.

words and deeds, events and happenings." Another layer is that of development, "applying such data to new situations, novel problems, and unforeseen circumstances." A final layer is that of creation, "not only composing new sayings and new stories but, above all, composing larger complexes that change their contents by that very process."[45] Crossan is very clear on the point that there is an integrity in the processes and results involved in all three layers. He hesitates, therefore, to speak of the final layer as "authentic," as if the other two were "inauthentic." "I talk of original, developmental, and compositional layers, or of retention, development, and creation, but I reject absolutely any pejorative language for those latter processes. Jesus left behind him thinkers not memorizers, disciples, not reciters, people not parrots."[46]

Crossan's task in *The Historical Jesus*, however, concentrates upon historical Jesus tradition instead of the later stages. To ascertain the genuine tradition, Crossan catalogues all the major sources and texts (canonical and noncanonical), determines where each source or text belongs in terms of four chronological strata from 30 to 150 CE, and identifies the stratum and the extent of independent attestation of the complexes of the Jesus tradition within the sources or texts. Crossan begins his work on Jesus with primary attention to those complexes of the first stratum (those complexes that can be dated from 30 to 60 CE) that have the highest count of independent attestation (avoiding any unit found in single attestation even within the first stratum). But the literary data highlighted in such a procedure cannot simply be joined together to form a coherent picture of the historical figure of Jesus. They demand some schemata, some frameworks within which they make sense. Crossan uses a broad-level schema (a macrocosmic level) involving cross-cultural and cross-temporal social anthropology and a medium-level schema (a mesocosmic level) of Hellenistic and Greco-Roman history. (The low-level schema is the literary-specific sayings and doings, stories and anecdotes, confessions, and interpretations concerning Jesus.)

Assumptions and decisions made in the inventory of all of the sources and determination of their place in the history of the tradition from 30 to 150 CE are vital. Instead of beginning with Mark, Q, M, and L, under-standing all of the sources as reflecting the different moments in the life

---

[45]John Dominic Crossan, *The Historical Jesus: The Life of a Mediterranean Jewish Peasant* (San Francisco: HarperSanFrancisco, 1991) xxxi.
[46]Ibid.

of the church from an Aramaic-speaking Palestinian church through the Greek-speaking Hellenistic church and any of the material, therefore, having the possibility of connection with the historical Jesus, Crossan begins with materials that can be dated in terms of the time of composition. He recognizes that material in a source in a later stratum can be as original as material in a source in an earlier stratum, but he begins with material he dates as *composed* in the period 30–60. (This is the first stratum. The second stratum is dated 60–80, the third 80–120, and the fourth 120–150.)

Thirteen sources or texts are situated by Crossan in the first stratum: four of Paul's letters (1 Thessalonians, Galatians, 1 Corinthinas, and Romans); the *Gospel of Thomas* I; the *Egerton Gospel*; the Papyrus Vindobonensis Greek 2325; Papyrus Oxyrhynchus 1224; the *Gospel of the Hebrews*; the *Sayings Gospel Q*; the *Miracles Collection*, the *Apocalyptic Scenario*; and the *Cross Gospel*. Crossan, then, does not give historical priority to the synoptic Gospels, assuming that noncanonical sources derive from canonical sources. In fact, of the thirteen sources in the first stratum, four (*Sayings Gospel Q*; *Miracles Collection, Apocalyptic Scenario*; and the *Cross Gospel*) are themselves sources for canonical Gospels and the other sources are independent of the canonical Gospels.

The daring presuppositions and decisions in Crossan's chronological stratification of Jesus tradition are based both on suggestions of other scholars and on Crossan's earlier work on sources. His placing of the "first layer" of the *Gospel of Thomas* in the first stratum is important. This layer, acccording to Crossan's tentative and experimental identification, "was composed by the fifties CE, possibly in Jerusalem, under the aegis of James's authority."[47] He places the *Secret Gospel of Mark* in the second stratum. This supposedly is the first version of the Gospel of Mark composed in the early 70s. It contained passages that were expurgated in the canonical Gospel of Mark that was completed by the end of the 70s. Here Crossan is dependent upon the work of Morton Smith[48] and his own earlier reactions to that work.[49] The Gospels of Matthew and

---

[47]Ibid., 427. Crossan is especially dependent upon the work of Stephen John Patterson, *The Gospel of Thomas within the Development of Early Christianity* (Ann Arbor MI: University Microfilm International, 1988).

[48]Smith, *The Secret Gospel: The Discovery and Interpretation of the Secret Gospel according to Mark* (New York: Harper & Row, 1973) and *Clement of Alexandria and a Secret Gospel of Mark* (Cambridge MA: Harvard University Press, 1973).

[49]Crossan, *Four Other Gospels: Shadows on the Contours of Canon* (Minneapolis:

Luke are placed in the third stratum and described in terms of sources used by those Gospels and in terms of use made by later writings of those Gospels. The Gospel of Matthew was "written around 90 CE and possibly at Syrian Antioch, [and] it used, apart from other data, the Gospel of Mark and the *Sayings Gospel Q* for its prepassion narrative, and the Gospel of Mark and the *Cross Gospel* for its passion and resurrection account." The Gospel of Luke was "written possibly as early as the nineties but before John 1–20, which used its passion and resurrection account. Like the Gospel of Matthew, it used, apart from much other data, the Gospel of Mark and the *Sayings Gospel Q* for its prepassion narrative, and the Gospel of Mark and *Cross Gospel* for its passion and resurrection account."[50]

Crossan's correlation of the literary data with the middle level or Hellenistic or Greco-Roman history is important. Here he uses materials that are familiar to students of the life of Jesus, such as the writings of Josephus. But more important is his correlation of the literary data and Hellenistic history with a higher-level schema. Here he is dependent upon studies that apply the social sciences to the historical study of the New Testament. Although these studies are relatively new, they have helped us realize that different societies operate with different worldviews and social norms and that this must be considered in the study of Jesus. Instead of placing a middle-class Jesus in a world essentially like our own, Crossan attempts to establish a clear connection with the history of first-century Palestine and with the "authentic" Jesus tradition by placing a peasant Jesus in an ancient Mediterranean culture in which there was a web of patronage and clientage involving "brokers" who sustained the relationship of client to patron and the relationship of patron to client.

The notion of brokerage, in fact, is the basis for the organization of Crossan's major work on Jesus. The first part ("Brokered Empire") covers the Roman world with its developed networks of master-slave and patron-client relationships. The second part ("Embattled Brokerage") deals with the Palestinian world and the activities and events leading to the war of 66–70 CE. The final part ("Brokerless Kingdom") discusses Jesus' own

---

Winston Press, Seabury Books, 1985).

[50]*The Historical Jesus*, 430-31. Crossan cites his own study, *The Cross that Spoke: The Origins of the Passion Narrative* (San Francisco: Harper & Row, 1988) in support of these assertions.

agenda and work. Jesus, as a peasant Jewish cynic, was trying to inaugurate "the brokerless kingdom of God."

> The historical Jesus was, then, a *peasant Jewish Cynic*. His peasant village was close enough to a Greco-Roman city like Sepphoris that sight and knowledge of Cynicism are neither inexplicable nor unlikely. But his work was among the farms and villages of Lower Galilee. His strategy, implicitly for himself and explicitly for his followers, was the combination of *free healing and common eating*, a religious and economic egalitarianism that negated alike and at once the hierarchical and patronal normalcies of Jewish religion and Roman power. And, lest he himself be interpreted as simply the new broker of a new God, he moved on constantly, settling down neither at Nazareth nor Capernaum. He was neither broker nor mediator but, somewhat paradoxically, the announcer that neither should exist between humanity and divinity or between humanity and itself. Miracle and parable, healing and eating were calculated to force individuals into unmediated physical and spiritual contact with God and unmediated physical and spiritual contact with one another. He announced, in other words, the brokerless kingdom of God.[51]

In an epilogue, Crossan traces his historical reconstruction of Jesus (and, indeed, all historical study of Jesus) within the larger context of Christianity. He asks: "Is an understanding of the historical Jesus of any permanent relevance to Christianity itself?" Crossan proposes that "at the heart of any Christianity there is always, covertly or overtly, a dialectic between a historically read Jesus and a theologically read Christ."[52] The New Testament contains a spectrum of different interpretations, each of which focuses on different aspects of the historical Jesus. Crossan indicates that we may speak of these as "historical Jesuses." A given tradition may emphasize the sayings, another the miracles, another the death of Jesus. Different visions of the historical Jesus "present a certain dialectic with different theological interpretations and . . . the New Testament itself is an obvious expression of that plurality's inevitability."[53] Crossan asks how his own historical reconstruction of Jesus' brokerless kingdom can be reconciled with Christian interpretations insisting that Jesus was "wholly God" and "wholly man." Crossan declares: "I find . . . no contradiction between the historical Jesus and the defined Christ, no

---

[51]*The Historical Jesus*, 421-22.
[52]Ibid., 423.
[53]Ibid.

betrayal whatsoever in the move from Jesus to Christ." In spite of the different visions of the historical Jesus and the legitimate move from Jesus to Christ, Crossan defends the scholarly reconstruction of the historical Jesus. He indicates that reconstructions or searches for the historical Jesus should not be dismissed as mere reconstruction, "as if reconstruction invalidated somehow the entire project."[54]

Third Questers and N. T. (Tom) Wright

Crossan's work is challenged at almost every point by Tom Wright who represents a traditional non-Bultmannian (or anti-Bultmannian) approach to the study of the historical Jesus. He situates himself in a "Third Quest" which, according to Wright, attempts "to do history seriously," is willing "to be guided by first-century sources," and situates Jesus within Judaism in general and within apocalyptic Jewish eschatology in particular.[55] A major difference between the work of scholars in the tradition of Bultmann (including Crossan and the Jesus Seminar) and Wright and the Third Questers is an assumption about the historical reliability of the Jesus tradition that leads to radically different methods of dealing with the tradition. Crossan, as representative of the Bultmann tradition, places the focus on the church, assuming that—unless established by severe and objective methods—the formation of the tradition is a result of the work of the early church. Wright, on the other hand, assumes that—unless established by severe and objective criteria—the tradition is authentic historically.

Instead of the reconstructing of traditions about Jesus according to their place in the history of the early church, then, Wright sees the task of historical-Jesus research as the "advancement of serious historical hypotheses—that is, the telling of large-scale narratives—about Jesus himself, and the examination of the prima facie relevant data to see how they fit."[56] He argues that this is the way other figures of the ancient past are studied. "Nobody grumbles at a book on Alexander the Great if, in telling the story, the author 'harmonizes' two or three sources; that is his or her job, to advance hypotheses which draw together the data into a

---

[54]Ibid., 426.
[55]N. T. Wright, *Jesus and the Victory of God*, vol. 2 of *Christian Origins and the Question of God* (Minneapolis: Fortress Press, 1996) 84-85.
[56]Ibid., 88.

coherent framework rather than leaving it scattered."[57] Wright connects the contemporary view of the work of the evangelists as works of literary art with such history and with his own historical agenda. "It is becoming apparent that the authors of at least the synoptic gospels, which still provide the bulk of the relevant source material, intended to write about Jesus, not just about their own churches and theology, and that they substantially succeeded in this intention."[58]

Wright clearly begins with assumptions about the literary sources that are directly opposite those of Crossan. But just as important is the overarching schema within which the literary data is to be interpreted. Crossan's schema is one provided by contemporary studies in social anthropology. The question with which Wright begins indicates a different schema: "How does Jesus fit into Judaism?" These different beginning points may be related to the different worlds assumed by Crossan and Wright, to the different sorts of readers to whom the books are addressed, or to the different sorts of people associated with Jesus in first-century Palestine. Crossan and Wright acknowledge such matters, but in their history writing, they do not emphasize history as involving perspectives and relationships. They assume that the Jesus presented in their reconstructions would be recognized by people of Jesus' day as today. If we look at the work of Crossan and Wright from a less positivistic perspective, we might ask what sort of readers would be able to see Jesus (with the eyes of Crossan) as a peasant Jewish cynic announcing the brokerless kingdom of God? And what sort of readers would be able to see Jesus (with the eyes of Wright) as an eschatological prophet/Messiah, announcing the kingdom, dying in order to bring it about, having the success of his task declared in his resurrection, and leaving to his followers the implementation of all he had achieved?

In a later book, Crossan speaks of his readers as those who want to know what they would have seen and heard if they had been more or less neutral observers in the early decades of the first century. He acknowledges that some people ignored Jesus, some worshipped him, and others crucified him. But Crossan wants to present "an accurate but impartial account of the historical Jesus as distinct from the confessional Christ."

---

[57]Ibid.
[58]Ibid., 89.

From his perspective, "that is what the academic or scholarly study of the historical Jesus is about."[59]

The final paragraph of Wright's book gives us insight into the sort of readers he would fashion. He declares that Schweitzer was wrong when he said that Jesus comes to us as one unknown. The reality is:

> We come to *him* as ones unknown, crawling back from the far country, where we had wasted our substance on riotious but ruinous historicism. But the swinehusks—the "assured results of modern criticism"—reminded us of that knowledge which arrogance had all but obliterated, and we began the journey home. But when we approached, as we have tried to do in this book, we found him running to us as one well known, whom we had spurned in the name of scholarship or even of faith, but who was still patiently waiting to be sought and found once more. And the ring on our finger and the shoes on our feet assure us that, in celebrating his kingdom and feasting at his table, we shall discover again and again not only who he is but who we ourselves are: as unknown and yet well known, as dying and behold we live.[60]

In the body of his book, Wright contrasts his view of Jesus as a prophet with the view of Jesus as simply a teacher of wisdom (although he sees that the model of Jesus as prophet has the capacity to draw in many of the features of Jesus' life and work that emphasize Jesus as a teacher of wisdom). Wright, then, sees Jesus as "a prophet bearing an urgent eschatological, and indeed apocalyptic, message for Israel." The main arguments for this prophetic portrayal "is the sense it makes in the total context of Judaism in general, of popular movements in particular, and of John the Baptist above all."[61]

As a Jewish prophet, Jesus shared the fundamental Jewish beliefs of monotheism, election, and eschatology. He believed "that there was one God who had made the world, and who had called Israel to be his people." Even though Jesus challenged current interpretations of election, Jesus believed "that Israel was the true people of the one creator God, called to be the light of the world, called to accomplish her vocation through suffering."[62] In terms of eschatology, Jesus believed in "the coming kingdom of Israel's god, which would bring about the real return

---

[59]Crossan, *Jesus: A Revolutionary Biography* (San Francisco: HarperSanFrancisco, 1994) xi.

[60]*Jesus and the Victory of God*, 662.

[61]Ibid., 150.

[62]Ibid., 652.

from exile, the final defeat of evil, and the return of YHWH to Zion." It was this Jewish hope that Jesus made thematic for his own work. The difference between the beliefs of Jesus and the Jews of his day was that Jesus believed that the kingdom was coming in and through his own work. The particular task of Jesus was "to a offer symbolic encoding (or decoding?) of this entire theology and expectation in terms of his own life and work."[63]

Wright does not conceive of Jesus' awareness of his vocation as the sort of "supernatural" awareness of himself envisioned by those who are concerned to maintain a "high" Christology. The knowledge of Jesus was of "a more risky" but perhaps more significant, sort: like knowing one is loved. "One cannot 'prove' it except by living by it. Jesus' prophetic vocation thus included within it the vocation to enact, symbolically, the return of YHWH to Zion. His messianic vocation included within it the vocation to attempt certain tasks which, according to scripture, YHWH had reserved for himself."[64]

Wright encourages his readers to focus

> on a young Jewish prophet telling a story about YHWH returning to Zion as judge and redeemer, and then embodying it by riding into the city in tears, symbolizing the Temple's destruction and celebrating the final exodus. I propose, as a matter of history, that Jesus of Nazareth was conscious of a vocation: a vocation, given him by the one he knew as "father," to enact in himself what, in Israel's scriptures, God had promised to accomplish all by himself. He would be the pillar of cloud and fire for the people of the new exodus. He would embody in himself the returning and redeeming action of the covenant God.[65]

Wright, then, returns to a radically apocalyptic perspective of Jesus. He shares this vision of Jesus with Schweitzer although he does not agree with Schweitzer's view of traditions in Mark as reflecting an ignorance of Jesus' own understanding that must be read into those traditions. He sees the Gospel writers as theologians who had "thought deeply and creatively about the Jewish scriptures, about Israel's god, about the achievement of this god in completing the story of those scriptures in Jesus, and about the tasks and problems of their own communities as the people of this god, summoned to a life of loyalty to this Jesus." But these

---

[63]Ibid.
[64]Ibid., 653.
[65]Ibid., 653.

theologians were dependent upon "some greater, more original, more subtle mind" in their writing.[66]

One result of connecting the Jesus of history with the evangelists is to conclude that Jesus was not mistaken in his apocalyptic vision. Here Wright is diametrically opposed to Schweitzer. Jesus does not see the cross as the end. The resurrection (however it is understood) is the reality that makes sense of the historical data of the Gospels and presents a meaningful agenda for the church today.

> The real problem . . . for historians and theologians alike, is not that Jesus expected the end of the world and it failed to happen; nor that the first generation of Christians expected the return of Jesus . . . within a generation and *it* failed to happen. Those are parodies of the real problem, which is this: Jesus interpreted his coming death, and the vindication he expected after that death, as the defeat of evil; but on the first Easter Monday evil still stalked the earth from Jerusalem to Gibraltar and beyond, and stalks it still.[67]

The customary ways of dealing with this problem are to postpone the effectiveness of his supposed victory to an afterlife or to transform it into the victory of true ideas over false ideas. These ways of dealing with the question take the program of Jesus outside of Judaism and fail to take seriously the prayer of Jesus for the kingdom to come and for God's will to be done on earth as it in heaven. These options noted above did not characterize the first generations of Christians. These Christians "announced and celebrated the victory of Jesus over evil as something that had already happened, something that related pretty directly to the real world, their world. There was still a mopping-up battle to be fought, but the real victory had been accomplished. . . . That was the basis of their remarkable joy, which was not merely the tasting of hope in advance, but had to do with past and present as well."[68]

Seeing Jesus as an eschatological prophet/messiah who announced the kingdom and who died in order to bring it about, "the resurrection would declare that he had in principle succeeded in his task, and that his earlier redefinitions of the coming kingdom had pointed to a further task awaiting his followers, that of *implementing* what he had achieved." Wright, then, viewing Jesus as a good first-century Jew believing that

---

[66]Ibid., 479.
[67]Ibid., 659.
[68]Ibid.

"Israel functioned to the rest of the world as the hinge to the door; what he had done for Israel, he had done in principle for the whole world," declares that it makes sense to suppose that Jesus "envisioned his followers becoming in their turn Isaianic herald lights to the world." The mission involves action: "the aim is not simply to believe as many true things as possible, but to act in obedience, implementing the achievement of Jesus while spurred and sustained by true belief."[69]

Wright's volumes on Jesus are clearly written from within a traditional Christian perspective for readers who are able to share his faith perspectives. Wright challenges some of the naïve assumptions and dogmatic beliefs of these readers, but he is not writing to make clear what neutral observers of the first century (or neutral scholars of the twentieth century) would have seen and heard in and from Jesus of Nazareth. As we have seen, Wright's choice of the schema of the religion of Judaism is basic for his reconstruction of Jesus.

Marcus J. Borg, a member of the Jesus Seminar, is a scholar who seems to coordinate the schema of Judaism and the schema of cross-temporal and cross-cultural social anthropology. That is, he speaks to readers who are interested in what neutral observers of the first century would have concluded about Jesus and what can be said from a religious perspective. The four or five strokes sketch of Jesus painted by Marcus Borg views Jesus as a religious ecstatic, healer, wisdom teacher, social prophet, and movement founder or catalyst. These are categories we are familiar with. Borg's portrait is not distinctly Christian; it is one that is understandable to contemporary people in general. Readers are able to use these frameworks for purely historical research, but they are able also to bring these understandings to bear on their religious experience. Borg himself indicates that his historical portrait of Jesus has made a difference to him religiously. Instead of a concentration upon dogma, he sees faith as believing in the following sense: "to give one's heart, one's self at its deepest level, to the post-Easter Jesus who is the living Lord, the side of God turned toward us, the face of God, the Lord who is also the Spirit."[70]

The work of Burton L. Mack must be mentioned as one appealing to those who would find mainline Christianity oppressive. This sort of Christianity (with emphasis on Jesus' saving death, the resurrection, the

---

[69]Ibid., 660.
[70]Borg, *Meeting Jesus Again for the First Time: The Historical Jesus & the Heart of Contemporary Faith* (San Francisco: HarperSanFrancisco, 1994) 137.

eucharist, and the church), according to Mack, was founded by Mark. Mack's Jesus is a social reformer whose teachings resemble most closely those of a Cynic sage, subverting his hearers' social and cultural worlds by means of extremely engaging aphorisms. "This turns the tables on older views of Jesus as an apocalyptic preacher and brings the message of Jesus around to another style of speech altogether."[71] The invitation offered by the historical Jesus is not seen by Mack in terms of Jewish concerns. "The invitation would have been to something like the Cynic's 'kingdom,' that is, to assume the Cynic's stance of confidence in the midst of confused and contrary social circumstance. Simply translated, Jesus' 'message' seems to have been, 'See how it's done? You can do it also.' "[72]

The Church and the Critical Study of Jesus

The answer to the question of the extent and manner of the church's involvement in the study of Jesus depends upon assumptions about the nature of faith, the extent of human knowledge, and the way faith and knowledge operate together in life. The suggestions in this section are made from a poetic and sectarian perspective. That is, Christian faith is presupposed, but this faith is not seen as an ecclesiastical or dogmatic straitjacket. New light is sought that assists in the Christian pilgrimage, the explication of doctrine, and the building up of the Christian communi-ty. The movement between faith and scripture is not merely an objective scientific historical-critical enterprise; it involves the creativity of individuals and the entire Christian community. From this perspective, the church should engage in the critical enterprise, but it should engage in the critical enterprise with full awareness of the constraints of modern critical approaches and the value, danger, and inevitability of ideological frameworks and worldviews. It should engage in both a narrow "skepti-cal" quest for authentic Jesus tradition and a broad advancing of hypotheses that cannot be validated by narrow criteria.

The enterprise concerned to analyze and authenticate Jesus tradition by the severest criteria is modeled by those using the criteria devised in the tradition of Rudolf Bultmann—beginning with the criterion of dissimilarity. Engagement in this sort of skeptical scholarship should be

---

[71]Mack, *A Myth of Innocence: Mark and Christian Origins* (Philadelphia: Fortress Press, 1988) 59.
[72]Ibid., 73.

maintained recognizing that the criteria will sift out tradition that could well be authentic. It is, then, only one methodological strategy. It indeed tends to problematize the broader Jewish nature of the historical Jesus and the distinctively Christian transformation of and/or challenge to this tradition. The church should also engage in the enterprise concerned to develop and use higher-level schemata that seek correlation and synthesis of tradition and guard against the methodological skepticism implicit in the effort to establish virtually infallible positions. Just as the skeptical analytic approach needs to be questioned, the affirmative synthetic approach needs to be challenged. As a historical-critical approach, it must not devolve into naïve gullibility. In order for the church's involvement in the critical enterprise to accomplish the purpose of relating the church to the world, preventing the church from living a ghetto existence, the method must be recognized as a legitimate method by secular scholars. The work of Adolf Schlatter in the early decades of this century and Peter Stuhlmacher in the present time collapse conventional historical method and a method that explicitly recognizes the sacred as involved in history. These and other believers are engaged in a legitimate and helpful task, but I would suggest that different tasks are involved and the question needs to be divided.

In the early part of this century, Schlatter protested the methodologically skeptical historical method (termed the "atheistic method"). According to Schlatter, criticism is required because a revelation that discloses God apart from and separate from human beings does not exist. The glory of God is not that God is capable of being the author of an inerrant book but that God has entered into a relationship with mortals so that as mortals they could speak God's word.[73] Criticism, however, is not simply exercised by an autonomous subject examining history as an object. It is exercised by observing the historical events that lie behind the traditional texts, events in which the certainty of God for individuals and for humankind as a whole is produced.[74] The theologian has the duty not only of observing the religious event but of grasping the event with a resolute devotion to the theologian's own purposes and perspectives.

---

[73] Adolf Schlatter, *Das Christliche Dogma*, 2nd ed. (Stuttgart: Calwer Verlag, 1923) 375.

[74] "Äthestische Methoden in der Theologie," in *Zur Theologie des Neuen Testaments und zur Dogmatik: Kleine Schriften mit einer Einführung* (Munich: Chr. Kaiser Verlag, 1969) 142-43.

The method of the historical exegete must be appropriate to the objectives of both the biblical text and the exegete.

> If we wish to explain religion from the perspective of the world, from the very beginning onward we set ourselves in a radical opposition to the subject matter which will not be explained from the perspective of the world but which asserts the idea of God loudly and persistently. Our object requires that we think of God; the neutral observer wishes to think "without including the idea of God." A sharp conflict of wills is evident; can we still perceive in spite of this? The more we desire not only to observe in a neutral fashion but also to explain and the more the object of religion is included in our complete schema, the more obvious the scientific caricature becomes and the more the alleged scientific method is transformed into a polemic against its real objective with a work of fiction resulting, a work that does not testify to the series of events but to the historian.[75]

Peter Stuhlmacher has recapitulated the arguments of Schlatter against the background of the work of Bultmann and his students. In two editions of his *Hermeneutics*,[76] Stuhmacher insists upon the historical nature of the biblical writings and the historical nature of the events to which they witness. In the first edition, Stuhlmacher gave attention to the modification of the historical method, with the assumption that a modified historical method will match the function of the Bible. The biblical texts witness to a reality that the principles of historical study, as enunciated by Troeltsch, are not capable of perceiving; a witness of God that transcends particular historical periods; a witness of truth that is constitutive for human life, the truth incarnate in Jesus Christ: a witness of the work of Jesus as Messanic reconciler. The purpose of the Bible, which is seen clearly by historical observation, is to engender faith. While the Bible serves as more than a historical collection, Stuhlmacher did not advocate a special hermeneutics for faith since the original historical purpose seen through historical research is consent (*Einverständnis*) to the biblical text. The purpose of the text may be carried out whether one is concerned with information as historical knowledge or information related to faith because the texts were written originally for the purpose of giving an

---

[75]Ibid., 148-49.

[76]Stuhlmacher, *Vom Verstehen des Neuen Testament: Eine Hermeneutik, Grundrisse zum Neuen Testament* (Göttingen: Vandenhoeck & Ruprecht, 1979 and 1986).

understandable report about Jesus' messianic work of reconciliation and engendering belief in him for those seeking information and direction.[77]

If historical method is necessary, and the method is to deal with life-giving and life-sustaining forces, with the witness of God made perceivable in the historical linguistic documents, then historical method must be more than or different from the conventional historical method. It must be an instrument that has the capacity for dealing with the purpose of confrontation with the biblical texts and their world. Stuhlmacher suggested that the principle of perception must be used alongside Troeltsch's principles of correlation, criticism, and analogy. Through the power of this principle, we may regain the possibility of discovering in history something new and without analogy. A new search may be inaugurated for the powers in the tradition that may establish and sustain life.

In a second edition of his *Hermeneutics*, Stuhlmacher does not allow even a modified historical criticism to carry the full weight of biblical study. Rather, he situates historical criticism within a more comprehensive model. He concludes with a reformulated model of biblical interpretation, about which he declares: "The ecclesiastical interpretation of scripture purposed by us is not exhausted with the description of the text as a historical phenomenon. It begins with and serves the present (ecclesiastical) use of scripture."[78] He distinguishes two major processes. An initial process of analysis involves the attempt to illuminate the texts themselves and the processes behind their creation and their historical individuality. The second phase grows out of this initial move. It is a process of interpretation that is accomplished in three steps.

In the first step the text is traced again as precisely as possible in its original setting and with all aspects of its "world" taken into consideration. The second step involves the placing of the particular text with its affirmations in the total canonical context of the Old and New Testaments and the evaluation of the texts in this framework. The final step is the development of an interpretation that speaks directly to the present.

> Through the conscious interlacing of historical analysis and dogmatically reflective interpretation we avoid a historical-critical biblicism that deludes itself into believing that it is exempt from all dogmatic responsi-

---

[77]*Vom Verstehen des Neuen Testament*, 1st ed., 218-19.
[78]*Vom Verstehen des Neuen Testament*, 2nd ed., 242.

bility, and also avoid the different varieties of a pure dogmatic use of Scripture that is no longer historically responsible.[79]

I would divide the question as raised by Schlatter and Stuhlmacher, suggesting that the church engage in conventional historical-critical study—not a modified historical-critical study, not one interlaced with dogma, but emphasizing that historical-critical study does not constitute the gatekeeper to all truth. The church should engage in a historical study that is recognized as historical-critical study by the academy. As the church engages in such study it cannot help but acknowledge to herself and to her fellow historians that for her history and the sacred cannot finally be divided. (The sacred is not to be simply identified with the history of the world, but the sacred cannot be isolated from the world.) The church can engage in historical-critical study with integrity as it sees history as real. History is not the enactment of a predetermined script. The sacred is related to history in a realistic not an idealistic fashion. God, the world, and the church are in dynamic process. The limitations involved in history are not only limitations in terms of method; they involve genuine divine as well as human contingency.

The church's engagement with political, social, cultural, and other this-worldly references, even though it is solidly historical, is penultimate to her own agenda and may be shaped in ways that impinge upon values that transcend these references, values that are more ultimate for the church. This is not an interlacing of pure history and dogma, for every history of Jesus will be a mixture of data gleamed from the Jesus tradition and a perspective from which that data is chosen and organized. We can tell the Jesus story conscious of Christian affirmations about Jesus as the Christ, and conscious of the constraints (limitations and requirements) of historical reconstruction. The story of Jesus will be recorded in a way as not to be inconsistent with the period of Jesus. What sorts of actions and teachings can be mapped with historical conviction from the world of Jesus to the life of Jesus. What can be understood from the human historical level that can at the same time be susceptible to transcendent realities?

The emphasis upon the Jewish context for understanding Jesus broadens the perspective in an appropriately scholarly fashion. E. P. Sanders, for example, begins with the assumption that Jesus is to be

---

[79]Ibid., 241-42.

understood within first-century Judaism, particularly within the context of Jewish restoration eschatology. Events in the life of Jesus are then interpreted within a religious framework. N. T. Wright's five specific questions guiding the work of the Third Questers are historical-critical sorts of questions that impinge upon the church's agenda: (1) How does Jesus fit into Judaism? (2) What was Jesus seeking to *do* within Judaism? (3) Why did Jesus die? (4) How and why did the early church begin? and (5) Why are the Gospels what they are? Wright lists a sixth question that leads directly into Christology: How is the Jesus we discover by doing history related to the contemporary church and world? The four- or five-stroke sketch of Jesus painted by Marcus Borg is a sketch that views Jesus as religious ecstatic, healer, wisdom teacher, social prophet, and movement founder or catalyst. Borg's sketch of Jesus is one understandable to non-Christians, and it gives a credibility to the traditions about Jesus. The suggestion of scholars (such as Burton Mack and John Dominic Crossan) that Jesus was a wandering cynic or a wandering Jewish cynic is a way of moving away from stifling overly cautious approaches.

In an essay "From the Humanity of Christ to Jesus of History: A Paradigm Shift in Catholic Christology," John Galvin delineates five issues "where historical information about Jesus is . . . of pivotal significance for the development of systematic theology."

> (1) The presuppositions in Jesus' own person for his preaching and public activity, (2) Jesus' understanding of his own salvific significance, (3) the coexistence of present and future dimensions in Jesus' proclamation of the kingdom of God, (4) Jesus' stance toward the approach of his own death, and (5) reference points in Jesus' public life and death for the emergence of the church and the origin of the sacraments.[80]

These items are susceptible to historical research, and they are matters that are central to theology. When scholars in the Catholic tradition come to historical study of Jesus in light of theological interests today, they are following a different paradigm than that which was dominant until the last quarter of this century. Until about 1970, Jesus was studied in relation to the foundation of faith, oriented toward the Chalcedonian dogma of Christ's two complete natures. The new paradigm focuses on the his-

---

[80]John P. Galvin "From the Humanity of Christ to Jesus of History: A Paradigm Shift in Catholic Christology," *Theological Studies* 55 (1994): 257-58.

torical Jesus, not on the theological definition of the humanity of Christ. The doctrine of Chalcedon is still affirmed, at least by most authors, but the Chalcedonian terminology no longer establishes the vocabulary and context for Christological investigation and reflection. Consistent with insights into contemporary study of the New Testament, the method of study in the new paradigm seeks bases for Christological affirmation no longer by "appeal to direct personal claims on Jesus' part" but rather "in Jesus' own life." This is due not only to the "lack (or paucity) of assured explicit Christological statement prior to Jesus' death and resurrection," but because "an isolation from implicit presuppositions, explicit verbal claims would in themselves be neither intelligible nor self justifying."[81]

The involvement of the church in historical-Jesus research will be encouraged and enhanced when it recognizes that historical discoveries and reconstructions cannot disprove Christian faith. Christian faith is not essentially dependent upon what can be discovered through any critical method. Dan Via raises the question as to "how much history must we be able to identify as the real historical past in order to justify the biblical claim that revelation occurs *in* history."[82] The question could be asked in a different fashion: What would have to be disproved to invalidate Christian faith? Avery Dulles lists both some facts that would seriously affect Christian faith if they were disproved and some points on which historians can confirm Christian faith.[83] These sorts of questions may reflect a lingering influence of a positivism that is no longer dominant in philosophy and theology. From a Christian perspective the question might take the form: What hermeneutical strategies allow us to correlate the Jesus tradition seen to be historically authentic with that which is more overtly a witness to the significance of Jesus as the Christ? What moves allow both of these sorts of tradition to bolster a contemporary belief in the God of Jesus Christ and foster an intellectual explication (not proof) of this belief?

---

[81]Ibid., 258-59.

[82]Via, *The Revelation of God and/as Human Reception in the New Testament* (Harrisburg PA: Trinity Press International, 1997) 43. Via does not think that the question can be finally answered, but he finds the question worth pursuing because historical critics continue to make determined efforts to acquire historical knowledge and because the pursuit of the question helps us gain some purchase on the nature of revelation in the New Testament—even without a final answer.

[83]"Historians and the Reality of Christ," *First Things* 28 (December 1992): 22, 24. Cited in Galvin, "From the Humanity of Christ to the Jesus of History: A Paradigm Shift in Catholic Christology," 257-58.

The answer as to how to move from the historical study of the traditions to belief and doctrine (and from belief and doctrine to the traditions)
may begin with the reverse of the perspective that historical-critical study
cannot *disprove* Christian faith: historical-critical study cannot *prove*
Christian faith. Historical-critical study itself cannot uncover a historical
figure who is the object of faith. Historical study as such, then, cannot
mediate an encounter with the Christ of faith. This encounter is mediated
in the community of faith through proclamation of the risen Lord. But the
one proclaimed is not a mythological figure. To convert the object of
Christian devotion into a mythological, nonhistorical figure would solve
certain dogmatic problems, but it would deny basic Christian convictions.
It would be comparable to choosing one of the poles of the discussion
concerning the humanity and divinity of Jesus Christ in an earlier epoch.
The church, nevertheless, can implement the claim of the continuity
between the risen Lord and the earthly Jesus by participation in historical
study of Jesus. The church's involvement in historical-critical study
emphasizes the historicity of Jesus. Jesus is not a Gnostic myth.

The historical study of Jesus, then, supports contemporary proclamation of the church as it clarifies the relationship between Jesus and the
Christ while it cautions that the Jesus rediscovered by historical research
is not the same as the Christ of Christian faith. Historical studies makes
it difficult to map the historical figure onto the dogmatic, but the solution
to this problem is not to forsake genuine historical-critical studies, but to
delve more deeply into the mystery of the relationship of history and the
sacred.

The contemporary exploration of the Gospels in the light of literary
experience and conventions allows us to reexamine and reevaluate the
dogmatic and historical affirmations and experiences of the church. Amos
Wilder is the literary critic and biblical scholar who opened the door for
correlation of genuine historical and literary study for many of us at a
time when Rudolf Bultmann's existential approach cast a shadow on
historical study and was out of tune with literary imagination. According
to Wilder,

> the parts and the wholes [of a Gospel] are not a self-enclosed sequence
> separate from the actualities which it recites or from their antecedents.
> The "story-world" is one face of a determining event-world. A literary
> reading a Gospel should take account of its poetics, but also of its
> semantics, and these will evoke a lived history reaching back into the
> past. The evangelist and his readers, before and apart from any written

Gospel, had already been shaped by a history both of language and events going back into the earliest tradition. It is therefore not only legitimate but mandatory to search out those latent strata and motifs in Mark's narrative in terms of which the new community had been oriented and empowered from its beginning, especially where, as in the case of the parables, they lie so close to the surface of the record. This kind of investigation should not be accused of "historicism." Reconstruction of earlier forms and "language events" underlying our Gospels is one aspect of our full encounter with what is written. The point is that "what is written," in the case of texts like these, is profoundly *referential* and does not belong only to some detached "story-world."[84]

The scholarly operations in bringing formative phases and events of the Christian community to life constitute an appropriate clarification of the church's life and memory. The Gospels are literary and historical products, containing literary narrative and discourses resulting from historical experiences, going back to Jesus and the earliest disciples but extending to the church of the New Testament and even to our day. Historical research by all scholars may help us to reestablish (hypothetically, to be sure) the this-worldly points of reference, the social, political, and religious circumstances of origin. The church may focus on faith perspectives. With the help of historical and literary tools, the critic may seek the different sorts of faith perspectives presupposed by and lying behind the literary forms of the proclamation in the Gospels. The historian may seek to establish some sort of continuity and/or discontinuity between later faith perspectives and earlier faith perspectives—even moving to the pre-Easter community of disciples. Detlev Dormeyer, for example, deals with the miracle stories as

> post-Easter constructions that are dependent on the charismatic healings and exorcisms of the pre-Easter Jesus. His healings and casting out of demons symbolized the dawning of the Kingdom of God, which broke the power of the demons that cause possession and illness. After Easter, the liberating memory of Jesus' healing activities was extended to the limits of death and the powers of nature as they affect humanity. Jesus as the bringer of the Kingdom of God leads to new levels of belief.[85]

---

[84]Amos N. Wilder, *Jesus' Parables and the War of Myths: Essays on Imagination in the Scriptures* (Philadelphia: Fortress Press, 1982) 30-31.

[85]Detlev Dormeyer, *The New Testament Among the Writings of Antiquity* (Sheffield: Sheffield Academic Press, 1998) 258.

Historical research may serve the church by calling into question inappropriate forms of faith. More importantly, the church may give attention to the faith perspectives behind the literary products in order to emulate them in appropriate fashion in the contemporary world. The assumption of such faith perspectives of course, is not demanded by the research. When Gospels as wholes and the different sorts of forms within the Gospels are approached as literature, however, the sharpest distinction made by Bultmann between the Christ of the proclamation and the Jesus of history may be blunted. To be sure the historical Jesus does not prove that the proclamation is true. The historical Jesus may not confront us with the sorts of ultimate decisions with which the proclaimed Christ presents us. But the same sorts of human responses are involved in literary interaction. We have in the New Testament the proclamation in the form of lasting fixed expressions—not simply of language, not simply of life in general, but of historical experience with life-giving and language-changing realities that both respond to and defy our objectivized methods of study.

The church can deal with the teachings of Jesus that can be authenticated from the historical perspective and from the faith perspectives uncovered by research. Again, the teachings may not be forced upon readers. But readers have resources to translate those teachings into appropriate contemporary sense and meaning when they see themselves in relation to the proclamation of the church as the ancient disciples were in relation to the proclamation of Jesus. The critical task is penultimate, a means to a relevant transcendent Word. Jesus' teachings, as they may be authenticated by contemporary historical-critical study, are important for Christian faith and life. Later teachings do not thereby become "inauthentic" for Christians. They may be examined historically in relation to Jesus' teachings and these too may be explicated in a fashion to become relevant for contemporary believers.

The church should engage in the study of the historical Jesus in light of its own commitments, allowing these commitments to be stated and restated in both the intellectual and faith terms and understandings that are accepted in the community of faith and in the intellectual community. Meaning will not be proved thereby, but intelligibility will be spread over the faith assumptions and conclusions. In this process, the historical-critical agenda may be correlated with the literary-critical and with the theological. Still, the integration will always be incomplete and dynamic. Different perspectives will facilitate different ways of seeing relationships.

As suggested earlier, biblical texts, including the Gospel text may be envisioned as food to be digested. The process of digestion is divided into stages of interaction between enzymes, acids, and nerve receptors. On every level some portion is assimilated but some is left undigested to be assimilated at another level. The application of historical-critical codes to the text is valuable but it does not exhaust the Gospel text. To accept only what can be authenticated historically leaves material undigested. So literary codes may be applied, and the results of such application may be correlated with results of the historical reading. Religious and theological codes offer further possibilities for reading the Gospel text.

The study of the historical Jesus has proceeded as a modern enterprise, with the rationalistic and empirical assumptions of the Enlightenment serving as a foundation. Biblical scholars often do not deal with the philosophical or even theological presuppositions of their study, but here is a case where we cannot afford to ignore the contemporary philosophical and theological context in which severe rationalistic presuppositions have been relativized. The modern world and modern ways of knowing are now seen as a subset of any real world and ways of knowing. Enlightenment rationality (modern ways of knowing) is seen as limited, instrumental, and penultimate. But such rationality is the basis of judgment and, therefore, any judgment shares the partial and instrumental nature of Enlightenment rationality. In light of our Western intellectual tradition, we want judgments to be validated as certain (at least virtually certain), from a position outside of history, and when this is impossible we use the term "relativity" which means uncertainty.

"Relativity" is a bad word. What if we changed the word to "relational"? Historical truth is always relational. It is not just that our knowledge of history is always related to our knowing; it is that historical events in and of themselves are real events that made a difference in the ebb and flow of history because they are dynamically related to the context in which they take place.

From a Platonic perspective what is really real is a world divorced from history. In Hegelian schemes, history is reduced to the movement toward absolute spirit. In severe apocalyptic schemes, history is devalued. It really doesn't make any difference, for example, whether we trash our earth or not. The God above history will sort it all out. Perhaps that is one reason that antiapocalyptic views of Jesus are attractive to some in our current phase of the historical study of Jesus. How can we conceive of God as related in a vital ongoing way to God's creation. Two factors, at least, would be involved. One would be the reconceptualization of God's relationship with the world so that God's transcendence does not preclude God's immanence. God is more than God's creation, but God is not absolutely other than God's creation. Another factor would be the reconceptualizing of human experience in terms of this immanent-transcendent God.

Karl Rahner, perhaps more than any other theologian, has attempted to deal with human openness to God as a human existential (a characteristic of human existing that makes it specifically human and distinguishes it from other modes of existence). Rahner's "Transcendental Method" is set within Roman Catholic thought, but it may be helpful for Protestants who have made such a radical separation between God and God's world and God and humankind. Rahner himself summarizes his purpose in his theological enterprise: "I really only want to tell the reader something very simple. Human persons in every age always and everywhere, whether they realize it and reflect upon it or not, are in relationship with the unutterable mystery of human life that we call God."[86] Marcus Borg has hinted at some of the things I am suggesting in his essay "A Renaissance in Jesus Studies."

> In my own work, the picture of Jesus as a charismatic or "holy man" vividly in touch with what the texts call "Spirit" radically challenges the flattened sense of reality pervading the modern worldview and much of the mainline church, and suggests that reality might indeed be far more mysterious than we suppose. It invites us to consider seriously the central claim of the Jewish-Christian tradition (and most religious traditions): that we are surrounded by an actual, even though nonmaterial, reality charged with energy and power with which it is possible to be in a relationship. Similarly, the picture of Jesus as a subversive sage undermining his culture's conventional assumptions, as a prophet calling it to change its historical direction, and as a revitalization movement founder seeking to create an alternate culture, all point to deep involvement in the life of history. The historical Jesus may well have been more historical than we supposed."[87]

We ought not equate God and God's action in an unproblematic fashion with the history that we uncover through historical research.

---

[86]*Karl Rahner in Dialogue: Conversations and Interviews, 1965–1982* (New York: Crossroad, 1986) 147.

[87]"A Renaissance in Jesus Studies, *Theology Today* 45 (1988–1989): 292.

God's Word in history is hidden, but present. But we may reevaluate our hesitancy at speaking of Jesus' experience of God and the disciples' experience of the God of Jesus Christ. Unless we are willing to reevaluate that, we may have trouble framing some way of understanding our actually being related to God in our day, being related in a way that makes a difference. Stanley Grenz and Roger Olson have examined twentieth-century theology in the interplay of transcendence and immanence. They conclude with a tilt toward the transcendent, but speak of God as

> imminent in our circumstances, sharing our present. . . . the God who addresses us from beyond—from the then-and-there—who is God who is with us in the present—in the here-and-now. Our realization of this truth lies at the heart of the theological balancing of the divine immanence with the divine transcendence.[88]

---

[88]Stanley J. Grenz and Roger E. Olson, *20ᵗʰ Century Theology: God and the World in a Transitional Age* (Downers Grove IL: InterVarsity Press, 1992) 315.

Chapter 8

The Significance of Literary Criticism for New Testament Hermeneutics: Bultmann Revisited

A pluralism of methods reigns today in biblical interpretation—ideological, historical, sociological, literary, and so on. New Testament scholars use a variety of methods, including a multitude of literary methods and different sorts of reader-oriented literary approaches. In this chapter I limit myself to a reader-oriented literary and hermeneutical method of biblical interpretation, one directed to meaning and significance for the contemporary reader. Since the theme is hermeneutics, the chapter must deal with the New Testament scholar of this century who established the ground rules and set the agenda for hermeneutics—Rudolf Bultmann.

I will begin with a summary of Bultmann's theological and existential hermeneutics, suggesting that Bultmann's concern for an existential interaction with the Bible—with questions of will, decision, choice, and intention—led to a failure to give due attention to the imaginative and the cognitive. A second section suggests why Bultmann failed to utilize the literary resources available to him. Then I will introduce some suggestions of the literary scholars Hans Robert Jauß and Wolfgang Iser to provide a reader-oriented literary framework that allows literary approaches to connect with theological hermeneutics. In a fourth section I will deal with the question of a concept of deity that is appropriate for an approach to the reading of the biblical text as an experience of transcendence. Finally, I will suggest the major values of a literary-oriented theological hermeneutics.

Rudolf Bultmann's Theological and Existential Approach to New Testament Hermeneutics

Biblical hermeneutics may be seen as a way of making a connection between the contemporary reader and the ancient biblical text. Believers and the believing community have always been able to make the connection. The ancient community of faith (the rabbis and primitive Christians, for example) developed rules by which they could take ancient legal material and apply it to ever-contemporary situations. They could also read the ancient stories of Israel as if the stories were referring to their own day. In Luke 4, for example, Jesus is in the synagogue in Nazareth where he reads from the prophet Isaiah and concludes: "Today this scripture has been fulfilled in your hearing." Distance between Isaiah and Jesus was dissolved. I was taught, along with all New Testament students of my day, to honor that distance. We were taught to reestablish the historical meaning and then to apply that meaning to the contemporary situation. One problem was that we could not establish the ancient meaning in a conclusive fashion. Another problem was that when we did establish a possible original meaning we did not have the tools to relate that meaning to our world. The Enlightenment had dug a ditch separating history and historical meaning from theology.

The New Testament scholar Rudolf Bultmann taught us that the ditch did not matter, that historical reconstruction as such is a "crutch" for faith and unnecessary (as well as impossible in terms of the story of Jesus). The theological approach of Bultmann can be seen in an essay he wrote before the years spent with Martin Heidegger at Marburg and before his demythologizing program. In his essay entitled "The Problem of a Theological Exegesis of the New Testament" published in 1925,[1] Bultmann evaluated contemporaneous methods of New Testament study and judged them all as insufficient because in them the original intention of the text is given up, the claim of the text upon the reader is forsaken. Instead of giving attention to the existential life of the reader, the text is observed for its own sake. Bultmann criticized in succession the different approaches: the older rationalism and its attempt to make universal truths out of

---

[1]Bultmann, "Das Problem einer theologischen Exegese des Neuen Testaments" in Jürgen Moltmann, ed., *Anfänge der dialectischen Theologie*, part 2 (Rudolf Bultmann, Friedrich Gogarten, Eduard Thurneysen), Theologische Bucherei 17/2 (München: C. Kaiser, 1963) 47-72.

the teachings in the biblical text; the historical approach and its attempt to see history as a closed system of cause and effect and its reduction of individual particulars to universal historical principles; the biological, sociological, and psychological reduction of humankind; and the romantic/aesthetic perspective of humankind.

> In all these cases the text is . . . seen from a distance. The critics sees "what is there" from the assumption that what is there is to be perceived, can only be perceived, independent of its own perspective, with the assumption that the texts can be interpreted without interpreting the subject matter that the texts refer to. On the basis of texts so interpreted history is understood without asking if there perhaps are not some essential realities in history that can be observed only if one is willing to give up the distancing process, when one is ready to take seriously the stance of the texts. . . . The historical-critical and history-of-religions exegesis in particular affirm that a certain event at a certain time under certain historical circumstances and psychological constraints was thought, said, and done, without reflecting on the meaning and claim of what is being said.[2]

Bultmann compares the existential perspective of human beings with that of idealism, romanticism, and psychology. The idealist sees humans in terms of reason, the romanticist sees human beings in terms of aesthetic perspectives and structures, the psychologist sees the human in terms of psychological circumstances, in terms of psychological drives and experiences. In all of these, human existence is seen as an existence that can be objectified, defined in terms of needs and uses, existence that can be made secure through our scientific processes.

With exegesis directed to the subject matter of existence another perspective of human being prevails:

> Human existence is not seen in the abstract whereby a human being is an exemplar of the type "humankind," but it is seen in terms of individual lives that move in time with their moments of uniqueness and unrepeatability, with their experiences and decisions. That means that our existence for ourselves is not secure and at our disposal but insecure, problematic, that we are therefore ready to hear words as words and to hear questions that mean decision for us, to hear the claim of a text as an authority, demanding a decision.[3]

---

[2]Ibid., 50.
[3]Ibid., 56.

In later work Bultmann will call on other ideas to add weight to his call for existential interpretation. The work of Heidegger on the philosophical question of being and the work of Hans Jonas on myth were important. Bultmann is searching for a way of knowing that is not limited to the constraints of scientific ways of knowing growing out of Enlightenment rationality. He speaks of these Enlightenment ways of knowing as objectifying thinking. Such scientific thinking does not come to final conclusions, but is always in process. Bultmann questions what meaning such a science could have for theology and the church—a science that always leads to relatively certain results. He acknowledges that in terms of ideas, interpretation is a continual process—but with understanding itself it is a different matter. A final understanding of a text is possible when that understanding has to do with an understanding of human existence from the perspective of the possibilities of the exegete's own existence. This understanding is not a result of continuing scientific research.

In his 1941 essay on demythologizing, Bultmann spoke of the relationship between Heidegger's analysis of human existence (Dasein) and the New Testament perspective on human existence.

> Above all, Martin Heidegger's existentialist analysis of human existence seems to be only a profane philosophical presentation of the New Testament view of who we are: beings existing historically in care for ourselves on the basis of anxiety, ever in the moment of decision between the past and the future, whether we will lose ourselves in the world of what is available and of the [impersonal] "one," or whether we will attain our authenticity by surrendering all securities and being unreservedly free for the future.[4]

Bultmann's differentiation between ideas and concepts of theology that are constantly changing and an existential understanding that does not change leads him to value Heidegger's analysis of *Dasein* ([human] being) as transcending objectifying methods. Heidegger's ideas are ideas that are not subject to alteration. In terms of the "existential understand-

---

[4]Bultmann, "Neues Testament und Mythologie: Das Problem der Entmythologisierung der neutestamentlischen Verkündigung," in *Kerygma und Mythos* 1, ed. H. W. Bartsch, 2nd ed. (Hamburg: Herbert Reich-Evangelischer Verlag, 1951) 41. ET: "New Testament and Mythology: The Problem of Demythologizing the New Testament Proclamation," in *New Testament and Mythology and Other Basic Writings*, selected, edited, and translated by Schubert M. Ogden (Philadelphia: Fortress Press, 1985) 23. For a variant translation, see "New Testament and Mythology," *Kerygma and Myth. A Theological Debate*, ed. Hans Werner Bartsch, trans. Reginald H. Fuller (London: S.P.C.K., 1953) 24-25.

ing of human being," Bultmann asserts, "one can certainly say that state-ments expressing it [the conclusions of philosophical analysis] have the meaning of timeless truths and, insofar as they are to the point, can be valid as such."[5]

Bultmann's Neglect of Literary Resources

We are now prepared to ask about Bultmann's view as to the value of literary perspectives and approaches for existential interpretation. Naturally Bultmann was well acquainted with classical and modern litera-ture. The question does not have to do with Bultmann's knowledge. Two major points are important. First of all, the text-intrinsic formalist approach that was dominant in the mid-twentieth century was methodo-logically and theoretically closed to extrinsic factors. A major impulse of this formalist method was dissatisfaction with the positivist (objectifying) assumptions that the literary work was to be interpreted only out of the sum of its historical constraints. The literary work was elevated from the effect of a historical cause to an independent object of research. Especially important were the description of linguistic means, structure, and compositional effect. The work-immanent method can be seen as a retreat not only from the positivism of literary history but also from the subjectivism of "the meaning of life." The impulse behind the text-intrinsic approach was not alien to Bultmann's agenda, but it did not lead immediately to existential interpretation. In "The Problem of Hermeneu-tics" (1950), Bultmann acknowledges the value of a formal analysis of literary works and the relationship of formal analysis to analysis of content. In a note he mentions the attempt of Ernst Bushor to correlate stylistic analysis and existential interpretation, but he indicates that this is not carried out with particularly clear categories.[6] Bultmann, then, senses the possibility of relating formalist literary interpretation to existential interpretation, but he does not make this move. Perhaps the supposed superficiality of literary meanings led to this neglect.

---

[5]Bultmann, "Zum Problem der Entmythologisierung," 179-208 in *Kerygma und Mythos. Ein theologisches Gespräch* II, ed. Hans Werner Bartsch (Hamburg: Ev. Verlag, 1952) 201. ET: "On the Problem of Demythologizing," in *New Testament and Mythology and Other Basic Writings*, 116.

[6]Bultmann, "Das Problem der Hermeneutik" (1950), 211-35 in *Glauben und Verstehen* II (Tübingen: Mohr, 1968) 224n.20. ET: "The Problem of Hermeneutics," in *New Testament and Mythology and Other Basic Writings*, 92n.20.

The second major reason Bultmann neglected using contemporary literary resources in his project, therefore, was his view that literary approaches and meanings operate at a superficial level. In his opinion, philosophical analysis moves to a deeper level than the meanings and effects at a literary level. The work of Wilhelm Dilthey forms the background not only for Bultmann's hermeneutics but also for his reaction to literary study. Dilthey saw hermeneutics as dealing with permanently fixed expressions of life. Some expressions of humankind are so fleeting that no method of understanding can be focused on them; some expressions are so simple as to be understood directly or so complex as to preclude understanding in a deep sense; but some expressions are permanently fixed expressions of life, and it is the interpretation of these that Dilthey finds significant. By "expressions" of life Dilthey means that life has stamped its mark on these literary pieces. And it is this life that Dilthey wants to recover from the literature. How can this life be deciphered? Poetics, or the creative capacity of the human being, is seen by Dilthey as the solution to the hermeneutical question.

Bultmann found part of Dilthey's work on human nature important for his own existential hermeneutics. He cites Dilthey in relation to the material means that allows the Bible to be interpreted in terms of human existence. The author of the text is the material means allowing such interpretation. Interpretation is possible because author and interpreter "have the same life relation to the subject matter under discussion or in question." Dilthey maintained that the basis of human nature as a whole is a condition for the possibility of understanding. Bultmann defined this further by saying that

> the condition for interpretation is the fact that interpreter and author are human beings who live in the same historical world in which human existence takes place as existence in an environment in understanding association with objects and other persons. Naturally, it belongs to such understanding association that it should also include questions and problems, struggle and suffering as well as resigned withdrawal.[7]

In his 1925 essay on "The Problem of a Theological Exegesis of the New Testament" Bultmann had seen the possibility of a romantic or an aesthetic perspective as a reaction against the scientific historical and

---

[7]Bultmann, "Das Problem der Hermeneutik," 219. ET: "The Problem of Hermeneutics," 74-76.

psychological laws of cause and effect. In such a perspective, the human being is seen as a gestalt that develops through the powers flowing from the center of personality. But Bultmann saw an objectifying biological perspective and domination reintroduced in such a move, and he did not follow that sort of literary approach. Actually Dilthey saw inner and outer factors at work in the dynamic unfolding of human personality. For Dilthey the human being was open, dynamic, and capable of development. (Dilthey was definitely not a behaviorist.)

Later in the same 1925 essay, Bultmann acknowledged in a footnote the work of Dilthey and his value for contemporary study of literature. R. Ungers in particular is mentioned: "In dependence upon Dilthey he [Ungers] sees literary art as life-meaning so that for him the history of literature becomes the history of problem with 'problem' understood not as a rational idea but as the idea of existence, so that the history of problem becomes not a dialectical movement of formal aesthetic ideas but a phenomenology of the problem of life." Bultmann, however, quickly cites philosophy as a necessary overarching method of conceptualization. Because the literary approach must finally seek a relationship with philosophy, there is no need to take a detour through literature.[8]

In an essay published in 1952 after reaction to his proposal on demythologizing, Bultmann deals with the objection that myth should be treated in literary terms, as symbols and poetic representations. The fact that mythological statements of the Bible have become poetic representations and have lost the mythical force of their origins is no justification for forsaking a radical existential interpretation. What is the meaning (*Sinn*)? The indirect, suggestive, fleeting meanings similar to the meanings in lyric poetry are not sufficient. In his discussion, an implicit objection to the plurality of literary meanings and an explicit objection to the dynamic nature of literary interpretation is to be found:

> Are mythological representations and concepts really indispensable? They may be so in a provisional sense insofar as truths are intended in them that cannot be expressed in the language of objectifying science. In that case mythological language provisionally expresses that for which adequate language must still be found. Thus, the task that is set for thinking (though not for the thinking of objectifying science!) can be formulated in mythological language in the way in which this happens in the Platonic

---

[8]"Das Problem einer theologischen Exegese des Neuen Testaments," in *Anfänge der dialectischen Theologie*, 2:65n.4.

myths. Nevertheless, the usual way of talking about mythical concepts and representations as "pictures" and "symbols" has to be patient of the question about the point of such pictures and symbols. For, clearly, they are supposed to express some point, and is it also to be formulated in mythological language, so that the point of this language must in turn be interpreted—and so on *in infinitum*? This is evidently absurd, and in fact even representatives of the symbol theory (if one may so speak of them) are given to offering interpretations in nonmythological language.[9]

Bultmann's concern for a scientific foundation for exegesis, for a questioning of scripture that can be answered in a satisfying philosophical fashion, caused him to bypass literary analysis as such. In his 1950 essay on "The Problem of Hermeneutics," Bultmann gives evidence of awareness of the way that art in general and literature in particular reveal "truth." He declares that "'The true' is made visible in literature and in art, and it is to be appropriated there by participatory understanding." But he quickly declares that the "truth" expressed in poetry and art is to be understood in a philosophically sophisticated way, that means as a present-day study of the problem of being and therefore of self-understanding.[10] Philosophy, then—not history or literature—is basic, a foundation. In application to the question of God and the interpretation of scripture, Bultmann acknowledges that at the level of actual experience, God is known and scripture is heard without consideration of philosophical assumptions or foundations. But Bultmann does not ask how scripture works at that level. That is too superficial a level. Bultmann's attention is not directed to such a level, but to the level of existential knowlege (with existential understood as having to do with constitutive elements in every person's humanity). For Bultmann, the surface level of experience of God and scripture is dependent upon and translatable into a foundational level. This foundational level was uncovered by Heidegger's analysis of understanding as a constitutive element of humanity as such and Heidegger's analysis of language as an expression of discourse that is equiprimordial with such understanding.

In Bultmann's day, in a world seeking foundations beyond the historical flux, foundations that makes human history meaningful, Bultmann's existential interpretation spoke a valid word for many intellectuals. In our

---

[9]"Zum Problem der Entmythologisierung," 186. ET: "On the Problem of Demythologizing," 100.
[10]"Das Problem der Hermeneutik," 220. ET: "The Problem of Hermeneutics," 78.

day, however, the intellectually scientific struggle to find ultimate foundations for our knowledge has been superceded by a so-called postmodern understanding. In a postmodern world more attention is given to the local, timely, historical. Attention is given to "difference," language as a reservoir of possibilities and meaning as a dynamic movement. Literary study is at the center of this movement away from the concern for foundations seen in Bultmann.

The New Literary Situation as Evidenced in the Work of Hans Robert Jauß and Wolfgang Iser

If we admit with Rudolf Bultmann that the older idea of the Bible as a collection of eternal dogmatic truths is not satisfying today and that a positivistic historical approach that reduces the Bible to objective historical facts is not sufficient, we must also admit that Bultmann's existential approach focuses the biblical texts too finely on existential ideas of decision, will, choice, and intention without tracing out how these ideas can be mapped onto the biblical text and related to other areas of human existence and experience. Is it possible for contemporary literary insights to assist in extending the hermeneutical vision of Bultmann and perhaps to modify that vision in the process.

The work of Hans-Robert Jauß and Wolfgang Iser allows us an entry into the question and provides a framework. In West German literary study, the Constance School of Jauß and Iser may be credited with making the reader a central factor in the study of literature. In an article entitled "A Change of Paradigm in Literary Criticism" Jauß declared that the impulse for a change of paradigm was the failure of the prevailing paradigm and its methodological axioms to provide what literary studies consistently require, which is, according to Jauß,

> the capacity to rescue works of art from the past by means of continually new interpretations, to transfer them into a new presence, to make the experience preserved in past art once more available, in other words: to ask questions—which must be discovered by each new generation—questions to which the art of the past can respond for us once again.[11]

Jauß lists literary approaches which in their day and in their turn were highly successful: the normative poetics of humanism and classicism, the

---

[11]"Paradigmawechsel in der Literaturwissenschaft," *Linguistische Berichte* 3 (1969): 54-55.

literary revolution of the Romantic period including the development of historical philological methods, and the formal method of stylistic criticism and text-intrinsic aesthetics. But these paradigms became exhausted when their methods of interpretations could no longer accomplish the actualization and transformation of past art into the present.

The contribution of the Constance School includes studies of the process by which a reader actualizes a text. This aspect has been stressed by Wolfgang Iser. Iser defines his approach to the reading process as "phenomenological," emphasizing that "in considering a literary work, one must take into account not only the actual text but also, and in equal measure, the actions involved in responding to that text"[12] Iser is concerned to formulate a theory of aesthetic response that has its roots in the text so he is at odds with a radical reader-oriented approach that allows the reader to do just about whatever the reader wishes. He and Stanley Fish of Duke University, for example, begin with quite different philosophical presuppositions. Iser is interested in the response-inviting structure of the text. Iser makes the "gaps" and completion of "gaps" by the reader the central factor in literary communication.

The view of reading advocated by Iser results in a reconceptionalization of the meaning of a literary text—meaning is an effect to be experienced, and this effective meaning depends upon the participation of the reader. The role prescribed by the text and the reader's own disposition operate together with the structure of the text allowing different ways of fulfilling the process.[13]

Other scholars have also made the actual reader and the event of reading the focus of their study. Umberto Eco emphasizes how a reader moves back and forth from the world of the text to the reader's own world.[14] Roman Ingarden emphasizes the role of the reader in making more concrete those elements of the text that cannot by the nature of the case be fully concretized textually.[15]

---

[12]Iser, "The Reading Process: A Phenomenological Approach," in *Reader-Response Criticism: From Formalism to Post-Structuralism*, ed. Jane P. Tompkins (Baltimore and London: Johns Hopkins University Press, 1980) 274.

[13]See Iser, *The Act of Reading: A Theory of Aesthetic Response* (London and Henley: Routledge & Kegan Paul, 1978).

[14]Umberto Eco, *The Role of the Reader: Explorations in the Semiotics of Texts* (Bloomington IN: Indiana University Press, 1979).

[15]Roman Ingarden, *The Cognition of the Literary Work of Art* (Evanston IL: Northwestern University Press, 1973).

But how are the reader-oriented approaches related to New Testament hermeneutics? I would make participatory understanding (rather than reflexive and investigative thought) primary and question about the sorts of truth that are discovered in such participatory understanding. From such a perspective, the debate over whether the New Testament text is the occasion for profound philosophical thought or for superficial "feeling" and enjoyment would be transformed. The text would be seen as an expression of the various sorts of experiences of the people of God brought into existence through Jesus Christ. As Dilthey saw the text as stamped by life, I see the New Testament text stamped by the life of religious experience. The Gospels as wholes and the various units of the Gospels grow out of and express in fixed written form and in appropriate refraction the historical experience of the church. This experience is an experience of the action of God, the word of God. Historically it may be seen in terms of the disciples' experience with Jesus, the primitive church's experience with the tradition and with the continuing act of God in ever new situations, the later evangelists' experiences in yet new contexts, the church in its existential formation and shaping of the material, and even canonization(s).

The experience of the action of God, the word of God, may be repeated in interaction with the text as a literary construction. This is not a static experience. It is a dynamic experience. The Roman Catholic New Testament scholar Sandra Schneiders has even spoken of the New Testament text becoming a "revelatory text" in the process of actualization. She cites the declaration of the Second Vatican Council that the church has always honored scripture "as it venerates the Body of the Lord" in the Eucharist. She says that this presents "a very useful model for understanding the nature of the Bible as sacred text. Scripture, like Eucharist, is best understood as sacrament."[16]

In my writings, I begin with the sorts of moves made by the formalists and new critics. I do not begin with historical reconstruction. The reader is confronted by words on the page. This basic data must be read or processed initially by linguistic and literary codes or conventions. Here the whole history of literature and our "inherited grammar of criticism"[17] come into play. The synthesis of meaning at the level of what

---

[16]Sandra Schneiders, *The Revelatory Text: Interpreting the New Testament as Sacred Scripture* (San Francisco: HarperSanFrancisco, 1991) 40.

[17]William Kurtz Wimsatt, *Hateful Contraries: Studies in Literature and Criticism*

is being said in the text begins as a simple task. The way a complete thought (a sentence) is created out of a collection of words may be taken as the pattern for reading at that level. It is a matter of selecting the meanings of words and sentences that result in an appropriate overall coordination. The words and sentences hang together in a meaning only when there is a topic or theme that ties them together. At the level of the entire text, the reader must supply an overall topic, theme, or meaning that will allow all of the text to have meaning. Sometimes, several possibilities must be entertained.

I emphasize in my writings not only the actualization of the text by the reader, but also the actualization of the reader by the text. In the process of reading biblical literature, the reader is affected in the same fashion as are readers of all literature. When the readers allows themselves to appreciate the play of language, there is intellectual and emotional pleasure as readers are able to analyse and synthesize the text on the various levels. But biblical literature is more than the occasion for intellectural and emotional pleasure, biblical literature introduces a transcendent world, and the reader must enter into that world at least momentarily in order to appreciate the text. The world uncovered or revealed by the biblical text is a world that is not created or essentially sustained by human will and effort. It is a world properly spoken of as a given, or a gift, that parallels the world of the achievements of humankind. Those who see the world as essentially a human quest are jolted by the picture of the world as a gracious gift. The reader's world may not only be challenged by the world of the text; it may be changed. We call that conversion. The conversion I am interested in is not simply the call for decision in an evangelistic sense. It is a lifetime project and it involving conversion on different levels. Bernard Lonergan speaks of different dimensions: intellectual, moral, psychological, affective, sociopolitical. These are different dimensions of our human drive to achieve meaning, and different New Testament texts may address different dimensions of this drive. The conversion is not only personal and internal. Lonergan speaks of conversion as the foundation for religion that is concrete, dynamic, personal, social, and historical.[18]

(Lexington: University of Kentucky Press, 1965) 217.

[18]See Lonergan, "Theology in Its New Context" and "The Dimensions of Conversion" in *Conversion: Perspectives on Personal and Social Transformation*, ed. Walter E. Conn (New York: Alba House, 1978) 3-21.

The Question of God

The power of the transcendent world of the Bible to achieve conversion, or (otherwise said) the capacity of the reader to appropriate the text in a transforming manner, is related to the ability of the reader to image God, more particularly, to image a God who enters into relations with God's creation and God's creatures. Christian faith is more than a taken-for-granted, naïve worldview that includes God. It is more than affirming that God is related to God's creation and humankind in a general way. But Christian faith is hard to keep alive apart from some conception of a God who is a reality beyond human will, desire, and choice. How can we relate transcendence and immanence? In Bultmann's 1925 essay with the title "What Sense Is It To Speak About God?", he indicates that "wherever the idea 'God' is thought, God is said to be the almighty, the reality that determines the universe. . . . But every 'speaking about' postulates a standpoint outside of which something is affirmed. A standpoint outside of God does not exist." Bultmann's major interest is not the possibility or impossibility of intellectual speculation about the concept of God. His existential concern comes to light in the very next statement: "God cannot be spoken about in abstract and general affirmations and truths that are valid without respect to the concrete existential situation of the one speaking."[19]

It was in an answer to the complaint that demythologizing leads to a pantheistic piety that Bultmann gives some hints that may be helpful in relating God and the world today. Pantheism, according to Bultmann, believes in the direct identity of a worldly event with divine action; but it asserts that a particular event is divine act in an abstract way and does not concern itself with what a particular event means as encounter.[20] Bultmann is interested not in an abstract universal system called God, but in the particulars of history and historical experience. And his criticism of abstraction and idealization may be directed to Hegelian systems of relating God to the world. Peter Hodgson of Vanderbilt University has attempted to revise the Hegelian system, but he acknowledges the validity

---

[19]"Welchen Sinn hat es, von Gott zu reden?" *Theologische Blätter* 4 (1925): 129. ET: "What Sense Is There to Speak of God?" *Christian Scholar* 43 (1960): 213.
[20]"Zum Problem der Entmythologisierung" (1952), 197. ET: "On the Problem of Demythologizing," 111-12.

of a Bultmannian critique. Hodgson summarizes Hegel's statements about the relationship of God and world:

> Though posited as free and independent, the world is not autonomous. It has its truth not in itself but in God; its truth is its ideality, not its reality. From God's point of view, it is but a "disappearing moment," "a flash of lightening that immediately vanishes, the sound of a word that is perceived and vanishes in its outward existence the instance it is spoken." It is an "appearance," whose characteristic is "to pass over, moving itself forward, so as to take itself back into the final idea."[21]

The particularity and historicity of human experience in the world is overshadowed by the idealism of Hegel's system.

Bultmann uses the vocabulary of Hegel in opposition to a closed static system:

> It becomes clear . . . that the world loses its character as a closed continuum for my existential life, which is realized in decisions in face of encounters. Put differently, in faith the closed continuum presented (or produced) by objectifying thinking is sublated—not of course in the manner of mythological thinking, so that it is thought of as disrupted, but in such a way that it is sublated as a whole when I talk about God's act. Actually it is already sublated when I talk about myself; for I myself, in my authentic being, am just as little to be seen and established within the world as is the act of God. When I look upon worldly occurrences as a closed continuum, which I have to do in the interest not only of scientific understanding but also of my daily life and work, then, indeed, there is no room for God's act. But the paradox of faith is that it understands an event that can be established in its natural and historical continuum as nevertheless God's act. This "nevertheless" is inseparable from faith.[22]

The appeal of Bultmann's existential hermeneutics may have been in its stress on existential vitality, the new possibilities offered in every concrete situation of life, the "I"–"you" (Du) relation in which we genuinely exist, in a personal confrontation with the reality of history. If we ask about a concept of God that is adequate for such an approach, we do not really get much specific help from Bultmann, but we are urged

---

[21]Peter C. Hodgson, *God in History: Shapes of Freedom* (Nashville: Abingdon Press, 1989) 71-72; cited from G. W. F. Hegel, *Lectures on the Philosophy of Religion*, ed. Peter C. Hodgson (Berkeley: University of California Press, 1985) 3:87-89.

[22]"Zum Problem der Entmythologisierung" (1952) 198. ET: "On the Problem of Demythologizing," 112-13.

away from a Platonic idealistic perspective toward a realist perspective that takes this world and God's activities in this world seriously. Today, as with Bultmann, there is dissatisfaction with abstract ideas of God's timelessness and immutability. There is a need to take seriously and nonmythically the biblical and Christian descriptions of God as creating, deciding, loving, acting graciously in relation to the world in general and in relation to humans in particular.

Hodgson suggests that we can begin with the quite powerful Hegelian system. It is true that Hegel's system tended toward an overarching rational synthesis that dissolves the particularity of things. But Hodgson suggests that Hegel can be reread or his triadic system can be used to reconceive of the relationship between God and world. The triadic dialectic can be summarized as follows: "The inner life of God becomes historical when the immanent distinctions within God are outwardly posited in the constitution of a world of space-time other than God, and when God enters into relationship with this world and returns to self spiritualized, historicized, temporalized."[23] As we have seen, with Hegel the contingent character of the central moment of historical existence was ignored in a stress on original and final identity. But when historicality is taken more seriously as it is today and considered in conjunction with the system of Hegel, God will be understood as incapable of being God apart from nature and history. The central moment and not the beginning and ending will become the focus. And action instead of ideas will form the foreground.

Hodgson presents his thesis concerning God and the world based on a rereading of Hegel:

> God is efficaciously present in the world, not as an individual agent performing observable acts, nor as a uniform inspiration or lure, nor as an abstract ideal, nor in the metaphorical role of companion or friend. Rather, God is present in specific shapes or patterns of praxis that have a configuring, transformative power within historical process, moving the process in a determinate direction, that of the creative unification of multiplicities of elements into new wholes, into creative syntheses that build human solidarity, enhance freedom, break systemic oppression, heal the injured and broken, and care for the natural.[24]

---

[23]*God in History*, 66.
[24]Ibid., 205.

The thought of Hodgson is influenced by postmodern thought that seeks to relativize the objectifying methods of science by expanding them to involve practical and emancipatory levels of knowledge. He is opposed to a postmodernism of radical relativism "for which nothing is known, believed, or acted upon."[25] He is indebted to Ernst Troeltsch who struggled with the relationship of God and history and "stressed the necessity of having the courage to act in situations of objective and intellectual uncertainty" with the understanding that "action can clarify and resolve things when theoretical questions remain irresolvable."[26] Hodgson declares that the relationship between God and history focuses at the point of

> praxis that is liberating, emancipatory, transfigurative. Freedom involves an activity of shaping, configuring, synthesizing, presencing; it is an activity in which we experience ultimacy and are empowered by it, but always in an unfinished, open, plural process, which includes reversals and defeats as well as advances. God is present in history in the many shapes of freedom, among which there is for Christians a paradigmatic gestalt, the shape of love in freedom associated with Jesus' proclamation and crucifixion.[27]

The process of revising of thought about the idea of God is not limited to one particular tradition. Catholic theology is provided a useful model in the work of Karl Rahner who stressed that ordinary human experience is unintelligible apart from the transcendent mystery called "God," that this mystery is to be encountered and known in and through the historical environment people experience daily.[28] The evangelical tradition is provided a model in the book by Clark Pinnock and three associates entitled *The Openness of God.* For the authors "the openness of God" means that

> God, in grace, grants humans significant freedom to cooperate with or work against God's will for their lives, and he enters into dynamic give-and-take relationships with us. The Christian life involves a genuine inter-action between God and human beings. We respond to God's gracious initiatives and God responds to our responses . . . and on it goes. God

---

[25]Ibid., 40.
[26]Ibid., 41.
[27]Ibid., 7.
[28]Karl Rahner, *Grundkurs des Glaubens. Einführung in den Begriff des Christentums* (Freiburg i.Br.: Herder, 1976).

takes risks in this give-and-take relationship, yet he is endlessly resource-ful and competent in working toward his ultimate goals. . . . God does not control everything that happens. Rather, he is open to receiving imput from his creatures. In loving dialogue, God invites us to participate with him to bring the future into being.[29]

In a most esoteric form, we have the suggestion of Mark C. Taylor. Taylor declares that the alternative of transcendence and immanence leaves out what is "neither representable in nor masterable by traditional philosophical and theological categories."[30] He contrasts Karl Barth's reassertion of divine transcendence with the work of the American death-of-God theologian Thomas J. J. Altizer. "Within Altizer's apocalyptic vision, the death of God is the condition of the possibility of the arrival of the Parousia. When the kingdom of God is at hand, authentic presence is totally realized here and now."[31] For Taylor, Altizer's radical imma-nence is not viable. What is viable is openness to the other, the death of God in and through which the sacred might be glimpsed, and the accep-tance of radical uncertainty. Bultmann's existential interpretation may be broadened by resources in various traditions to include concerns other than human decision, choice, and will. The biblical text will effectively mediate the variegated historical experience of the people of God as we correlate anthropology and theology by a contemporary (and ancient) con-ception of God as active in the human history of God's people.

Values of Literary Approaches for Hermeneutics

In conclusion, I would suggest some specific values of a reader-ori-ented literary approach to the Bible in combination with Bultmann's exis-tential interpretation.

1. Serious interaction with the text is facilitated by reader-oriented approaches. Such approaches are for biblical studies what the text-imma-

---

[29]Clark Pinnock et al., *The Openness of God: A Biblical Challenge to the Traditional Understanding of God* (Downers Grove IL: InterVarsity Press, 1994) 7.

[30]Taylor, "The End(s) of Theology," in *Theology at the End of Modernity*, ed. Sheila Greeve Davaney (Philadelphia: Trinity Press International, 1991) 241.

[31]Ibid., 239. Other scholars offer valuable insights into the reasons for the loss of transcendence and ways to reconceptualize the relationship of the world of immanence and the world of transcendence. See, for example, Jerry H. Gill, *Mediated Transcendence: A Postmodern Reflection* (Macon GA: Mercer University Press, 1989) and Ted Peters, *God as Trinity: Relationality and Temporality in Divine Life* (Louisville: Westminster/ John Knox Press, 1993).

nent criticism in Europe and New Criticism in America were for literature in general and what Bultmann sought in his approach—to free the biblical text from its domination by objectifying disciplines such as history, sociology, and psychology.

2. Reader-response emphases represent a victory for the reader. Readers are freed to make sense for themselves. This method allows readers to interact with the text in light of their own context, linguistic and literary competence, and need, as well as in light of the potentialities of the text. Confidence and further literary competence are developed as readers discover and create meanings in light of their own "language."

3. Such approaches allow the obvious religious concerns of the text to impinge upon reading in a way appropriate to the concerns of the reader. A type of knowledge may result from the experience of reading that is different from the knowledge gained by scientific methodologies. Levels of meaning and knowledge may be experienced which became lost with the Enlightment paradigm.

4. Reader-response approaches are capable of accommodating and utilizing approaches followed in more conventional biblical and literary studies. Historical and sociological exegesis, for example, are not precluded in reader-response criticism. They are reconceptualized and relativized, but not made illegitimate as such.

5. Finally, I must admit that literary approaches are very unsettling and overwhelming for "modern" readers who want to control the text and discover the meaning on the basis of a secure foundation. Reader-response criticism often gives the impression of an excess of critical resources and of readings that outdo each other and the text itself in complexity and creativity. This characterization is valid. But we ought to expect such complexity and creativity—given the nature and potentiality of biblical texts and the developing capacity of readers.

Chapter 9

A Sheep in Wolf's Clothing: Feminist and Sectarian Hermeneutics

Literary approaches to the New Testament function within the context of different agendas and disciplines and respond to the different constraints and needs of those agendas. Historical, literary, hermeneutical, and other agendas cooperate and conflict in the study of the New Testament. In a gracious review of my *Postmodern Use of the Bible*, A. K. M. Adam warns readers that my work could be seen by radical postmodernists as a "sheep in wolf's clothing" because I utilize literary criticism, including the strategies developed with the close reading of New Criticism, for constructive purposes.[1] I am interested in the meaning of the constructive moment even though it is local, ad hoc, and provisional—and thus can be deconstructed in its turn.

This essay is designed to explore the hermeneutical use of literary insights in a postmodern mode by comparing feminist and sectarian interpretation. Since my own entry into literary study of the New Testament helps to explain my concern with the hermeneutical agenda, the first part of the chapter will be autobiographical. Important philosophical and political differences in the total enterprise of New Testament studies will be disclosed in my experience. A second part will situate postmodern literary study in the hermeneutical tradition and delineate the dissatisfaction not only of severe postmodern critics but also of antipostmodernists in the hermeneutical tradition. The final major section of the chapter will compare and contrast the agendas and approaches of the Radical Reformation and contemporary feminists to show how a contemporary approach may be fashioned to do justice to postmodern antifoundational insights and to the need for critical criteria for reading and interpretation.

---

[1]Adam, A. K. M., "Review of *Postmodern Use of the Bible* by Edgar V. McKnight," *Catholic Biblical Quarterly* 52 (1990): 758-59.

Autobiographical: Entry into the Literary World

In the early 1970s I began investigating the potential of reader-oriented literary approaches for the rehabilitation of hermeneutics in the Schleiermacher-Bultmann tradition, giving attention to meaning for the ever-contemporary reader. The beginning was a simple proposal for a dissertation at Oxford University during my first sabbatical from college teaching, an investigation into the relationship between diachronic historical approaches using historical linguistics as a model and synchronic literary approaches using structural linguistics as a model. In 1972, I had been asked by the book review editor of the *Journal of Biblical Literature* to review for American readers a book by Erhardt Güttgemanns that had caused some stir in German New Testament circles.[2] The book was entitled *Offene Fragen zur Formgeschichte des Evangeliums*[3] but it was much more than a series of "Offene Fragen" ("Candid Questions"); it was a declaration that the whole tradition of New Testament scholarship has to be shelved. Historical criticism had to be replaced by a linguistic exegesis based on the principles of structural linguistics. Form criticism was the first opponent to be demolished in Güttgemanns's work, for (according to him) history and the sociological situation of the early church had nothing to do with the essence of the self-contained small units or forms of the synoptic Gospels. The forms on a deep level grow out of nonhistorical anthropological and linguistic factors. My review of the book caused me to rethink the whole set of assumptions and practices of historical criticism. Is the form and meaning of the text the result of historical and cultural factors or of nonhistorical, transhistorical factors that might even govern the perception of history and culture?

As I proceeded in the work under the tutelage of Professor John Macquarrie (the dissertation was in philosophical theology rather than biblical studies because of the orientation of the faculty in biblical studies), I discovered a structuralism earlier than that of the French

---

[2]McKnight, Edgar V., "Review of *Offene Fragen zur Formgeschichte des Evangeliums* by Erhardt Güttgemanns, *Journal of Biblical Literature* 91 (1972): 554-57.

[3]Erhardt Güttgemanns, *Offene Fragen zur Formgeschichte des Evangeliums: Eine methodische Skizze der Grundlagenproblematik der Form- und Redaktionsgeschichte,* Beiträge zur evangelischen Theologie 54 (Munich: Chr. Kaiser Verlag, 1970). ET: *Candid Questions concerning Gospel Form Criticism: A Methodological Sketch of the Fundamental Problematics of Form and Redaction Criticism,* trans. William G. Doty, Pittsburgh Theological Monograph series 26 (Pittsburg: Pickwick Press, 1979).

"narratologists" who influenced the work of Erhardt Güttgemanns. East European structuralism or formalism provided theoretical and practical resources for development and use of a view of textual unity or structure that is energetic and dynamic and capable of responding to cultural and individual development and valuation. Nonliterary factors influence literature not in a direct way or in a way to change the nature of literature and the literary work as a nexus of relationships. Literary structure is dynamic and not static, capable of responding to its different contexts and maintaining the nexus of internal relationships. The "determinate" structure of meaning is not a static "summative whole," but it exists in a ceaseless stage of movement.

My dissertation, "The Significance of the Structural Study of Narrative for New Testament Hermeneutics," introduced me to all sorts of questions: the different levels and kinds of literary structures, the dynamic relationship between the nexus of literary factors and the reader, the dynamic relationship between the reader and the community, and the dynamic structure of readers themselves.

Conversation with my two examiners upon the completion of my dissertation made me realize that I had moved far away from foundationalist historical-critical assumptions that were accepted by many (at least at Oxford in the 1970s) as facts instead of hypotheses. The examiners were an English tutor and an Old Testament professor. The major objection of both examiners was the very orientation of my study, the hermeneutical context. I assumed the validity of hermeneutics, and (in order to carry out my more ultimate goal) I attempted to show the importance of a synchronic as well as a diachronic perspective and the interdependence of elements not only within the text but also outside the text, including the reader and the reader's culture. I was proposing an open, corrigible, structure, not the timeless ahistorical structure of structuralism but one that is understood and informed by hermeneutical insights and decisions.

I was working on a metacritical level, submitting both the structuralist and hermeneutical critical agendas to a yet higher level of critical evaluation. My examiners were situated at the critical level, which requires a basis of comparison accepted as a given, a foundation from which secure results follow. At the critical level, critics assume they are employing criteria that are foundational in some final sense. In fact, they are employing criteria that are accepted as foundational because of the influence of their academic communities. The metacritical level of evaluation moves away from secure foundations. There seem to be no objective criteria independent of the aims and interests of those involved in the process of reading and interpretation.

My examiners represented historical linguistics and the historical approach and wanted me to "reduce" my study to such a model. The English tutor suggested that I adopt the view of E. D. Hirsch, Jr. and make a distinction between the meaning of the text, which can be detected by historical approaches, and the application of that meaning, which is not subject to historical-critical strictures. The Old Testament professor suggested that I should begin with the historically oriented biblical studies of C. H. Dodd—rather than the theologically oriented New Testament hermeneutics of Rudolf Bultmann.[4]

Postmodern Literary Study
from Hermeneutical Perspectives

For conventional historical-critical critics, a New Testament hermeneutics informed by nonfoundationalist reader-oriented literary approaches is suspect because it problematizes the firm mooring of history. For the postmodern literary critic, however, a reader-oriented hermeneutical approach to biblical literature is a sheep in wolf's clothing. The wolf's clothing is a result of postmodern questioning of assumptions of conventional critical approaches (such as the independence of fact and meaning from value and interpretation, the stability of texts and even the autonomy of the self and the nature of reality). The sheep-like quality? The refusal to acknowledge that the questioning of such assumptions must conclude with a nihilistic skepticism. This refusal may be rationalized as it is situated in the literary and hermeneutical traditions.

Before the mid-twentieth century, literary studies moved from historical domestication of the text to new-critical formalist analysis, and then to rehabilitation of historical, social, and psychological factors (not simply as extrinsic, but also as intrinsic factors), and more recently to a radical theoretical and practical decontextualizing and deconstruction.

---

[4]The dissertation, essentially as it was deposited in the Bodleian Library at Oxford, was published by Fortress Press in 1978 with the title *Meaning in Texts: The Historical Shaping of a Narrative Hermeneutics.* The book received an award in 1978 at the annual meeting of the Modern Language Association of America from the Conference on Christianity and Literature for furthering the dialogue between Christianity and literature. The difference in the reception by my examiners and members of the Conference on Christianity and Literature may well represent the difference between British and American attitudes in the 1970s toward Continental modes of literary analysis.

Developments in structural semiotics, poststructuralism, and deconstruc-tion associated with scholars such as Roland Barthes, Umberto Eco, and Jacques Derrida became important. Barthes sees the structure of a text as dynamic and involving the reader in a process of analysis without a final synthesis or end.[5] Eco sees the process of reading as involving moves both within the text (intensional) and outside the text (extensional). The various levels and sublevels of textual and extratextual realities are interconnected, and the reader moves back and forth within and without the text to produce meaning.[6] Derrida sets knowledge, language, meaning, and interpretation not simply within a dynamic cultural context but within a larger context of power and authority.[7] Reading in the conventional mode is a synthesizing process with the subject/reader being governed (as the subject/author) by language. But a deconstructive reading gives conscious attention to the impulse toward and result of the synthesizing of the conventional reading process in order to break its "domination."

The positive and negative reactions to semiotics, poststructuralism, and deconstruction in America may be explained in part by the fact that the dominant American brand of deconstruction is a result of a bypassing of the hermeneutical tradition of Schleiermacher, Dilthey, Heidegger, and Gadamer. The deconstructionist critic is then merely a distanced observer of the "scene of textuality" who refines all writing into "free-floating" texts. The continually unsituated deconstructionist critic is characterized by a forever new or unmastered irony. A mastered irony does not ignore the valid insight of deconstruction but does not remain forever unsitu-ated.[8] When reader-oriented interpretation comes to biblical texts through the hermeneutical tradition, it seeks to situate possibility in an actual worldly relation; it is a sheep in wolf's clothing.

Theoretical and practical resources are available to provide a post-modern or a postcritical rationale for and program of hermeneutics, but the "modern" Enlightenment quest for intellectual certainty and concentra-

---

[5]Roland Barthes, *S/Z*, trans. Richard Miller (London: Jonathan Cape, 1975).

[6]Umberto Eco, *The Role of the Reader: Explorations in the Semiotics of Texts* (Bloomington: Indiana University Press, 1979).

[7]Jacques Derrida, *Of Grammatology*, trans. G. C. Spivak (Baltimore: Johns Hopkins University Press, 1976) 158.

[8]See Søren Kierkegaard, *The Concept of Irony with Constant Reference to Socrates*, trans. with intro. and notes by Lee M. Capel, A Midland Book MB111 (Bloomington: Indiana University Press, 1968) for a discussion of "mastered" and "unmastered" irony that has influenced the hermeneutical tradition.

tion on empirical data continues to influence us, as does Immanuel Kant's attempt to transcend the level of empirical data by a metacritical elucidation of forms and categories making possible the cognitive activities of the human subject. The history of the Enlightenment is the history of shifts back and forth between epistemological idealism and realism, but Kant shifted the center of philosophical inquiry to an examination of the concepts and categories in terms of which we think and reason. Kant disagreed with a severe empiricism by holding that there are a priori elements in cognition. These a priori concepts are indispensable for knowledge of objects.[9]

Kant made a basic epistemological distinction between knowledge of phenomena (empirical data) and understanding of transcendental noumenal realities. Kant's was an epistemological dualism, not an ontological dualism. This epistemological distinction, however, became an ontological dualism. Phenomenal reality became distinct from noumenal reality. Developments after Kant may be seen first (in the "modern" phase) as the inability to accommodate transcendence in any traditional sense whatsoever and then (in a "postmodern" phase) as the inability to achieve the desired certainty in dealing with the natural world.

Attempts to maintain a "modern" Enlightenment rationality and raise it to a metacritical level to serve as a foundation constitutes a recapitulation of Kantian thought—albeit a reversal in that a foundation for the knowledge of phenomena (empirical data) as well as (or instead of) a foundation for understanding of transcendental noumenal realities is sought. Attempts to rehabilitate rationalism do not have the goal of a complete and coherent theoretical absolute that can be articulated fully either deductively or inductively. Enlightenment rationalism has been judged universally to be instrumental, always operating upon subordinate levels from within superior levels that the given rationalism is unable to reach. Acknowledgment of the limits of Enlightenment rationality, however, does not mean devolution into irrationalism.

Hans-Georg Gadamer is the scholar claimed not only by postmodernism but also by a revitalized, albeit relativized, modernism. Gadamer's acceptance of Wilhelm von Humboldt's view of language as an unbordered creative power of thought and speech making unlimited use of

---

[9]Immanuel Kant, "Transcendental Deduction of the Categories," in *Critique of Pure Reason*, trans. J. M. D. Meiklejohn, Great Books of the Western World 42 (Chicago: Encyclopaedia Britannica, 1952).

limited materials allows both moves. Gadamer developed a hermeneutics giving attention to historical consciousness and expanding hermeneutical options beyond the Romanticism of Schleiermacher and Dilthey and the existentialism of Heidegger and his heirs. We do not simply question the work with our scientific methods or simply see in the work what we bring; we come to the work participating in the same structure of being that is the basis for our understanding of what was intended in the work.[10]

Gadamer's view of the historically constrained and finite nature of the hermeneutical actualization of texts and traditions may be emphasized. But his indication of the universality of language may also be emphasized; and within the hermeneutic tradition a broader base than Enlightenment rationality is sought by such scholars as Jürgen Habermas and Karl-Otto Apel. They do not deny that truth always and of necessity exceeds method (a fact emphasized by Gadamer), but they posit some kind of provisional notion of the universal, which is then used as basis for a metacriticism that is able to acknowledge and contain the relativity of Enlightenment rationalism. Habermas and Apel seek to expand and not to undermine traditional epistemology. The actual pragmatic function of tradition and communities of interpreters is not denied; what is denied is the conclusion that a particular tradition and community of interpreters is unrelated to universal norms. They seek a transcendental dimension that is not merely contextually internal to particular societies but that will allow a critique of particular societies. Apel depends upon a hypothesis of universal commensurability whereby languages are intertranslatable and "language games" overlap, merge, fall apart, and reintegrate. The historically constituted life form of a given society (language) is

> not only the normatively binding "institution of institutions" . . . it is also the "metainstitution" of all dogmatically established institutions. As a metainstitution, it represents the instance of criticism for all unreflected social norms, and . . . it does not abandon the individual persons to their merely subjective reasoning.[11]

The modern mentality that cannot abide skepticism and that searches for new foundations is the result of confidence in its capacity to achieve

---

[10]Hans-Georg Gadamer, *Truth and Method*, translation edited by Garrett Barden and John Cumming (New York: Seabury, 1975) 430.

[11]Karl-Otto Apel, *Towards a Transformation of Philosophy*, trans. Glyn Adey and David Frisby, International Library of Phenomenology and Moral Sciences (London and Boston: Routledge & Kegan Paul, 1980) 119.

its rational and material goals here on earth, and in historical time, an optimism that led to major advances in moral, political, and social thought as well as in the natural sciences.[12] Acknowledgment of the impossibility of the ideal of Enlightenment certainty may result in a nihilistic debilitating skepticism but it may result in a positive skepticism. This sort of skepticism would acknowledge that our rational processes are essentially defined by and dependent upon historical and social contexts. It would not only have a toleration for other contexts with their questions and answers, it would even question the finality of the validity of one's own answers in one's own context—but it would not be disabled by such questioning.

The Radical Reformation and Contemporary Feminists

In this section I will use the experiences and approaches of the Radical Reformation and contemporary feminists to reformulate a hermeneutics that utilizes and matches postmodern philosophical and literary insights. I will first suggest a reformulated hermeneutics with these two groups in mind. Then I will examine the agendas of these two groups and correlate them with the hermeneutical tradition.

Reformulation of Hermeneutics. In a reformulated hermeneutical approach, the importance of texts and the assumption that readers can make sense of texts are important. The problematizing of "texts," "readers," and "sense" in the postmodern epoch is taken seriously but not allowed to disable the hermeneutical drive for meaning. All of the resources of linguistics, the natural language of texts, and the languages of literature are utilized. Extrinsic approaches such as history, sociology, psychology, and anthropology provide an understanding of the originating circumstances (personal, social, historical, and so on) for the hermeneutical approach. A hermeneutical concern for present meaning cannot reduce meaning to some ostensible original historical meaning or to other extrinsic causes. The view of the text as a scientific object as such precludes achievement of meaning-for-the-reader.

The hermeneutical approach posits a meaning beyond the meanings of words and sentences, a meaning that does not simply derive from the words and sentences. It posits a meaning that is not obtained from a

---

[12]Stephen Edelston Toulmin, *Cosmopolis: The Hidden Agenda of Modernity* (New York: The Free Press, 1990) ix.

simple recovery of the originating circumstances. The knowledge sought in hermeneutics is as complicated as the knowledge of other persons—and the procedure just as complicated. Schleiermacher's system of hermeneutics involves a dynamic procedure allowing the achievement of the desired sort of meaning by the coordination of a series of polarities or contrasts. The dynamic procedure whereby these polarities are coordinated and the series of polarities harmonized calls upon imagination (divination) as well as criticism (comparison). The relationship between parts and wholes (with the parts determined by the whole and the whole determined by its parts) is one polarity; and the same sort of relationship exists between individual thinking and social speaking, language as a general system and language in particular use, and grammatical interpretation involving language and psychological interpretation involving human beings and their expressions of thought.

The interest or focus of interpretation has changed in the history of hermeneutics from Schleiermacher's feeling for the infinite to Dilthey's life, Heidegger's being, Bultmann's possibilities of human existence, the New Hermeneutic's language event and so on. In order to achieve the level and sort of interest seen as appropriate, hermeneutics had made a distinction between a surface level (what the text says) and a deeper level of intention, but in his treatment of myth Bultmann came to see the radical relativity of language as an objectifying of understanding, the objectification in myth being contrary to the understanding seeking expression in it. Bultmann, on the basis of his conclusion as to the subject matter of Scripture, finds that myth, instead of really intending to give an objective worldview or to tell of divine powers, expresses the way humans understand themselves in their world. With Bultmann, a process of demythologizing was proposed in order to arrive at the genuine subject matter of the text. With the New Hermeneutic, the dialectic changed from myth versus understanding of existence to language versus language-event. The issuing of the utterance is the performing of an action.

The hermeneutic tradition of Bultmann and the New Hermeneutic stagnated because the resources of the hermeneutical tradition of Heidegger were unable to provide the means of achieving the interests and goals involved. The present task may be envisioned as the revitalization of the hermeneutic tradition by means of resources in the European hermeneutic tradition and American literary studies. Particular hermeneutical interests will (as they always have) direct the utilization of these resources. The process of deconstruction, for example (as suggested earlier), will be accommodated to the hermeneutical agenda. Deconstruction is comparable to the demythologizing of Bultmann. It is capable of allowing readers to move beyond readings that have become dogmatized and that do not speak to those readers. Demythologizing as a hermeneutical strategy, however, has an ultimately positive presupposition about the possibility of meaning and significance. Deconstruction's position about textual meaning is more problematic. So a hermeneutical approach will utilize strategies of deconstruction with assumptions somewhat in tension with the philosophy of deconstruction. But only somewhat in tension, for a postmodern hermeneutical approach will continue to be skeptical while benefiting from the local, ad hoc and provisional meaning that is found.

The same sort of system of polarities and contrasts that we find in Schleiermacher are appropriate for a postmodern hermeneutical approach. Some of these polarities include (1) modernism versus postmodernism—with the postmodern being defined in relation to the modern and remaining related to the modern in a dialectical fashion; (2) historical criticism (and other critical approaches) as foundational versus historical criticism (and other critical approaches) as instrumental; (3) the text as a historical artifact to be distanced for scientific study versus the text as a literary source of meaning and significance with which rapport is sought; (4) the intention of the author versus the intention of readers; (5) logic versus the imagination; (6) intellectual certainty involving the universal, general, and timeless that can be established with mathematical exactitude and logical rigor versus a benign skepticism concerned with truthfulness related to the particular, local, and timely.

Feminists and the Hermeneutics of the Radical Reformation. The Radical Reformers and their descendants have found a positive skepticism to be necessary and satisfying. Contemporary feminism will benefit from a view of interpretation and humankind implied in such a positive skepticism. The Radical Reformers and their descendants may be compared and contrasted with the Catholic and Protestant scholasticism and rationalism prevailing in their origin and history. In overly simplistic terms, the Catholic reading of the Bible was constrained by the church as a known extrinsic institution. The church was a foundational beginning and ending point. The Protestant reading was constrained by doctrine—an extrinsic principle such as *sola fide*—again, a foundational beginning and ending point. (The existential philosophy and categories that served Rudolf Bultmann are comparable to these churchly foundations.) The Radical Reformers were concerned with both church and doctrine, but the way they saw themselves as church influenced their reading of the Bible and their concern for doctrine. They existed as church in the present. But that present Christian community was aware of itself as the primitive and the eschatological community. The Bible, then, had contemporary and not mere antiquarian relevance. The Radical Reformers were like the Qumran community in that they read the Bible as referring to them and their lives in the present. They were like the Jesus of Luke's Gospel who indicated that the Scripture he had just read in the synagogue in Nazareth "has been fulfilled in your hearing" (Luke 4:21).

Doctrine was important to the Radical Reformation, but doctrine stood in relation to the life and practice of the church as primitive and eschatological community. A dialectical relationship existed between doctrine and practice, which meant that a doctrine satisfying at one time was unsatisfying at another. James Wm. McClendon, Jr. and James M. Smith have explicated a "principle of fallibility" that was characteristic of the Radical Reformers: "Even one's most cherished and tenaciously held convictions might be false and are in principle always subject to rejection, reformulation, improvement, or reformation."[13]

The effort at this point is to gain from the Radical Reformation a key to a postmodern reading of the Bible that is properly skeptical but not nihilistic. The importance of ideological "location" is obvious, with earlier interpretations and formulations always subject to reformulation, not through the securing of better information or the devising of a more effective way of reasoning, but through the dynamics of life itself. With the Enlightenment ideal of certainty (as Toulmin[14] stressed), the particular gave way to the universal, the local to the general, the timely to the timeless. The rhetorical context of arguments did not matter—only the rational. With the Radical Reformers, the religious context was most important, and this context was most frequently some dominant state and/or churchly power to which the Radical Reformers were reacting. For descendants of the Radical Reformers, the context is often social. As McClendon points out, with the Swiss brethren in the sixteenth century, it was Catholic views of sacrament and society and Zwinglian Evangelicalism. With Roger Williams in the seventeenth century, it was Puritan models and assumptions. With Issac Backus in the eighteenth century, it

---

[13]James Wm. McClendon, Jr. and James M. Smith, *Convictions: Diffusing Religious Relativism* (Valley Forge PA: Trinity Press International, 1994) 112.
[14]*Cosmopolis*, 29

was New England's struggle for religious liberty. With Thomas and Alexander Campbell in the nineteenth century, it was Locke, the Scottish Enlightenment, and the American frontier. With Walter Rauschenbusch in the twentieth century, it was urban industrialization and poverty.[15]

In the face of a dominant political, religious, and/or social "establishment" with its reading (or domestication) of the Bible, the Radical Reformation carried out a counterideological reading. First, however, came the prevailing reading. This reading was necessary so as to "try" the conventional position. This attempt to naturalize or make their own the sense made of the Bible by others is cited by McClendon as a principle paralleling the principle of fallibility. It is the principle stated by Roger Williams:

> It is the command of Christ Jesus to his scholars [a title Williams felt belonged to all believers] to try all things: and liberty of trying what a friend, yea what an (esteemed) enemy presents hath ever (in point of Christianity) proved one especial means of attaining to the truth of Christ.[16]

The trying of the prevailing reading was, of course, in light of the reformers' perception of themselves as the primitive and eschatological community. And this was the norm for their counterreading.

The agenda of the Radical Reformers and their strategy of reading are not as obvious today as in earlier epochs because their descendants have become the victims of others' agendas and have not been faithful to their own guiding vision. In this last decade of the twentieth century, feminist criticism may provide more persuasive patterns for interpretation that give conscious attention to general cultural norms and ideologies at odds with ideological perspectives and goals of interpreters.[17] Is it possible that the continuing dynamic relationship between extraliterary life and the literary

---

[15]James Wm. McClendon, Jr., *Ethics*, vol. 1 of *Systematic Theology* (Nashville: Abingdon Press, 1986) 37.

[16]Roger Williams, *The Hireling Ministry None of Christ's, or A Discourse Touching the Propogating of the Gospel of Christ Jesus* (1652), in *The Complete Writings Writings of Roger Williams*, vol. 7, ed. Perry Miller (New York: Russell and Russell, 1963) 29.

[17]For various perspectives on the relationship of feminism to postmodernism, see *Feminism/Postmodernism*, ed. Linda Nicholson (London: Routledge & Kegan Paul, 1990). Janice Capel Anderson ("Mapping Feminist Biblical Criticism: The American Scene, 1983–1990," in *Critical Review of Books in Religion* [1991]: 21-44) surveys recent feminist biblical criticism. I am indebted in this section especially to Patrocinio P. Schweickart, "Reading Ourselves: Toward a Feminist Theory of Reading," in *Speaking of Gender*, ed. E. Showalter (London: Routledge & Kegan Paul, 1989) 17-44.

text and its interpretation is not yet appreciated fully by feminists because they (we) are in the midst of a particular struggle against general cultural norms and ideologies and find it difficult to affirm the principle of fallibility of the Radical Reformers for themselves? Feminists are caught up in the Enlightenment ideal of certainty—at least as a strategy in their struggle. I begin, then, with an illustration from experiences of Jean E. Kennard of the way that changes in extraliterary life affect literary life and conventions; this illustration will provide opportunity for highlighting some factors in feminist interpretation and imply the challenge of seeing feminist criticism in dynamic terms.

Kennard cites a section from Northrop Frye's *Anatomy of Criticism*:

> All humor demands agreement that certain things, such as a picture of a wife beating her husband in a comic strip, are conventionally funny. To introduce a comic strip in which a husband beats his wife would distress the reader, because it would mean learning a new convention.[18]

Kennard acknowledges that she first read the book fifteen years earlier and had reread the book several times. Only in the late 1970s and early 1980s did the sentences become objectionable. Her objection was not with a concept of "a convention as an agreement which allows art to communicate." Rather it was in Frye's choice of an example.

> For me, obviously, a convention had changed, and some of the reasons at least seemed apparent. Such extraliterary experiences as talking with friends who worked with battered women, an increased awareness of violence in every city I visited, together with reading feminist scholarship, had led me to formulate values which resisted the convention Frye named. I no longer agreed to find it funny.[19]

Before Kennard experienced resistance to Frye's example, she experienced an appreciation of texts in general and the text of Frye in particular. She assumed that something could be gained from reading and interpretation. An early conventional processing of the text was made possible, then, by a language and worldview shared by author and reader. Had Kennard first come to the text in the 1990s with convictions of the

---

[18]Northrop Frye, *Anatomy of Criticism: Four Essays* (Princeton NJ: Princeton University Press, 1957) 225.

[19]Jean E. Kennard, "Convention Coverage or How to Read Your Own Life," *New Literary History* 18 (1981): 69.

1990s she might have been forced to reconstruct the worldview of Frye in order to appreciate how the text would have been processed originally.

A feminist reading will begin by following conventional approaches, uncritically synthesizing the text as it unfolds and/or critically seeking the "intention" of the author. But this is a beginning and a strategy. The goal of feminism precludes this as the final aim! The meaning obtained in an initial reading is relativized from a metacritical perspective in at least two ways. It is relativized because it is seen as a representation created by a reader. It is also relativized because it is represented or actualized in terms of what the author may have meant to a reader at a particular time. This representation or "meaning" is not one that is normative for all time. A metacritical perspective allows a reader to free herself from the power of what may be taken to be the "obvious" meaning.

Beyond this initial interaction with the text are further positive and negative moves dependent not only upon the power assumed by the reader vis-à-vis the text but also upon the feminist location. The text has the power to structure the experience of the reader, and the female reader may simply accept the values implicit in the text—values that must be observed and assumed provisionally in an initial uncritical reading or in a critical reading directed to the author's intention. But the reader may become conscious of what is happening in the reading and recognize that the power of the text is matched by the essential role of the reader and the process of reading. To read in light of feminist perspectives and goals the reader must learn to resist any androcentric bias of the text, the literary canon, and traditional critical approaches. For a feminist, according to Patrocinio Schweickart, androcentricity is "a sufficient condition for the process of emasculation."[20] A text that serves the male reader positively as "the meeting ground of the personal and the universal"[21] becomes oppressive to the woman reader. (Recall the experience of Jean Kennard.) Schweickart suggests the negative hermeneutic of "ideological unmasking." "The reader recalls and examines how she would 'naturally' read a male text in order to understand and therefore undermine the subjective predispositions that had rendered her vulnerable to its designs."[22]

The negative hermeneutic is possible only because of the possibility of a positive hermeneutic "whose aim is the recovery and cultivation of

---

[20]Schweickart, "Reading Ourselves: Toward a Feminist Theory of Reading," 26.
[21]Ibid.
[22]Ibid., 34.

women's culture."[23] The normative dimension of the feminist story makes visible and pushes beyond the reading that denies women's culture (perhaps only implicitly and unconsciously, but thereby more powerfully). Just as the Radical Reformers and their descendants interpreted the Bible against the horizon of a dominant church, state, and society, feminist critics interpret literature against the horizon of a male-oriented context of writers and interpreters. If they wish the text to serve as the meeting ground for the personal and universal for themselves, feminists must go beyond contemporary male-oriented interpretation, beyond the text, but by means of the text. Theory and strategy are devised and followed in view of a more comprehensive praxis. "Feminist criticism . . . is a mode of praxis. The point is not merely to interpret literature in various ways; the point is to change the world."[24] Schweikart indicates that this involves the producing of "a community of feminist readers and writers" with the hope that ultimately "this community will expand to include everyone."[25]

The "evangelistic" goal of feminism requires theory and strategy that has a validity beyond feminism. What is desired is a concept of validity comparable in power to that which has supported male academic assertions of validity that have excluded women. In the view of some feminists (operating from a "modernist" perspective), feminist criticism benefits from the Enlightenment view of certainty that has supported male agendas. In their view, it is only from such a perspective that the feminist agenda can be validated and carried out effectively. Christine DiStefano asks if postmodernism may not be a theory whose time has come for men but not for women. Since men have had their Enlightenment, they can afford the claims of postmodernism. But women cannot afford a sense of humbleness regarding the coherence and truth of their claims.[26]

Feminist criticism, then, is thrust squarely into the contemporary hermeneutical debate between scholars such as Habermas and Apel and scholars such as Stanley Fish and Richard Rorty. Schweikart offers a criterion that is helpful to feminist biblical scholars, the criterion of an expanding community and continuing dialogue.[27] But this criterion cannot

---

[23]Ibid., 35.

[24]Ibid., 24.

[25]Ibid., 39.

[26]Christine DiStefano, "Dilemmas of Difference: Feminism, Modernity, and Postmodernism," in Nicholson, ed., *Feminism/Postmodernism*, 63-82.

[27]She is using Habermas's idea that consensus obtained through domination-free discourse is the warrant for truth; see Jürgen Habermas, "Wahrheitstheorien," in

simply be pronounced; it must be situated in terms of existing criteria. Historically oriented biblical scholars have absorbed a foundationalist approach, and they are able to operate effectively within historical criticism by reconstructing the life worlds behind biblical texts in a way to rehabilitate biblical texts for the feminist agenda. Phyllis Trible[28] and Elisabeth Schüssler Fiorenza,[29] in particular, have done a remarkable job of placing feminist biblical interpretation at the bar of conventional historical-critical norms. Some critics, however, have noted that this historical-critical scholarship is not "objective," that social and hermeneutical interests determine the weighing of hypotheses and even the selection of hypotheses to be considered.[30]

Mary Ann Tolbert is more comfortable than Trible and Schüssler Fiorenza with the functional or instrumental use of criticism. She is fully aware that reason functions within a community's advocacy of its agenda.

> To assert that all scholarship is advocacy is not . . . to chart new ground and invite anarchy. It is only to admit honestly what the case has been and still is. The criteria of public evidence, logical argument, reasonable hypotheses, and intellectual sophistication still adjudicate acceptable and unacceptable positions.[31]

It is these criteria themselves that raise additional problems. "The 'public' who determines what is reasonable, who form a 'consensus view' are special interest groups with different cannons of validity. . . . No value-neutral position exists nor ever has."[32]

With Tolbert we find satisfaction with an instrumental rationality constrained by interest groups. Rationality is not denied; it is located. Can feminists save themselves from the charge of simply being constrained by one interest while male scholars are constrained by another, with no basis for adjudication? The goal of feminist criticism requires a particular location, but in order to maintain validity that location must be at least

---

Wirklichkeit und Reflexion, ed. H. Fahrenbach (Pfullingen: Nesge, 1973).

[28]See Trible, *Texts of Terror: Literary-Feminist Readings of Biblical Narratives* (Philadelphia: Fortress Press, 1984).

[29]See Schüssler Fiorenza, *In Memory of Her: A Feminist Theological Reconstruction of Christian Origins* (New York: Crossroad; London: SCM Press, 1983).

[30]See Antony C. Thiselton, *New Horizons in Hermeneutics* (Grand Rapids: Zondervan, 1992) 439-52.

[31]Mary Ann Tolbert, "Defining the Problem: The Bible and Feminist Hermeneutics," *Semeia* 28 (1983): 118.

[32]Ibid.

theoretically expanded beyond that location. In feminist interpretation, then, the end that justifies and guides interpretation is not a self-serving parochial agenda but one that extends beyond feminism. I would suggest that it involves at the same time a redefinition of what it means to make sense of texts and what it means to be human.

In both the hermeneutical tradition and in postmodernism we find implicit and explicit challenges to prevailing notions of interpretation that are related to the question of what it means to be a human being. Schleiermacher and the Romantics shared a distrust of what could be achieved by rational argument alone and emphasized feeling, life, imagination, and the sense of the infinite. Schleiermacher emphasized "divination" (imagination) and indicated that this must interact with comparison (criticism). The creative, intuitive capacity is associated with the feminine and the comparative with the masculine.

> Divinatory knowledge is the feminine strength in knowing people; comparative knowledge, the masculine. . . . [T]he divinatory is based on the assumption that each person is not only a unique individual in his own right, but that he has a receptivity to the uniqueness of every other person.[33]

In the postmodern epoch, there is a distrust of rational argumentation akin to the Romantics' distrust and an attempt to relate the affective (feminine) and cognitive (masculine). Geoffrey Hartman proposes a role for literary study in the deconstructionist or postmodern mode: "to word a wound words have made." Hartman's proposal maintains a polarity between the modern and the postmodern. Antirepresentational modes of questioning deconstruct the illusion that particular texts "have a direct, even original, relation to what they represent." What seems to be a cause (reality, presence) is in fact an effect, an illusion of depth. Hartman, however, sees that there is "a reality of the effect" that is inseparable from the "reality of words." The movement of liberation of language from representational concepts "should not cheapen the mimetic and affectional power of words, their interpersonal impact." The wounding results from the equivocal nature of words and the lack of satisfaction of demands of the psyche that a self be defined or constituted by words. But literature has a "medicinal function," which is "to word a wound words have

---

[33]Friedrich Schleiermacher, *Hermeneutics: The Handwritten Manuscripts*, ed. Heinz Kimmerle, trans. James Duke and Jack Forstman (Missoula MT: Scholars Press, 1977) 150.

made." Words themselves help us tolerate the normal conditions of "partial knowledge," which is the condition of living in the context of words.[34]

Hartman contrasts the cognitive function and the "recognitive" function. The cognitive has to do with truth and evidence. A true statement is something that we know or do not know. This is the arena of instrumental rationality. A truthful statement is validated by different criteria than a true statement. A truthful statement is one that we can acknowledge or fail to acknowledge. For Hartman, acknowledgment is the "recognition" that is beyond cognition and that brings closure and the healing of the wounded spirit.[35]

James S. Hans suggests that the new way of conceiving of language is in reality a new concept of humankind. Hans, too, maintains a dialectical relationship between the modern and the postmodern. After a lengthy history of trying to subjugate the world by means of language and to subjugate language itself, "we have arrived at the point where we should be capable of listening to language and allowing ourselves to played by it."[36] When we speak of the end of humankind, it is not

> to deny the human or to act as if it doesn't exist: it is simply a way to reenregister our views of the activities in which we participate in a way which places the human in a more modest, though still important, place. Our location is never central because there never is a central location.[37]

In this sense the end of humankind is really a beginning of a different kind of human. The play of language from this perspective is inaugurated by the orientation of readers. Language is an instrument in the same sense that feet are instruments: "Our language takes us where we want to go, but we often don't know precisely where we want to go, so, given a general direction, we follow the play of language that is inaugurated by our orientation."[38]

That language "takes us down paths we hadn't originally foreseen," is true, but true also is the fact that "we have provided the general

---

[34]Geoffrey H. Hartman, 1981 *Saving the Text* (Baltimore: Johns Hopkins University Press, 1981) 121, 131, 133, 137.

[35]Ibid., 155.

[36]James S. Hans, *The Play of the World* (Amherst: University of Massachusetts Press, 1981) 104.

[37]Ibid., 198.

[38]Ibid., 105.

direction ourselves." When the play of language takes over, it places our specific purposes into the larger perspective of its own play. This play of language, then, "is one of the chief ways through which we confirm or deny the value for different propositions for which we are using language at any particular time."[39] The readers' instrumental approach to language allows the play within the field of language. This play of language then doubles back to the instrumental use. In the process, conventions of perception and orientation are generated, but those conventions are constantly changed through interaction with other fields. We do not arrive at some foundation outside of life, for this more comprehensive play is one that is activated by the orientation humans apply, through language, to the situations that confront them.

The insights of Hartman and Hans concerning the nature of literature and the human in the new context are especially important for feminist criticism. In the functioning of language in a postmodern mode, historical-critical theory and practice (and other particular critical tools) must be seen as instrumental, penultimate not ultimate. To capitulate to modern Enlightenment critical ideas for temporary strategic advantage is not only to retreat from our contemporary worldview but it is to deny the genuine basis for validity. There is a contemporary yearning for validity, then, but when the Enlightenment view of validity is evaluated from postmodern and feminist perspectives, that view becomes suspect. Yet, a validity is possible. This validity is a result of the reading's connecting not with the author of the original text but with a community of readers. To the extent that that connection is made by a feminist, according to Schweikart, and "to the extent that the community is potentially all embracing, her interpretation has that degree of validity."[40]

A challenge for feminist critics is to operate in their local context but to see that context as embracing more than the local. To whatever extent the universal is to be seen, it is seen in the local. In the midst of conflict, the community assuring validity may have a distorted vision; it may be a limited and limiting community. It is that sort of limited community and that sort of limiting validation that Anthony C. Thiselton has in mind when he challenges the sociopragmatic approaches of Stanley Fish and Richard Rorty:

---

[39]Ibid.
[40]Schweickart, "Reading Ourselves: Toward a Feminist Theory of Reading," 39.

If there can be no critique from outside of a community, hermeneutics serves only to affirm its corporate self, its structures, and its corporate values. It can use texts only by the same ploy as that which oppressors and oppressive power structures use, namely in the service of its own interests.[41]

This clear danger is avoided by maintaining the same sort of suspicion vis à vis the reading of the community as is maintained vis à vis oppressive readings. We are back to the principle of fallibility of the Radical Reformers.

Conclusion

The reading of the Bible by the Radical Reformers and their descendants and the reading of literature (including biblical literature) by feminists, then, are similar at the formal level. Both take the text seriously. Although feminists are not content to deal with "male" texts at a superficial level of the author's intention, they acknowledge that male texts play upon authentic liberatory aspirations. Community is important, a community defined in part over against a dominant group and/or ideology. Both are consciously concerned with texts for ideological reasons related to the praxis of the group. In order to obtain the appropriate reading, both must read against the grain of the dominant reading— against the grain of what has become the "obvious" reading. Both must move beyond the superficial level to a level that informs their life and practice. Both are "evangelistic" in that they have a utopian dream that their community will expand to include everyone. The reorientation of hermeneutics in general may be informed, then, by the reading of the Radical Reformers and their descendants and by contemporary feminists. Finality in terms of meaning is not claimed. The meaning achieved, limited and ad hoc as it is, provides satisfaction in terms of criteria of praxis, openness, and continuing communication.

---

[41]Antony C. Thiselton, *New Horizons in Hermeneutics* (Grand Rapids MI: Zondervan, 1992) 7.

Chapter 10

How to Read
and How Not to Read the Bible:
Lessons from the Münster Anabaptists

Validation in reading and interpretation of literature in general and the Bible in particular has always been problematic. Philosophical and theological presuppositions about what is really real and how that reality is known continue to influence biblical interpretation today and lead to debate within religious communities and between those communities and so-called secular communities of interpretation.

In 1995–1996 I was on sabbatical at the University of Münster where I team-taught a course in newer literary methods of New Testament interpretation with colleagues in the Institute for Teacher Training of the Catholic Faculty of the University. I also worshipped with the small Baptist congregation in Münster and participated in activities with the Protestant faculty. This chapter is a result of reflections on the problem of the context and practice of interpretation, particularly on the problem of validity in interpretation. I begin with the biblical interpretation of the Münster Anabaptists of the sixteenth century and Anabaptists in general and I end with an apology for an open-ended circular system of interpretation with a system-oriented self-criticism and self-validation modeled on the Anabaptists.[1]

---

[1]I would like to express appreciation to my colleagues at Münster, especially to Professor Detlev Dormeyer, now of the University of Dortmund, and Doctor Ingrid Rosa Kitzberger with whom I team-taught the course at the University of Münster in 1996. I also would like to express gratitude to Professor James McClendon, Distinguished Scholar in Residence at Fuller Theological Seminary, from whom I have learned much about Free Church ("baptist," to use McClendon's nomenclature) doctrine and biblical interpretation.

Münster and the Anabaptist Vision

All of my Baptist life I have heard of Münster in relation to a radical group of Anabaptists who assumed political and religious control of the city in 1534 and 1535. Present-day visitors discover that the city of Münster has made the Anabaptists central in the telling of its own story. Tour guides point to three metal cages hanging on the tower of a church located on the principal market street of the city, alongside the town hall and other buildings from the Middle Ages. The guides tell the story of the three Anabaptist leaders of the sixteenth century who were executed and whose bodies were placed in those cages in January 1536.[2] The Münster Anabaptists may be seen as something of an aberration of a larger sixteenth-century movement of Radical Reformers. Eric W. Gritsch fits the Münster Anabaptists into events surrounding the birth of the Baptist movement by showing how these Anabaptists were related to Melchior Hoffmann (ca. 1495–1543/1544), a widely traveled Lutheran preacher who was influenced by prevailing sixteenth-century notions of the imminent end of the world and by the Bible's language about this end time. Followers of Hoffmann were called "Melchiorites" and were found in northern Germany and in the Netherlands. They remained a secret party within the church, obedient to Hoffmann's admonition to wait for the time when Hoffmann would be led to establish a new and final Christian assembly on earth just prior to the end.

Jan Matthys (Matthijs), the leader of the secret Dutch Anabaptist party and whom Hoffmann baptized, was the link between the Melchiorites and the Münster Anabaptists. Matthys sent emissaries to the city of Münster, near the Dutch border. They were accepted by the Anabaptists in Münster and persuaded a local Lutheran pastor, Bernard Rothmann, to adopt their ideas and programs. Rothmann became the chief theologian and preacher for the Anabaptists.

---

[2]In the summer of 1995, on city tours, and tours of the cathedral, as well as tours of St. Lambert Church, I heard the guides recounting with obvious relish how the Anabaptists established a new Zion in the city of Münster, practiced a form of communal living, passed a law allowing a man to have more than one wife, and so on. When one of the officials of the cathedral showed me the astronomical clock, he indicated with dismay that the clock was not completely original because it had been destroyed by the Anabaptists due to their opposition to the displaying of pictures in the church.

The radical wing of the Melchiorites soon won control of the city by emotional preaching and manipulation of the several thousand inhabitants. A political opportunist named Knipperdolling became the mayor of the city in February 1534, bringing to power with him several radicals who advocated the establishment of an "eternal kingdom" in the city. Within days, things had gotten out of hand. Twelve appointed "apostles" were led by a former innkeeper from Leiden, Beuckelsz who introduced polygamy and ordered the execution of anyone who disobeyed him. "Prophet" Beuckelsz and "King" Jan married several wives, ordered all goods to be shared in common, burned all books except the Bibles, and established a reign of holy terror until the Catholic bishop of the region, Franz von Waldeck, besieged and conquered the city with the help of Protestant princes and their mercenaries in June 1535. The leaders of the "eternal kingdom" were executed, their corpses hung in iron cages from the tower of St. Lambert Church where they [the iron cages] still can be seen today.[3]

In a recent retelling of the story of Münster, Tal Howard declared that "the violent attempt by the Melchiorite Anabaptists in 1534/1535 to establish the 'New Jerusalem' in the city of Münster represents one of the most bizarre events of the Reformation."

The whole crisis is often construed as an extreme outworking of some latent tendencies within Reformation thought. Luther's widespread influence had greatly diminished the role of the priest as a mediator between the layman and God, thereby increasing the importance of the Bible and personal conscience in directing the layman's spiritual journey. The outcome of this change was that many laymen gave birth to radical interpretations of scripture—interpretations which often carried dangerous social and political implications. The prophetic claims of the two principal prophets at Münster, Jan Matthys and Jan Bockelszoon van Leiden, support this view. Both men drew an enormous amount of prophetic authority from scripture and wielded it with disastrous social and political consequences.[4]

Any contemporary Christian may hesitate before claiming relationship with Anabaptists in general, much less with the Münster Anabaptists. But the Anabaptists are the ancestors of the "Free Church" or "Believers'

---

[3]Eric W. Gritsch, "Birth of the Baptist Movement," historical introduction to *Cecelia's Sin*, by Will D. Campbell (Macon GA: Mercer University Press, 1983) 7-8.

[4]Tal Howard, "Charisma and History: The Case of Münster, Westphalia, 1534–1535," *Essays in History* 35 (1993): 48.

Church" (or what James McClendon calls the "*b*aptists," a practice I follow in this chapter), and their use and misuse of the Bible provides guidance for hermeneutics today. The Münster Anabaptists may be considered an example that "proves the rule" and allows us to see clearly some of the characteristics of Anabaptist hermeneutics.

McClendon has provided a set of persistent marks of the heirs of the Radical Reformation that can serve as a beginning point for appreciation of the hermeneutics of the Münster Anabaptists and for developing a contemporary baptist or Free-Church hermeneutical stance that can be defined in relation to Roman Catholic, Protestant, and nonconfessional and critical modes of interpretation. Five marks are noted by McClendon: (1) *biblicism*, understood as "humble acceptance of the authority of scripture for both faith and practice"; (2) *mission* (or evangelism, understood as "the responsibility to witness to Christ—and accept the suffering that witness entails"; (3) *liberty*, or soul competence, understood as "the God-given freedom to respond to God without the intervention of the state or other powers"; (4) *discipleship*, understood as "life transformed into service by the lordship of Jesus Christ"; and (5) *community*, understood as "sharing together in a storied life of obedient service to and with Christ."[5]

McClendon is interested in how these marks may be drawn together into a "baptist vision" that is adequate for the generation of a theology and to give form to a shared life in Christ Jesus. In this chapter, interest is focused on the way these characteristics provide a vision for hermeneutics. Indeed, McClendon finds the role of scripture to be the clue to the way the marks noted above are drawn together to form a "baptist vision." He chooses not to use the term "biblicism" because it has the sound of a weary old controversy, an agenda that really is not central to baptist life and thought. "Rather," says McClendon,

> say that Scripture in this vision effects a link between the church of the apostles and our own. So the vision can be expressed as a hermeneutical motto, which is shared awareness of *the present Christian community as the primitive community and the eschatological community*. In other words, the church now is the primitive church and the church on the day

---

[5]James Wm. McClendon, Jr., *Ethics*, vol. 1 of *Systematic Theology* (Nashville: Abingdon Press, 1986) 28.

of judgment is the church now; the obedience and liberty of the followers of Jesus of Nazareth is *our* liberty, *our* obedience.[6]

By means of this vision of the constitution of a people's identity, "narratives that are historically set in another time and place" are freed to "display redemptive power here and now." This is a hermeneutical program that moves beyond historical questioning and critical understanding of the Bible. Doing church and reading the Bible are coordinate activities.

At the time of the Münster Anabaptists, three different ways of doing church and reading the Bible were available. The Roman Catholic Church emphasized tradition and authority and understood the Bible within that sociological and ecclesiastical framework. Luther and the other Protestant Reformers stressed the authority of the Bible and the doctrine of justification by faith alone over against the authority and doctrine of the Roman Catholic Church and the papacy; the Reformers were interested in getting the doctrine right. If the Roman Catholics were characterized by traditional authority, the Reformers were characterized by a rational-legal authority. Anabaptists, for their part, felt that the Protestant Reformers had not completed the Reformation. The Reformers' subservience to the state authorities and particularly their failure to return to what the Anabaptists saw as the New Testament church created the Anabaptist movement in German-speaking countries.

The Free, Direct, and Interactive Reading of the Anabaptists

The Anabaptists felt that they had gotten the Bible right! The authentication and validation of their reading, however, was quite different from validation in the Roman Catholic tradition and in the Reformation tradition. The Anabaptists of Münster, along with other Anabaptists, read the Bible from the perspective of Erasmus, Calvin, and Zwingli, from the perspective of Luther and the proposition that justification by faith alone

---

[6]Ibid., 31. In *Doctrine*, vol. 2 of *Systematic Theology* (Nashville: Abingdon, 1994), McClendon summarizes his thesis: "The baptist vision is the way the Bible is read by those who (1) accept the plain sense of Scripture as its dominant sense and recognize their continuity with the story it tells, and who (2) acknowledge that finding the point of that story leads them to its application, and who also (3) see past and present and future linked by a 'this is that' and 'then is now' vision, a trope of mystical identity binding the story now to the story then, and the story then and now to God's future yet to come" (45).

is the basis of our standing before God. But the Anabaptists were radical in their application of Reformation tenets. There was a radicality related to the concept of the church as a gathered community. It was a gathered community of believers that constituted nothing less than the primitive community of New Testament days and the eschatological community. The chief theologian and preacher for the Münster Anabaptists, Bernard Rothmann, spoke of the Anabaptist congregation as being reconstituted by God as the church was in the beginning, particularly as it is described in the Book of Acts.

There was an immediacy and self-authentication in the encounter between believers and the biblical text. The context of a new people of God, directed toward Christian lifestyle and discipleship provided control, direction, and vitality. Political and ecclesiastical controls and barriers were removed. This involves a freedom, a liberty of conscience, that was politically and ecclesiastically dangerous in the sixteenth century. The freedom assumed by the Anabaptists permeated and distinguished the other marks of biblical authority, mission, discipleship, and community. Today, this idea of freedom is so prevalent that we find it hard to appreciate the distinctiveness of those Anabaptists and their descendants.

The freedom assumed by the Anabaptists of Münster moved into license and excess. The Münster Anabaptists could be accused of reading themselves into the scriptures as the eschatological people of God in such a literal and political fashion that other legitimate and important teachings and practices became lost or distorted. Rothmann had declared that it was clear and obvious that Christ in that very period of time in the sixteenth century would appear to assume his reign and to destroy his enemies. The Münster Anabaptists may be seen as confusing the spiritual reality expressed in the apocalyptic vision with a literal understanding that became the basis for interpreting events and doing church in Münster. The intellectual basis for this interpretation, as indicated earlier, was the work of Melchior Hoffmann, who saw himself as Elijah, the first witness of the apocalypse, and preached that the city of Strasbourg was the site of the future New Jerusalem. Hoffmann did not use violent means to achieve his ends; yet he was imprisoned by the authorities at Strasbourg. After his imprisonment, his ideas assumed a life of their own in the Netherlands, with Jan Matthys proclaiming himself to be Enoch, the second witness of the apocalypse. When conditions in Münster were seen by Matthys to coincide with Hoffmann's eschatological hopes for Strasbourg, Matthys concluded that the New Jerusalem would now be Münster.

From the perspective of the systemic approach supported by the correlation of different marks of Anabaptists, error and excess could arise at other points. The nature of the church would allow dictatorial leaders who imposed their wills and agendas upon the members.[7] The functions of the church, moreover, could become confused with political agendas.[8]

The apocalyptic interpretation and application of the Münster Anabaptists shows that the Bible was interfaced with the Christian community in a more-or-less direct fashion, not indirectly by way of creeds, traditions, or university-trained linguistic experts (as with the Reformers.) The proclamation by Matthys on 15 March 1534, that all writings other than the Old and New Testaments were be brought to the cathedral square and burned may be seen as an anti-intellectual act and/or as a final instance of the authoritarian control exercised by Matthys. But it may be seen as movement toward immediate access to the message of scripture. In fact, Rothmann had declared that since the Holy Scriptures had become darkened through human writings and teachings, the almighty had decreed that writings other than the Holy Scriptures be banned.

The Münster Anabaptists (utilizing figural and typological approaches provided in the Bible itself and in Christian history) could apply language about one set of events and circumstances in scripture to other events and circumstances and all of these together to events and circumstances in their day.[9] The emphasis that the church now *is* the primitive church and

---

[7]Howard sees the events at Münster in light of the use and misuse of authority. Hoffmann "established his authority simply by personal appeal and the content of his message. Matthys . . . represents a devolution into authoritarian measures. His use of violence, his tactics of information control, and the opposition which he received from the citizens in Münster testify to his inability to maintain a sense of authority in the basis of charisma alone. . . . Finally . . . Bokelszoon represents only the extreme propulsion of authoritarian tendencies already originating with Matthys" ("Charisma and History," 64).

[8]The life and work of Menno Simons and the establishment of an Anabaptist movement that vowed never again to violate its promise to remain pacifist supports this view.

[9]The Anabaptists were using literary, typological, and allegorical methods of interpretation found throughout the Bible and early church history, made problematic with historical-critical emphases upon historical origin and/or the intention of the original author(s), and rediscovered in contemporary approaches to literary intertextuality. The Exodus from Egypt was not only an event for ancient Israel, it was the pattern for understanding the return from Babylonian Exile, the model for appreciating the liberation gained through Christ, and for appreciating the freedom of the contemporary believer. At its worst this literary and theological practice is a superficial joining of verses that are not related in any fashion. At its best, it is a sensing that biblical events are more than past events. They have been appropriated over and over again and can be appropriated in the present. In the biblical text, we have fixed expressions of the significance of those events

the church of the end time and that the biblical message is directed to the church now *as* the primitive and eschatological people of God gives a focus to the reading of the Bible, but it can be the source of disastrous delusion as well as of authentic insight and direction. To guard against false interpretation, the *is* can become legal and institutional (with ideas of succession and/or development). But when viewed artistically and poetically, the baptist *is* makes the church and Bible reading dynamic and alive.

Excesses and Churchly Validation

The traditional, institutional, and rational-legal approaches of the Roman Catholics and Reformers guard against the excesses made possible in artistic and poetic approaches. Can such excesses be avoided without abandoning the baptist vision? The church's concern with hermeneutics arose because of the excesses of the heresies of Marcion and the Gnostics. Principles of hermeneutics were developed by Irenaeus in his work *Against Heresies* to deal with these excesses. The principles of Irenaeus do not allow perfect knowledge, but this is due not to the nature of scripture but to human limitations. Irenaeus indicated that "perfect knowledge cannot be attained in the present life: many questions must be submissively left in the hands of God." This lack of complete knowledge is a result of the fact that although the scriptures "are indeed perfect, since they were spoken by the Word of God and His Spirit," we are "inferior to, and later in existence than, the Word of God and His Spirit."[10] The principles of Irenaeus may be summarized as follows.

> Scripture is to be read as a whole. Any one text is to be understood within the whole of Scripture. Scripture is a whole because it tells one story, and readers need to know what the story is all about in order to understand any part of the story. The church knows what the story is all about, for the church is in continuity with that story. The "rule of faith" constitutes the church's knowledge of what the Bible is all about. So the Bible is to be read in light of that "rule of faith."[11]

---

and by means of the biblical text the significance of those events can be reexperienced.

[10]Irenaeus, *Against Heresies* 2.28.2.

[11]Robert W. Jenson has commended and commented on the rules of Irenaeus in an essay entitled "Hermeneutics and the Life of the Church" in *Reclaiming the Bible for the Church*, ed. Carl E. Braaten and Robert W. Jenson (Grand Rapids MI: Eerdmans, 1995) 89-105.

Irenaeus's appeal to the wholeness of scripture emerges in his polemics against Marcion who divorced the Old Testament from the New. Irenaeus believed that every part of scripture points ultimately to Christ, and in his actual interpretation Irenaeus uses allegory and typology to relate the two Testaments. Irenaeus relates the fact that "the hidden treasure in the Scriptures is Christ" (the basis of the wholeness of scripture) to the proposition that "the true exposition of the Scripture is to be found in the church alone" by explaining first of all that Christ is the treasure that was hid in the "field" (referring to the parable of Matthew 13:44) in Old Testament types and prophecies, but not understood until the advent of Christ. When the law is read to those who do not know Christ, "it is like a fable; for they do not possess the explanation of all things pertaining to the advent of the Son of God, which took place in human nature."[12] When the law is read by Christians, the treasure hid in the field is "brought to light by the cross of Christ, and explained." Irenaeus declares that this way of understanding the scriptures goes back to the discourse between Jesus and the disciples following the resurrection, when Jesus proved to them from the Scriptures that "Christ must suffer, and enter into His glory, and that remission of sins should be preached in His name throughout all the world" (Luke 24:26, 47). Irenaeus concludes:

> Wherefore it is incumbent to obey the presbyters who are in the Church—those who . . . together with the succession of the episcopate, have received the certain gift of truth, according to the good pleasure of the Father. But [it is also incumbent] to hold in suspicion others who depart from the primitive succession, and assemble themselves together in any place whatsoever . . . For all these have fallen from the truth.[13]

By the very nature of the debate in which he was engaged with Marcion and the Gnostics, Irenaeus was interested in a foundation for interpretation, a basis for ruling out the views of his opponents. In his discussion of the interpretation of parables and obscure passages of scripture, Irenaeus warns against applying "expressions which are not clear or evident" to the interpretation of the parables with the result that different individuals discover for themselves different truths.

---

[12]*Against Heresies* 4.26.1.
[13]*Against Heresies* 4.26.2.

[I]n this way no one will possess the rule of truth; but in accordance with the number of persons who explain the parables will be found the various systems of truth, in mutual opposition to each other. . . . According to this course of procedure, therefore, man would always be inquiring but never finding, because he has rejected the very method of discovery.[14]

Irenaeus argues the case for understanding the Bible in close connection with the tradition of the church in opposition to the heretics who "follow neither Scripture nor tradition." Irenaeus sees a dialectical relationship between scripture and tradition, with priority claimed for the tradition but appealed to as a means for determining the true sense of the scriptures. Irenaeus asks what would be done if scripture did not exist. To what would we appeal?

[H]ow should it be if the apostles themselves had not left us writings? Would it not be necessary, [in that case,] to follow the course of the tradition which they handed down to those to whom they did commit the Churches?[15]

Irenaeus assumed that the apostles are the ultimate authority, but appeal to the apostles in person is no longer possible. Their representatives and successors are still to be found in the churches however. Irenaeus appeals to the church at Rome and sees a dialectical relationship between that church and the other churches, the church at Rome being the one church in the West able to claim apostolic foundation and being the church most conspicuous and so under the judgment of other churches that no innovation there could escape notice and criticism.[16]

In his essay "On Reclaiming the Bible for Christian Theology," Brevard Childs indicates the relevance of the interdependence of the different factors involved in Irenaeus' principles of interpretation for contemporary interpretation:

Scripture does not bring forth a witness to itself, but points to God's Word calling the church into existence. Yet the community of faith actively received, shaped, and transmitted the Scriptures and the church provides the context for its correct interpretation for faith and practice. This means that proper interpretation does not consist of an initial stance of seeking a purely objective or neutral reading to which the element of

---

[14]*Against Heresies* 2.27.1-2.
[15]*Against Heresies* 3.4.1.
[16]*Against Heresies* 3.3.2.

faith is added subsequently, but rather, from the start, the Christian reader receives a particular point of standing from which to identify with the apostolic faith in awaiting a fresh word from God through the Spirit."[17]

Childs is less interested in the limiting rule of faith than he is in the church's activity in the formation of the canon and the potential the canon presents for contemporary interpretation. Both of these (the rule of faith and the result of the historical shaping of the canon) are certainly constraints upon excesses. Perhaps the canonical criticism of Childs is more amiable to a baptist approach than an unimaginative application of the rule of faith. But a baptist vision begins with a different view of church and doing church than the vision of Irenaeus. James McClendon has restated this baptist vision for our day. In his chapter on the church entitled "The Quest for Christian Community," McClendon cites the work of Ernst Troeltsch (who recognized "mystical," "church," and "sect" types of European ecclesiology); Franklin H. Littell (who maintained that the Anabaptists proper were the Radical Reformers who gathered and disciplined a "true church"); Harold S. Bender and his students (who emphasized the entire baptist movement as a community originating in more than one place and characterized by discipline, peace, and love); and Leslie Newbigen (who recognized that neither Protestant orthodoxy of doctrine nor Catholic impeccability of succession can take the place of the presence and power of the Holy Spirit). McClendon sees that baptists understand church in a unique way: "It is local, Spirit-filled, mission-oriented, its discipleship always shaped by a practice of discernment."[18]

The challenge I have given as a title for this chapter ("How to Read and How Not to Read the Bible") and the problem facing Irenaeus as to how to recognize truth from error in biblical interpretation is answered by McClendon in the "practice of discernment" and McClendon emphasizes that discernment involves the two motifs of the baptist vision: "this is that" and "then is now." The first motif is the vision of the church now being seen in the frame of the New Testament church. In certain ways this is the vision of Irenaeus. The context of self-interpretation is the Christian community that grew up from the ministry of Jesus Christ on earth.

---

[17]*Reclaiming the Bible for the Church*, 10.
[18]*Systematic Theology: Doctrine*, 342-43.

> It requires that the reading method by which the first Christians once approached the Bible (a method they learned from the Bible itself) be again employed by Christians today so that their understanding of Christian community is framed, shaped, by that original benchmark of understanding.[19]

These features are realized for McClendon, however, through independent discernment as the living church reads afresh, not through the fixities of canon law or tradition. The other motif of the baptist vision is "then is now." "The church on judgment day, the church that must give final answer only to Jesus the Lord, is already present—it is the church today." The church, then, sees itself in the frame of biblical expectation. In both aspects of the baptist vision, there is an expectancy, an openness to the future.[20]

The frame of biblical expectation and correction is seen clearly in the advice given by John Robinson to the pilgrims before they left for America:

> I cannot sufficiently bewail the condition of the Reformed Churches, who are come to a Period in Religion and will go at present no further than the instruments of their Reformation. The Lutherans can't be drawn to go beyond what Luther saw; whatever part of His will our God has revealed to Calvin, they would rather die than embrace it; and the Calvinists, you see, stick fast where they were left by that great man of God, who yet saw not all things. . . . I beseech you remember it is an article of your church covenant, that you be ready to receive whatever truth shall be made known to you from the written Word of God.[21]

The call for interpretation of the Bible within the church and the provisional nature of the present church results in a dynamic biblical hermeneutics. Could the present-day coexistence of different ideas and practices of church provide direction for a more inclusive and dynamic hermeneutics. I would suggest that McClendon's understanding of baptist ecclesiology as provisional allows not only a view of self-correction of baptist ecclesiology (and interpretation) in the historical process, it allows the coexistence of other forms of ecclesiology (and interpretation). McClendon sees that from an ecumenical perspective "the forms of

---

[19]Ibid., 344.

[20]Ibid.

[21]Daniel Neal, *History of the Puritans*, part 2, chap. 2. Quoted in Ernest Payne, *The Fellowship of Believers* (London: Cary Kingsgate Press, 1952) 74.

Christian community so far achieved are at best tentative or provisional steps toward the full unity Christ commanded." The fact that three major styles of being church have made their appearance and that no one type of Christian community is capable of absorbing the other two suggests "that all three types may be provisional."[22]

In actual practice, the different forms of doing church are often interdependent. In my stay in Münster, I participated in activities among Protestants, Free-Church congregations, and Roman Catholics. The 300-member Baptist congregation with which I was associated existed within or in tandem with the political, social, and even ecclesiastical frameworks produced and dominated by the Roman Catholic Church in that section of Germany. In certain respects, the Roman Catholic bishop could and did speak for all Christians in the area, including Free-Church congregations. But within the Roman Catholic church, there were evidences of a Free-Church mentality. During my stay in Germany, a "petition of the people of the church" was distributed and signed by many Roman Catholics throughout the country demanding a "renewal of the church in the spirit of Jesus." As the Free-Church congregations rely upon certain traditions and foundations sustained by the Roman Catholic Church, the Roman Catholic Church is influenced by the dynamic movement allowed by the less hierarchically organized congregations. To the extent that the Roman Catholic Church is influenced by Vatican II, both the baptists and Roman Catholics may see the church as *ecclesia semper reformanda*—the eternally self-reforming church.[23]

This chapter is less concerned with the accommodation of the different understandings of church and in ways of doing church than with the sort of biblical interpretation facilitating and being facilitated by these eccelesiologies. How might a baptist emphasis benefit from and/or contribute to the Roman Catholic emphasis upon apostolicity. Attention directed *only* to doctrinal purity and the role of the episcopal hierarchy (incomplete without the papacy), does not tend toward mutuality and appreciation. In my work, I emphasize continuity by suggesting that the biblical text is shaped by or stamped with and expresses the experience

---

[22]*Systematic Theology: Doctrine*, 344.

[23]In America, certain of the Free-Church groups have assumed the dominate stances taken by the Roman Catholic and Protestants churches in Europe. Sociologically, they attempt to assume the stance of "church" as well as "sect."

of the people of God and that this experience can be recapitulated in different times and places by reading of the Bible.[24]

Sandra Schneiders has discussed the hermeneutical dialectic between scripture and tradition and the place of the ordinary or extraordinary magisterium of the Roman Catholic Church. She indicates that the approach that attempts to declare once and for all either the superiority of scripture to tradition or the superiority of tradition to scripture is futile and undermines the value in both positions. Scripture and tradition

> constitute a single reality, the historical consciousness of the Church insofar as this is explicitly appropriated and deliberately transmitted from generation to generation with the intention that what is transmitted will function as effective historical consciousness in the ongoing experience of the Church. The important distinction is not that between tradition and scripture but that between the apostolic tradition . . . and postapostolic tradition.

The apostolic tradition includes "both the written and unwritten witness to the foundational revelation experience" and the postapostolic tradition includes "both the written and unwritten expression and transmission of the subsequent living of that revelation experience."[25] In her discussion of the official teaching of the church, Schneiders indicates the difficulty with determining official teaching "because it is nowhere written down and because it must constantly be reactualized in terms of new situations."[26]

> The magisterium is not empowered to invent the tradition out of whole cloth, to impose on the People of God what Jesus does not call them to, or to sit in judgment on the foundational revelation. If at times it has seemed (to Protestants and even to Catholics) to do so, either it has been misunderstood or it has misunderstood itself and overstepped its bounds. Both have happened. But the fact remains that valid tradition must have at its heart apostolic tradition, and the touchstone of apostolic tradition is the New Testament."[27]

---

[24]See McKnight, "Der hermeneutische Gewinn der neuen literarischen Zugänge in der neutestamentlichen Bibelinterpretation," *Biblische Zeitschrift* (1997): 161-73.

[25]Schneiders, *The Revelatory Text: Interpreting the New Testament as Sacred Scripture* (San Francisco: HarperSanFrancisco, 1991) 81.

[26]Ibid., 79.

[27]Ibid., 80.

The quest for doctrinal purity must be redefined from a baptist perspective. Doctrine is not simply a matter of "getting it right" intellectually. McClendon not only sees Christian doctrine intertwined with Bible reading, he also distinguishes between Christian doctrines and "the practice of doctrine." By "practice" McClendon means "a complex series of human actions involving definite practitioners who by these means and in accordance with these rules together seek the intended end." He uses the term "convictions" in his relating of Christian doctrines to practice. According to McClendon,

> convictions are not just beliefs or opinions, but are deeply self-involving. By coming to understanding our convictions, we can come to know ourselves as we truly are. For our convictions show themselves not merely in our professions of belief or disbelief, but in all our attitudes and actions. Thus . . . convictions have an affective dimension, while . . . they also have cognitive content, and . . . they entail our intentions as well as our action.[28]

From the Roman Catholic side, Schneiders has discussed doctrine or "faith affirmative" in relation to practice, faith, and intellectual insight. She discusses how the doctrines of creation and incarnation are related to their subject matter and to other kinds of affirmations.

> To affirm that God *created* the universe is not to affirm that God performed the chronologically first act in the causal series that scientists call evolution. . . . To affirm creation is to live in a new world, a world one shares with the Creator. The affirmation of creation is not primarily an intellectual assent to a proposition about reality but a personal engagement characterized by humility, gratitude, reverence, and all those other qualities that define the properly religious attitude of the human being before God.[29]

The faith affirmation of the *incarnation* is not a matter of reasoning logically from sayings and/or deeds of Jesus to Jesus' divinity. To affirm that Jesus is divine "is to profess having perceived in him something that could be but does not have to be perceived, namely, the definitive historical instance of the full coincidence between divine self-giving and

---

[28] *Systematic Theology: Doctrine*, 29.
[29] *The Revelatory Text*, 49.

human experience." In his words and deeds we experience Jesus as "disclosive of the self-giving God and therefore affirm his divinity."[30]

The rule of faith of the Catholic Church and the corresponding doctrinal positions of the Reformers are problematic standards. They establish stops or barriers beyond which believers are not to go. Can we find a constraining force guarding against error (a "red light") that is at the same time a liberating force (a "green light")? Augustine's distinctions between signs, things to be used, and things to be enjoyed may be profitable in coordinating constraints operating in conjunction with creative freedom. For Augustine, signs (words, language) and things to be used operate at subordinate levels. At a higher level are things to be enjoyed. For the Christian, signs and things to be used function in relation to true objects of enjoyment which are the Father, the Son, and the Holy Spirit. The scriptures themselves are to be used in relation to these more ultimate realities: "The end of the law, and of all holy scripture, is the love of an object which is to be enjoyed, and the love of an object which can enjoy that other in fellowship with ourselves."[31]

Augustine, of course, is referring to the love of God and the love of neighbor. This is the end of scripture. Irenaeus said that when we come to something that is not clear, we interpret it in light of the rule of faith.[32] For Augustine, love of God and love of neighbor are the primary hermeneutical guides. Augustine declared that the purpose of a biblical text could be reached even when the meaning drawn from the text is not the meaning intended by the author. The primacy of enjoyment of God and love of neighbor relativize even such matters as textual criticism and translation. There was a coordination of conventional signs and things to be used with the true objects of enjoyment, but the true objects of enjoyment were superior schemata.

---

[30]Ibid.

[31]Augustine, *On Christian Doctrine* 1.35.39.

[32]Irenaeus indicated that true knowledge consists not only of the doctrine of the apostles, the ancient constitution of the church, the succession of the bishops, and so on, but also of "the preeminent gift of love, which is more precious than knowledge, more glorious than prophecy, and which excels all the other gifts [of God]" (*Against Heresies* 4.33.8). Operationally, of course, the rule of faith is primary.

Historical Criticism and a Circle of Circles

The contemporary challenge for most readers is the appropriate coordination of critical (primarily historical-critical) approaches and theological reading and construction. In the churchly interpretation emphasized to this point, the Bible provides the unquestioned premises for the faithful. It was revelation. What was needed was an appropriate method for securing what was revealed. With the Enlightenment, the Bible began to be treated as data to be subjected to critical investigation. The view of the nature of biblical revelation was altered in the critical investigation. But the faithful discovered ways to correlate some concept of the Bible as authority with critical investigation. Schleiermacher, for example, understood religion as having to do with feeling, immediate prereflective self-consciousness, or the feeling of absolute dependence. The task of the theologian is to develop the conceptions of God and the world that are implied in the religious consciousness and that are representative of that consciousness. The human reality of religion disclosed by scholarship leaves open the question of God because scholarship cannot settle the question through its rational procedures. The question of God is left genuinely open; believers are able to affirm it on other than rational grounds and procedures.

Critical believers since the Enlightenment have faced the challenge of remaining critical and utilizing criticism in their appropriation of scripture. My experience is the experience of many of my generation. I began with a noncritical (not anticritical) reading of the Bible in a small farming community in South Carolina. Life centered around the Methodist church. We read the Bible in a simple way, correlating the biblical texts with life in the community. As a youngster, it seemed to me that rules and regulations having to do with Sabbath observance were primary. By the time I got to high school, we had moved to Charleston where I became a Baptist and participated in the various activities of my local congregation, including the regular reading of scripture. With the devotional sort of reading we engaged in, I was not assisted in sorting out some simple hermeneutical principles—such as distinguishing between the New Testament and the Old Testament—and had to come to some practical procedures on my own.

As a Methodist-Baptist I had some problems with the question of falling from grace and the perseverance of the saints. The historical-critical method, learned first in the study of history at the College of

Charleston, became a means of deliverance in terms of interpretation. An event, an idea, a writing (such as the Book of Hebrews with its talk of apostasy) makes sense in light of its historical setting. From a dogmatic beginning point, historical-critical insights were very productive. I even wrote a little book—*Opening the Bible: A Guide to Understanding the Scriptures*[33]—that was an introduction to historical-critical insights for lay readers.

A historical-critical method in tandem with a dogmatic system is not to be sneered at! But the historical-critical approach in itself is incapable of arriving at the sort of conclusions found acceptable in the philosophical and theological enterprises. G. E. Lessing emphasized that truths of fact cannot be raised to the level of truths of reason, and the ditch between these two levels has played its part in the development of the different systems of theology and biblical studies. Ernst Troeltsch helped to clarify what historical study involves and why historical study is incapable of reaching beyond the historical nexus.[34] A "crisis of historicism" was generated, according to Troeltsch, by awareness of the conflict between claims to absolute or normative truth and historical relativism. Troeltsch worked at the task of achieving a synthesis whereby the absolute can be given the form possible to it at a given moment that remains true to its inherent limitations as approximations of universal values. He concluded that there is a vital and creative absolute within the relative.

Peter C. Hodgson has utilized Troeltsch's later thought in a revision of idealistic views of God. According to Hodgson, Troeltsch "stressed the necessity of having the courage to act in situations of objective and intellectual uncertainty, for action can clarify and resolve things when theoretical questions remain irresolvable; and he called for the creation of a new synthesis of cultural values, the beginning of a process of a new, postbourgeois society."[35]

One of the characters in a novel by a student of Troeltsch expresses (according to Hodgson) the vision of Troeltsch:

---

[33](Nashville: Broadman Press, 1967).

[34]Ernst Troeltsch, "Historiography," in *Encyclopedia of Religion and Ethics*, ed. James Hastings (New York: Charles Scribner's Sons, 1925) 4:718. See also his essay on "Contingency."

[35]Peter C. Hodgson, *God in History: Shapes of Freedom* (Nashville: Abingdon, 1989) 41.

We cannot assure ourselves of the ultimate mysteries except by a bold leap into their depth. This leap is an enormous daring; it is an entirely personal decision, but we can act on it despite the dangers and the apparent uncertainty that are involved in it, because it is no blind accident that we entertain such and such ideas about the ultimate mysteries, for these ideas are effected in us by the divine life itself.[36]

Praxis and thought, action and theory, are interdependent. Action both precedes and gives rise to thought. The prophetic vision of Troeltsch was not heeded and he died before he was able to contribute to its realization. Positivism instead of Troeltsch's modification of Hegel's idealism was in the ascendancy in Troeltsch's day. Positivism recognized only assured facts and the connections between them, with the facts and connections turned over to schemata and criteria related to the completion of human existence itself. That is, in its essential form, the historical-critical approach of the Enlightenment presupposed a closed system of cause and effect on the human plane.

If the Roman Catholic rule of faith and Reformation doctrine could form a wedge between the Bible and the believing readers, how much more can the historical-critical method when it becomes the doorkeeper to all possibilities of truth. In "Introduction: Gospel, Church, and Scripture," a preamble to a series of essays entitled *Reclaiming the Bible for the Church*, Carl E. Braaten and Robert W. Jenson evaluate such a view of the historical-critical method:

> The historical-critical method was a gift to the church of the Enlightenment. At first the historical approach was rejected by the theologians of Protestant Orthodoxy and Pietism, but then it gradually gained acceptance among mediating theologians who attempted to reconcile the traditional faith of the church with principles of modern reason. However the marriage between scholarly criticism of the Bible as a collection of ancient documents and the church's belief in its divinely inspired message of salvation has ever since proved to be unstable. The methods of critical reason have tended to take over the entire operation of biblical interpretation, marginalizing the faith of the church and dissolving the unity of the Bible as a whole into a multiplicity of

---

[36]Gertrud von le Fort, *Der Kranz der Engel*, 6th ed. (Munich: Ehrenwirth Verlag, 1953) 210. English translation of text cited in *God in History* from Wilhelm Pauck, *Harnack and Troeltsch: Two Historical Theologies* (New York: Oxford University Press, 1968) 91n.

unrelated fragments. The academy has replaced the church as the home of biblical interpretation. Biblical critics frequently claim that their use of the historical-critical method is free of confessional assumptions and theological motivations, that their approach enjoys the status of objective historical science. Upon close scrutiny, however, it is possible to show that historical critics approach the texts with their own set of prior commitments, sometimes hiddenly linked to ideologies alien or hostile to the faith of the Christian church.[37]

In the present day we are witnessing what is called a "postmodern" or a "postcritical" mindset that is consonant in many ways with Troeltsch's thought. It is a recognition that rational and empirical assumptions and approaches of the Enlightenment overreached themselves. The suggestions of scholars as to how deal with the new postcritical situation may be helpful for us in biblical interpretation. Scholars on the continent of Europe and in England and America acknowledge that Enlightenment rationality is not complete in and of itself. Enlightenment rationality is the rationality that has helped us learn facts about the natural world from given perspectives. But what we learn depends upon our perspectives and our questions. European scholars would still want to find some metacritical or overarching position, some Archimedian point, from which modern scientific study would be validated. They speak of levels of practical and emancipatory knowledge involving interpersonal understanding, social cooperation, and freedom from ideological constraints. Functions of knowledge exist that transcend the purely cognitive.[38] Anglo-American scholars emphasize the social and pragmatic construction of realities beyond those that can be manipulated scientifically. One individual's understanding of truth is tested in relation to his or her colleagues' understanding of truth, and this truth is not treated as something fixed and final but is subject to a continuing history of study and interpretation.[39]

---

[37]*Reclaiming the Bible for the Church*, x-xi.

[38]Perhaps we can find some parallels between the interests of continental scholars in nonobjectivizing frameworks and the emphasis of Irenaeus upon the necessity of the "rule of faith" or Augustine's emphasis upon love of God and love of neighbor as the overarching criteria and schemata for interpretation. We continue with whatever scientific tools we have at our disposal, language (knowledge of the biblical languages), archaeology, history, sociology, and so on. But these tools of themselves do not bring us to the matter with which the Bible is concerned. These tools objectify. They may help us see what a text is saying—but only partly, for what a text is saying is related to what the text is speaking about.

[39]Anglo-American interests may be seen as paralleling Anabaptists and their descen-

A comprehensive nonfoundationalist approach to the reading of the Bible begins somewhere, and the beginning point is important. But hidden behind that beginning point are "prior" (chronologically and/or ideologically) "beginning points." We may begin with dogma, but we do not reduce the Bible to dogma. If we already know what the Bible has said or can say to us, we are unable to hear a new word in our reading of the Scripture. We may begin with history, or sociology, or anthropology, or psychology, but we do not reduce the Bible to any object of scientific research. We may begin with readers in communities of faith with confidence that the Bible speaks, because it has spoken. But when we begin there, we become suspicious when we see the excesses— whether of ancient Gnostics, or sixteenth-century Anabaptists in Münster, or modern-day enthusiasts. We must clothe impressions (or guesses, or wagers) concerning what the Bible is saying to us with intelligibility, with different sorts of intelligibility. We must give attention to the question of validity in interpretation. Instead of attempting to reconstruct a post-modern foundation, I suggest the appreciation and utilization of circles which hang together in an interlocking fashion and form a dynamic unity. Changes in one will affect other circles and the whole dynamic unity.

One circle is the circle of praxis, the practice of religion in terms of individual piety, congregational worship and service, and involvement in the larger world of God's creation. We are learning about this circle and the primacy of this circle from Third World Christians who are not really concerned with the theories of continental and Anglo-American scholars. They are teaching us that understanding of the Bible does not move in a logical fashion from theory to praxis. Bernard Lategan has studied the interpretation of Romans 13 in the South African context, highlighting reading strategies affirming or resisting what appears to be a requirement of Christians to obey the state.[40] Some of the interpretations that Lategan studied were the work of groups of South African biblical scholars who had seen the effects of official practices of apartheid upon their fellow

---

dants who maintained a "principle of fallibility" that stressed that "even one's most cherished and tenaciously held convictions might be false and are in principle always subject to rejection, reformulation, improvement, or reformation." James Wm. McClendon, Jr. and James M. Smith, *Convictions: Diffusing Religious Relativism*, rev. ed. (Valley Forge PA: Trinity Press International, 1994) 112.

[40]Bernard Lategan, "Reading Romans 13 in a South African Context," *The Reader and Beyond: Theory and Practice in South African Studies*, ed. Bernard Lategan (Pretoria: Human Sciences Research Council, 1992) 115-33.

South Africans. They were concerned with the text of Romans that declares Christians are to be subject to governing authorities because the Dutch Reformed Church had used that text to support the system of apartheid. The scholars wanted to challenge the interpretation of the Dutch Reformed Church. They often organized their arguments in logical fashion, moving from questions of language, to questions of history, to questions of praxis. But in fact they began with praxis. They knew that apartheid was wrong and needed to be abolished. They began with praxis and developed theory adequate for praxis.

Doctrine is another circle. James McClendon reminds us that this circle is dynamic in and of itself. The first-order task is the teaching of Christian doctrine. The second-order task is the theological task of critically examining and revising that teaching.[41] Different levels are involved in the critical theological task: biblical theology, systematic theology, and comparative theology. The correlation of the sacred with criteria related to the completion of human existence is a challenge for all levels of the theological enterprise. Severely abstract idealistic views of the sacred and severely anthropomorphic views of God are unsatisfying. And some popular concepts of God are in fact seen to be in conflict with completion of human existence. Instead of maintaining a dialogue between the human and divine dimensions, some must deny the divine in order to allow the human to grow and prosper. Some biblical scholars, then, not only exclude the sacred methodologically in their study of biblical literature, they exclude the sacred on philosophical and theological grounds in order to enhance the human. The "death of God" is recapitulated, even in a postcritical epoch. Believers engage in the critical theological task, and that task is correlated with the teaching of doctrine. But, as shown earlier, we also move behind the teaching of doctrine to the practice of doctrine. In the practice of doctrine, perhaps, some of the theoretical aspects of the theological enterprise are subsumed or transformed. At any rate, doctrine and theology is a dynamic circle involved implicitly or explicitly in the comprehensive system of hermeneutics.

History and historical study constitute a circle that cannot be ignored in our era. In our postmodern world we recognize the limitations of historical study. We recognize that our historical tools as such are unable to uncover the connection of the eternal with the finite in historical experience. This is not due to a lack of connection! It is due to a methodologi-

---

[41]*Systematic Theology: Doctrine*, 33.

cal assumption of the historical approach itself. Some theologians in our day are dissatisfied with the ideology resulting from the methodological exclusion of any sort of transcendence in historical research. Peter Hodgson has been cited as a theologian who uses the work of Ernst Troeltsch to revise the (Hegelian) view of God as a Platonic Idea above the play of history. Hodgson does not desire to represent God as "an individual agent performing observable acts," or as "a uniform inspiration or lure," or as "an abstract ideal," or "in the metaphorical role of companion or friend." Nevertheless, Hodgson affirms that God is effectively present in the world in specific patterns of praxis that operate within historical process and move that process in specific directions.[42]

Historical-critical scholars who cannot entertain any traditional concept of the sacred may establish for themselves values that transcend isolated transient historical events. They may then read biblical texts in light of those abiding values and correlate biblical texts from different historical epochs in light of those values. Believers, of course, may deal consciously with biblical texts with different methodological assumptions— with more-or-less positivistic historical assumptions, with assumptions of transcendent human values, and/or with assumptions of the sacred that do not violate but rather enhance the possibilities of the completion of human existence.

The circles of language and literature play their important part in the system of hermeneutics. Language can be seen as a scientific discipline, a tool of humankind. But it can also be seen as a capacity of humankind that exceeds any and all human languages, as an essential property of humankind that is prior to any speaking. From perspectives on language as such (moving from Heidegger and Saussure to Derrida), we are given confidence to treat the Bible as a text that is open to our appropriation while we are cautioned against claiming that the biblical text in and of itself is able to make fully present what it presents. My most recent work has been an attempt to advance the hermeneutical task through an appreciation of the New Testament as literature. Biblical texts are linguistic structures. The same linguistic and literary principles at work in the case of literary masterpieces are at work in the case of biblical writings. Readers can come to the biblical text as they come to other literature and exercise their creativity and faith. A rich difference of opinion exists today over the relative importance of the text and reader and the best

---

[42]*God and History: Shapes of Freedom*, 205.

ways of conceptualizing the activities of the reader in actualizing the text. But there is unanimity of opinion that the reader is necessarily and legitimately involved in the process of reading.

I have already suggested that a literary approach to biblical texts allows modern-day readers to recapitulate the significance of the historical experiences of the people of God. The circle of literature, then, is related to the circles of history, doctrine, and theology. The literary units of the Bible may be seen as growing out of and expressing in fixed literary form the historical experiences of the people of God. Through historical study we can do something with the circumstances of origin of the biblical texts and the historical circumstances of the transmission and alteration of the texts that allowed the significance of the texts to be appropriated by a succession of peoples. The historical facts depicted and the circumstances of origin and transmission uncovered *as such* do not really touch our lives, however. They remain historical data. Through our present-day appropriation of the literature growing out of the historical experiences of the people of God, however, we can experience the sacred.

Sandra Schneiders, speaking of the New Testament as a "revelatory text" comparable with the sacrament of the Eucharist,[43] declares that "it is sacrament in the fully actualized sense of the word only when it is being read, when it is coming to event as meaning through interpretation. However, the book that preserves and localizes for us the possibility of such events of meaning and that stabilizes the meaning and so gives it continuity in the community is a symbolic object that is fittingly venerated so long as it plays its proper role in the context of the entire mystery."[44] Schneiders is using a Roman Catholic conceptualization and vocabulary to affirm a Radical Reformation appreciation of the Bible as a text overflowing with meaning, capable of matching the needs and capacity of different generations.

As literature, scripture may function to enable readers to appropriate the experiences stamped upon the literature. This takes place as the reader interacts with the text and the world of the text in and through elements from the reader's world and the totality of the reader's world itself. A new world presents itself. A world of grace and a world of challenge on

---

[43] *The Revelatory Text*, 40. Schneiders quotes from "Dei Verbum" (Dogmatic Constitution on Divine Revelation of Vatican Council II) in *Documents of Vatican II*, vol. 1, ed. Austin P. Flannery (Grand Rapids MI: Eerdmans, 1984) vi:21.

[44] *The Revelatory Text*, 43.

the basis of that grace. The failure, captivity, and redemption of the people of God is the basic story. It is presented over and over again in the Old and New Testaments so that any one telling of the story is reinforced and interpreted by other forms of the story. The Exodus, then, is superimposed on the whole of the Bible. The story of Jesus and the story of the Exodus are read together. And we do not benefit from that story simply by reestablishing historical facts. We experience Exodus.

From the perspective of the Bible as literature, discovery and explication of factual scientific information about the history of the peoples involved with the Bible and with their religious and social convictions and traditions is secondary (but vital) as is the discovery and display of dogmatic truth. These circles remain related to the circle of literature, however. For example, concepts of God and how God may be experienced in history, that is, concepts of the Kingdom of God, influence the way we read the Bible in a literary fashion.

We move backward and forward to other circles from the experience of the Bible as literature. We may check our experience with data from these other circles. Does the language allow our reading? What about history and theology? We may relate the biblical material to our lives by retelling, by transformation into the various artistic forms, by preaching, or by fitting the Bible into theological conceptualizations. An inclusion of the literary circle into the hermeneutic circle of circles does fuller justice to the biblical text and its claims upon our lives intellectually, emotionally, and spiritually.

This chapter began with the Anabaptists in Münster who were used as a beginning point for a discussion on how to read and not read the Scriptures. Their reading of the Scriptures so as to engender an encounter between believers and the text was applauded. But the actual excesses of the Anabaptists raised the question of the validity of interpretation and the need for some principles to give guidance. Dogmatic and historical frameworks provide guidance and control but alter the immediacy between the reader and the biblical text when used as the "gatekeepers" for all truth. A comprehensive hermeneutical system in which movement is made within circles and from circle to circle provides freedom and control.

Conclusion

How "Must" and/or How "May"
We Interpret Jesus?

The study of Jesus has been dominated by a perspective emphasizing the correct interpretation—how Jesus *must* be interpreted. This perspective permeated the precritical and critical approaches and remains the horizon for contemporary approaches. The resources for study have varied—philosophical, theological, historical, literary—but the idea that there is one proper and correct interpretation has continued.

A stance influenced by the poetic and the sectarian begins with interest in how Jesus *may* be understood and interpreted. When past as well as present writers are seen as exercising a variety of creative and artistic talents and tools as well as objective and critical methods, sense can be made of the entire history of Jesus research. The ostensible question, for example, is: What interpretation of Jesus does the language of the Gospels require? But the question from a poetic perspective is: What does the language of the Gospels allow? This framing of the question makes clear that other questions, which must be similarly framed, are involved: What do the originating historical and sociological circumstances allow? What does the worldview of readers allow? What do the presuppositions concerning the sacred allow?

Scholars in the critical period—even through the post-Bultmannian quest—were able to construct compelling interpretations of Jesus and frame them within the positivist perspective that demands such interpretations. What really happened, however, was that various textual and extra-textual elements and factors were fitted together in a compelling fashion. This does not mean that any interpretation was acceptable; the language will not allow just anything, the postulated originating circumstances will not allow just anything, and so on. Marcus Borg's confession of the significance of his study of Jesus—that his Jesus, for example, challenges the modern flattened sense of reality, undermines conventional religious assumptions, and points to deep involvement in the life of history—could be paralleled by other scholars. Such confessions do not result from finally "getting it right" from some position transcending historical experience. It is the result of putting together the various elements so that the result speaks to the reader/scholar.

If this is the case, the task for readers today is not the acceptance of one or another scholar as providing the final answer (though a reader may begin with a particular reconstruction—ancient or modern—in the reader's own creation). The task is to recapitulate what was involved in the writing of the Gospels in the first place and what has been involved in every portrait of Jesus. The sources are to be read in light of a faith perspective and refined in a fashion consistent with scientific and poetic constraints and resources. Such a portrait will be compelling because it matches the reader's competence and faith.

In *Meaning in Texts: The Historical Shaping of a Narrative Hermeneutics*, I saw the various moves in biblical interpretation in a developmental scheme with (1) critical moves validated within recognized and accepted critical frameworks, (2) symbolic interpretations governed by already existing symbolic systems, and (3) prospective symbolism in which readers appropriate texts as a vehicle for new meaning matching their needs and competence.[1] Today, I would emphasize these moves in the interpretation of Jesus, but I would see them as coexisting, with hermeneutical concern for meaning-for-the-reader involved at every critical and interpretative level. Readers will be concerned with historical meaning that is the circumstance for "original" meaning but not as the gatekeeper to all meaning and significance. They will be concerned with the way scholars have approached the texts so as to find historical and historic meaning and significance. But in the process they *may* (not *must*) be aware of the different drives for meaning in their own lives—the sorts of "conversions" enumerated by Bernard Lonergan—intellectual, moral, psychological, affective, sociopolitical; and they may be aware of a drive for religion that is concrete, dynamic, personal, social, and historical. These drives will not be met by conventional historical-critical approaches alone. But they may be met by the comprehensive approach advocated in this book.

---

[1](Philadelphia: Fortress Press, 1978) 215-25.

The establishment of some sort of fit or equilibrium in terms of a specific sort or sorts of conversion ought to be celebrated as this equilibrium is achieved by individuals and in communities of believers. An individual may discover meaning that is personal and combines both the intellectual and the affective. But life and history move on and other sorts of conversion become important. The social side of religion with moral and sociopolitical conversions may become paramount.

The stress on the ways we may interpret Jesus has ethical and religious significance. What we demand for ourselves—the ability to match our needs and competence—we demand for others, within and without religious communities. This does not forsake meaning of Jesus Christ for us in our pilgrimage. Rather, it enhances meaning as it influences our understanding of interpretation and even our understanding of what it means to be human.

Index

Jesus Christ in History and Scripture.
A Poetic and Sectarian Perspective.
   by Edgar V. McKnight.

Mercer University Press, Macon, Georgia 31210-3960.
Isbn 0-86554-653-3 (casebound). MUP/H486.
Isbn 0-86554-677-0 (perfectbound). MUP/P202.
Text and interior design and composition by Edmon L. Rowell, Jr.
Cover design by Jim Burt.
Cover illustration: *Resurrection,* by Agnolo Bronzino (1552).
Camera-ready pages composed via dos WordPerfect 5.1
      and WordPerfect for Windows 5.1/5.2,
            and printed on a LaserMaster 1000.
Text fonts: TimesNewRomanPS 11/13 + ATECH Hebrew and Greek.
Display fonts: Helvetica + TimesNewRomanPS.
Printed and bound by BookCrafters, Chelsea, Michigan,
      via offset lithography on 60# Booktext Natural (420 ppi).
Perfectbound: bound into 10-pt. cls stock,
      cover printed four-color process and with lay-flat matte film lamination.
Casebound: Smyth sewn (32s) and cased into .088" binder's boards
      and Roxite C cloth, with 80# plain matching endsheets,
            with one-hit foil stamping on spine and c. 4 with imitation gold foil.
      Dust jacket printed four-color process and lay-flat matte film laminated.

091599elr.